Official TOEFL iBT® Tests Volume 1 5th Edition 온라인 실전 테스트 사용법

설치

웹사이트 www.mhprofessional.com/totvol1을 방문하면 책에 있는 접속 코드를 입력하라는 메시지가 뜹니다. 이 코드는 책 구매자에 한해 최대 2회까지 이용할 수 있습니다. 접속 코드를 입력하면 자동으로 다운로드가 시작됩니다.

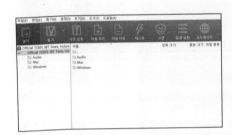

프로그램 실행

오디오 파일뿐만 아니라 PC와 Mac® 포맷의 실전 테스트 파일도 함께 다운로드 됩니다. 이 중 Windows PC를 사용하신다면 Windows 폴더를 클릭하여 TOEFL Tests Volume 1 Setup 파일을 실행하면 됩니다.

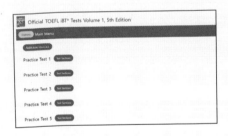

온라인 실전 테스트

프로그램을 실행하면 다음과 같은 화면이 나타납니다. Main Menu 에서 Practice Test 1, 2, 3, 4, 5 중 수행하고 싶은 테스트를 선택합니다. 그런 다음 읽기, 듣기, 말하기, 쓰기 등 수행하고 싶은 영역을 선택합니다. 각 영역은 한 번 이상 풀어 볼 수 있습니다.

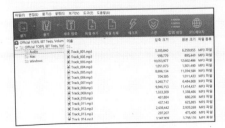

MP3 오디오 파일 활용

컴퓨터가 아니라 책에 인쇄된 실전 테스트로 공부할 때도 오디오 트랙을 들어야 합니다. 'Audio'라는 폴더를 컴퓨터에 복사하면, 교재에 표시된 오디오 트랙 번호와 일치하는 파일을 찾아 들을 수 있습니다.

Digital Access Code

✳toefl ibt®

Official TOEFL iBT® TESTS

VOLUME **1** 5TH EDITION

Official TOEFL iBT Tests Volume 1, 5ᵗʰ Edition

Original: Official TOEFL iBT Tests Volume 1, 5ᵗʰ Edition © 2024
        By Educational Testing Service (ETS)
        ISBN 978-1-265-47907-7

TOEFL is a registered trademark of ETS, Princeton, New Jersey, U.S.A. and is used under license.

ETS, the ETS logo, TOEFL, TOEFL iBT and MyBest Score are registered trademarks of ETS
in the United States and other countries.

This authorized Korean language edition is published by YBM, Inc. in arrangement with McGraw-Hill Education Korea, Ltd.
This edition is authorized for sale in the Republic of Korea.

This Korean language edition is exclusively distributed by YBM, Inc. in the Republic of Korea.

When ordering this title, please use ISBN 978-89-17-23997-3

Printed in Korea

Official TOEFL iBT® Tests Volume 1 | Fifth Edition

발행인	허문호
발행처	YBM

저자	Educational Testing Service (ETS)
편집	정윤영, 이시현
마케팅	정연철, 박천산, 고영노, 김동진, 박찬경, 김윤하

초판인쇄	2024년 10월 16일
초판발행	2024년 10월 31일

신고일자	1964년 3월 28일
신고번호	제 1964-000003호

주소	서울시 종로구 종로 104
전화	(02) 2000-0515[구입문의] / (02) 2000-0328[내용문의]
팩스	(02) 2285-1523
홈페이지	www.ybmbooks.com

ISBN 978-89-17-23997-3

Contents

Introduction

About the TOEFL iBT® Test

호주, 캐나다, 뉴질랜드, 미국, 영국, 그리고 유럽 및 아시아를 포함한 160개국 이상에서 만 2천여 개 대학과 기관, 기타 단체가 TOEFL iBT® 점수를 입학 또는 입사 기준의 일부로 인정하고 있으며 TOEFL iBT® 시험은 세계에서 가장 널리 공신력을 확보한 영어 시험으로 자리매김했다.

TOEFL iBT® 시험에는 읽기, 듣기, 말하기, 쓰기 네 가지 영역이 포함된다. 이 영역들에서 묻는 질문은 얼마나 능숙하게 영어로 **읽고, 듣고, 말하고, 쓸** 수 있는지를 평가한다. 또한 이 능력들을 함께 구사할 수 있는 역량도 평가하므로, 어떤 경우에는 복수의 능력을 통합해서 답변해야 한다. 예를 들어, 지문을 읽거나 강의를 들은 다음 이해한 내용에 관해 쓰거나 말해야 한다. 다음은 각 영역에 대한 간략한 설명으로, 해당 영역에서 평가하는 항목과 질문 유형이 정리되어 있다.

Reading Section

읽기 영역은 영어로 저술된 학술 관련 지문을 이해하는 능력을 평가한다. 대학 입문 과정에 활용하기에 적합한 교재와 책에서 발췌한 내용이 지문으로 나온다.

읽기 지문에는 질문에 답하는 데 필요한 정보가 전부 포함되어 있으므로, 응시자가 지문에서 다루는 주제에 대해 배경지식을 갖출 필요는 전혀 없다. 이 영역에서는 서술된 정보를 이해하는 능력, 추론하는 능력, 부차적인 정보와 골자가 되는 개념을 구별하는 능력을 판단하기 위한 문제가 출제된다.

읽기 영역의 문제 유형과 각 유형에서 요구되는 사항은 다음과 같다.

기초 이해 문제

세부 사항 찾기	지문에 명시된 사실 정보를 식별한다.
틀린 정보 찾기	사실인 정보와 사실이 아닌 정보나 지문에 포함되지 않은 정보를 구별한다.
어휘	개별 단어나 구가 *지문에서 사용된 의미*를 식별한다.
지시 대상 찾기	지문에서 언급된 개념과 개념을 가리키는 표현 사이의 연관성을 식별하는 능력을 평가한다. 예를 들어, 개념이 제시되고 다른 문장에서 이를 "This idea"라고 언급했다면, "This idea"가 의미하는 바를 묻는다.
문장 재구성	지문에 있는 특정 문장과 본질적으로 의미가 동일한 문장을 선택한다.

추론 문제

내용 추론	지문에 명시적으로 제시되지는 않았지만 암시되어 있는 정보에 대해 질문한다.
수사학적 의도 파악	지문에 제시된 특정 정보의 수사학적 기능에 대해 질문한다. 저자가 특정 정보를 언급하거나 지문에 포함시킨 *이유*나 *방식*을 묻는다. 일부 문항은 저자가 지문에서 정보를 구성한 방식을 묻는다.
문장 삽입	새로운 문장을 제시하고 해당 문장이 들어가기에 가장 적절한 곳을 묻는다.

논지 파악 문제

지문 요약하기	지문에 제시된 주요 논지를 식별하고 이 논지들을 사소한 논지나 지문에서 제시되지 않은 논지와 구별한다. 정답을 고르기 위해서는 지문에 포함된 다양한 정보들이 상대적으로 얼마나 중요한지를 이해하고 지문에 제시된 주요 논지를 아우르는 보기들을 파악할 수 있어야 한다. 항상 읽기 영역에서 마지막 문제로 출제되며 배점은 2점이다. 정답 3개를 모두 고르면 2점, 2개만 고르면 1점을 받는다.

Listening Section

이 영역은 영어로 이루어지는 대화와 학술 강의를 이해하는 능력을 평가한다.

두 가지 대화 유형이 등장한다. 한 가지 유형은 교수 연구실에서 이루어지는 대화로, 학술 자료나 강의에서 요구되는 사항과 관련된 내용이 포함될 수 있다. 두 번째 유형은 대학 캠퍼스에서 이루어지는 대화로 학문과 상관없는, 대학 생활과 관련된 내용이 포함된다. 각 대화가 끝나면 5문항이 출제된다.

덧붙여 다양한 주제를 다루는 세 가지 강의를 들려준다. 교수 혼자서 쭉 진행하는 강의도 있고, 학생들이 토론에 참여하는 강의도 있는데, 교수가 토론 중인 주제에 대해 학생들에게 질문하거나 학생들의 질문에 대답하기도 한다. 강의가 끝나면 6문항이 출제된다.

모든 대화와 강의는 한 번만 들려주며, 화자/화자들이 등장하는 상황 사진이 포함되어 있다. 일부 대화와 강의에는 전문적인 어휘나 흔하지 않은 이름이 적힌 칠판 등 다른 시각 자료가 포함되어 있다.

다음은 듣기 영역의 문제 유형과 각 유형에 대한 설명이다.

기초 이해 문제

핵심 내용 파악	강의나 대화의 핵심 개념을 식별한다.
주된 목적 파악	강의나 대화의 주된 목적을 식별한다.
세부 사항 찾기	강의나 대화의 중요한 세부 사항을 파악한다.

화용론적 이해 문제

기능 또는 목적	대화나 강의에서 화자가 진술한 발언의 기능이나 목적을 식별한다.
화자의 태도	화자의 태도, 의견, 또는 확신 정도를 식별한다.

정보 연결 문제

구성 파악	강의에서 정보가 어떻게 조직되어 있는지 파악한다.
내용 연결하기	강의나 대화에 나온 개념 간 관계를 파악하거나, 논의된 요지를 바탕으로 추론한다.

대다수 문항은 정답이 하나인 다지선다형 문제이며 일부 문항은 정답을 둘 이상 골라야 한다. 또한 진행 단계를 순서대로 배치하거나 표에 체크 표시를 하는 문제도 출제되며, 대화 또는 강의 일부를 다시 듣고 푸는 문제도 있다.

Speaking Section

말하기 영역은 다양한 주제에 관해 영어로 말하는 능력을 평가한다.

문제마다 답변을 준비할 수 있는 짧은 시간이 부여된다. 준비 시간이 끝나면 해당 문항에서 표시된 시간에 가능한 한 충실하게 답변한다. 이 책에 수록된 문제를 풀 때는 답변을 녹음장치에 담아야 한다. 이렇게 하면 나중에 녹음된 답변을 검토하면서 이 책 정답란에 있는 해설이나 채점 기준과 비교해 볼 수 있다.

첫 번째 문제는 '양자택일'로, 익숙한 주제에 대한 응시자 자신의 의견을 제시해야 한다. 자신의 의견을 밝히고 그러한 의견을 견지하는 이유를 설명해야 한다.

두 번째 문제는 '찬반 파악 및 설명'으로, 먼저 짧은 지문을 읽고, 같은 주제를 두고 나누는 대화를 듣거나 대화를 기록한 원고를 읽는다. 뒤이어 지문과 대화를 모두 포괄하는 문제가 출제된다. 완성도 높은 답변을 하려면 지문과 대화에 나온 관련 정보를 종합해야 한다. 명료하고 조리 있게 말하는 능력, 지문과 대화에 담긴 정보를 정확하게 전달하는 능력에 따라 채점이 이루어진다.

세 번째 문제는 '일반론/각론'으로, 먼저 학술 주제에 대한 짧은 지문을 읽고 같은 주제를 다룬 강의를 듣거나 강의를 기록한 원고를 읽는다. 뒤이어 지문과 강의를 모두 포괄하는 문제가 출제된다. 명료하고 조리 있게 말하는 능력, 지문과 강의의 핵심 정보를 종합해서 전달하는 능력에 따라 채점이 이루어진다.

마지막 문제는 '요약하기'로 강의 일부를 듣거나 강의 일부를 기록한 원고를 읽는다. 뒤이어 강의에 대한 문제가 출제된다. 채점은 명료하고 조리 있게 말하는 능력, 강의에 담긴 정보를 정확하게 전달하는 능력에 따라 이루어진다.

말하기 답변은 세 가지 중요한 기준인 전달력과 언어 구사력, 주제 전개 위주로 채점이 이루어진다. 답변을 평가할 때는 세 가지 기준이 모두 동일하게 고려되며, 다른 기준들에 비해 특정 기준에 가중치를 두지 않는다.

Writing Section

쓰기 영역은 학업 환경에서 영어 글쓰기를 통해 의사소통할 수 있는 능력을 평가한다.

쓰기 영역 1번 문제에서는 지문을 읽고 강의를 듣거나 강의를 기록한 원고를 읽는다. 뒤이어 독해 지문과 강의의 연관성을 묻는 문제가 출제된다. 20분 동안 답안을 구상하고 글을 작성해야 한다. 읽기 지문과 강의 양쪽의 정보를 모두 활용해 가능한 한 완성도 높은 답안을 작성하도록 노력해야 한다. 응시자 개인의 의견을 표명하는 것은 문제에서 요구하는 바가 아니다. 답안을 작성할 때가 되면 응시자가 참고할 수 있도록 다시 화면에 독해 지문이 나타난다. 통상 완성도를 갖춘 답안은 최소 150단어 분량으로 구성된다. 답안의 수준, 내용의 완성도와 정확도에 따라 평가가 이루어진다.

쓰기 영역 2번 문제는 학술 토론을 위한 쓰기로, 온라인 토론에서 교수의 질문과 다른 학생들의 답변을 읽는다. 그런 다음 토론 중인 주제에 기여하는 의견을 진술하고 근거를 제시하라는 과제가 제시된다. 게시물을 읽고 답변을 작성하는 시간은 10분이다. 어느 정도 완성도를 갖추려면 통상 최소 100단어 이상이어야 한다. 얼마나 토론과 연관성이 밀접하며 명확한 표현으로 온라인 토론에 기여했는지, 그리고 일관되고 능숙한 언어 구사력을 보여주는지 여부에 따라 평가가 이루어진다.

How to Use This Book/Digital Resources

Official TOEFL iBT® Tests Volume 1은 시험 준비에 도움이 될 수 있다. 이 책에는 TOEFL iBT® 5개 세트가 수록되어 있다. 일부 문항은 기출 변형 형태이지만 모든 시험 문제는 실제로 출제된 TOEFL iBT® 기출 문항이다. (말하기 영역을 풀 때는 녹음 장치를 사용해야 한다)

두 가지 방식으로 테스트를 풀어볼 수 있다.

- 책을 이용할 때는 펜이나 연필을 사용해 답을 표시하거나 답안을 작성한다. 음원을 들어야 할 때마다 페이지에 헤드폰 모양 아이콘이 인쇄되어 있다. 듣기 영역의 음원은 디지털 다운로드에서 제공된다. Audio 폴더를 열면 번호별로 트랙이 나열되므로 책에서 지시하는 대로 각 항목을 선택하면 된다
- 컴퓨터로는 디지털 다운로드에서 제공되는 쌍방향 테스트를 이용한다. 책의 맨 앞에 있는 '온라인 실전 테스트 사용법'의 지침을 따르면 된다. 답을 선택하고 지침에 따라 답안을 작성해 입력한다. 문제가 화면에 표시되면 음원이 자동으로 재생된다

음원의 원고는 '해설 및 정답'에 수록되어 있다. 만약 음원을 이용할 수 없다면 영어 발음이 좋은 사람에게 원고를 큰 소리로 읽어 달라고 요청한다. 원고를 들으면서 연습하는 편이 혼자 원고를 읽는 것보다 효과가 좋다. 만약 누군가가 원고를 읽어준다면, 들으면서 사진 자료 등을 놓치지 않도록 유의한다.

인쇄된 지면 테스트를 이용할 경우, 음원은 한 번만 듣는다. 실제 시험처럼 듣는 동안 메모를 할 수 있으며 답변할 때 메모를 활용해도 좋다.

Answers

이 책에 수록된 각 테스트에 대한 정답은 '해설 및 정답' 별책에 제공된다.

읽기 및 듣기 영역의 경우 정답이 제공된다.

말하기 및 쓰기 영역의 경우 유일한 정답이 존재하지 않으므로 해설 및 정답에서 고득점을 받을 수 있는 요령을 밝히고 있다. Appendix에 제공된 채점 기준을 이용해 자신의 답변을 평가해 볼 수 있다.

말하기 영역에서 녹음 장치에 답변을 녹음했다면 해설 및 정답의 설명 및 Appendix의 채점 기준과 자신의 답변을 비교할 수 있다.

컴퓨터로 문제를 푼다면 화면에 나타나는 지침에 따라 읽기 및 듣기 영역 정답과 말하기 및 쓰기 영역의 답안 설명을 확인한다.

Rubrics

이 채점 기준은 채점자가 말하기 및 쓰기 영역의 답변을 평가하는 데 활용되는 지침이다. TOEFL iBT® 테스트 채점 기준은 Appendix에서 확인할 수 있다.

말하기 점수는 의도한 메시지를 어느 정도 제대로 전달하고 있는지를 전반적으로 판단한다. **전달력** 및 **언어 구사력**은 채점자가 말하기 영역의 4개 문항에 대한 답변을 채점할 때 고려하는 두 가지 주요 범주이며, 세 번째 범주가 **주제 전개**이다. 말하기 영역 독립형 문제의 경우, 주제 전개는 전반적인 일관성뿐만 아니라 답변에 제시된 내용이 얼마나 알찬지 충실도를 판단한다. 미리 암기한 답변이나 예시는 점수를 깎는 요인이 되므로 사용하지 않도록 한다. ETS 채점자는 암기한 답변과 자연스럽게 나오는 즉흥적인 답변을 쉽게 구별할 수 있다. 말하기 영역 통합형 문제의 경우 주제 전개는 전반적인 일관성뿐만 아니라 답변에 제공된 내용의 정확도와 완성도로 평가된다.

쓰기 점수 역시 의도한 메시지를 어느 정도 제대로 전달하고 있는지를 전반적으로 판단한다. **작문의 수준**은 채점자들이 통합형 쓰기 문제(1번 문항)와 학술 토론을 위한 쓰기 문제(2번 문항)에 대한 답변을 채점할 때 고려하는 핵심 특성이다. 통합형 쓰기 문제에서 수준 높은 작문은 문법과 어휘의 적절하고 정확한 활용이 특징이다. 학술 토론을 위한 쓰기 문제 역시 탄탄한 근거와 예시를 통해 자신의 의견을 뒷받침해야 하며 명확하게 표현해야 한다. 답안이 온라인 게시물 형태로 나타나므로 여러 단락으로 나누어 구성할 필요는 없다. 하지만 개념 간 연관성이 밀접하며 조리 있고 명료해야 한다. 서로 연관관계가 뚜렷하지 않으며 주장을 뒷받침하는 데 기여하지 않는 단어와 문장을 많이 사용하면 낮은 점수를 받게 된다. 단어 수나 답변 분량을 늘리려고 도입부나 결말에서 암기한 문구나 문장을 장황하게 이어가면 안 된다. 이런 글은 진정성이 결여되어 있으며, 온라인 토론에서 사용되는 글쓰기 유형에도 부합하지 않는다.

내용의 완성도와 정확도는 채점자가 통합형 쓰기 문제 답안을 채점할 때 고려하는 핵심 요소다. 완성도 높고 정확한 답안을 작성하려면 강의와 지문 양쪽 모두에서 적절한 주요 논점들을 제시하고 중요한 사항 간의 연관성을 드러내는 한편 강의에서 논거를 뒷받침하는 중요한 세부 내용을 모두 포함해야 한다. 강의와 지문 이외 출처에서 나온 정보는 배제해야 한다. 학술 토론을 위한 쓰기 문제에서 토론에 대한 기여는 답안을 평가하는 데 사용되는 매우 중요한 기준이다. 토론에는 교수의 질문뿐만 아니라 다른 학생들의 게시물도 포함된다. 반드시 새로운 아이디어를 많이 낸다고 해서 토론에 기여하는 것은 아니다. 다른 사람이 이미 작성한 글에 동의하거나 반대한 다음 자신의 관점으로 이유를 설명하는 방식으로 토론에 기여할 수도 있다. 다른 사람이 쓴 글을 그대로 반복하지 말고, 독창적인 표현과 관점을 활용해 독자적인 방식으로 개념을 다듬어야 한다.

More Official Resources

ETS는 다음 자료를 비롯해 TOEFL iBT® 시험을 준비하는 데 도움이 되는 공식 자료를 다수 보유하고 있다.

- The Official Guide to the TOEFL® Test
- TOEFL® Practice Online
- "Inside the TOEFL® Test" Video Series
- TOEFL® Test Preparation: The Insider's Guide (MOOC)
- Official TOEFL iBT® Prep Course

www.ets.org/toefl에서 이 자료들을 비롯한 다양한 자료를 확인하고 시험 접수도 할 수 있다.

TOEFL iBT® Test 1

READING

In this section, you will be able to demonstrate your ability to understand academic passages in English. You will read and answer questions about **two passages**.

In the actual test, you will have 36 minutes total to read both passages and answer the questions. A clock will indicate how much time remains.

Some passages may include one or more notes explaining words or phrases. The words or phrases are marked with footnote numbers, and the notes explaining them appear at the end of the passage.

Most questions are worth 1 point, but the last question for each passage is worth 2 points.

You may review and revise your answers in this section as long as time remains.

At the end of this practice test, you will find an answer key.

Directions: Read the passage. Then answer the questions. You have 18 minutes on average to answer the questions.

DEER POPULATIONS OF THE PUGET SOUND

Two species of deer have been prevalent in the Puget Sound area of Washington state in the Pacific Northwest of the United States. The black-tailed deer, a lowland, west-side cousin of the mule deer of eastern Washington, is now the most common. The other species, the Columbian white-tailed deer, in earlier times was common in the open prairie country; it is now restricted to the low, marshy islands and flood plains along the lower Columbia River.

Nearly any kind of plant of the forest understory can be part of a deer's diet. Where the forest inhibits the growth of grass and other meadow plants, the black-tailed deer browses on huckleberry, salal, dogwood, and almost any other shrub or herb. But this is fair-weather feeding. What keeps the black-tailed deer alive in the harsher seasons of plant decay and dormancy? One compensation for not hibernating is the built-in urge to migrate. Deer may move from high-elevation browse areas in summer down to the lowland areas in late fall. Even with snow on the ground, the high bushy understory is exposed; also snow and wind bring down leafy branches of cedar, hemlock, red alder, and other arboreal fodder.

The numbers of deer have fluctuated markedly since the entry of Europeans into Puget Sound country. The early explorers and settlers told of abundant deer in the early 1800s and yet almost in the same breath bemoaned the lack of this succulent game animal. Famous explorers of the North American frontier, Lewis and Clark arrived at the mouth of the Columbia River on November 14, 1805, in nearly starved circumstances. They had experienced great difficulty finding game west of the Rockies and not until the second of December did they kill their first elk. To keep 40 people alive that winter, they consumed approximately 150 elk and 20 deer. And when game moved out of the lowlands in early spring, the expedition decided to return east rather than face possible starvation. Later on in the early years of the nineteenth century, when Fort Vancouver became the headquarters for the Hudson's Bay Company, deer populations continued to fluctuate. David Douglas, Scottish botanical explorer of the 1830s, found a disturbing change in the animal life around the fort during the period between his first visit in 1825 and his final contact with the fort in 1832. A recent Douglas biographer states: "The deer which once picturesquely dotted the meadows around the fort were gone [in 1832], hunted to extermination in order to protect the crops."

Reduction in numbers of game should have boded ill for their survival in later times. A worsening of the plight of deer was to be expected as settlers encroached on the land, logging, burning, and clearing, eventually replacing a wilderness landscape with roads, cities, towns, and factories. No doubt the numbers of deer declined still further. Recall the fate of the Columbian white-tailed deer, now in a protected status. But for the black-tailed deer, human pressure has had just the opposite effect. Wildlife zoologist Helmut Buechner (1953), in reviewing the nature of biotic changes in Washington through recorded time, says that "since the early 1940s, the state has had more deer than at any other time in its history, the winter population fluctuating around approximately 320,000 deer (mule and black-tailed deer), which will yield about 65,000 of either sex and any age annually for an indefinite period."

The causes of this population rebound are consequences of other human actions. First, the major predators of deer—wolves, cougar, and lynx—have been greatly reduced in numbers. Second, conservation has been insured by limiting times for and types of hunting. But the most profound reason for the restoration of high population numbers has been the fate of the forests. Great tracts of lowland country deforested by logging, fire, or both have become ideal feeding grounds for deer. In addition to finding an increase of suitable browse, like huckleberry and vine maple, Arthur Einarsen, longtime game biologist in the Pacific Northwest, found quality of browse in the open areas to be substantially more nutritive. The protein content of shade-grown vegetation, for example, was much lower than that for plants grown in clearings.

Directions: Now answer the questions.

PARAGRAPH 1

Two species of deer have been prevalent in the Puget Sound area of Washington state in the Pacific Northwest of the United States. The black-tailed deer, a lowland, west-side cousin of the mule deer of eastern Washington, is now the most common. The other species, the Columbian white-tailed deer, in earlier times was common in the open prairie country; it is now restricted to the low, marshy islands and flood plains along the lower Columbia River.

1. According to paragraph 1, which of the following is true of the white-tailed deer of Puget Sound?

    (A) It is native to lowlands and marshes.
    (B) It is more closely related to the mule deer of eastern Washington than to other types of deer.
    (C) It has replaced the black-tailed deer in the open prairie.
    (D) It no longer lives in a particular type of habitat that it once occupied.

PARAGRAPH 2

Nearly any kind of plant of the forest understory can be part of a deer's diet. Where the forest inhibits the growth of grass and other meadow plants, the black-tailed deer browses on huckleberry, salal, dogwood, and almost any other shrub or herb. But this is fair-weather feeding. What keeps the black-tailed deer alive in the harsher seasons of plant decay and dormancy? One compensation for not hibernating is the built-in urge to migrate. Deer may move from high-elevation browse areas in summer down to the lowland areas in late fall. Even with snow on the ground, the high bushy understory is exposed; also snow and wind bring down leafy branches of cedar, hemlock, red alder, and other arboreal fodder.

2. It can be inferred from the discussion in paragraph 2 that winter conditions

   Ⓐ cause some deer to hibernate
   Ⓑ make food unavailable in the highlands for deer
   Ⓒ make it easier for deer to locate understory plants
   Ⓓ prevent deer from migrating during the winter

PARAGRAPH 3

The numbers of deer have fluctuated markedly since the entry of Europeans into Puget Sound country. The early explorers and settlers told of abundant deer in the early 1800s and yet almost in the same breath bemoaned the lack of this succulent game animal. Famous explorers of the North American frontier, Lewis and Clark arrived at the mouth of the Columbia River on November 14, 1805, in nearly starved circumstances. They had experienced great difficulty finding game west of the Rockies and not until the second of December did they kill their first elk. To keep 40 people alive that winter, they consumed approximately 150 elk and 20 deer. And when game moved out of the lowlands in early spring, the expedition decided to return east rather than face possible starvation. Later on in the early years of the nineteenth century, when Fort Vancouver became the headquarters for the Hudson's Bay Company, deer populations continued to fluctuate. David Douglas, Scottish botanical explorer of the 1830s, found a disturbing change in the animal life around the fort during the period between his first visit in 1825 and his final contact with the fort in 1832. A recent Douglas biographer states: "The deer which once picturesquely dotted the meadows around the fort were gone [in 1832], hunted to extermination in order to protect the crops."

3. The author tells the story of the explorers Lewis and Clark in paragraph 3 in order to illustrate which of the following points?

   Ⓐ The number of deer within the Puget Sound region has varied over time.
   Ⓑ Most of the explorers who came to the Puget Sound area were primarily interested in hunting game.
   Ⓒ There was more game for hunting in the East of the United States than in the West.
   Ⓓ Individual explorers were not as successful at locating game as were the trading companies.

4. According to paragraph 3, how had Fort Vancouver changed by the time David Douglas returned in 1832?

Ⓐ The fort had become the headquarters for the Hudson's Bay Company.
Ⓑ Deer had begun populating the meadows around the fort.
Ⓒ Deer populations near the fort had been destroyed.
Ⓓ Crop yields in the area around the fort had decreased.

PARAGRAPH 4

Reduction in numbers of game should have boded ill for their survival in later times. A worsening of the plight of deer was to be expected as settlers encroached on the land, logging, burning, and clearing, eventually replacing a wilderness landscape with roads, cities, towns, and factories. No doubt the numbers of deer declined still further. Recall **the fate of the Columbian white-tailed deer**, now in a protected status. But for the black-tailed deer, human pressure has had just the opposite effect. Wildlife zoologist Helmut Buechner (1953), in reviewing the nature of biotic changes in Washington through recorded time, says that "since the early 1940s, the state has had more deer than at any other time in its history, the winter population fluctuating around approximately 320,000 deer (mule and black-tailed deer), which will yield about 65,000 of either sex and any age annually for an **indefinite period**."

5. Why does the author ask readers to recall "**the fate of the Columbian white-tailed deer**" in the discussion of changes in the wilderness landscape?

Ⓐ To provide support for the idea that habitat destruction would lead to population decline
Ⓑ To compare how two species of deer caused biotic changes in the wilderness environment
Ⓒ To provide an example of a species of deer that has successfully adapted to human settlement
Ⓓ To argue that some deer species must be given a protected status

6. The phrase "**indefinite period**" in the passage is closest in meaning to a period

Ⓐ whose end has not been determined
Ⓑ that does not begin when expected
Ⓒ that lasts only briefly
Ⓓ whose importance remains unknown

7. Which of the following statements about deer populations is supported by the information in paragraph 4?

Ⓐ Deer populations reached their highest point during the 1940s and then began to decline.
Ⓑ The activities of settlers contributed in unexpected ways to the growth of some deer populations in later times.
Ⓒ The clearing of wilderness land for construction caused biotic changes from which the black-tailed deer population has never recovered.
Ⓓ Since the 1940s the winter populations of deer have fluctuated more than the summer populations have.

PARAGRAPH 5

The causes of this population rebound are consequences of other human actions. First, the major predators of deer—wolves, cougar, and lynx—have been greatly reduced in numbers. Second, conservation has been insured by limiting times for and types of hunting. But the most profound reason for the restoration of high population numbers has been the fate of the forests. Great tracts of lowland country deforested by logging, fire, or both have become ideal feeding grounds for deer. **In addition to finding an increase of suitable browse, like huckleberry and vine maple, Arthur Einarsen, longtime game biologist in the Pacific Northwest, found quality of browse in the open areas to be substantially more nutritive.** The protein content of shade-grown vegetation, for example, was much lower than that for plants grown in clearings.

8. Which of the sentences below best expresses the essential information in the highlighted sentence in paragraph 5? Incorrect choices change the meaning in important ways or leave out essential information.

   Ⓐ Arthur Einarsen's longtime familiarity with the Pacific Northwest helped him discover areas where deer had an increase in suitable browse.
   Ⓑ Arthur Einarsen found that deforested feeding grounds provided deer with more and better food.
   Ⓒ Biologists like Einarsen believe it is important to find additional open areas with suitable browse for deer to inhabit.
   Ⓓ According to Einarsen, huckleberry and vine maple are examples of vegetation that may someday improve the nutrition of deer in the open areas of the Pacific Northwest.

PARAGRAPHS 2 & 3

What keeps the black-tailed deer alive in the harsher seasons of plant decay and dormancy? One compensation for not hibernating is the built-in urge to migrate. **(A)** Deer may move from high-elevation browse areas in summer down to the lowland areas in late fall. **(B)** Even with snow on the ground, the high bushy understory is exposed; also snow and wind bring down leafy branches of cedar, hemlock, red alder, and other arboreal fodder. **(C)**

The numbers of deer have fluctuated markedly since the entry of Europeans into Puget Sound country. **(D)** The early explorers and settlers told of abundant deer in the early 1800s and yet almost in the same breath bemoaned the lack of this succulent game animal.

9. Look at the part of the passage that is displayed above. The letters **(A)**, **(B)**, **(C)**, and **(D)** indicate where the following sentence could be added.

   There food is available and accessible throughout the winter.

   Where would the sentence best fit?

   Ⓐ Choice A
   Ⓑ Choice B
   Ⓒ Choice C
   Ⓓ Choice D

10. **Directions**: An introductory sentence for a brief summary of the passage is provided below. Complete the summary by selecting the THREE answer choices that express the most important ideas in the passage. Some sentences do not belong in the summary because they express ideas that are not presented in the passage or are minor ideas in the the passage. **This question is worth 2 points.**

Write your answer choices in the spaces where they belong. You can either write the letter of your answer choice or you can copy the sentence.

> **Deer in the Puget Sound area eat a wide variety of foods and migrate seasonally to find food.**
>
> ●
>
> ●
>
> ●

Answer Choices

A The balance of deer species in the Puget Sound region has changed over time, with the Columbian white-tailed deer now outnumbering other types of deer.

B Because Puget Sound deer migrate, it was and still remains difficult to determine accurately how many deer are living at any one time in the western United States.

C Deer populations naturally fluctuate, but early settlers in the Puget Sound environment caused an overall decline in the deer populations of the area at that time.

D Although it was believed that human settlement of the American West would cause the total number of deer to decrease permanently, the opposite has actually occurred for certain types of deer.

E In the long term, black-tailed deer in the Puget Sound area have benefitted from human activities through the elimination of their natural predators, and more and better food in deforested areas.

F Wildlife biologists have long been concerned that the loss of forests may create nutritional deficiencies for deer.

Directions: Read the passage. Then answer the questions. You have 18 minutes on average to answer the questions.

CAVE ART IN EUROPE

The earliest discovered traces of art are beads and carvings, and then paintings, from sites dating back to the Upper Paleolithic period. We might expect that early artistic efforts would be crude, but the cave paintings of Spain and southern France show a marked degree of skill. So do the naturalistic paintings on slabs of stone excavated in southern Africa. Some of those slabs appear to have been painted as much as 28,000 years ago, which suggests that painting in Africa is as old as painting in Europe. But painting may be even older than that. The early Australians may have painted on the walls of rock shelters and cliff faces at least 30,000 years ago, and maybe as much as 60,000 years ago.

The researchers Peter Ucko and Andrée Rosenfeld identified three principal locations of paintings in the caves of western Europe: (1) in obviously inhabited rock shelters and cave entrances; (2) in galleries immediately off the inhabited areas of caves; and (3) in the inner reaches of caves, whose difficulty of access has been interpreted by some as a sign that magical-religious activities were performed there.

The subjects of the paintings are mostly animals. The paintings rest on bare walls, with no backdrops or environmental trappings. Perhaps, like many contemporary peoples, Upper Paleolithic men and women believed that the drawing of a human image could cause death or injury, and if that were indeed their belief, it might explain why human figures are rarely depicted in cave art. Another explanation for the focus on animals might be that these people sought to improve their luck at hunting. This theory is suggested by evidence of chips in the painted figures, perhaps made by spears thrown at the drawings. But if improving their hunting luck was the chief motivation for the paintings, it is difficult to explain why only a few show signs of having been speared. Perhaps the paintings were inspired by the need to increase the supply of animals. Cave art seems to have reached a peak toward the end of the Upper Paleolithic period, when the herds of game were decreasing.

The particular symbolic significance of the cave paintings in southwestern France is more explicitly revealed, perhaps, by the results of a study conducted by researchers Patricia Rice and Ann Paterson. The data they present suggest that the animals portrayed in the cave paintings were mostly the ones that the painters preferred for meat and for materials such as hides. For example, wild cattle (bovines) and horses are portrayed more often than we would expect by chance, probably because they were larger and heavier (meatier) than other animals in the environment. In addition, the paintings mostly portray animals that the painters may have feared the most because of their size, speed, natural weapons such as tusks and horns, and the unpredictability of their behavior. That is, mammoths, bovines, and horses are portrayed more often than deer and reindeer. Thus, the paintings are consistent with the idea that the art is related to the importance of hunting in the economy of Upper Paleolithic people. Consistent with this idea, according to the investigators, is the fact that the art of the cultural period that followed the Upper Paleolithic also seems to reflect how people got their food. But in that period, when getting food no longer depended on hunting large game animals (because they were becoming extinct), the art ceased to focus on portrayals of animals.

Upper Paleolithic art was not confined to cave paintings. Many shafts of spears and similar objects were decorated with figures of animals. The anthropologist Alexander Marshack has an interesting interpretation of some of the engravings made during the Upper Paleolithic. He believes that as far back as 30,000 B.C., hunters may have used a system of notation, engraved on bone and stone, to mark phases of the Moon. If this is true, it would mean that Upper Paleolithic people were capable of complex thought and were consciously aware of their environment. In addition to other artworks, figurines representing the human female in exaggerated form have also been found at Upper Paleolithic sites. It has been suggested that these figurines were an ideal type or an expression of a desire for fertility.

Directions: Now answer the questions.

PARAGRAPH 1

The earliest discovered traces of art are beads and carvings, and then paintings, from sites dating back to the Upper Paleolithic period. We might expect that early artistic efforts would be crude, but the cave paintings of Spain and southern France show a **marked** degree of skill. So do the naturalistic paintings on slabs of stone excavated in southern Africa. Some of those slabs appear to have been painted as much as 28,000 years ago, which suggests that painting in Africa is as old as painting in Europe. But painting may be even older than that. The early Australians may have painted on the walls of rock shelters and cliff faces at least 30,000 years ago, and maybe as much as 60,000 years ago.

11. The word "**marked**" in the passage is closest in meaning to
    - (A) considerable
    - (B) surprising
    - (C) limited
    - (D) adequate

12. Paragraph 1 supports which of the following statements about painting in Europe?
    - (A) It is much older than painting in Australia.
    - (B) It is as much as 28,000 years old.
    - (C) It is not as old as painting in southern Africa.
    - (D) It is much more than 30,000 years old.

<table>
<tr><td>P A R A G R A P H 2</td><td>The researchers Peter Ucko and Andrée Rosenfeld identified three principal locations of paintings in the caves of western Europe: (1) in obviously inhabited rock shelters and cave entrances; (2) in galleries immediately off the inhabited areas of caves; and (3) in the inner reaches of caves, whose difficulty of access has been interpreted by some as a sign that magical-religious activities were performed there.</td></tr>
</table>

13. According to paragraph 2, what makes some researchers think that certain cave paintings were connected with magical-religious activities?

   Ⓐ The paintings were located where many people could easily see them, allowing groups of people to participate in the magical-religious activities.
   Ⓑ Upper Paleolithic people shared similar beliefs with contemporary peoples who use paintings of animals in their magical-religious rituals.
   Ⓒ Evidence of magical-religious activities has been found in galleries immediately off the inhabited areas of caves.
   Ⓓ The paintings were found in hard-to-reach places away from the inhabited parts of the cave.

<table>
<tr><td>P A R A G R A P H 3</td><td>The subjects of the paintings are mostly animals. The paintings rest on bare walls, with no backdrops or environmental trappings. Perhaps, like many contemporary peoples, Upper Paleolithic men and women believed that the drawing of a human image could cause death or injury, and if that were indeed their belief, it might explain why human figures are rarely depicted in cave art. Another explanation for the focus on animals might be that these people sought to improve their luck at hunting. This theory is suggested by evidence of chips in the painted figures, perhaps made by spears thrown at the drawings. But if improving their hunting luck was the chief motivation for the paintings, it is difficult to explain why only a few show signs of having been speared. Perhaps the paintings were inspired by the need to increase the supply of animals. Cave art seems to have **reached a peak toward the end of the Upper Paleolithic period, when the herds of game were decreasing**.</td></tr>
</table>

14. According to paragraph 3, scholars explained chips in the painted figures of animals by proposing that

   Ⓐ Upper Paleolithic artists used marks to record the animals they had seen
   Ⓑ the paintings were inspired by the need to increase the supply of animals for hunting
   Ⓒ the artists had removed rough spots on the cave walls
   Ⓓ Upper Paleolithic people used the paintings to increase their luck at hunting

15. Why does the author mention that Upper Paleolithic cave art seemed to have "**reached a peak toward the end of the Upper Paleolithic period, when the herds of game were decreasing**"?

Ⓐ To argue that Upper Paleolithic art ceased to include animals when herds of game became scarce

Ⓑ To provide support for the idea that the aim of the paintings was to increase the supply of animals for hunting

Ⓒ To emphasize the continued improvement in the quality of cave art throughout the Upper Paleolithic period

Ⓓ To show the direct connection between the decrease in herds of game and the end of the Upper Paleolithic period

PARAGRAPH 4

The particular symbolic significance of the cave paintings in southwestern France is more explicitly revealed, perhaps, by the results of a study conducted by researchers Patricia Rice and Ann Paterson. The data they present suggest that the animals portrayed in the cave paintings were mostly the ones that the painters preferred for meat and for materials such as hides. For example, wild cattle (bovines) and horses are portrayed more often than we would expect by chance, probably because they were larger and heavier (meatier) than other animals in the environment. In addition, the paintings mostly portray animals that the painters may have feared the most because of their size, speed, natural weapons such as tusks and horns, and the unpredictability of their behavior. That is, mammoths, bovines, and horses are portrayed more often than deer and reindeer. Thus, the paintings are consistent with the idea that the art is related to the importance of hunting in the economy of Upper Paleolithic people. Consistent with this idea, according to the investigators, is the fact that the art of the cultural period that followed the Upper Paleolithic also seems to reflect how people got their food. But in that period, when getting food no longer depended on hunting large game animals (because they were becoming extinct), the art ceased to focus on portrayals of animals.

16. According to paragraph 4, which of the following may best represent the attitude of hunters toward deer and reindeer in the Upper Paleolithic period?

Ⓐ Hunters did not fear deer and reindeer as much as they did large game animals such as horses and mammoths.

Ⓑ Hunters were not interested in hunting deer and reindeer because of their size and speed.

Ⓒ Hunters preferred the meat and hides of deer and reindeer to those of other animals.

Ⓓ Hunters avoided deer and reindeer because of their natural weapons, such as horns.

17. According to paragraph 4, what change is evident in the art of the period following the Upper Paleolithic?

Ⓐ This new art starts to depict small animals rather than large ones.

Ⓑ This new art ceases to reflect the ways in which people obtained their food.

Ⓒ This new art no longer consists mostly of representations of animals.

Ⓓ This new art begins to show the importance of hunting to the economy.

PARAGRAPH 5

Upper Paleolithic art was not confined to cave paintings. Many shafts of spears and similar objects were decorated with figures of animals. The anthropologist Alexander Marshack has an interesting interpretation of some of the engravings made during the Upper Paleolithic. He believes that as far back as 30,000 B.C., hunters may have used a system of notation, engraved on bone and stone, to mark phases of the Moon. If this is true, it would mean that Upper Paleolithic people were capable of complex thought and were consciously aware of their environment. In addition to other artworks, figurines representing the human female in exaggerated form have also been found at Upper Paleolithic sites. It has been suggested that these figurines were an ideal type or an expression of a desire for fertility.

18. According to paragraph 5, which of the following has been used as evidence to suggest that Upper Paleolithic people were capable of complex thought and conscious awareness of their environment?

Ⓐ They engraved animal figures on the shafts of spears and other objects.

Ⓑ They may have used engraved signs to record the phases of the Moon.

Ⓒ Their figurines represented the human female in exaggerated form.

Ⓓ They may have used figurines to portray an ideal type or to express a desire for fertility.

The subjects of the paintings are mostly animals. The paintings rest on bare walls, with no backdrops or environmental trappings. Perhaps, like many contemporary peoples, Upper Paleolithic men and women believed that the drawing of a human image could cause death or injury, and if that were indeed their belief, it might explain why human figures are rarely depicted in cave art. Another explanation for the focus on animals might be that these people sought to improve their luck at hunting. **(A)** This theory is suggested by evidence of chips in the painted figures, perhaps made by spears thrown at the drawings. **(B)** But if improving their hunting luck was the chief motivation for the paintings, it is difficult to explain why only a few show signs of having been speared. **(C)** Perhaps the paintings were inspired by the need to increase the supply of animals. Cave art seems to have reached a peak toward the end of the Upper Paleolithic period, when the herds of game were decreasing. **(D)**

19. Look at the part of the passage that is displayed above. The letters **(A)**, **(B)**, **(C)**, and **(D)** indicate where the following sentence could be added.

Therefore, if the paintings were connected with hunting, some other explanation is needed.

Where would the sentence best fit?

Ⓐ Choice A
Ⓑ Choice B
Ⓒ Choice C
Ⓓ Choice D

20. **Directions**: An introductory sentence for a brief summary of the passage is provided below. Complete the summary by selecting the THREE answer choices that express the most important ideas in the passage. Some sentences do not belong in the summary because they express ideas that are not presented in the passage or are minor ideas in the passage. **This question is worth 2 points.**

Write your answer choices in the spaces where they belong. You can either write the letter of your answer choice or you can copy the sentence.

> **Upper Paleolithic cave paintings in western Europe are among humanity's earliest artistic efforts.**
>
> ●
>
> ●
>
> ●

Answer Choices

A Researchers have proposed several different explanations for the fact that animals were the most common subjects in the cave paintings.

B The cave paintings focus on portraying animals without also depicting the natural environments in which these animals are typically found.

C The art of the cultural period that followed the Upper Paleolithic ceased to portray large game animals and focused instead on the kinds of animals that people of that period preferred to hunt.

D Some researchers have argued that the cave paintings mostly portrayed large animals that provided Upper Paleolithic people with meat and materials.

E Some researchers believe that the paintings found in France provide more explicit evidence of their symbolic significance than those found in Spain, southern Africa, and Australia.

F Besides cave paintings, Upper Paleolithic people produced several other kinds of artwork, one of which has been thought to provide evidence of complex thought.

LISTENING

In this section, you will be able to demonstrate your ability to understand conversations and lectures in English.

In the actual test, the section is divided into two separately timed parts. You will hear each conversation or lecture only one time. A clock will indicate how much time remains. The clock will count down only while you are answering questions, not while you are listening. You may take up to 16.5 minutes to answer the questions.

In this practice test, there is no time limit for answering questions.

You may take notes while you listen. You may use your notes to help you answer the questions. Your notes will not be scored.

Answer the questions based on what is stated or implied by the speakers.

In some questions, you will see this icon: 🎧. This means that you will hear, but not see, part of the question.

In the actual test, you must answer each question. You cannot return to previous questions.

At the end of this practice test, you will find an answer key.

Directions: Listen to Track 1.

Directions: Now answer the questions.

1. Why does the man need the woman's assistance? *Select 2 answers.*

   - ☐A He does not know the publication date of some reviews he needs.
   - ☐B He does not know the location of the library's video collection of plays.
   - ☐C He does not know how to find out where the play is currently being performed.
   - ☐D He does not know how to determine which newspapers he should look at.

2. What does the woman imply about critical reaction to the play *Happy Strangers*?

   - Ⓐ Negative critical reaction led to its content being revised after it premiered.
   - Ⓑ The play has always been quite popular among university students.
   - Ⓒ Reactions to the play are more positive nowadays than they were in the past.
   - Ⓓ The play is rarely performed nowadays because critics have never liked it.

3. What does the woman say about her experience seeing a performance of *Happy Strangers* when she was younger? *Select 2 answers.*

   - ☐A It was the first play she had seen performed professionally.
   - ☐B She saw it against the wishes of her parents.
   - ☐C She was surprised at how traditional the performance was.
   - ☐D She had a variety of emotional reactions to the play.

4. What is the man's attitude toward his current assignment?

   - Ⓐ He is not confident that he will find the materials he needs.
   - Ⓑ He feels that performing in a play is less boring than reading one.
   - Ⓒ He thinks his review of the play will be more objective than the contemporary reviews were.
   - Ⓓ He is optimistic that he will learn to appreciate the play he is researching.

5. *Listen again to part of the conversation by playing Track 2.* 🎧 *Then answer the question.*

   Why does the woman say this?
   - Ⓐ To ask the man to clarify his request
   - Ⓑ To state the man's request more precisely
   - Ⓒ To make sure that she heard the man correctly
   - Ⓓ To correct a mistake the man has made

Directions: Listen to Track 3.

Biology

disinhibition

displacement activity

Directions: Now answer the questions.

6. What is the lecture mainly about?

    (A) Methods of observing unusual animal behavior

    (B) A theory about ways birds attract mates

    (C) Ways animals behave when they have conflicting drives

    (D) Criteria for classifying animal behaviors

7. Indicate whether each of the activities below describes a displacement activity. *Put a check (✓) in the correct boxes.*

	Yes	No
An animal attacks the ground instead of its enemy.		
An animal falls asleep in the middle of a mating ritual.		
An animal eats some food when confronted by its enemy.		
An animal takes a drink of water after grooming itself.		

8. What does the professor say about disinhibition?

    (A) It can prevent displacement activities from occurring.

    (B) It can cause animals to act on more than one drive at a time.

    (C) It is not useful for explaining many types of displacement activities.

    (D) It is responsible for the appearance of seemingly irrelevant behavior.

9. According to the lecture, what is one possible reason that displacement activities are often grooming behaviors?

    (A) Grooming may cause an enemy or predator to be confused.

    (B) Grooming is a convenient and accessible behavior.

    (C) Grooming often occurs before eating and drinking.

    (D) Grooming is a common social activity.

10. Why does the professor mention the wood thrush?

    (A) To contrast its displacement activities with those of other animal species

    (B) To explain that some animals display displacement activities other than grooming

    (C) To point out how displacement activities are influenced by the environment

    (D) To give an example of an animal that does not display displacement activities

11. *Listen again to part of the lecture by playing Track 4.* 🎧 *Then answer the question.*

What does the professor mean when she says this?

    (A) She is impressed by how much the student knows about redirecting.

    (B) She thinks it is time to move on to the next part of this lecture.

    (C) The student's answer is not an example of a displacement activity.

    (D) The student should suggest a different animal behavior to discuss next.

Directions: Listen to Track 5.

Literature

Directions: Now answer the questions.

12. What is the main purpose of the lecture?

    Ⓐ To point out similarities in Emerson's essays and poems
    Ⓑ To prepare the students to read an essay by Emerson
    Ⓒ To compare Emerson's concept of universal truth to that of other authors
    Ⓓ To show the influence of early United States society on Emerson's writing

13. On what basis did Emerson criticize the people of his time?

    Ⓐ They refused to recognize universal truths.
    Ⓑ They did not recognize the genius of certain authors.
    Ⓒ Their convictions were not well-defined.
    Ⓓ They were too interested in conformity.

14. What does Emerson say about the past?

    Ⓐ It should guide a person's present actions.
    Ⓑ It must be examined closely.
    Ⓒ It is less important than the future.
    Ⓓ It lacks both clarity and universal truth.

15. What point does the professor make when he mentions a ship's path?

    Ⓐ It is easy for people to lose sight of their true path.
    Ⓑ Most people are not capable of deciding which path is best for them.
    Ⓒ The path a person takes can only be seen clearly after the destination has been reached.
    Ⓓ A person should establish a goal before deciding which path to take.

16. What does the professor imply about himself when he recounts some life experiences he had before becoming a literature professor? *Select 2 answers.*

    Ⓐ He did not consider the consequences of his decisions.
    Ⓑ He did not plan to become a literature professor.
    Ⓒ He has always tried to act consistently.
    Ⓓ He has trusted in himself and his decisions.

17. *Listen again to part of the lecture by playing Track 6.* 🎧 *Then answer the question.*

    Why does the professor say this?

    Ⓐ To suggest that United States citizens have not changed much over time
    Ⓑ To encourage the class to find more information about this time period
    Ⓒ To explain why Emerson's essay has lost some relevance
    Ⓓ To provide background for the concept he is explaining

Directions: Listen to Track 7.

Directions: Now answer the questions.

18. What is the conversation mainly about?
    - Ⓐ Methods for finding appropriate sources for a project
    - Ⓑ Reasons the woman is having difficulties with a project
    - Ⓒ Criteria the professor uses to evaluate group projects
    - Ⓓ Ways to develop the skills needed to work in groups

19. Why does the professor mention the "free-rider" problem?
    - Ⓐ To review a concept he explained in class
    - Ⓑ To give the student a plan to solve her problem
    - Ⓒ To clarify the problem the student is facing
    - Ⓓ To explain a benefit of working in groups

20. What is the professor's opinion of the other students in the woman's group?
    - Ⓐ They try to take credit for work they did not do.
    - Ⓑ They did not perform well in previous courses with him.
    - Ⓒ They are more motivated when they are working in a group.
    - Ⓓ They do good work when they are interested in the subject.

21. Why did the woman choose property rights as a topic?
    - Ⓐ The professor recommended the topic.
    - Ⓑ She already had a lot of reference materials on the subject.
    - Ⓒ She wanted to learn something new.
    - Ⓓ It was easy to research at the school library.

22. What mistakes does the professor imply the woman has made while working on a project? *Select 2 answers.*
    - A Finding sources for her group partners
    - B Writing the weekly progress reports for her group
    - C Forgetting to pay attention to the project's deadlines
    - D Failing to involve the group members in the selection of a topic

Directions: Listen to Track 8.

United States Government

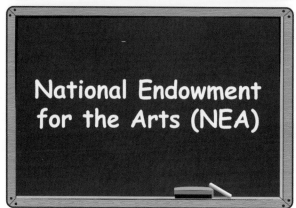

Directions: Now answer the questions.

23. What is the discussion mainly about?

    Ⓐ Reasons the United States government should not support the arts

    Ⓑ The history of government support for the arts in the United States

    Ⓒ Strengths and weaknesses of different government-sponsored arts programs

    Ⓓ Different ways in which governments can help support artists

24. According to the discussion, in what two ways was the Federal Art Project successful? *Choose 2 answers.*

    Ａ It established standards for art schools.

    Ｂ It provided jobs for many artists.

    Ｃ It produced many excellent artists.

    Ｄ It gave many people greater access to the arts.

25. The class discusses some important events related to government support for the arts in the United States. Put the events in order from earliest to latest.

Write your answer choices in the spaces where they belong. You can either write the letter of your answer choice or you can copy the sentence. The first one is done for you.

1. The government provided no official support for the arts.
2.
3.
4.
5.

Answer Choices

    Ａ Arts councils were established in all 50 states of the country.

    Ｂ The federal budget supporting the arts was reduced by half.

    Ｃ The Federal Art Project helped reduce unemployment.

    Ｄ The National Endowment for the Arts was established.

26. Why does the professor mention the Kennedy Center and Lincoln Center?

    Ⓐ To give examples of institutions that benefit from corporate support

    Ⓑ To illustrate why some artists oppose the building of cultural centers

    Ⓒ To show how two centers were named after presidents who supported the arts

    Ⓓ To name two art centers built by the government during the Depression

27. What does the professor say about artists' opinions of government support for the arts?

   Ⓐ Most artists believe that the government should provide more funding for the arts.

   Ⓑ Most artists approve of the ways in which the government supports the arts.

   Ⓒ Even artists do not agree on whether the government should support the arts.

   Ⓓ Even artists have a low opinion of government support for the arts.

28. *Listen again to part of the discussion by playing Track 9.* 🎧 *Then answer the question.*

   What does the professor imply when she says this?.

   Ⓐ Other students should comment on the man's remark.

   Ⓑ Most people would agree with the man's opinion.

   Ⓒ Artwork funded by the government is usually of excellent quality.

   Ⓓ The government project was not a waste of money.

SPEAKING

In this section, you will be able to demonstrate your ability to speak about a variety of topics.

In the actual test, the Speaking section will last approximately 16 minutes. You will answer four questions by speaking into the microphone. You may take notes while you listen. You may use your notes to help you answer the questions. Your notes will not be scored. For each question, you will have time to prepare before giving your response. You should answer the questions as completely as possible in the time allowed.

For this practice test, you may want to use a personal recording device to record and play back your responses.

For each question, play the audio track listed and follow the directions to complete the task.

At the end of this practice test, you will find important points about each question.

1. You will now give your opinion about a familiar topic. After you hear the question, you should give yourself 15 seconds to prepare and 45 seconds to speak.

Listen to Track 10.

> Many universities now offer academic courses over the Internet. However, some people still prefer learning in traditional classrooms. Which do you think is better? Explain why.
>
> | **Preparation Time: 15 seconds** |
> |:---:|
> | **Response Time: 45 seconds** |

2. Now you will read a passage about a campus situation and then listen to a conversation about the same topic. You will then answer a question, using information from both the reading passage and the conversation. You should give yourself 30 seconds to prepare and 60 seconds to speak.

Listen to Track 11.

Reading Time: 45 seconds

Evening Computer Classes May Be Added

The computer department is considering offering evening classes in the fall. The proposal to add the classes is a response to student complaints that day-time computer classes have become increasingly overcrowded and there are no longer enough computers available. The department has decided that despite some added expense, the most cost-effective way of addressing this problem is by adding computer classes in the evening. It is hoped that this change will decrease the number of students enrolled in day classes and thus guarantee individual access to computers for all students in computer classes.

Listen to Track 12.

The man expresses his opinion about the proposal described in the article. Briefly summarize the proposal. Then state his opinion about the proposal and explain the reasons he gives for holding that opinion.

Preparation Time: 30 seconds
Response Time: 60 seconds

3. Now you will read a passage about an academic subject and then listen to a lecture on the same topic. You will then answer a question, using information from both the reading passage and the lecture. You should give yourself 30 seconds to prepare and 60 seconds to speak.

Listen to Track 13.

Reading Time: 45 seconds

Verbal and Nonverbal Communication

When we speak with other people face-to-face, the nonverbal signals we give—our facial expressions, hand gestures, body movements, and tone of voice—often communicate as much as, or more than, the words we utter. When our nonverbal signals, which we often produce unconsciously, agree with our verbal message, the verbal message is enhanced and supported, made more convincing. But when they conflict with the verbal message, we may be communicating an entirely different and more accurate message than what we intend.

Listen to Track 14.

Explain how the examples from the professor's lecture illustrate the relationship between verbal and nonverbal communication.

Preparation Time: 30 seconds
Response Time: 60 seconds

4. Now you will listen to a lecture. You will then be asked to summarize the lecture. You should give yourself 20 seconds to prepare and 60 seconds to speak.

Listen to Track 15.

Using points and examples from the lecture, explain the importance of visual elements in painting.

Preparation Time: 20 seconds
Response Time: 60 seconds

WRITING

In this section, you will be able to demonstrate your ability to use writing to communicate in an academic environment. There will be two writing tasks.

At the end of this practice test, you will find topic notes for each question.

Turn the page to see the directions for the first writing task.

Writing Based on Reading and Listening

For this task, you will read a passage about an academic topic. Then you will listen to a lecture about the same topic. You may take notes while you listen.

In your response, provide a detailed summary of the lecture and explain how the lecture relates to the reading passage.

In the actual test, you will have 3 minutes to read the passage and 20 minutes to write your response. While you write, you will be able to see the reading passage. If you finish your response before time is up, you may go on to the second writing task.

Reading Time: 3 minutes

Endotherms are animals such as modern birds and mammals that keep their body temperatures constant. For instance, humans are endotherms and maintain an internal temperature of 37°C, no matter whether the environment is warm or cold. Because dinosaurs were reptiles, and modern reptiles are not endotherms, it was long assumed that dinosaurs were not endotherms. However, dinosaurs differ in many ways from modern reptiles, and there is now considerable evidence that dinosaurs were, in fact, endotherms.

Polar dinosaurs

One reason for believing that dinosaurs were endotherms is that dinosaur fossils have been discovered in polar regions. Only animals that can maintain a temperature well above that of the surrounding environment could be active in such cold climates.

Leg position and movement

There is a connection between endothermy and the position and movement of the legs. The physiology of endothermy allows sustained physical activity, such as running. But running is efficient only if an animal's legs are positioned underneath its body, not at the body's side, as they are for crocodiles and many lizards. The legs of all modern endotherms are underneath the body, and so were the legs of dinosaurs. This strongly suggests that dinosaurs were endotherms.

Haversian canals

There is also a connection between endothermy and bone structure. The bones of endotherms usually include structures called Haversian canals. These canals house nerves and blood vessels that allow the living animal to grow quickly, and rapid body growth is in fact a characteristic of endothermy. The presence of Haversian canals in bone is a strong indicator that the animal is an endotherm, and fossilized bones of dinosaurs are usually dense with Haversian canals.

Listen to Track 16.

Directions: You have 20 minutes to plan and write your response. Your response will be judged on the basis of the quality of your writing and on how well your response presents the points in the lecture and their relationship to the reading passage. Typically, an effective response will contain a minimum of 150 words.

Listen to Track 17.

Response Time: 20 minutes

Question 1

Summarize the points made in the lecture, being sure to explain how they challenge the specific points made in the reading passage.

_____

_____

_____

_____

_____

_____

_____

_____

_____

Writing for an Academic Discussion

For this task, you will read an online discussion. A professor has posted a question about a topic, and some classmates have responded with their ideas.

In the actual test, you will have 10 minutes to write a response that contributes to the discussion.

Question 2

Your professor is teaching a class on sociology. Write a post responding to the professor's question.

In your response, you should do the following.
- Express and support your opinion.
- Make a contribution to the discussion in your own words.

An effective response will contain at least 100 words.

Dr. Achebe

Recently economic and technological changes have made it possible for some people to give up the idea of a "home" as a city or town where one resides for many years, thus becoming more nomadic—living and working from place to place, without ever "settling down" in one location. For those with the means to accomplish it, this lifestyle might be very fulfilling or liberating, but there must be disadvantages as well. What do you think those disadvantages are?

Claire

I think this is a romantic idea that is only realistic for younger people. As people age, they need more and more support. For example, it is helpful for them to have a regular doctor who knows their medical history. That sort of support can't happen if you're always moving.

Kelly

Being a modern nomad seems appealing, but how empowering is it? The disadvantage to this lifestyle is that you will likely feel like a foreigner in the places you spend your time, and that can be an obstacle to your success. Only at "home," where you feel culturally connected to other people within familiar surroundings, can you really thrive.

Response Time: 10 minutes

TOEFL iBT® Test 2

READING

In this section, you will be able to demonstrate your ability to understand academic passages in English. You will read and answer questions about **two passages**.

In the actual test, you will have 36 minutes total to read both passages and answer the questions. A clock will indicate how much time remains.

Some passages may include one or more notes explaining words or phrases. The words or phrases are marked with footnote numbers, and the notes explaining them appear at the end of the passage.

Most questions are worth 1 point, but the last question for each passage is worth 2 points.

You may review and revise your answers in this section as long as time remains.

At the end of this practice test, you will find an answer key.

Directions: Read the passage. Then answer the questions. You have 18 minutes on average to answer the questions.

MINERALS AND PLANTS

Research has shown that certain minerals are required by plants for normal growth and development. The soil is the source of these minerals, which are absorbed by the plant with the water from the soil. Even nitrogen, which is a gas in its elemental state, is normally absorbed from the soil as nitrate ions. Some soils are notoriously deficient in micro nutrients and are therefore unable to support most plant life. So-called serpentine soils, for example, are deficient in calcium, and only plants able to tolerate low levels of this mineral can survive. In modern agriculture, mineral depletion of soils is a major concern, since harvesting crops interrupts the recycling of nutrients back to the soil.

Mineral deficiencies can often be detected by specific symptoms such as chlorosis (loss of chlorophyll resulting in yellow or white leaf tissue), necrosis (isolated dead patches), anthocyanin formation (development of deep red pigmentation of leaves or stem), stunted growth, and development of woody tissue in an herbaceous plant. Soils are most commonly deficient in nitrogen and phosphorus. Nitrogen-deficient plants exhibit many of the symptoms just described. Leaves develop chlorosis; stems are short and slender; and anthocyanin discoloration occurs on stems, petioles, and lower leaf surfaces. Phosphorus-deficient plants are often stunted, with leaves turning a characteristic dark green, often with the accumulation of anthocyanin. Typically, older leaves are affected first as the phosphorus is mobilized to young growing tissue. Iron deficiency is characterized by chlorosis between veins in young leaves.

Much of the research on nutrient deficiencies is based on growing plants hydroponically, that is, in soilless liquid nutrient solutions. This technique allows researchers to create solutions that selectively omit certain nutrients and then observe the resulting effects on the plants. Hydroponics has applications beyond basic research, since it facilitates the growing of greenhouse vegetables during winter. Aeroponics, a technique in which plants are suspended and the roots misted with a nutrient solution, is another method for growing plants without soil.

While mineral deficiencies can limit the growth of plants, an overabundance of certain minerals can be toxic and can also limit growth. Saline soils, which have high concentrations of sodium chloride and other salts, limit plant growth, and research continues to focus on developing salt-tolerant varieties of agricultural crops. Research has focused on the toxic effects of heavy metals such as lead, cadmium, mercury, and aluminum; however, even copper and zinc, which are essential elements, can become toxic in high concentrations. Although most plants cannot survive in these soils, certain plants have the ability to tolerate high levels of these minerals.

Scientists have known for some time that certain plants, called hyperaccumulators, can concentrate minerals at levels a hundredfold or greater than normal. A survey of known hyperaccumulators identified that 75 percent of them amassed nickel; cobalt, copper, zinc, manganese, lead, and cadmium are other minerals of choice. Hyperaccumulators run the entire range of the plant world. They may be herbs, shrubs, or trees. Many members of the mustard family, spurge family, legume family, and grass family are top hyperaccumulators. Many are found in tropical and subtropical areas of the world, where accumulation of high concentrations of metals may afford some protection against plant-eating insects and microbial pathogens.

Only recently have investigators considered using these plants to clean up soil and waste sites that have been contaminated by toxic levels of heavy metals—an environmentally friendly approach known as phytoremediation. This scenario begins with the planting of hyperaccumulating species in the target area, such as an abandoned mine or an irrigation pond contaminated by runoff. Toxic minerals would first be absorbed by roots but later relocated to the stem and leaves. A harvest of the shoots would remove the toxic compounds off site to be burned or composted to recover the metal for industrial uses. After several years of cultivation and harvest, the site would be restored at a cost much lower than the price of excavation and reburial, the standard practice for remediation of contaminated soils. For example, in field trials, the plant alpine pennycress removed zinc and cadmium from soils near a zinc smelter, and Indian mustard, native to Pakistan and India, has been effective in reducing levels of selenium salts by 50 percent in contaminated soils.

Directions: Now answer the questions.

PARAGRAPH 1

Research has shown that certain minerals are required by plants for normal growth and development. The soil is the source of these minerals, which are absorbed by the plant with the water from the soil. Even nitrogen, which is a gas in its elemental state, is normally absorbed from the soil as nitrate ions. Some soils are notoriously deficient in micro nutrients and are therefore unable to support most plant life. So-called serpentine soils, for example, are deficient in calcium, and only plants able to tolerate low levels of this mineral can survive. In modern agriculture, mineral depletion of soils is a major concern, since harvesting crops interrupts the recycling of nutrients back to the soil.

1. According to paragraph 1, what is true of plants that can grow in serpentine soils?
   - (A) They absorb micronutrients unusually well.
   - (B) They require far less calcium than most plants do.
   - (C) They are able to absorb nitrogen in its elemental state.
   - (D) They are typically crops raised for food.

PARAGRAPH 2

Mineral deficiencies can often be detected by specific symptoms such as chlorosis (loss of chlorophyll resulting in yellow or white leaf tissue), necrosis (isolated dead patches), anthocyanin formation (development of deep red pigmentation of leaves or stem), stunted growth, and development of woody tissue in an herbaceous plant. Soils are most commonly deficient in nitrogen and phosphorus. Nitrogen-deficient plants exhibit many of the symptoms just described. Leaves develop chlorosis; stems are short and slender; and anthocyanin discoloration occurs on stems, petioles, and lower leaf surfaces. Phosphorus-deficient plants are often stunted, with leaves turning a characteristic dark green, often with the accumulation of anthocyanin. Typically, older leaves are affected first as the phosphorus is mobilized to young growing tissue. Iron deficiency is characterized by chlorosis between veins in young leaves.

2. According to paragraph 2, which of the following symptoms occurs in phosphorus-deficient plants but not in plants deficient in nitrogen or iron?

   Ⓐ Chlorosis on leaves
   Ⓑ Change in leaf pigmentation to a dark shade of green
   Ⓒ Short, stunted appearance of stems
   Ⓓ Reddish pigmentation on the leaves or stem

3. According to paragraph 2, a symptom of iron deficiency is the presence in young leaves of

   Ⓐ deep red discoloration between the veins
   Ⓑ white or yellow tissue between the veins
   Ⓒ dead spots between the veins
   Ⓓ characteristic dark green veins

PARAGRAPH 3

Much of the research on nutrient deficiencies is based on growing plants hydroponically, that is, in soilless liquid nutrient solutions. This technique allows researchers to create solutions that selectively omit certain nutrients and then observe the resulting effects on the plants. Hydroponics has applications beyond basic research, since it **facilitates** the growing of greenhouse vegetables during winter. Aeroponics, a technique in which plants are suspended and the roots misted with a nutrient solution, is another method for growing plants without soil.

4. The word "**facilitates**" in the passage is closest in meaning to

   Ⓐ slows down
   Ⓑ affects
   Ⓒ makes easier
   Ⓓ focuses on

5. According to paragraph 3, what is the advantage of hydroponics for research on nutrient deficiencies in plants?

   Ⓐ It allows researchers to control what nutrients a plant receives.

   Ⓑ It allows researchers to observe the growth of a large number of plants simultaneously.

   Ⓒ It is possible to directly observe the roots of plants.

   Ⓓ It is unnecessary to keep misting plants with nutrient solutions.

Scientists have known for some time that certain plants, called hyperaccumulators, can concentrate minerals at levels a hundredfold or greater than normal. A survey of known hyperaccumulators identified that 75 percent of them amassed nickel; cobalt, copper, zinc, manganese, lead, and cadmium are other minerals of choice. Hyperaccumulators run the entire range of the plant world. They may be **herbs**, **shrubs**, or **trees**. Many members of the mustard family, spurge family, legume family, and grass family are top hyperaccumulators. Many are found in tropical and subtropical areas of the world, where accumulation of high concentrations of metals may afford some protection against plant-eating insects and microbial pathogens.

6. Why does the author mention "**herbs**," "**shrubs**," and "**trees**"?

   Ⓐ To provide examples of plant types that cannot tolerate high levels of harmful minerals

   Ⓑ To show why so many plants are hyperaccumulators

   Ⓒ To help explain why hyperaccumulators can be found in so many different places

   Ⓓ To emphasize that hyperaccumulators occur in a wide range of plant types

Only recently have investigators considered using these plants to clean up soil and waste sites that have been contaminated by toxic levels of heavy metals—an environmentally friendly approach known as phytoremediation. **This scenario begins with the planting of hyperaccumulating species in the target area, such as an abandoned mine or an irrigation pond contaminated by runoff.** Toxic minerals would first be absorbed by roots but later relocated to the stem and leaves. A harvest of the shoots would remove the toxic compounds off site to be burned or composted to recover the metal for industrial uses. After several years of cultivation and harvest, the site would be restored at a cost much lower than the price of excavation and reburial, the standard practice for remediation of contaminated soils. For example, in field trials, the plant alpine pennycress removed zinc and cadmium from soils near a zinc smelter, and Indian mustard, native to Pakistan and India, has been effective in reducing levels of selenium salts by 50 percent in contaminated soils.

7. Which of the sentences below best expresses the essential information in the highlighted sentence in paragraph 6? Incorrect choices change the meaning in important ways or leave out essential information.

   (A) Before considering phytoremediation, hyperaccumulating species of plants local to the target area must be identified.
   (B) The investigation begins with an evaluation of toxic sites in the target area to determine the extent of contamination.
   (C) The first step in phytoremediation is the planting of hyperaccumulating plants in the area to be cleaned up.
   (D) Mines and irrigation ponds can be kept from becoming contaminated by planting hyperaccumulating species in targeted areas.

8. It can be inferred from paragraph 6 that compared with standard practices for remediation of contaminated soils, phytoremediation

   (A) does not allow for the use of the removed minerals for industrial purposes
   (B) can be faster to implement
   (C) is equally friendly to the environment
   (D) is less suitable for soils that need to be used within a short period of time

Scientists have known for some time that certain plants, called hyperaccumulators, can concentrate minerals at levels a hundredfold or greater than normal. **(A)** A survey of known hyperaccumulators identified that 75 percent of them amassed nickel; cobalt, copper, zinc, manganese, lead, and cadmium are other minerals of choice. **(B)** Hyperaccumulators run the entire range of the plant world. **(C)** They may be herbs, shrubs, or trees. **(D)** Many members of the mustard family, spurge family, legume family, and grass family are top hyperaccumulators. Many are found in tropical and subtropical areas of the world, where accumulation of high concentrations of metals may afford some protection against plant-eating insects and microbial pathogens.

9. Look at the part of the passage that is displayed above. The letters **(A)**, **(B)**, **(C)**, and **(D)** indicate where the following sentence could be added.

    Certain minerals are more likely to be accumulated in large quantities than others.

    Where would the sentence best fit?

    (A) Choice A
    (B) Choice B
    (C) Choice C
    (D) Choice D

10. **Directions:** An introductory sentence for a brief summary of the passage is provided below. Complete the summary by selecting the THREE answer choices that express the most important ideas in the passage. Some sentences do not belong in the summary because they express ideas that are not presented in the passage or are minor ideas in the passage. **This question is worth 2 points.**

Write your answer choices in the spaces where they belong. You can either write the letter of your answer choice or you can copy the sentence.

> **Plants need to absorb certain minerals from the soil in adequate quantities for normal growth and development.**
>
> ●
>
> ●
>
> ●

Answer Choices

A Some plants can tolerate comparatively low levels of certain minerals, but such plants are of little use for recycling nutrients back into depleted soils.

B When plants do not absorb sufficient amounts of essential minerals, characteristic abnormalities result.

C Mineral deficiencies in many plants can be cured by misting their roots with a nutrient solution or by transferring the plants to a soilless nutrient solution.

D Though beneficial in lower levels, high levels of salts, other minerals, and heavy metals can be harmful to plants.

E Because high concentrations of sodium chloride and other salts limit growth in most plants, much research has been done in an effort to develop salt-tolerant agricultural crops.

F Some plants are able to accumulate extremely high levels of certain minerals and thus can be used to clean up soils contaminated with toxic levels of these minerals.

Directions: Read the passage. Then answer the questions. You have 18 minutes on average to answer the questions.

THE ORIGIN OF THE PACIFIC ISLAND PEOPLE

The greater Pacific region, traditionally called Oceania, consists of three cultural areas: Melanesia, Micronesia, and Polynesia. Melanesia, in the southwest Pacific, contains the large islands of New Guinea, the Solomons, Vanuatu, and New Caledonia. Micronesia, the area north of Melanesia, consists primarily of small scattered islands. Polynesia is the central Pacific area in the great triangle defined by Hawaii, Easter Island, and New Zealand. Before the arrival of Europeans, the islands in the two largest cultural areas, Polynesia and Micronesia, together contained a population estimated at 700,000.

Speculation on the origin of these Pacific islanders began as soon as outsiders encountered them; in the absence of solid linguistic, archaeological, and biological data, many fanciful and mutually exclusive theories were devised. Pacific islanders were variously thought to have come from North America, South America, Egypt, Israel, and India, as well as Southeast Asia. Many older theories implicitly deprecated the navigational abilities and overall cultural creativity of the Pacific islanders. For example, British anthropologists G. Elliot Smith and W. J. Perry assumed that only Egyptians would have been skilled enough to navigate and colonize the Pacific. They speculated that the Egyptians even crossed the Pacific to found the great civilizations of the New World (North and South America). In 1947 Norwegian adventurer Thor Heyerdahl drifted on a balsa-log raft westward with the winds and currents across the Pacific from South America to prove his theory that Pacific islanders were Native Americans (also called American Indians). Later Heyerdahl suggested that the Pacific was peopled by three migrations: by Native Americans from the Pacific Northwest of North America drifting to Hawaii, by Peruvians drifting to Easter Island, and by Melanesians. In 1969 he crossed the Atlantic in an Egyptian-style reed boat to prove Egyptian influences in the Americas. Contrary to these theorists, the overwhelming evidence of physical anthropology, linguistics, and archaeology shows that the Pacific islanders came from Southeast Asia and were skilled enough as navigators to sail against the prevailing winds and currents.

The basic cultural requirements for the successful colonization of the Pacific islands include the appropriate boat-building, sailing, and navigation skills to get to the islands in the first place; domesticated plants and gardening skills suited to often marginal conditions; and a varied inventory of fishing implements and techniques. It is now generally believed that these prerequisites originated with peoples speaking Austronesian languages (a group of several hundred related languages) and began to emerge in Southeast Asia by about 5000 B.C.E. The culture of that time, based on archaeology and linguistic reconstruction, is assumed to have had a broad inventory of cultivated plants including taro, yams, banana, sugarcane, breadfruit, coconut, sago, and rice. Just as important, the culture also possessed the basic foundation for an effective maritime adaptation, including outrigger canoes and a variety of fishing techniques that could be effective for overseas voyaging.

Contrary to the arguments of some that much of the Pacific was settled by Polynesians accidentally marooned after being lost and adrift, it seems reasonable that this feat was accomplished by deliberate colonization expeditions that set out fully stocked with food and domesticated plants and animals. Detailed studies of the winds and currents using computer simulations suggest that drifting canoes would have been a most unlikely means of colonizing the Pacific. These expeditions were likely driven by population growth and political dynamics on the home islands, as well as the challenge and excitement of exploring unknown waters. Because all Polynesians, Micronesians, and many Melanesians speak Austronesian languages and grow crops derived from Southeast Asia, all these peoples most certainly derived from that region and not the New World or elsewhere. The undisputed pre-Columbian presence in Oceania of the sweet potato, which is a New World domesticate, has sometimes been used to support Heyerdahl's "American Indians in the Pacific" theories. However, this is one plant out of a long list of Southeast Asian domesticates. As Patrick Kirch, an American anthropologist, points out, rather than being brought by rafting South Americans, sweet potatoes might just have easily been brought back by returning Polynesian navigators who could have reached the west coast of South America.

Directions: Now answer the questions.

PARAGRAPH 2

Speculation on the origin of these Pacific islanders began as soon as outsiders encountered them; in the absence of solid linguistic, archaeological, and biological data, many fanciful and **mutually exclusive** theories were devised. Pacific islanders were variously thought to have come from North America, South America, Egypt, Israel, and India, as well as Southeast Asia. Many older theories implicitly deprecated the navigational abilities and overall cultural creativity of the Pacific islanders. For example, British anthropologists G. Elliot Smith and W. J. Perry assumed that only Egyptians would have been skilled enough to navigate and colonize the Pacific. They speculated that the Egyptians even crossed the Pacific to found the great civilizations of the New World (North and South America). In 1947 Norwegian adventurer Thor Heyerdahl drifted on a balsa-log raft westward with the winds and currents across the Pacific from South America to prove his theory that Pacific islanders were Native Americans (also called American Indians). Later Heyerdahl suggested that the Pacific was peopled by three migrations: by Native Americans from the Pacific Northwest of North America drifting to Hawaii, by Peruvians drifting to Easter Island, and by Melanesians. In 1969 he crossed the Atlantic in an Egyptian-style reed boat to prove Egyptian influences in the Americas. Contrary to these theorists, the overwhelming evidence of physical anthropology, linguistics, and archaeology shows that the Pacific islanders came from Southeast Asia and were skilled enough as navigators to sail against the prevailing winds and currents.

11. By stating that the theories are "**mutually exclusive**" the author means that

    (A) if one of the theories is true, then all the others must be false
    (B) the differences between the theories are unimportant
    (C) taken together, the theories cover all possibilities
    (D) the theories support each other

12. According to paragraph 2, which of the following led some early researchers to believe that the Pacific islanders originally came from Egypt?

    (A) Egyptians were known to have founded other great civilizations.
    (B) Sailors from other parts of the world were believed to lack the skills needed to travel across the ocean.
    (C) Linguistic, archaeological, and biological data connected the islands to Egypt.
    (D) Egyptian accounts claimed responsibility for colonizing the Pacific as well as the Americas.

PARAGRAPH 3

The basic cultural requirements for the successful colonization of the Pacific islands include the appropriate boat-building, sailing, and navigation skills to get to the islands in the first place; domesticated plants and gardening skills suited to often marginal conditions; and a varied inventory of fishing **implements** and techniques. It is now generally believed that these prerequisites originated with peoples speaking Austronesian languages (a group of several hundred related languages) and began to emerge in Southeast Asia by about 5000 B.C.E. The culture of that time, based on archaeology and linguistic reconstruction, is assumed to have had a broad inventory of cultivated plants including taro, yams, banana, sugarcane, breadfruit, coconut, sago, and rice. Just as important, the culture also possessed the basic foundation for an effective maritime adaptation, including outrigger canoes and a variety of fishing techniques that could be effective for overseas voyaging.

13. The word "**implements**" in the passage is closest in meaning to

    (A) skills
    (B) tools
    (C) opportunities
    (D) practices

14. All of the following are mentioned in paragraph 3 as required for successful colonization of the Pacific islands EXCEPT

    (A) knowledge of various Austronesian languages
    (B) a variety of fishing techniques
    (C) navigational skills
    (D) knowledge of plant cultivation

15. In paragraph 3, why does the author provide information about the types of crops grown and boats used in Southeast Asia during the period around 5000 B.C.E.?

Ⓐ To evaluate the relative importance of agriculture and fishing to early Austronesian peoples

Ⓑ To illustrate the effectiveness of archaeological and linguistic methods in discovering details about life in ancient times

Ⓒ To contrast living conditions on the continent of Asia with living conditions on the Pacific islands

Ⓓ To demonstrate that people from this region had the skills and resources necessary to travel to and survive on the Pacific islands

PARAGRAPH 4

Contrary to the arguments of some that much of the Pacific was settled by Polynesians accidentally marooned after being lost and adrift, it seems reasonable that this feat was accomplished by deliberate colonization expeditions that set out fully stocked with food and domesticated plants and animals. Detailed studies of the winds and currents using computer simulations suggest that drifting canoes would have been a most unlikely means of colonizing the Pacific. These expeditions were likely driven by population growth and political dynamics on the home islands, as well as the challenge and excitement of exploring unknown waters. Because all Polynesians, Micronesians, and many Melanesians speak Austronesian languages and grow crops derived from Southeast Asia, all these peoples most certainly derived from that region and not the New World or elsewhere. The undisputed pre-Columbian presence in Oceania of the sweet potato, which is a New World domesticate, has sometimes been used to support Heyerdahl's "American Indians in the Pacific" theories. However, this is one plant out of a long list of Southeast Asian domesticates. As **Patrick Kirch**, an American anthropologist, points out, rather than being brought by rafting South Americans, sweet potatoes might just have easily been brought back by returning Polynesian navigators who could have reached the west coast of South America.

16. Which of the sentences below best expresses the essential information in the highlighted sentence in paragraph 4? Incorrect choices change the meaning in important ways or leave out essential information.

Ⓐ Some people have argued that the Pacific was settled by traders who became lost while transporting domesticated plants and animals.

Ⓑ The original Polynesian settlers were probably marooned on the islands, but they may have been joined later by carefully prepared colonization expeditions.

Ⓒ Although it seems reasonable to believe that colonization expeditions would set out fully stocked, this is contradicted by much of the evidence.

Ⓓ The settlement of the Pacific islands was probably intentional and well planned rather than accidental as some people have proposed.

17. According to paragraph 4, which of the following is NOT an explanation for why a group of people might have wanted to colonize the Pacific islands?

   Ⓐ As their numbers increased, they needed additional territory.

   Ⓑ The winds and currents made the islands easy to reach.

   Ⓒ The political situation at home made emigration desirable.

   Ⓓ They found exploration challenging and exciting.

18. Why does the author mention the views of "**Patrick Kirch**"?

   Ⓐ To present evidence in favor of Heyerdahl's idea about American Indians reaching Oceania

   Ⓑ To emphasize the familiarity of Pacific islanders with crops from many different regions of the world

   Ⓒ To indicate that a supposed proof for Heyerdahl's theory has an alternative explanation

   Ⓓ To demonstrate that some of the same crops were cultivated in both South America and Oceania

PARAGRAPH 2

Speculation on the origin of these Pacific islanders began as soon as outsiders encountered them; in the absence of solid linguistic, archaeological, and biological data, many fanciful and mutually exclusive theories were devised. Pacific islanders were variously thought to have come from North America, South America, Egypt, Israel, and India, as well as Southeast Asia. **(A)** Many older theories implicitly deprecated the navigational abilities and overall cultural creativity of the Pacific islanders. **(B)** For example, British anthropologists G. Elliot Smith and W. J. Perry assumed that only Egyptians would have been skilled enough to navigate and colonize the Pacific. **(C)** They speculated that the Egyptians even crossed the Pacific to found the great civilizations of the New World (North and South America). **(D)** In 1947 Norwegian adventurer Thor Heyerdahl drifted on a balsa-log raft westward with the winds and currents across the Pacific from South America to prove his theory that Pacific islanders were Native Americans (also called American Indians). Later Heyerdahl suggested that the Pacific was peopled by three migrations: by Native Americans from the Pacific Northwest of North America drifting to Hawaii, by Peruvians drifting to Easter Island, and by Melanesians. In 1969 he crossed the Atlantic in an Egyptian-style reed boat to prove Egyptian influences in the Americas. Contrary to these theorists, the overwhelming evidence of physical anthropology, linguistics, and archaeology shows that the Pacific islanders came from Southeast Asia and were skilled enough as navigators to sail against the prevailing winds and currents.

19. Look at the part of the passage that is displayed above. The letters **(A)**, **(B)**, **(C)**, and **(D)** indicate where the following sentence could be added.

   Later theories concentrated on journeys in the other direction.

   Where would the sentence best fit?

   Ⓐ Choice A   Ⓑ Choice B   Ⓒ Choice C   Ⓓ Choice D

20. **Directions:** An introductory sentence for a brief summary of the passage is provided below. Complete the summary by selecting the THREE answer choices that express the most important ideas in the passage. Some sentences do not belong in the summary because they express ideas that are not presented in the passage or are minor ideas in the passage. **This question is worth 2 points.**

Write your answer choices in the spaces where they belong. You can either write the letter of your answer choice or you can copy the sentence.

> **Together, Melanesia, Micronesia, and Polynesia make up the region described as the Pacific islands, or Oceania.**
>
> ●
>
> ●
>
> ●

Answer Choices

A Many theories about how inhabitants first came to the islands have been proposed, including the idea that North and South Americans simply drifted across the ocean.

B Although early colonizers of the islands probably came from agriculture-based societies, they were obliged to adopt an economy based on fishing.

C New evidence suggests that, rather than being isolated, Pacific islanders engaged in trade and social interaction with peoples living in Southeast Asia.

D Computer simulations of the winds and currents in the Pacific have shown that reaching the Pacific Islands was probably much easier than previously thought.

E It is now believed that the process of colonization required a great deal of skill, determination, and planning and could not have happened by chance.

F Using linguistic and archaeological evidence, anthropologists have determined that the first Pacific islanders were Austronesian people from Southeast Asia.

LISTENING

In this section, you will be able to demonstrate your ability to understand conversations and lectures in English.

In the actual test, the section is divided into two separately timed parts. You will hear each conversation or lecture only one time. A clock will indicate how much time remains. The clock will count down only while you are answering questions, not while you are listening. You may take up to 16.5 minutes to answer the questions.

In this practice test, there is no time limit for answering questions.

You may take notes while you listen. You may use your notes to help you answer the questions. Your notes will not be scored.

Answer the questions based on what is stated or implied by the speakers.

In some questions, you will see this icon: 🎧. This means that you will hear, but not see, part of the question.

In the actual test, you must answer each question. You cannot return to previous questions.

At the end of this practice test, you will find an answer key.

Directions: Listen to Track 18.

Directions: Now answer the questions.

1. What do the speakers mainly discuss?

   (A) Why the woman has little in common with her roommates

   (B) How the woman can keep up in her academic studies

   (C) The woman's adjustment to life at the university

   (D) The woman's decision to transfer to another university

2. Why does the woman mention her hometown?

   (A) To draw a contrast to her current situation

   (B) To acknowledge that she is accustomed to living in big cities

   (C) To indicate that she has known some people on campus for a long time

   (D) To emphasize her previous success in academic studies

3. What does the woman imply about the incident that occurred in her sociology class?

   (A) She was embarrassed because she gave an incorrect answer.

   (B) She was upset because the professor seemed to ignore her.

   (C) She was confused by the organization of the professor's lecture.

   (D) She was surprised by the comments of the other students.

4. According to the counselor, why should the woman visit her professor's office?
   Select 2 answers.

   A To offer a compliment

   B To offer to help other students

   C To introduce herself

   D To suggest ways of making the class more personal

5. What does the woman imply about joining the string quartet?

   (A) It would enable her to continue a hobby she gave up when she was ten.

   (B) It would allow her to spend more time in her major area of study.

   (C) It would help her stop worrying about her academic studies.

   (D) It would be a way to meet students with similar interests.

Directions: Listen to Track 19.

Sociology

meme

replicator

longevity

longevity
fecundity

longevity
fecundity
fidelity

Directions: Now answer the questions.

6. What is the main purpose of the lecture?

   (A) To introduce a method that can help students remember new information

   (B) To introduce a way to study how information passes from one person to another

   (C) To explain the differences between biological information and cultural information

   (D) To explain the differences between stories, songs, and other pieces of information

7. Why does the professor tell the story about alligators?

   (A) To explain the difference between true and false stories

   (B) To draw an analogy between alligator reproduction and cultural transmission

   (C) To give an example of a piece of information that functions as a meme

   (D) To show how a story can gradually change into a song

8. According to the professor, which of the following are examples of meme transfer? *Select 2 answers.*

   A Telling familiar stories

   B Sharing feelings

   C Composing original music

   D Learning a scientific theory

9. What example does the professor give of a meme's longevity?

   (A) A story has been changing since it first appeared in the 1930s.

   (B) A person remembers a story for many years.

   (C) A gene is passed on through many generations without changing.

   (D) A song quickly becomes popular all over the world.

10. What does the professor compare to a housefly laying many eggs?

    (A) A child learning many different ideas from his or her parents

    (B) Alligators reproducing in New York sewers

    (C) Different people remembering different versions of a story

    (D) A person singing the "Twinkle, twinkle" song many times

11. *Listen to Track 20 to answer the question.*

    Why does the professor say this?

    (A) To explain why some memes do not change much

    (B) To ask the students for their opinion about songs as memes

    (C) To acknowledge a problem with the meme theory

    (D) To ask the students to test an idea about memes

Directions: Listen to Track 21.

Earth Science

12. What do the speakers mainly discuss?

    Ⓐ Stories told by desert travelers throughout history

    Ⓑ Efforts to locate unique sand formations in deserts around the world

    Ⓒ An effect caused by sand sliding down the slopes of some dunes

    Ⓓ Evidence that sound travels farthest in the driest regions of the world

13. What can be inferred from the students' reactions when the professor begins to discuss sand dunes?

    Ⓐ They appreciate the professor's unusual way of summarizing the previous discussion.

    Ⓑ They suspect that the professor is not completely serious.

    Ⓒ They would prefer to learn more about beach sand before beginning a new topic.

    Ⓓ They look forward to asking the professor about a topic they have wondered about for a long time.

14. Why does the professor mention an airplane?

    Ⓐ To describe a sound that is sometimes heard in the desert

    Ⓑ To emphasize the wide geographic distribution of sand dunes

    Ⓒ To introduce an anecdote about doing research in the desert

    Ⓓ To illustrate the power of a desert sandstorm

15. According to the professor's description of the unusual dunes, how does the sand in the outer layer typically differ from the sand underneath? *Select two answers.*

    Ⓐ The sand in the outer layer is extremely dry.

    Ⓑ The sand in the outer layer is packed less tightly.

    Ⓒ The grains of sand in the outer layer are smaller.

    Ⓓ The grains of sand in the outer layer are less uniform in size.

16. Why does one of the students refer to dormitory stairways?

    Ⓐ To estimate the steepness of the slope on the side of a sand dune

    Ⓑ To emphasize that scientific proof is a step-by-step process

    Ⓒ To suggest that the human voice may be compared to a musical instrument

    Ⓓ To demonstrate her understanding of the professor's explanation

17. *Listen to Track 22 to answer the question.*

    What does the professor imply when he says this?

    Ⓐ Most experts would agree that the comparison is correct.

    Ⓑ The comparison seems reasonable but is not actually true.

    Ⓒ The student has not explained his point clearly.

    Ⓓ The student has used an unusual approach to reach the same conclusion that the professor does.

Directions: Listen to Track 23.

Directions: Now answer the questions.

18. What is the conversation mainly about?

    Ⓐ An assignment about which the student would like advice
    Ⓑ Concerns as to whether the student should be in the professor's course
    Ⓒ The selection of films to be viewed by students in a film theory course
    Ⓓ The structure and sequence of courses in the Film Department

19. What is the professor's attitude toward the student's high school film course?

    Ⓐ He does not consider it satisfactory preparation for the class he teaches.
    Ⓑ He does not think that literary works should be discussed in film classes.
    Ⓒ He believes that this type of course often confuses inexperienced students.
    Ⓓ He feels that the approach taken in this course is the best way to learn about film.

20 Why was the student permitted to sign up for the professor's film theory course?

    Ⓐ Her high school course fulfilled the requirement for previous course work.
    Ⓑ The computer system that usually blocks students was not working properly.
    Ⓒ An employee in the department did not follow instructions.
    Ⓓ The professor made an exception in her case.

21. Why does the professor decide to allow the student to remain in his class?
    Select 2 answers.

    Ⓐ She needs to take the course in order to graduate.
    Ⓑ He is impressed with her eagerness to continue.
    Ⓒ She convinces him that she does have adequate preparation for the course.
    Ⓓ He learns that she is not studying film as her main course of study.

22. What does the professor advise the student to do in order to keep up with the class she is in?

    Ⓐ Take the introductory course
    Ⓑ Watch some video recordings
    Ⓒ Do extra reading
    Ⓓ Drop out of her marketing class

Directions: Listen to Track 24.

Literature

Directions: Now answer the questions.

23. What is the lecture mainly about?

    Ⓐ Oral traditions in folktales and fairy tales
    Ⓑ Common characters and plots in folktales and fairy tales
    Ⓒ Differences between folktales and fairy tales
    Ⓓ Hidden meanings in folktales and fairy tales

24. What does the professor mean when he says that folktales are communal?

    Ⓐ They vary little from one community to another.
    Ⓑ They serve to strengthen ties among individuals within a community.
    Ⓒ They relate important events in the history of a community.
    Ⓓ They can be adapted to meet the needs of a community.

25. Why does the professor clarify the concept of a "fairy"?

    Ⓐ To explain the origins of the term "fairy tale"
    Ⓑ To eliminate a possible definition of the term "fairy tale"
    Ⓒ To support a claim about the function of fairy tales
    Ⓓ To indicate that fairies are a major element in fairy tales

26. What does the professor say about the setting of fairy tales?

    Ⓐ The tales are usually set in a nonspecific location.
    Ⓑ The location is determined by the country of origin of a tale.
    Ⓒ The tales are set in a location familiar to the author.
    Ⓓ A storyteller varies the location of a tale depending on the audience.

27. In the lecture, the professor discusses characteristics of folktales and fairy tales. Indicate the characteristics of each type of tale. *Put a check in the correct boxes.*

	Folktales	Fairy Tales
Their appeal is now mainly to children.		
The plot is the only stable element.		
The tales are transmitted orally.		
There is one accepted version.		
Characters are well developed.		
The language is relatively formal.		

28. *Listen again to part of the lecture by playing Track 25.* 🎧 *Then answer the question.*

Why does the professor say this?

Ⓐ To support the student's statement
Ⓑ To ask the student to clarify her statement
Ⓒ To find out if the students know what story the line comes from
Ⓓ To clarify the relationship between time and space in fairy tales

SPEAKING

In this section, you will be able to demonstrate your ability to speak about a variety of topics.

In the actual test, the Speaking section will last approximately 16 minutes. You will answer four questions by speaking into the microphone. You may take notes while you listen. You may use your notes to help you answer the questions. Your notes will not be scored. For each question, you will have time to prepare before giving your response. You should answer the questions as completely as possible in the time allowed.

For this practice test, you may want to use a personal recording device to record and play back your responses.

For each question, play the audio track listed and follow the directions to complete the task.

At the end of this practice test, you will find important points about each question.

1. You will now give your opinion about a familiar topic. After you hear the question, you should give yourself 15 seconds to prepare and 45 seconds to speak.

   Listen to Track 26.

   > Do you agree or disagree with the following statement? Why or why not? Use details and examples to explain your answer.
   >
   > **It is more important to study math or science than it is to study art or literature.**
   >
   > | Preparation Time: 15 seconds |
   > | :---: |
   > | **Response Time: 45 seconds** |

2. Now you will read a passage about a campus situation and then listen to a conversation about the same topic. You will then answer a question, using information from both the reading passage and the conversation. You should give yourself 30 seconds to prepare and 60 seconds to speak.

   Listen to Track 27.

Reading Time: 50 seconds

   > ### Campus Dining Club Announced
   >
   > Starting this year, the university dining hall will be transformed into The Campus Dining Club for one week at the end of each semester. During the last week of each semester, the dining hall will feature special meals prepared by the university's culinary arts students. The school feels that this will give students who are studying cooking and food preparation valuable experience that will help them later, when they pursue careers. The university has announced that it will charge a small additional fee for these dinners in order to pay for the special gourmet food ingredients that will be required.

Listen to Track 28.

> The man expresses his opinion about the plan described in the article. Briefly summarize the plan. Then state his opinion about the plan and explain the reasons he gives for holding that opinion.
>
> **Preparation Time: 30 seconds**
> **Response Time: 60 seconds**

3. Now you will read a passage about an academic subject and then listen to a lecture on the same topic. You will then answer a question, using information from both the reading passage and the lecture. You should give yourself 30 seconds to prepare and 60 seconds to speak.

Listen to Track 29.

Reading Time: 45 seconds

> ### Target Marketing
>
> Advertisers in the past have used radio and television in an attempt to provide information about their products to large, general audiences; it was once thought that the best way to sell a product was to advertise it to as many people as possible. However, more recent trends in advertising have turned toward target marketing. Target marketing is the strategy of advertising to smaller, very specific audiences—audiences that have been determined to have the greatest need or desire for the product being marketed. Target marketing has proved to be very effective in reaching potential customers.

Listen to Track 30. 🎧

Using the professor's examples, explain the advertising technique of target marketing.

Preparation Time: 30 seconds
Response Time: 60 seconds

4. Now you will listen to a lecture. You will then be asked to summarize the lecture. You should give yourself 20 seconds to prepare and 60 seconds to speak.

Listen to Track 31. 🎧

Using points and examples from the talk, explain the two types of motivation.

Preparation Time: 20 seconds
Response Time: 60 seconds

WRITING

In this section, you will be able to demonstrate your ability to use writing to communicate in an academic environment. There will be two writing tasks.

At the end of this practice test, you will find topic notes for each question.

Turn the page to see the directions for the first writing task.

Writing Based on Reading and Listening

For this task, you will read a passage about an academic topic. Then you will listen to a lecture about the same topic. You may take notes while you listen.

In your response, provide a detailed summary of the lecture and explain how the lecture relates to the reading passage.

In the actual test, you will have 3 minutes to read the passage and 20 minutes to write your response. While you write, you will be able to see the reading passage. If you finish your response before time is up, you may go on to the second writing task.

Reading Time: 3 minutes

As early as the twelfth century A.D., the settlements of Chaco Canyon in New Mexico in the American Southwest were notable for their "great houses," massive stone buildings that contain hundreds of rooms and often stand three or four stories high. Archaeologists have been trying to determine how the buildings were used. While there is still no universally agreed upon explanation, there are three competing theories.

One theory holds that the Chaco structures were purely residential, with each housing hundreds of people. Supporters of this theory have interpreted Chaco great houses as earlier versions of the architecture seen in more recent Southwest societies. In particular, the Chaco houses appear strikingly similar to the large, well-known "apartment buildings" at Taos, New Mexico, in which many people have been living for centuries.

A second theory contends that the Chaco structures were used to store food supplies. One of the main crops of the Chaco people was grain maize, which could be stored for long periods of time without spoiling and could serve as a long-lasting supply of food. The supplies of maize had to be stored somewhere, and the size of the great houses would make them very suitable for the purpose.

A third theory proposes that houses were used as ceremonial centers. Close to one house, called Pueblo Alto, archaeologists identified an enormous mound formed by a pile of old material. Excavations of the mound revealed deposits containing a surprisingly large number of broken pots. This finding has been interpreted as evidence that people gathered at Pueblo Alto for special ceremonies. At the ceremonies, they ate festive meals and then discarded the pots in which the meals had been prepared or served. Such ceremonies have been documented for other Native American cultures.

Listen to Track 32.

Directions: You have 20 minutes to plan and write your response. Your response will be judged on the basis of the quality of your writing and on how well your response presents the points in the lecture and their relationship to the reading passage. Typically, an effective response will contain a minimum of 150 words.

Listen to Track 33.

Response Time: 20 minutes

Question 1

Summarize the points made in the lecture, being sure to explain how they cast doubt on the specific theories discussed in the reading passage.

_____

_____

_____

_____

_____

_____

_____

_____

_____

Writing for an Academic Discussion

For this task, you will read an online discussion. A professor has posted a question about a topic, and some classmates have responded with their ideas.

In the actual test, you will have 10 minutes to write a response that contributes to the discussion.

Question 2

Your professor is teaching a class on public policy. Write a post responding to the professor's question.

In your response, you should do the following.

- Express and support your opinion.
- Make a contribution to the discussion in your own words.

An effective response will contain at least 100 words.

Dr. Diaz

Next week we are scheduled to discuss the economic impacts of tourism. Tourism is a source of income for many cities and regions around the world. On the other hand, tourism can also bring with it a number of well-known disadvantages. In general, do you think governments should continue to develop and encourage a tourism industry in their countries? Why or why not?

Kelly

Even considering the economic argument, I think it's time for governments to stop encouraging tourism. That's because the tourist economy is unstable. Tourists may visit a region for a while, but then people's preferences change, and tourists stop coming. It's economically better for a country to promote other industries that are more stable.

Paul

I see your point, Kelly, but I believe tourism is almost always helpful for a country—and not just for economic reasons. If a city is made more attractive for tourists, it will also become more livable for the residents. To lure tourists, cities are often made safer and cleaner, for example, and they add attractions such as museums.

Response Time: 10 minutes

TOEFL iBT® Test 3

READING

In this section, you will be able to demonstrate your ability to understand academic passages in English. You will read and answer questions about **two passages**.

In the actual test, you will have 36 minutes total to read both passages and answer the questions. A clock will indicate how much time remains.

Some passages may include one or more notes explaining words or phrases. The words or phrases are marked with footnote numbers, and the notes explaining them appear at the end of the passage.

Most questions are worth 1 point, but the last question for each passage is worth 2 points.

You may review and revise your answers in this section as long as time remains.

At the end of this practice test, you will find an answer key.

Directions: Read the passage. Then answer the questions. You have 18 minutes on average to answer the questions.

POWERING THE INDUSTRIAL REVOLUTION

In Britain one of the most dramatic changes of the Industrial Revolution was the harnessing of power. Until the reign of George III (1760–1820), available sources of power for work and travel had not increased since the Middle Ages. There were three sources of power: animal or human muscles; the wind, operating on sail or windmill; and running water. Only the last of these was suited at all to the continuous operating of machines, and although waterpower abounded in Lancashire and Scotland and ran grain mills as well as textile mills, it had one great disadvantage: streams flowed where nature intended them to, and water-driven factories had to be located on their banks, whether or not the location was desirable for other reasons. Furthermore, even the most reliable waterpower varied with the seasons and disappeared in a drought. The new age of machinery, in short, could not have been born without a new source of both movable and constant power.

The source had long been known but not exploited. Early in the century, a pump had come into use in which expanding steam raised a piston in a cylinder, and atmospheric pressure brought it down again when the steam condensed inside the cylinder to form a vacuum. This "atmospheric engine," invented by Thomas Savery and vastly improved by his partner, Thomas Newcomen, embodied revolutionary principles, but it was so slow and wasteful of fuel that it could not be employed outside the coal mines for which it had been designed. In the 1760s, James Watt perfected a separate condenser for the steam, so that the cylinder did not have to be cooled at every stroke; then he devised a way to make the piston turn a wheel and thus convert reciprocating (back and forth) motion into rotary motion. He thereby transformed an inefficient pump of limited use into a steam engine of a thousand uses. The final step came when steam was introduced into the cylinder to drive the piston backward as well as forward, thereby increasing the speed of the engine and cutting its fuel consumption.

Watt's steam engine soon showed what it could do. It liberated industry from dependence on running water. The engine eliminated water in the mines by driving efficient pumps, which made possible deeper and deeper mining. The ready availability of coal inspired William Murdoch during the 1790s to develop the first new form of nighttime illumination to be discovered in a millennium and a half. Coal gas rivaled smoky oil lamps and flickering candles, and early in the new century, well-to-do Londoners grew accustomed to gaslit houses and even streets. Iron manufacturers, which had starved for fuel while depending on charcoal, also benefited from ever-increasing supplies of coal; blast furnaces with steam-powered bellows turned out more iron and steel for the new machinery. Steam became the motive force of the Industrial Revolution, as coal and iron ore were the raw materials.

By 1800 more than a thousand steam engines were in use in the British Isles, and Britain retained a virtual monopoly on steam engine production until the 1830s. Steam power did not merely spin cotton and roll iron; early in the new century, it also multiplied ten times over the amount of paper that a single worker could produce in a day. At the same time, operators of the first printing presses run by steam rather than by hand found it possible to produce a thousand pages in an hour rather than thirty. Steam also promised to eliminate a transportation problem not fully solved by either canal boats or turnpikes. Boats could carry heavy weights, but canals could not cross hilly terrain; turnpikes could cross the hills, but the roadbeds could not stand up under great weights. These problems needed still another solution, and the ingredients for it lay close at hand. In some industrial regions, heavily laden wagons, with flanged wheels, were being hauled by horses along metal rails; and the stationary steam engine was puffing in the factory and mine. Another generation passed before inventors succeeded in combining these ingredients, by putting the engine on wheels and the wheels on the rails, so as to provide a machine to take the place of the horse. Thus the railroad age sprang from what had already happened in the eighteenth century.

Directions: Now answer the questions.

P A R A G R A P H S 1 & 2

In Britain one of the most dramatic changes of the Industrial Revolution was the harnessing of power. Until the reign of George III (1760–1820), available sources of power for work and travel had not increased since the Middle Ages. There were three sources of power: animal or human muscles; the wind, operating on sail or windmill; and running water. **Only the last of these was suited at all to the continuous operating of machines, and although waterpower abounded in Lancashire and Scotland and ran grain mills as well as textile mills, it had one great disadvantage: streams flowed where nature intended them to, and water-driven factories had to be located on their banks, whether or not the location was desirable for other reasons.** Furthermore, even the most reliable waterpower varied with the seasons and disappeared in a drought. The new age of machinery, in short, could not have been born without a new source of both movable and constant power.

The source had long been known but not exploited. Early in the century, a pump had come into use in which expanding steam raised a piston in a cylinder, and atmospheric pressure brought it down again when the steam condensed inside the cylinder to form a vacuum. This "atmospheric engine," invented by Thomas Savery and vastly improved by his partner, Thomas Newcomen, embodied revolutionary principles, but it was so slow and wasteful of fuel that it could not be employed outside the coal mines for which it had been designed. In the 1760s, James Watt perfected a separate condenser for the steam, so that the cylinder did not have to be cooled at every stroke; then he devised a way to make the piston turn a wheel and thus convert reciprocating (back and forth) motion into rotary motion. He thereby transformed an inefficient pump of limited use into a steam engine of a thousand uses. The final step came when steam was introduced into the cylinder to drive the piston backward as well as forward, thereby increasing the speed of the engine and cutting its fuel consumption.

1. Which of the sentences below best expresses the essential information in the highlighted sentence in paragraph 1? Incorrect choices change the meaning in important ways or leave out essential information.

   Ⓐ Running water was the best power source for factories since it could keep machines operating continuously, but since it was abundant only in Lancashire and Scotland, most mills and factories that were located elsewhere could not be water driven.

   Ⓑ The disadvantage of using waterpower is that streams do not necessarily flow in places that are the most suitable for factories, which explains why so many water-powered grain and textile mills were located in undesirable places.

   Ⓒ Since machines could be operated continuously only where running water was abundant, grain and textile mills, as well as other factories, tended to be located only in Lancashire and Scotland.

   Ⓓ Running water was the only source of power that was suitable for the continuous operation of machines, but to make use of it, factories had to be located where the water was, regardless of whether such locations made sense otherwise.

2. Which of the following best describes the relation of paragraph 2 to paragraph 1?

   Ⓐ Paragraph 2 shows how the problem discussed in paragraph 1 arose.

   Ⓑ Paragraph 2 explains how the problem presented in paragraph 1 came to be solved.

   Ⓒ Paragraph 2 provides a more technical discussion of the problem introduced in paragraph 1.

   Ⓓ Paragraph 2 shows why the problem discussed in paragraph 1 was especially important to solve.

3. According to paragraph 2, the "atmospheric engine" was slow because

   Ⓐ it had been designed to be used in coal mines

   Ⓑ the cylinder had to cool between each stroke

   Ⓒ it made use of expanding steam to raise the piston in its cylinder

   Ⓓ it could be operated only when a large supply of fuel was available

4. According to paragraph 2, Watt's steam engine differed from earlier steam engines in each of the following ways EXCEPT:

   Ⓐ It used steam to move a piston in a cylinder.

   Ⓑ It worked with greater speed.

   Ⓒ It was more efficient in its use of fuel.

   Ⓓ It could be used in many different ways.

PARAGRAPH 3

Watt's steam engine soon showed what it could do. It liberated industry from dependence on running water. The engine eliminated water in the mines by driving efficient pumps, which made possible deeper and deeper mining. The ready availability of coal inspired William Murdoch during the 1790s to develop the first new form of nighttime illumination to be discovered in a millennium and a half. Coal gas rivaled smoky oil lamps and flickering candles, and early in the new century, well-to-do Londoners **grew accustomed to** gaslit houses and even streets. Iron manufacturers, which had starved for fuel while depending on charcoal, also benefited from ever-increasing supplies of coal; blast furnaces with steam-powered bellows turned out more iron and steel for the new machinery. Steam became the motive force of the Industrial Revolution, as coal and iron ore were the raw materials.

5. In paragraph 3, the author mentions William Murdoch's invention of a new form of nighttime illumination in order to

Ⓐ indicate one of the important developments made possible by the introduction of Watt's steam engine

Ⓑ make the point that Watt's steam engine was not the only invention of importance to the Industrial Revolution

Ⓒ illustrate how important coal was as a raw material for the Industrial Revolution

Ⓓ provide an example of another eighteenth-century invention that used steam as a power source

6. The phrase "**grew accustomed to**" in the passage is closest in meaning to

Ⓐ began to prefer

Ⓑ wanted to have

Ⓒ became used to

Ⓓ insisted on

By 1800 more than a thousand steam engines were in use in the British Isles, and Britain retained a virtual monopoly on steam engine production until the 1830s. Steam power did not merely spin cotton and roll iron; early in the new century, it also multiplied ten times over the amount of paper that a single worker could produce in a day. At the same time, operators of the first printing presses run by steam rather than by hand found it possible to produce a thousand pages in an hour rather than thirty. Steam also promised to eliminate a transportation problem not fully solved by either canal boats or turnpikes. Boats could carry heavy weights, but canals could not cross hilly terrain; turnpikes could cross the hills, but the roadbeds could not stand up under great weights. These problems needed still another solution, and the ingredients for it lay close at hand. In some industrial regions, heavily laden wagons, with flanged wheels, were being hauled by horses along metal rails; and the stationary steam engine was puffing in the factory and mine. Another generation passed before inventors succeeded in combining these ingredients, by putting the engine on wheels and the wheels on the rails, so as to provide a machine to take the place of the horse. Thus the railroad age sprang from what had already happened in the eighteenth century.

7. According to paragraph 4, which of the following statements about steam engines is true?

Ⓐ They were used for the production of paper but not for printing.
Ⓑ By 1800, significant numbers of them were produced outside of Britain.
Ⓒ They were used in factories before they were used to power trains.
Ⓓ They were used in the construction of canals and turnpikes.

8. According to paragraph 4, providing a machine to take the place of the horse involved combining which two previously separate ingredients?

Ⓐ Turnpikes and canals
Ⓑ Stationary steam engines and wagons with flanged wheels
Ⓒ Metal rails in roadbeds and wagons capable of carrying heavy loads
Ⓓ Canal boats and heavily laden wagons

PARAGRAPH 3

(A) Watt's steam engine soon showed what it could do. **(B)** It liberated industry from dependence on running water. **(C)** The engine eliminated water in the mines by driving efficient pumps, which made possible deeper and deeper mining. **(D)** The ready availability of coal inspired William Murdoch during the 1790s to develop the first new form of nighttime illumination to be discovered in a millennium and a half. Coal gas rivaled smoky oil lamps and flickering candles, and early in the new century, well-to-do Londoners grew accustomed to gaslit houses and even streets. Iron manufacturers, which had starved for fuel while depending on charcoal, also benefited from ever-increasing supplies of coal; blast furnaces with steam-powered bellows turned out more iron and steel for the new machinery. Steam became the motive force of the Industrial Revolution, as coal and iron ore were the raw materials.

9. Look at the part of the passage that is displayed above. The letters **(A)**, **(B)**, **(C)**, and **(D)** indicate where the following sentence could be added.

   The factories did not have to go to the streams when power could come to the factories.

   Where would the sentence best fit?

   Ⓐ Choice A
   Ⓑ Choice B
   Ⓒ Choice C
   Ⓓ Choice D

10. **Directions**: An introductory sentence for a brief summary of the passage is provided on the next page. Complete the summary by selecting the THREE answer choices that express the most important ideas in the passage. Some sentences do not belong in the summary because they express ideas that are not presented in the passage or are minor ideas in the passage. **This question is worth 2 points.**

Write your answer choices in the spaces where they belong. You can either write the letter of your answer choice or you can copy the sentence.

> **The Industrial Revolution would not have been possible without a new source of power that was efficient, movable, and continuously available.**
>
> •
>
> •
>
> •

Answer Choices

A In the early eighteenth century, Savery and Newcomen discovered that expanding steam could be used to raise a piston in a cylinder.

B In the mid-1700s, James Watt transformed an inefficient steam pump into a fast, flexible, fuel-efficient engine.

C Watt's steam engine played a leading role in greatly increasing industrial production of all kinds.

D In the 1790s, William Murdoch developed a new way of lighting houses and streets using coal gas.

E Until the 1830s, Britain was the world's major producer of steam engines.

F The availability of steam engines was a major factor in the development of railroads, which solved a major transportation problem.

Directions: Read the passage. Then answer the questions. You have 18 minutes on average to answer the questions.

PEST CONTROL

Many pest species that are native to North America, such as white-footed mice and ground moles, are more nuisance pests and are usually regulated by native predators and parasites. This situation is not true for nonindigenous pests in North America, such as brown rats and cockroaches. After centuries, it is evident that these pests cannot be eradicated. The best that can be done is to introduce pest control measures that will control their numbers.

An ancient and popular means of pest control is chemical. For example, the Sumerians used sulfur to combat crop pests, and by the early 1800s such chemicals as arsenic were used to combat insect and fungal pests.

However, chemical control has its dark side. Chemical pesticides have many unintended consequences through their effects not just on the target species but on a wide array of nontarget species as well, often eliminating them and thereby upsetting the existing food webs, especially through the suppression of native predator species. The surviving pests then rebound in greater numbers than ever.

Perhaps more insidious is that a pesticide loses its effectiveness because the target species evolves resistance to it. As one pesticide replaces another, the pests acquire a resistance to them all. Some species, notably certain mosquitoes, have overcome the toxic effects of every pesticide to which they have been exposed. Insect pests need only about five years to evolve pesticide resistance; their predators do so much more slowly. So after the pest develops resistance, pest outbreaks become even more disastrous.

Farmers long ago observed that enemies of pests act as controls. As early as 300 c.e., the Chinese were introducing predatory ants into their citrus orchards to control leaf-eating caterpillars. Insect pests have their own array of enemies in their native habitats. When an animal or plant is introduced, intentionally or unintentionally, into a new habitat outside of its natural range, it may adapt to the new environment and leave its enemies behind. Freed from predation and finding an abundance of resources, the species quickly becomes a pest or a weed. This fact has led to the search for natural enemies to introduce into populations of pests to reduce their populations.

Because the serious pest is usually a nonnative species, biological control involves the introduction of a nonindigenous predator or parasite to control the pest. The introduction of the cactus-eating moth, a native of Argentina, into Australia effectively reduced and controlled the rapidly spreading prickly pear, which had been introduced into Australia in 1901.

But biological control, like chemical control, can backfire. The success of the cactus-feeding moth in controlling prickly pear in Australia encouraged its introduction to several West Indies islands to control prickly pear there. In time the moth made its way to Florida, where it now threatens the existence of several native prickly pear species. The moral is that although using nonindigenous predators as biological controls can be effective, these species possess their own inherent dangers that must be assessed before they are released. They, too, can become alien invaders.

Because chemical, biological, and other methods used individually are obviously not the solution to pest control, entomologists have developed a holistic approach to pest control, called integrated pest management (IPM). IPM considers the biological, ecological, economic, social, and even aesthetic aspects of pest control and employs a variety of techniques. The objective of IPM is to control the pest not at the time of a major outbreak but at an earlier time, when the size of the population is easier to control. The approach is to rely first on natural mortality caused by weather and natural enemies, with as little disruption of the natural system as possible, and to use other methods only if they are needed to hold the pest below the economic injury level.

Successful IPM requires the knowledge of the population ecology of each pest and its associated species and the dynamics of the host species. It involves considerable fieldwork monitoring the pest species and its natural enemies by such techniques as egg counts and the trapping of adults to acquire information to determine the necessity, timing, and intensity of control measures. These control measures must be adjusted to the situation, which may vary from one location to another. The intensity of control or no control is based on the degree of pest damage that can be tolerated, the costs of control, and the benefits to be derived.

Directions: Now answer the questions.

PARAGRAPH 1

Many pest species that are native to North America, such as white-footed mice and ground moles, are more nuisance pests and are usually regulated by native predators and parasites. This situation is not true for nonindigenous pests in North America, such as brown rats and cockroaches. After centuries, it is evident that these pests cannot be eradicated. The best that can be done is to introduce pest control measures that will control their numbers.

11. What can be inferred from paragraph 1 about nonindigenous pests such as brown rats and cockroaches?

Ⓐ Attempts to limit the size of their populations have been unsuccessful.

Ⓑ They have inhabited North America longer than white-footed mice and ground moles.

Ⓒ Their numbers cannot usually be controlled by native predators and parasites.

Ⓓ They do not pose as many problems for humans as do white-footed mice and ground moles.

PARAGRAPH 3

However, chemical control has its dark side. **Chemical pesticides have many unintended consequences through their effects not just on the target species but on a wide array of nontarget species as well, often eliminating them and thereby upsetting the existing food webs, especially through the suppression of native predator species.** The surviving pests then rebound in greater numbers than ever.

12. Which of the sentences below best expresses the essential information in the highlighted sentence in the passage? Incorrect choices change the meaning in important ways or leave out essential information.

   (A) Chemical pesticides often eliminate species other than the intended target and thereby upset food webs, especially by suppressing native predator species.

   (B) Native predator species are often eliminated by chemical pesticides that are intended to have consequences for other pests.

   (C) Chemical pesticides upset existing food webs by eliminating native species and by increasing the number of nonnative predators.

   (D) The effects of chemical pesticides on a wide array of food webs and native predators are often unintended.

PARAGRAPH 5

Farmers long ago observed that enemies of pests act as controls. As early as 300 c.e., the Chinese were introducing predatory ants into their citrus orchards to control leaf-eating caterpillars. Insect pests have their own array of enemies in their native habitats. When an animal or plant is introduced, intentionally or unintentionally, into a new habitat outside of its natural range, it may adapt to the new environment and leave its enemies behind. Freed from predation and finding an abundance of resources, the species quickly becomes a pest or a weed. This fact has led to the search for natural enemies to introduce into populations of pests to reduce their populations.

13. According to paragraph 5, why is a species likely to become a pest when it is introduced into a new habitat?

   (A) The species becomes more effective at escaping from its enemies.

   (B) The species has no natural predators in its new habitat.

   (C) The species adapts to habitats outside its natural range.

   (D) The species does not have to compete for resources with other plants and animals.

Because the serious pest is usually a nonnative species, biological control involves the introduction of a nonindigenous predator or parasite to control the pest. The introduction of the cactus-eating moth, a native of Argentina, into Australia effectively reduced and controlled the rapidly spreading prickly pear, which had been introduced into Australia in 1901.

14. In paragraph 6, the discussion of the cactus-eating moth and the prickly pear in Australia illustrates which of the following about biological control?

Ⓐ Nonnative pests cannot be controlled through biological means once they have begun to spread rapidly.

Ⓑ A nonnative pest can sometimes be controlled by the introduction of a nonnative predator.

Ⓒ A nonindigenous pest can be controlled only by a predator that comes from the same original habitat as the pest.

Ⓓ A native pest can be controlled by either a native or a nonnative predator.

But biological control, like chemical control, can backfire. The success of the cactus-feeding moth in controlling prickly pear in Australia encouraged its introduction to several West Indies islands to control prickly pear there. In time the moth made its way to **Florida**, where it now threatens the existence of several native prickly pear species. The moral is that although using nonindigenous predators as biological controls can be effective, these species possess their own inherent dangers that must be **assessed** before they are released. They, too, can become alien invaders.

15. The word "**assessed**" in the passage is closest in meaning to

Ⓐ minimized

Ⓑ identified

Ⓒ evaluated

Ⓓ dealt with

16. The author discusses the cactus-feeding moth in "**Florida**" in order to

Ⓐ explain why the prickly pear species that are native to Florida have no indigenous predators

Ⓑ show how a predator spreads more rapidly in alien environments than it does in its native environment

Ⓒ indicate that a single nonindigenous predator species can be effective against a wide array of nonindigenous pest species

Ⓓ argue that controlling pests with nonindigenous predators can have unintended consequences

PARAGRAPH 8

Because chemical, biological, and other methods used individually are obviously not the solution to pest control, entomologists have developed a holistic approach to pest control, called integrated pest management (IPM). IPM considers the biological, ecological, economic, social, and even aesthetic aspects of pest control and employs a variety of techniques. The objective of IPM is to control the pest not at the time of a major outbreak but at an earlier time, when the size of the population is easier to control. The approach is to rely first on natural mortality caused by weather and natural enemies, with as little disruption of the natural system as possible, and to use other methods only if they are needed to hold the pest below the economic injury level.

17. According to paragraph 8, each of the following is a principle of integrated pest management EXCEPT

Ⓐ to control pest populations before a major outbreak occurs
Ⓑ to first determine if weather and natural enemies are able to control a pest
Ⓒ to increase the populations of the pest's natural enemies during certain seasons of the year
Ⓓ to use artificial methods of pest control only when pests begin to cause economic injury

PARAGRAPH 9

Successful IPM requires the knowledge of the population ecology of each pest and its associated species and the dynamics of the host species. It involves considerable fieldwork monitoring the pest species and its natural enemies by such techniques as egg counts and the trapping of adults to acquire information to determine the necessity, timing, and intensity of control measures. These control measures must be adjusted to the situation, which may vary from one location to another. The intensity of control or no control is based on the degree of pest damage that can be tolerated, the costs of control, and the benefits to be derived.

18. According to paragraph 9, each of the following helps to determine how intensely to apply pest control measures EXCEPT

Ⓐ how much pest damage can be tolerated
Ⓑ the cost of pest control measures
Ⓒ what can be gained through pest control measures
Ⓓ whether pest control measures have been used before

Perhaps more insidious is that a pesticide loses its effectiveness because the target species evolves resistance to it. As one pesticide replaces another, the pests acquire a resistance to them all. **(A)** Some species, notably certain mosquitoes, have overcome the toxic effects of every pesticide to which they have been exposed. **(B)** Insect pests need only about five years to evolve pesticide resistance; their predators do so much more slowly. **(C)** So after the pest develops resistance, pest outbreaks become even more disastrous. **(D)**

Farmers long ago observed that enemies of pests act as controls. As early as 300 c.e, the Chinese were introducing predatory ants into their citrus orchards to control leaf-eating caterpillars. Insect pests have their own array of enemies in their native habitats. When an animal or plant is introduced, intentionally or unintentionally, into a new habitat outside of its natural range, it may adapt to the new environment and leave its enemies behind. Freed from predation and finding an abundance of resources, the species quickly becomes a pest or a weed. This fact has led to the search for natural enemies to introduce into populations of pests to reduce their populations.

19. Look at the part of the passage that is displayed above. The letters **(A)**, **(B)**, **(C)**, and **(D)** indicate where the following sentence could be added.

   These flare-ups continue to occur until a new pesticide is developed, at which time the cycle begins anew.

   Where would the sentence best fit?
   Ⓐ Choice A
   Ⓑ Choice B
   Ⓒ Choice C
   Ⓓ Choice D

20. **Directions:** An introductory sentence for a brief summary of the passage is provided below. Complete the summary by selecting the THREE answer choices that express the most important ideas in the passage. Some sentences do not belong in the summary because they express ideas that are not presented in the passage or are minor ideas in the passage. **This question is worth 2 points.**

Write your answer choices in the spaces where they belong. You can either write the letter of your answer choice or you can copy the sentence.

Pest control measures vary in their approach and overall degree of success.

-
-
-

Answer Choices

A Biological methods of pest control were introduced by the ancient Sumerians, and chemical control was first used in ancient China.

B Pesticides are limited in their usefulness because pests quickly become resistant to them, and because they can harm species for which they were not intended.

C Biological control, for example, the use of natural enemies of pests, has been effective at regulating nonnative pests, though it can also threaten the existence of native species.

D The success of biological and chemical approaches to pest control has been difficult to measure because situations vary significantly from one location to another.

E Integrated pest management is a holistic approach that has been successful at controlling major pest outbreaks in locations where chemical and biological control have already failed.

F Integrated pest management, an approach that considers biological, ecological, economic, and aesthetic aspects of pest control, uses a variety of techniques adjusted to specific situations.

LISTENING

In this section, you will be able to demonstrate your ability to understand conversations and lectures in English.

In the actual test, the section is divided into two separately timed parts. You will hear each conversation or lecture only one time. A clock will indicate how much time remains. The clock will count down only while you are answering questions, not while you are listening. You may take up to 16.5 minutes to answer the questions.

In this practice test, there is no time limit for answering questions.

You may take notes while you listen. You may use your notes to help you answer the questions. Your notes will not be scored.

Answer the questions based on what is stated or implied by the speakers.

In some questions, you will see this icon: 🎧 . This means that you will hear, but not see, part of the question.

In the actual test, you must answer each question. You cannot return to previous questions.

At the end of this practice test, you will find an answer key.

Directions: Listen to Track 34.

Directions: Now answer the questions.

1. Why does the student go to the career services office?

    Ⓐ To confirm the date and time of the career fair
    Ⓑ To learn the location of the career fair
    Ⓒ To find out if he is allowed to attend the career fair
    Ⓓ To get advice about interviewing at the career fair

2. Why does the student think that companies' representatives would not be interested in talking to him?

    Ⓐ He will not be graduating this year.
    Ⓑ He is not currently taking business classes.
    Ⓒ He has not declared a major yet.
    Ⓓ He does not have a current résumé.

3. What does the woman imply about the small print on the career fair posters and flyers?

    Ⓐ The information in the small print was incomplete.
    Ⓑ The print was smaller than she expected it to be.
    Ⓒ The information the small print contains will be updated.
    Ⓓ The information in the small print will be presented in a more noticeable way.

4. What does the woman say is a good way for the student to prepare for speaking to companies' representatives? *Select 2 answers.*

    Ａ Take some business classes
    Ｂ Familiarize himself with certain businesses beforehand
    Ｃ Have questions ready to ask the representatives
    Ｄ Talk to people who work for accounting firms

5. *Listen to Track 35 to answer the question.*

    Why does the student say this?

    (A) To acknowledge that he cannot go to this year's career fair
    (B) To acknowledge the amount of preparation he will have
    (C) To indicate that he has schoolwork he must complete before the career fair
    (D) To indicate that he needs to go to his job now

Directions: Listen to Track 36.

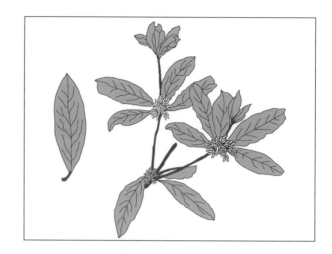

Directions: Now answer the questions.

6. What topics related to the Nightcap Oak does the professor mainly discuss?
    Select 2 answers.

    A   Factors that relate to the size of the area in which it grows
    B   The size of its population over the last few centuries
    C   Whether anything can be done to ensure its survival
    D   Why it did not change much over the last one hundred million years

7. According to the professor, what led scientists to characterize the Nightcap Oak as primitive?

    Ⓐ It has no evolutionary connection to other trees growing in Australia today.
    Ⓑ It has an inefficient reproductive system.
    Ⓒ Its flowers are located at the bases of the leaves.
    Ⓓ It is similar to some ancient fossils.

8. What point does the professor make about the Nightcap Oak's habitat?

    Ⓐ It is stable despite its limited size.
    Ⓑ Unlike the habitats of many plants, it is expanding.
    Ⓒ Its recent changes have left the Nightcap Oak struggling to adapt.
    Ⓓ Its size is much larger than the area where the Nightcap Oak grows.

9. According to the professor, what are two factors that prevent the Nightcap Oak population from spreading? *Choose 2 answers.*

    A   The complex conditions required for the trees to produce fruit
    B   The fact that the seed cannot germinate while locked inside the shell
    C   The limited time the seed retains the ability to germinate
    D   Competition with tree species that evolved more recently

10. Why does the professor mention the size of the Nightcap Oak population over the last few hundred years?

    Ⓐ To explain why it is likely that the Nightcap Oak population will increase in the future
    Ⓑ To point out that the Nightcap Oak's limited reproductive success has not led to a decrease in its population
    Ⓒ To present evidence that the Nightcap Oak is able to tolerate major changes in its environment
    Ⓓ To point out that the Nightcap Oak is able to resist diseases that have destroyed other tree species

11. *Listen again to part of the lecture by playing Track 37.* 🎧 *Then answer the question.*

    Why does the professor say this?

    Ⓐ She wants the students to think about a possible connection.
    Ⓑ She wants to know if the students have any questions.
    Ⓒ She is implying that researchers have been asking the wrong questions.
    Ⓓ She is implying that there may be no connection between the questions.

Directions: Listen to Track 38.

Directions: Now answer the questions.

12. Why does the student go to see the professor?

    Ⓐ She is having trouble finding a topic for her term paper.
    Ⓑ She needs his help to find resource materials.
    Ⓒ She wants to ask him for an extension on a term paper.
    Ⓓ She wants him to approve her plans for a term paper.

13. Why is the student interested in learning more about dialects?

    Ⓐ She often has trouble understanding what other students are saying.
    Ⓑ She is trying to change the way she speaks.
    Ⓒ She is aware that her own dialect differs from those of her roommates.
    Ⓓ She spent her childhood in various places where different dialects are spoken.

14. Based on the conversation, what can be concluded about "dialect accommodation"? *Select 2 answers.*

    Ⓐ It is a largely subconscious process.
    Ⓑ It is a process that applies only to some dialects.
    Ⓒ It is a very common phenomenon.
    Ⓓ It is a topic that has not been explored extensively.

15. What does the professor want the student to do next?

    Ⓐ Read some articles he has recommended
    Ⓑ Present her proposal before the entire class
    Ⓒ Submit a design plan for the project
    Ⓓ Listen to recordings of different dialects

16. *Listen again to part of the conversation by playing Track 39.* 🎧 *Then answer the question.*

    What can be inferred about the professor when he says this?

    Ⓐ He thinks the topic goes beyond his expertise.
    Ⓑ He thinks the topic is too broad for the student to manage.
    Ⓒ He thinks the topic is not relevant for a linguistics class.
    Ⓓ He thinks other students may have chosen the same topic.

Directions: Listen to Track 40.

Directions: Now answer the questions.

17. What aspect of creative writing does the professor mainly discuss?

    Ⓐ How to keep a reader's interest
    Ⓑ How to create believable characters
    Ⓒ Key differences between major and minor characters
    Ⓓ Techniques for developing short-story plots

18. Why does the professor recommend that students pay attention to the people they see every day?

    Ⓐ The behavior and characteristics of these people can be used in character sketches.
    Ⓑ Observing people in real-life situations can provide ideas for story plots.
    Ⓒ It is easier to observe the behavior of familiar people than of new people.
    Ⓓ Students can gather accurate physical descriptions for their characters.

19. The professor discusses an example of three friends who run out of gas. What point does he use the example to illustrate?

    Ⓐ Writers should know their characters as well as they know their friends.
    Ⓑ Writers should create characters that interact in complex ways.
    Ⓒ Friends do not always behave the way we expect them to behave.
    Ⓓ Friends' behavior is often more predictable than fictional characters' behavior.

20. What warning does the professor give when he talks about the man who lives on the mountain?

    Ⓐ Avoid placing characters in remote settings
    Ⓑ Avoid having more than one major character
    Ⓒ Avoid using people as models whose lives are unusual
    Ⓓ Avoid making characters into stereotypes

21. What does the professor imply is the importance of flat characters?

    Ⓐ They act more predictably than other characters.
    Ⓑ They are difficult for readers to understand.
    Ⓒ They help reveal the main character's personality.
    Ⓓ They are the only characters able to experience defeat.

22. *Listen again to part of the lecture by playing Track 41.* 🎧 *Then answer the question.*

    Why does the professor say this?

    Ⓐ To indicate that he is about to explain what type of drawing he wants
    Ⓑ To help students understand a term that may be confusing
    Ⓒ To indicate that he used the wrong word earlier
    Ⓓ To motivate the students to do better work

Directions: Listen to Track 42.

Earth Science

Sahara Desert

Directions: Now answer the questions.

23. What is the lecture mainly about?

    Ⓐ An example of rapid climate change
    Ⓑ A comparison of two mechanisms of climate change
    Ⓒ The weather conditions in the present-day Sahara
    Ⓓ Recent geological findings made in the Sahara

24. Not long ago, the Sahara had a different climate. What evidence does the professor mention to support this? *Select 3 answers.*

    A Ancient pollen
    B Bones from large animals
    C Rock paintings
    D Agriculture in ancient Egypt
    E Underground water

25. In the lecture, what do the Ice Age and the creation of the Sahara Desert both illustrate about past climate changes? *Select 2 answers.*

    A That some climate changes benefitted the development of civilization
    B That some climate changes were not caused by human activity
    C That some climate changes were caused by a decrease of moisture in the atmosphere
    D That some climate changes were caused by changes in Earth's motion and position

26. What started the runaway effect that led to the Sahara area of North Africa becoming a desert?

    Ⓐ The prevailing winds became stronger.
    Ⓑ The seasonal rains moved to a different area.
    Ⓒ The vegetation started to die off in large areas.
    Ⓓ The soil lost its ability to retain rainwater.

27. The professor mentions a theory that people migrating from the Sahara were important to the development of the Egyptian civilization. Which sentence best describes the professor's attitude toward this theory?

    Ⓐ It is exciting because it perfectly explains recent archaeological discoveries.
    Ⓑ It is problematic because it goes too far beyond the generally available data.
    Ⓒ It raises an interesting possibility and he hopes to see more evidence for it.
    Ⓓ It cannot be taken seriously until it explains how the migrants got to Egypt.

28. *Listen again to part of the lecture by playing Track 43.* 🎧 *Then answer the question.*

Why does the professor say this?

Ⓐ To correct a misstatement he made about the Sahara's climate

Ⓑ To suggest that the current dryness of the Sahara is exaggerated

Ⓒ To indicate that scientists are not in agreement about the Sahara's past climate

Ⓓ To emphasize the difference between the current and past climates of the Sahara

SPEAKING

In the actual test, the Speaking section will last approximately 16 minutes. You will answer four questions by speaking into the microphone. You may take notes while you listen. You may use your notes to help you answer the questions. Your notes will not be scored. For each question, you will have time to prepare before giving your response. You should answer the questions as completely as possible in the time allowed.

For this practice test, you may want to use a personal recording device to record and play back your responses.

For each question, play the audio track listed and follow the directions to complete the task.

At the end of this practice test, you will find important points about each question.

1. You will now give your opinion about a familiar topic. After you hear the question, you should give yourself 15 seconds to prepare and 45 seconds to speak.

    Listen to Track 44.

    > Some people have one career throughout their lives. Other people do different kinds of work at different points in their lives. Which do you think is better? Explain why.
    >
    > | **Preparation Time: 15 seconds** |
    > | --- |
    > | **Response Time: 45 seconds** |

2. Now you will read a passage about a campus situation and then listen to a conversation about the same topic. You will then answer a question, using information from both the reading passage and the conversation. You should give yourself 30 seconds to prepare and 60 seconds to speak.

    Listen to Track 45.

Reading Time: 50 seconds

    ### History Seminars Should Be Shorter

    Currently, all of the seminar classes in the history department are three hours long. I would like to propose that history seminars be shortened to two hours. I make this proposal for two reasons. First, most students just cannot concentrate for three hours straight. I myself have taken these three-hour seminars and found them tiring and sometimes boring. Also, when a seminar lasts that long, people stop concentrating and stop learning, so the third hour of a three-hour seminar is a waste of everyone's time. Two-hour seminars would be much more efficient.

    Sincerely,

    Tim Lawson

Listen to Track 46.

The woman expresses her opinion about the proposal described in the letter. Briefly summarize the proposal. Then state her opinion about the proposal and explain the reasons she gives for holding that opinion.

Preparation Time: 30 seconds
Response Time: 60 seconds

3. Now you will read a passage about an academic subject and then listen to a lecture on the same topic. Answer the question, using information from both the reading passage and the lecture. Give yourself 30 seconds to prepare and 60 seconds to speak.

Listen to Track 47.

Reading Time: 45 seconds

Explicit Memories and Implicit Memories

In everyday life, when people speak of memory, they are almost always speaking about what psychologists would call explicit memories. An explicit memory is a conscious or intentional recollection, usually of facts, names, events, or other things that a person can state or declare. There is another kind of memory that is not conscious. Memories of this kind are called implicit memories. An individual can have an experience that he or she cannot consciously recall yet still display reactions that indicate the experience has been somehow recorded in his or her brain.

Listen to Track 48.

Using the example of the car advertisement, explain what is meant by implicit memory.

Preparation Time: 30 seconds
Response Time: 60 seconds

4. Now you will listen to a lecture. You will then be asked to summarize the lecture. You should give yourself 20 seconds to prepare and 60 seconds to speak.

Listen to Track 49.

Using points and examples from the talk, explain the difference between active and passive attention.

Preparation Time: 20 seconds
Response Time: 60 seconds

WRITING

In this section, you will be able to demonstrate your ability to use writing to communicate in an academic environment. There will be two writing tasks.

At the end of this practice test, you will find topic notes for each question.

Turn the page to see the directions for the first writing task.

Writing Based on Reading and Listening

For this task, you will read a passage about an academic topic. Then you will listen to a lecture about the same topic. You may take notes while you listen.

In your response, provide a detailed summary of the lecture and explain how the lecture relates to the reading passage.

In the actual test, you will have 3 minutes to read the passage and 20 minutes to write your response. While you write, you will be able to see the reading passage. If you finish your response before time is up, you may go on to the second writing task.

Reading Time: 3 minutes

Communal online encyclopedias represent one of the latest resources to be found on the Internet. They are in many respects like traditional printed encyclopedias: collections of articles on various subjects. What is specific to these online encyclopedias, however, is that any Internet user can contribute a new article or make an editorial change in an existing one. As a result, the encyclopedia is authored by the whole community of Internet users. The idea might sound attractive, but the communal online encyclopedias have several important problems that make them much less valuable than traditional, printed encyclopedias.

First, contributors to a communal online encyclopedia often lack academic credentials, thereby making their contributions partially informed at best and downright inaccurate in many cases. Traditional encyclopedias are written by trained experts who adhere to standards of academic rigor that nonspecialists cannot really achieve.

Second, even if the original entry in the online encyclopedia is correct, the communal nature of these online encyclopedias gives unscrupulous users and vandals or hackers the opportunity to fabricate, delete, and corrupt information in the encyclopedia. Once changes have been made to the original text, an unsuspecting user cannot tell the entry has been tampered with. None of this is possible with a traditional encyclopedia.

Third, the communal encyclopedias focus too frequently, and in too great a depth, on trivial and popular topics, which creates a false impression of what is important and what is not. A child doing research for a school project may discover that a major historical event receives as much attention in an online encyclopedia as, say, a single long-running television program. The traditional encyclopedia provides a considered view of what topics to include or exclude and contains a sense of proportion that online "democratic" communal encyclopedias do not.

Listen to Track 50.

Directions: You have 20 minutes to plan and write your response. Your response will be judged on the basis of the quality of your writing and on how well your response presents the points in the lecture and their relationship to the reading passage. Typically, an effective response will contain a minimum of 150 words.

Listen to Track 51.

Response Time: 20 minutes

Question 1

Summarize the points made in the lecture, being sure to explain how they oppose the specific points made in the reading passage.

_____

_____

_____

_____

_____

_____

_____

_____

_____

Writing for an Academic Discussion

For this task, you will read an online discussion. A professor has posted a question about a topic, and some classmates have responded with their ideas.

In the actual test, you will have 10 minutes to write a response that contributes to the discussion.

Question 2

Your professor is teaching a class on advertising. Write a post responding to the professor's question.

In your response, you should do the following.
- Express and support your opinion.
- Make a contribution to the discussion in your own words.

An effective response will contain at least 100 words.

Dr. Achebe

Let's discuss advertising for organizations that do charitable work. Many of these organizations use images, particularly photographs, in their advertisements to motivate people to donate money or goods to support their charity. Some use sad images, for example, photographs of people who are in difficult situations and need help. Others use happy or inspirational images, for example, of people already receiving help. In your view, which strategy is more effective to bring in donations—using sad or happy images? Why?

Claire

I think you've got to show the problem if you want people to understand that it's serious and help is truly needed. Consider a charity that builds schools and provides school supplies. If their advertisements only show happy children attending nice schools, why is my donation necessary?

Paul

Let's not forget that people often see lots of advertisements from many different charities—too many to even keep track of. Honestly, many potential donors may not want to look at advertisements containing unpleasant or sad images. In my opinion, inspirational images of all the good a charity does will get more attention and ultimately bring in more donations.

Response Time: 10 minutes

TOEFL iBT® Test 4

READING

In this section, you will be able to demonstrate your ability to understand academic passages in English. You will read and answer questions about **two passages**.

In the actual test, you will have 36 minutes total to read both passages and answer the questions. A clock will indicate how much time remains.

Some passages may include one or more notes explaining words or phrases. The words or phrases are marked with footnote numbers, and the notes explaining them appear at the end of the passage.

Most questions are worth 1 point, but the last question for each passage is worth 2 points.

You may review and revise your answers in this section as long as time remains.

At the end of this practice test, you will find an answer key.

Directions: Read the passage. Then answer the questions. You have 18 minutes on average to answer the questions.

UNDERSTANDING ANCIENT MESOAMERICAN ART

Starting at the end of the eighteenth century and continuing up to the present, explorers have searched for the ruins of ancient Mesoamerica, a region that includes Central America and central and southern Mexico. With the progress of time, archaeologists have unearthed civilizations increasingly remote in age. It is as if with each new century in the modern era an earlier stratum of antiquity has been revealed. Nineteenth-century explorers, particularly John Lloyd Stephens and Frederick Catherwood, came upon Maya cities in the jungle, as well as evidence of other Classic cultures. Twentieth-century research revealed a much earlier high civilization, the Olmec. It now scarcely seems possible that the frontiers of early Mesoamerican civilization can be pushed back any further, although new work—such as in Oaxaca, southern Mexico—will continue to fill in details of the picture.

The process of discovery often shapes what we know about the history of Mesoamerican art. New finds are just as often made accidentally as intentionally. In 1971 workers installing sound and light equipment under the Pyramid of the Sun at Teotihuacán stumbled upon a remarkable cave that has since been interpreted by some scholars as a royal burial chamber. Archaeology has its own fashions too: the isolation of new sites may be the prime goal in one decade and the excavation of pyramids the focus in the next. In a third decade, outlying structures rather than principal buildings may absorb archaeologists' energies. Nor should one forget that excavators are vulnerable to local interests. At one point, reconstruction of pyramids to attract tourism may be desired; at another, archaeologists may be precluded from working at what has already become a tourist attraction. Also, modern construction often determines which ancient sites can be excavated. In Mexico City, for example, the building of the subway initiated the excavations there and renewed interest in the old Aztec capital.

But the study of Mesoamerican art is not based exclusively on archaeology. Much useful information about the native populations was written down in the sixteenth century, particularly in central Mexico, and it can help us unravel the pre-Columbian past (the time prior to the arrival of Columbus in the Americas in 1492). Although many sources exist, the single most important one to the art historian is Bernardino de Sahagún's *General History of the Things of New Spain*. A Franciscan friar (member of the Roman Catholic religious order), Sahagún recorded for posterity many aspects of pre-Hispanic life in his encyclopedia of twelve books, including history, ideology, and cosmogony (theories of the origin of the universe), as well as detailed information on the materials and methods of the skilled native craft workers. Furthermore, traditional ways of life survive among the native peoples of Mesoamerica, and scholars have increasingly found that modern practice and belief can decode the past. Remarkably, some scholars have even turned this process around, teaching ancient writing to modern peoples who may use it to articulate their identity in the twenty-first century.

During the past 40 years, scholars also have made great progress in deciphering and interpreting ancient Mesoamerican writing systems, a breakthrough that has transformed our understanding of the pre-Columbian mind. Classic Maya inscriptions, for example—long thought to record only calendrical information and astrological incantations—can now be read, and we find that most of them glorify family and ancestry by displaying the right of individual sovereigns to rule. The carvings can thus be seen as portraits or public records of dynastic power. Although scholars long believed that Mesoamerican artists did not sign their works, Mayanist scholar David Stuart's 1986 deciphering of the Maya glyphs (written symbols) for "scribe" and "to write" opened a window on Maya practice; now we know at least one painter of ceramic vessels was the son of a king. Knowledge of the minor arts has also come in large part through an active art market. Thousands more small-scale objects are known now than in the twentieth century, although at a terrible cost to the ancient ruins from which they have been plundered.

Directions: Now answer the questions.

PARAGRAPH 1

Starting at the end of the eighteenth century and continuing up to the present, explorers have searched for the ruins of ancient Mesoamerica, a region that includes Central America and central and southern Mexico. With the progress of time, archaeologists have unearthed civilizations increasingly remote in age. It is as if with each new century in the modern era an earlier stratum of antiquity has been revealed. Nineteenth-century explorers, particularly John Lloyd Stephens and Frederick Catherwood, came upon Maya cities in the jungle, as well as evidence of other Classic cultures. Twentieth-century research revealed a much earlier high civilization, the Olmec. It now scarcely seems possible that the frontiers of early Mesoamerican civilization can be pushed back any further, although new work—such as in Oaxaca, southern Mexico—will continue to fill in details of the picture.

1. Paragraph 1 supports which of the following statements about the revealing of early Mesoamerican civilization?
   (A) The Maya and Olmec civilizations were discovered by explorers at approximately the same time.
   (B) Most of our understanding of Mesoamerican civilization comes from discoveries made in the twentieth century.
   (C) The discoveries made at Oaxaca in southern Mexico show that the Olmec civilization had its origins there.
   (D) Evidence still to be found in Oaxaca, Mexico, is likely to provide additional information about the high civilization of early Mesoamerica.

The process of discovery often shapes what we know about the history of Mesoamerican art. New finds are just as often made accidentally as intentionally. In 1971 workers installing sound and light equipment under the Pyramid of the Sun at Teotihuacán stumbled upon a remarkable cave that has since been interpreted by some scholars as a royal burial chamber. Archaeology has its own fashions too: the isolation of new sites may be the prime goal in one decade and the excavation of pyramids the focus in the next. In a third decade, **outlying** structures rather than principal buildings may absorb archaeologists' energies. Nor should one forget that excavators are vulnerable to local interests. At one point, reconstruction of pyramids to attract tourism may be desired; at another, archaeologists may be precluded from working at what has already become a tourist attraction. Also, modern construction often determines which ancient sites can be excavated. In Mexico City, for example, the building of the subway initiated the excavations there and renewed interest in the old Aztec capital.

2. The word "**outlying**" in the passage is closest in meaning to

Ⓐ ceremonial
Ⓑ temporary
Ⓒ far from the center
Ⓓ simple

3. In paragraph 2, why does the author discuss the Pyramid of the Sun at Teotihuacán?

Ⓐ To introduce the discussion of a specific style of Mesoamerican art
Ⓑ To illustrate the importance of an accidental discovery
Ⓒ To emphasize the necessity of systematic study
Ⓓ To argue against the use of modern equipment in archaeology

4. Which of the following is NOT mentioned in paragraph 2 as a factor affecting the process of discovery in archaeology?

Ⓐ Fashions that change over time
Ⓑ The popularity of archaeology as a field of study
Ⓒ The interests of local inhabitants
Ⓓ The building of modern structures

P A R A G R A P H 3

But the study of Mesoamerican art is not based **exclusively** on archaeology. Much useful information about the native populations was written down in the sixteenth century, particularly in central Mexico, and it can help us unravel the pre-Columbian past (the time prior to the arrival of Columbus in the Americas in 1492). Although many sources exist, the single most important one to the art historian is Bernardino de Sahagún's *General History of the Things of New Spain*. A Franciscan friar (member of the Roman Catholic religious order), Sahagún recorded for posterity many aspects of pre-Hispanic life in his encyclopedia of twelve books, including history, ideology, and cosmogony (theories of the origin of the universe), as well as detailed information on the materials and methods of the skilled native craft workers. Furthermore, traditional ways of life survive among the native peoples of Mesoamerica, and scholars have increasingly found that modern practice and belief can decode the past. Remarkably, some scholars have even turned this process around, teaching ancient writing to modern peoples who may use it to articulate their identity in the twenty-first century.

5. The word "**exclusively**" in the passage is closest in meaning to

   Ⓐ exactly
   Ⓑ solely
   Ⓒ traditionally
   Ⓓ primarily

6. According to paragraph 3, why was Bernardino de Sahagún important to the study of Mesoamerican art?

   Ⓐ He recorded detailed information about native populations in the sixteenth century.
   Ⓑ He made important archaeological discoveries in central Mexico.
   Ⓒ He studied the methods and materials of skilled Mesoamerican craft workers as a basis for his own art.
   Ⓓ He encouraged native people to preserve their traditional ways of life.

7. According to paragraph 3, which of the following is true of ancient Mesoamerican writing?

   Ⓐ It is very similar to the modern writing of Mesoamerican peoples.
   Ⓑ It is not as old as originally thought.
   Ⓒ It can be used by modern peoples to express their own identities.
   Ⓓ It is most thoroughly understood by skilled native craft workers.

During the past 40 years, scholars also have made great progress in deciphering and interpreting ancient Mesoamerican writing systems, a breakthrough that has transformed our understanding of the pre-Columbian mind. Classic Maya inscriptions, for example—long thought to record only calendrical information and astrological incantations—can now be read, and we find that most of them glorify family and ancestry by displaying the right of individual sovereigns to rule. The carvings can thus be seen as portraits or public records of dynastic power. Although scholars long believed that Mesoamerican artists did not sign their works, Mayanist scholar David Stuart's 1986 deciphering of the Maya glyphs (written symbols) for "scribe" and "to write" opened a window on Maya practice; now we know at least one painter of ceramic vessels was the son of a king. Knowledge of the minor arts has also come in large part through an active art market. Thousands more small-scale objects are known now than in the twentieth century, although at a terrible cost to the ancient ruins from which they have been plundered.

PARAGRAPH 4

8. According to paragraph 4, all of the following are true of Mayanist scholar David Stuart's 1986 discovery EXCEPT:

    Ⓐ It reversed a belief held by earlier scholars.
    Ⓑ It uncovered long lists of royal dynastic records.
    Ⓒ It allowed scholars to understand two glyphs for the first time.
    Ⓓ It revealed that at least one Maya painter was a king's son.

The process of discovery often shapes what we know about the history of Mesoamerican art. New finds are just as often made accidentally as intentionally. **(A)** In 1971 workers installing sound and light equipment under the Pyramid of the Sun at Teotihuacán stumbled upon a remarkable cave that has since been interpreted by some scholars as a royal burial chamber. **(B)** Archaeology has its own fashions too: the isolation of new sites may be the prime goal in one decade and the excavation of pyramids the focus in the next. In a third decade, outlying structures rather than principal buildings may absorb archaeologists' energies. **(C)** Nor should one forget that excavators are vulnerable to local interests. **(D)** At one point, reconstruction of pyramids to attract tourism may be desired; at another, archaeologists may be precluded from working at what has already become a tourist attraction. Also, modern construction often determines which ancient sites can be excavated. In Mexico City, for example, the building of the subway initiated the excavations there and renewed interest in the old Aztec capital.

PARAGRAPH 2

9. Look at the part of the passage that is displayed above. The letters **(A)**, **(B)**, **(C)**, an **(D)** indicate where the following sentence could be added.

    This chance discovery has done as much for our understanding of the pyramid as any systematic study would have.

    Where would the sentence best fit?

    Ⓐ Choice A
    Ⓑ Choice B
    Ⓒ Choice C
    Ⓓ Choice D

10. **Directions:** An introductory sentence for a brief summary of the passage is provided below. Complete the summary by selecting the THREE answer choices that express the most important ideas in the passage. Some sentences do not belong in the summary because they express ideas that are not presented in the passage or are minor ideas in the passage. **This question is worth 2 points.**

> **Our knowledge of Mesoamerican art has grown since explorers first began searching for ruins of ancient Mesoamerica.**
>
> ●
>
> ●
>
> ●

Answer Choices

A   John Lloyd Stephens and Frederick Catherwood used the ruins of Maya cities in the jungle as evidence that the Maya civilization was older than the Olmec civilization.

B   Often discovered accidentally, Mesoamerican pyramids not only contain numerous samples of native art but also attract tourism.

C   Classic Maya inscriptions primarily recorded calendrical information, astrological incantations, and signatures of artists.

D   Accidental discoveries, fashions in archaeology, and local interests have shaped our knowledge of Mesoamerican art.

E   Much information about Mesoamerican art exists in sixteenth-century writings and in surviving traditions and practices in Mesoamerica.

F   Progress in deciphering ancient writing systems and active art markets have contributed to knowledge of Mesoamerican art.

Directions: Read the passage. Then answer the questions. You have 18 minutes on average to answer the questions.

WHAT IS A COMMUNITY?

The Black Hills forest, the prairie riparian forest, and other forests of the western United States can be separated by the distinctly different combinations of species they comprise. It is easy to distinguish between prairie riparian forest and Black Hills forest—one is a broad-leaved forest of ash and cottonwood trees, the other is a coniferous forest of ponderosa pine and white spruce trees. One has kingbirds; the other, juncos (birds with white outer tail feathers). The fact that ecological communities are, indeed, recognizable clusters of species led some early ecologists, particularly those living in the beginning of the twentieth century, to claim that communities are highly integrated, precisely balanced assemblages. This claim harkens back to even earlier arguments about the existence of a balance of nature, where every species is there for a specific purpose, like a vital part in a complex machine. Such a belief would suggest that to remove any species, whether it be plant, bird, or insect, would somehow disrupt the balance, and the habitat would begin to deteriorate. Likewise, to add a species may be equally disruptive.

One of these pioneer ecologists was Frederick Clements, who studied ecology extensively throughout the Midwest and other areas in North America. He held that within any given region of climate, ecological communities tended to slowly converge toward a single endpoint, which he called the "climatic climax." This "climax" community was, in Clements's mind, the most well-balanced, integrated grouping of species that could occur within that particular region. Clements even thought that the process of ecological succession—the replacement of some species by others over time—was somewhat akin to the development of an organism, from embryo to adult. Clements thought that succession represented discrete stages in the development of the community (rather like infancy, childhood, and adolescence), terminating in the climatic "adult" stage, when the community became self-reproducing and succession ceased. Clements's view of the ecological community reflected the notion of a precise balance of nature.

Clements was challenged by another pioneer ecologist, Henry Gleason, who took the opposite view. Gleason viewed the community as largely a group of species with similar tolerances to the stresses imposed by climate and other factors typical of the region. Gleason saw the element of chance as important in influencing where species occurred. His concept of the community suggests that nature is not highly integrated. Gleason thought succession could take numerous directions, depending upon local circumstances.

Who was right? Many ecologists have made precise measurements, designed to test the assumptions of both the Clements and Gleason models. For instance, along mountain slopes, does one life zone, or habitat type, grade sharply or gradually into another? If the divisions are sharp, perhaps the reason is that the community is so well integrated, so holistic, so like Clements viewed it, that whole clusters of species must remain together. If the divisions are gradual, perhaps, as Gleason suggested, each species is responding individually to its environment, and clusters of species are not so integrated that they must always occur together.

It now appears that Gleason was far closer to the truth than Clements. The ecological community is largely an accidental assemblage of species with similar responses to a particular climate. Green ash trees are found in association with plains cottonwood trees because both can survive well on floodplains and the competition between them is not so strong that only one can persevere. One ecological community often flows into another so gradually that it is next to impossible to say where one leaves off and the other begins. Communities are individualistic.

This is not to say that precise harmonies are not present within communities. Most flowering plants could not exist were it not for their pollinators—and vice versa. Predators, disease organisms, and competitors all influence the abundance and distribution of everything from oak trees to field mice. But if we see a precise balance of nature, it is largely an artifact of our perception, due to the illusion that nature, especially a complex system like a forest, seems so unchanging from one day to the next.

Directions: Now answer the questions.

PARAGRAPH 1

The Black Hills forest, the prairie riparian forest, and other forests of the western United States can be separated by the distinctly different combinations of species they comprise. It is easy to distinguish between prairie riparian forest and Black Hills forest—one is a broad-leaved forest of ash and cottonwood trees, the other is a coniferous forest of ponderosa pine and white spruce trees. One has kingbirds; the other, juncos (birds with white outer tail feathers). The fact that ecological communities are, indeed, recognizable clusters of species led some early ecologists, particularly those living in the beginning of the twentieth century, to claim that communities are highly integrated, precisely balanced assemblages. This claim harkens back to even earlier arguments about the existence of a balance of nature, where every species is there for a specific purpose, like a vital part in a complex machine. Such a belief would suggest that to remove any species, whether it be plant, bird, or insect, would somehow disrupt the balance, and the habitat would begin to deteriorate. Likewise, to add a species may be equally disruptive.

11. In paragraph 1, why does the author distinguish between prairie riparian forest and Black Hills forest?

   (A) To highlight the difference between the views of various ecologists about the nature of ecological communities

   (B) To illustrate why some ecologists tended to view ecological communities as highly integrated

   (C) To demonstrate that one forest has a greater variety of species than the other

   (D) To show how these two forests differ from others in the United States

12. According to paragraph 1, what was a common claim about ecological communities before the early twentieth century?

   (A) Every species in a community has a specific role in that community.

   (B) It is important to protect communities by removing certain species.

   (C) A precise balance is difficult to maintain in an ecological community.

   (D) It is necessary for new species to be added quickly as ecological communities develop.

13. According to paragraph 1, the belief in a balance of nature suggests that removing a species from an ecological community would have which of the following effects?

   Ⓐ It would reduce competition between the remaining species of the community.
   Ⓑ It would produce a different, but equally balanced, community.
   Ⓒ It would lead to a decline in the community.
   Ⓓ It would cause more harm than adding a species to the community.

PARAGRAPH 2

One of these pioneer ecologists was Frederick Clements, who studied ecology extensively throughout the Midwest and other areas in North America. He held that within any given region of climate, ecological communities tended to slowly converge toward a single endpoint, which he called the "climatic climax." This "climax" community was, in Clements's mind, the most well-balanced, integrated grouping of species that could occur within that particular region. Clements even thought that the process of ecological succession—the replacement of some species by others over time—was somewhat akin to the development of an organism, from embryo to adult. Clements thought that succession represented discrete stages in the development of the community (rather like infancy, childhood, and adolescence), terminating in the climatic "adult" stage, when the community became self-reproducing and succession ceased. Clements's view of the ecological community reflected the notion of a precise balance of nature.

14. Which of the following best represents the view of ecological communities associated with Frederick Clements in paragraph 2?

   Ⓐ Only when all species in a community are at the reproductive stage of development is an ecological community precisely balanced.
   Ⓑ When an ecological community achieves "climatic climax," it begins to decline.
   Ⓒ All climates have similar climax communities.
   Ⓓ Ecological communities eventually reach the maximum level of balance that is possible for their region.

PARAGRAPH 3

Clements was challenged by another pioneer ecologist, Henry Gleason, who took the opposite view. Gleason viewed the community as largely a group of species with similar tolerances to the stresses imposed by climate and other factors typical of the region. Gleason saw the element of chance as important in influencing where species occurred. His concept of the community suggests that nature is not highly integrated. Gleason thought succession could take numerous directions, depending upon local circumstances.

15. According to Gleason in paragraph 3, the occurrence of a species in a particular community is influenced by

   Ⓐ unpredictable events
   Ⓑ how individualistic the species is
   Ⓒ the number of other species present
   Ⓓ the tolerance of other species to stresses

Who was right? Many ecologists have made precise measurements, designed to test the assumptions of both the Clements and Gleason models. For instance, along mountain slopes, does one life zone, or habitat type, grade sharply or gradually into another? If the divisions are sharp, perhaps the reason is that the community is so well integrated, so holistic, so like Clements viewed it, that whole clusters of species must remain together. If the divisions are gradual, perhaps, as Gleason suggested, each species is responding individually to its environment, and clusters of species are not so integrated that they must always occur together.

16. What did the ecologists in paragraph 4 hope to determine with their measurements?

   Ⓐ Whether different species compete for the same environments
   Ⓑ Whether habitats are sharply separated or gradually flow into each other
   Ⓒ Whether succession differs in different types of habitats
   Ⓓ Whether integrated communities survive better than independent communities

It now appears that Gleason was far closer to the truth than Clements. The ecological community is largely an accidental assemblage of species with similar responses to a particular climate. Green ash trees are found in association with plains cottonwood trees because both can survive well on floodplains and the competition between them is not so strong that only one can **persevere**. One ecological community often flows into another so gradually that it is next to impossible to say where one leaves off and the other begins. Communities are individualistic.

17. The word "**persevere**" in the passage is closest in meaning to

   Ⓐ reproduce
   Ⓑ fail
   Ⓒ expand
   Ⓓ continue

This is not to say that precise harmonies are not present within communities. Most flowering plants could not exist were it not for their pollinators—and vice versa. Predators, disease organisms, and competitors all influence the abundance and distribution of everything from oak trees to field mice. **But if we see a precise balance of nature, it is largely an artifact of our perception, due to the illusion that nature, especially a complex system like a forest, seems so unchanging from one day to the next.**

18. Which of the sentences below best expresses the essential information in the highlighted sentence in paragraph 6? Incorrect choices change the meaning in important ways or leave out essential information.

   Ⓐ We see nature as precisely balanced because nature is unchanging.
   Ⓑ A precise balance of nature is not possible because of the complexity of natural systems.
   Ⓒ Our sense that nature is precisely balanced results from the illusion that it is unchanging.
   Ⓓ Because nature is precisely balanced, complex systems do not seem to change.

(A) Who was right? **(B)** Many ecologists have made precise measurements, designed to test the assumptions of both the Clements and Gleason models. **(C)** For instance, along mountain slopes, does one life zone, or habitat type, grade sharply or gradually into another? **(D)** If the divisions are sharp, perhaps the reason is that the community is so well integrated, so holistic, so like Clements viewed it, that whole clusters of species must remain together. If the divisions are gradual, perhaps, as Gleason suggested, each species is responding individually to its environment, and clusters of species are not so integrated that they must always occur together.

19. Look at the part of the passage that is displayed above. The letters **(A)**, **(B)**, **(C)**, and **(D)** indicate where the following sentence could be added.

    Their research has helped to decide between the two views because it has focused on questions to which Clements and Gleason would give opposing answers.

    Where would the sentence best fit?

    Ⓐ Choice A
    Ⓑ Choice B
    Ⓒ Choice C
    Ⓓ Choice D

20. **Directions:** An introductory sentence for a brief summary of the passage is provided below. Complete the summary by selecting the THREE answer choices that express the most important ideas in the passage. Some sentences do not belong in the summary because they express ideas that are not presented in the passage or are minor ideas in the passage. **This question is worth 2 points.**

Write your answer choices in the spaces where they belong. You can either write the letter of your answer choice or you can copy the sentence.

> **Over time, many views have been formed on the structure of ecological communities.**
>
> ●
>
> ●
>
> ●

Answer Choices

A   Clements held that ecological communities were like organisms that compete with each other for dominance in a particular climatic region.

B   Clements saw the community as a collection of thoroughly interdependent species progressing toward a single climax community.

C   Gleason held that within a single climatic region, differing local factors would cause ecological communities to develop in different ways.

D   Gleason believed that sharp divisions would exist between species in different habitats.

E   Today's ecologists recognize that ecological communities must be precisely and permanently balanced.

F   The current thinking is that communities are individualistic and largely accidental collections of species with similar needs and tolerances.

LISTENING

In this section, you will be able to demonstrate your ability to understand conversations and lectures in English.

In the actual test, the section is divided into two separately timed parts. You will hear each conversation or lecture only one time. A clock will indicate how much time remains. The clock will count down only while you are answering questions, not while you are listening. You may take up to 16.5 minutes to answer the questions.

In this practice test, there is no time limit for answering questions.

You may take notes while you listen. You may use your notes to help you answer the questions. Your notes will not be scored.

Answer the questions based on what is stated or implied by the speakers.

In some questions, you will see this icon: 🎧. This means that you will hear, but not see, part of the question.

In the actual test, you must answer each question. You cannot return to previous questions.

At the end of this practice test, you will find an answer key.

ekphrastic

William Carlos Williams
Pieter Bruegel

Directions: Now answer the questions.

1. Why does the woman want to talk with the man?

   Ⓐ To give him information he needs to become a docent
   Ⓑ To discuss his role in an upcoming writing competition
   Ⓒ To get his opinion about a competition she is planning
   Ⓓ To find out what he knows about the Art of India exhibit

2. What was the focus of the newspaper advertisement that the woman mentions?

   Ⓐ An ekphrastic poetry course that she helped develop
   Ⓑ A new collection of Indian art at the museum
   Ⓒ A student teaching position at a local high school
   Ⓓ A part-time volunteer position at the art museum

3. What does the woman say about William Carlos Williams' poem "The Hunter in the Snow"?

   Ⓐ It inspired an artist to paint a snowy scene.
   Ⓑ It was inspired by an old landscape painting.
   Ⓒ It is Williams' longest poem.
   Ⓓ It is Williams' best-known poem.

4. What is indicated about the paintings that students will write about for the poetry contest?

   Ⓐ Each student may select up to three paintings.
   Ⓑ Students may write more than one poem about a single painting.
   Ⓒ All the paintings are associated with one specific exhibit.
   Ⓓ All the paintings are by Pieter Bruegel.

5. What is the man's attitude when he learns that he will be giving an hour-long tour in the Art of India exhibit?

   Ⓐ Nervous, because he is not familiar with most of the paintings there
   Ⓑ Disappointed, because the exhibit is not one of his favorites
   Ⓒ Enthusiastic, because he can choose which paintings to talk about
   Ⓓ Surprised, because the Art of India exhibit is relatively small

Directions: Listen to Track 53.

Directions: Now answer the questions.

6. What is the lecture mainly about?
   (A) Ways to limit the expansion of international trade
   (B) How restrictions on international trade can cause economic harm
   (C) Factors that influence the distribution of exports
   (D) Why international trade has expanded in recent years

7. According to the professor, why do many people want imports to be regulated?
   (A) To allow for price increases in domestic products
   (B) To make the prices of exports more competitive
   (C) To protect against domestic unemployment
   (D) To encourage the economic growth of certain industries

8. According to the professor, what is a negative result of limiting imports?
   (A) The pace of technological innovation slows down.
   (B) The number of domestic low-paying jobs decreases.
   (C) People move to areas where income is lower.
   (D) The potential income from exports is reduced.

9. What does the professor imply about the sugar industry in Florida?
   (A) It is a good source of high-paying jobs.
   (B) It should not be protected from competition from imports.
   (C) It is a good example of the effect of international specialization.
   (D) It is managed cost effectively.

10. What does the professor imply about the effect of increasing imports?
    (A) It will eventually result in a decrease in exports.
    (B) It is not necessarily bad for the economy.
    (C) It creates domestic economic problems that are easily solved.
    (D) Its impact on the economy is immediately apparent.

11. What is the professor's opinion of retraining and relocating unemployed people?
    (A) It is more expensive over time than blocking imports.
    (B) It can sometimes have unintended consequences.
    (C) It is one possible way to adapt to an increase in imports.
    (D) It maintains the production levels of inefficient industries.

Directions: Listen to Track 54.

Directions: Now answer the questions.

12. Why does the student go to see her advisor, Professor Anderson?

    Ⓐ She wants Professor Anderson's help with her research.

    Ⓑ She is responding to Professor Anderson's invitation.

    Ⓒ She has a complaint about another professor.

    Ⓓ She wants to get a letter of recommendation to law school.

13. Why does the student mention Professor Connelly's class?

    Ⓐ She was not happy with the grade she received in the class.

    Ⓑ She might be able to expand the research she did in the class.

    Ⓒ It was the most difficult class she ever took.

    Ⓓ Professor Connelly took the class on a trip to Venezuela.

14. What does the student tell Professor Anderson she will do before their next meeting?

    Ⓐ Register for Professor Connelly's class

    Ⓑ Begin to write her honors thesis

    Ⓒ Turn in her honors project to Professor Connelly

    Ⓓ Talk to Professor Connelly about doing an honors project

15. *Listen to Track 55 to answer the question.*

What does Professor Anderson imply when he says this?.

    Ⓐ Very few students are asked to consider writing an honors thesis.

    Ⓑ The woman has shown poor research skills in the past.

    Ⓒ An honors thesis could help the woman get into law school.

    Ⓓ The woman should write a proposal outlining her research skills.

16. *Listen to Track 56 to answer the question.*

What does the woman imply when she says this?

    Ⓐ She is uncertain about her ability to write an honors thesis.

    Ⓑ She does not think an honors thesis would be useful to her.

    Ⓒ She considers herself to be a good writer.

    Ⓓ She has only written one research paper before.

Directions: Listen to Track 57.

Journalism

Directions: Now answer the questions.

17. What is the lecture mainly about?

    Ⓐ Why some newspapers do not improve their services

    Ⓑ What newspapers can do to increase their readership

    Ⓒ Why local newspapers cannot compete with major newspapers

    Ⓓ How the topics that interest readers have changed over the years

18. According to the professor, what topics are newspaper readers most interested in? *Select 2 answers.*

    A Political issues

    B Entertainment and weather

    C Natural disasters and accidents

    D Ordinary people

19. According to the professor, how can newspapers attract readers to serious stories?

    Ⓐ By including photos that provide background information

    Ⓑ By making minor revisions to the content of the story

    Ⓒ By making the format more appealing to readers

    Ⓓ By gradually increasing the number of serious stories

20. What does the professor imply about the use of colors in newspapers?

    Ⓐ It has been greatly influenced by reader preferences.

    Ⓑ It is more effective than early research indicated.

    Ⓒ It has not resulted in significant increases in the number of readers.

    Ⓓ It has been neglected in the study of journalism.

21. *Listen to Track 58 to answer the question.*

    What does the student imply when he says this?

    Ⓐ He agrees with the professor completely.

    Ⓑ He is surprised by the professor's point of view.

    Ⓒ He is not familiar with the topic the professor is discussing.

    Ⓓ He can offer a solution to the problem being discussed.

22. *Listen again to part of the lecture by playing Track 59.* *Then answer the question.*

    What does the professor imply when he says this?

    Ⓐ He fully supports the student's statement.

    Ⓑ His experience this morning was unexpected.

    Ⓒ He was not affected by what happened this morning.

    Ⓓ The student should not complain.

Directions: Listen to Track 60.

Geology

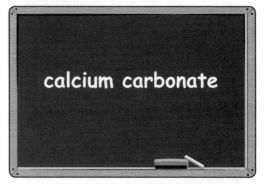

calcium carbonate

erratics

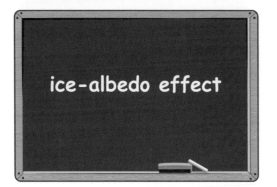

ice-albedo effect

Directions: Now answer the questions.

23. What aspect of the Earth 750 million years ago is the lecture mainly about?

    Ⓐ The changes in locations of the continents
    Ⓑ The effect of greenhouse gases on the atmosphere
    Ⓒ Factors that influenced the ocean currents
    Ⓓ Factors that contributed to a global freeze

24. According to the professor, how do geologists interpret the presence of erratics in the tropics?

    Ⓐ It indicates that carbon-dioxide levels were once higher there.
    Ⓑ It is evidence of global glaciation.
    Ⓒ It indicates that the Earth may cool off at some point in the future.
    Ⓓ It is evidence that some glaciers originated there.

25. What is the ice-albedo effect?

    Ⓐ Global warming is balanced by carbon dioxide in the oceans.
    Ⓑ Solar radiation retained in the atmosphere melts ice.
    Ⓒ Large amounts of carbon dioxide are removed from the atmosphere.
    Ⓓ Reflection of heat by glaciers contributes to their growth.

26. What is the relationship between carbon dioxide and silicate rocks?

    Ⓐ Silicate rocks are largely composed of carbon dioxide.
    Ⓑ Silicate rocks contribute to the creation of carbon dioxide.
    Ⓒ The erosion of silicate rocks reduces carbon-dioxide levels in the atmosphere.
    Ⓓ The formation of silicate rocks removes carbon dioxide from the oceans.

27. What was one feature of the Earth that contributed to the runaway freeze 750 million years ago?

    Ⓐ Carbon-dioxide levels in the oceans were low.
    Ⓑ The continents were located close to the equator.
    Ⓒ The movement of glaciers carried away large quantities of rock.
    Ⓓ The level of greenhouse gases in the atmosphere was high.

28. *Listen to Track 61 to answer the question.*

    Why does the professor say this?

    Ⓐ To compare an unfamiliar object to a familiar one
    Ⓑ To reveal evidence that contradicts his point
    Ⓒ To indicate uncertainty as to what deposits from glaciers look like
    Ⓓ To encourage students to examine rocks in streams

SPEAKING

In this section, you will be able to demonstrate your ability to speak about a variety of topics.

In the actual test, the Speaking section will last approximately 16 minutes. You will answer four questions by speaking into the microphone. You may take notes while you listen. You may use your notes to help you answer the questions. Your notes will not be scored. For each question, you will have time to prepare before giving your response. You should answer the questions as completely as possible in the time allowed.

For this practice test, you may want to use a personal recording device to record and play back your responses.

For each question, play the audio track listed and follow the directions to complete the task.

At the end of this practice test, you will find important points about each question.

1. You will now give your opinion about a familiar topic. After you hear the question, you should give yourself 15 seconds to prepare and 45 seconds to speak.

   Listen to Track 62.

   > When some people visit a city or country for the first time, they prefer to take an organized tour. Other people prefer to explore new places on their own. Which do you prefer and why?
   >
   > | **Preparation Time: 15 seconds** |
   > | --- |
   > | **Response Time: 45 seconds** |

2. Now you will read a passage about a campus situation and then listen to a conversation about the same topic. You will then answer a question, using information from both the reading passage and the conversation. You should give yourself 30 seconds to prepare and 60 seconds to speak.

   Listen to Track 63.

Reading Time: 45 seconds

   Professor Fox Accepts New Position

   We are happy to announce that Professor Fox will be filling the vacant Dean of Students position. Strong organizational skills are important for this position. Professor Fox has demonstrated such skills in her role as Head of the Philosophy Department, where she has coordinated department affairs for five years. Additionally, the Dean of Students must be someone who is able to work well with students, since responsibilities include counseling and advising students who are dealing with personal problems. As our head women's soccer coach, Professor Fox has proven to be a supportive role model for team members, always offering assistance when they ask for personal guidance.

Listen to Track 64.

> The woman expresses her opinion about the change described in the article. Briefly summarize the change. Then state her opinion about the change and explain the reasons she gives for holding that opinion.
>
> **Preparation Time: 30 seconds**
> **Response Time: 60 seconds**

3. Now you will read a passage about an academic subject and then listen to a lecture on the same topic. You will then answer a question, using information from both the reading passage and the lecture. You should give yourself 30 seconds to prepare and 60 seconds to speak.

Listen to Track 65.

Reading Time: 45 seconds

> **Critical Period**
>
> It is generally believed that for many organisms, there is a specific time period, a so-called "window of opportunity," during which the organism must receive crucial input from its environment in order for normal development to occur. This period is called the *critical period*. If the needed environmental input is not received during this period, the normal development of certain physical attributes or behaviors may never occur. In other words, if the organism is not provided with the needed stimulus or influence during the critical period, it may permanently lose the capacity to ever obtain a particular physical attribute or behavior.

Listen to Track 66. 🎧

Using the examples of kittens and geese, explain the idea of a critical period.

Preparation Time: 30 seconds
Response Time: 60 seconds

4. Now you will listen to a lecture. You will then be asked to summarize the lecture. You should give yourself 20 seconds to prepare and 60 seconds to speak.

Listen to Track 67.

Using the example of the vacuum cleaner, explain when it is legally acceptable to use exaggeration in advertising and when it is not.

Preparation Time: 20 seconds
Response Time: 60 seconds

WRITING

In this section, you will be able to demonstrate your ability to use writing to communicate in an academic environment. There will be two writing tasks.

At the end of this practice test, you will find topic notes for each question.

Turn the page to see the directions for the first writing task.

Writing Based on Reading and Listening

For this task, you will read a passage about an academic topic. Then you will listen to a lecture about the same topic. You may take notes while you listen.

In your response, provide a detailed summary of the lecture and explain how the lecture relates to the reading passage.

In the actual test, you will have 3 minutes to read the passage and 20 minutes to write your response. While you write, you will be able to see the reading passage. If you finish your response before time is up, you may go on to the second writing task.

Reading Time: 3 minutes

Many people dream of owning their own business but are afraid of the risks. Instead of starting a new business, however, one can buy a franchise. A franchise is a license issued by a large, usually well-known, company to a small business owner. Under the license, the owner acquires the right to use the company's brand name and agrees to sell its products. In return, the franchising company receives a percent of the sales.

A major problem for first-time business owners is finding reliable suppliers of the goods and services they need: equipment, raw materials, maintenance, etc. It is easy to choose the wrong supplier, and doing so can be costly. Buying a franchise eliminates much of this problem. Most franchising companies have already found reliable suppliers, and franchise contracts typically specify which suppliers are to be used. This protects franchise owners from the risk of serious losses.

Another advantage of a franchise is that it can save a new business a lot of money on advertising. Advertising one's product to potential customers is a crucial factor in a business's success. A franchise owner, however, sells an already popular and recognized brand and also gets the benefit of sophisticated and expensive advertising paid by the parent company.

Finally, a franchise offers more security than starting an independent (nonfranchise) business. The failure rate for starting independent businesses is very high during the first few years; the failure rate for starting franchises is much lower. Finding one's own way in today's competitive business environment is difficult, and buying a franchise allows an inexperienced business owner to use a proven business model.

Listen to Track 68.

Directions: You have 20 minutes to plan and write your response. Your response will be judged on the basis of the quality of your writing and on how well your response presents the points in the lecture and their relationship to the reading passage. Typically, an effective response will contain a minimum of 150 words.

Listen to Track 69.

Response Time: 20 minutes

Question 1

Summarize the points made in the lecture, being sure to explain how they challenge specific points made in the reading passage.

_____

_____

_____

_____

_____

_____

_____

_____

_____

Writing for an Academic Discussion

For this task, you will read an online discussion. A professor has posted a question about a topic, and some classmates have responded with their ideas.

In the actual test, you will have 10 minutes to write a response that contributes to the discussion.

Question 2

Your professor is teaching a class on sociology. Write a post responding to the professor's question.

In your response, you should do the following.
- Express and support your opinion.
- Make a contribution to the discussion in your own words.

An effective response will contain at least 100 words.

Dr. Diaz

As we discuss rules that societies expect their members to follow, let's focus specifically on how young people perceive those rules. Sometimes young people consider those rules to be too strict or unfair, and they take action to try to loosen the rules or change them. How important is it for young people to try to change rules that they consider to be unfair?

Kelly

It is so easy for some young people to get into trouble with illegal things. Parents should create rules to prevent that, and kids should not challenge those rules. Kids do not have the life experience to understand how, for example, their parents' rules about not staying out late at night are helping them stay out of trouble.

Paul

As a young person, I think the society I live in has certain rules that are in many respects unwise and unfair; for example, the rules in my country do not allow teachers to discuss certain controversial subjects in school that are important to young people. Young people should challenge those rules.

Response Time: 10 minutes

TOEFL iBT® Test 5

READING

In this section, you will be able to demonstrate your ability to understand academic passages in English. You will read and answer questions about **two passages**.

In the actual test, you will have 36 minutes total to read both passages and answer the questions. A clock will indicate how much time remains.

Some passages may include one or more notes explaining words or phrases. The words or phrases are marked with footnote numbers, and the notes explaining them appear at the end of the passage.

Most questions are worth 1 point, but the last question for each passage is worth 2 points.

You may review and revise your answers in this section as long as time remains.

At the end of this practice test, you will find an answer key.

Directions: Read the passage. Then answer the questions. You have 18 minutes on average to answer the questions.

HABITATS AND CHIPMUNK SPECIES

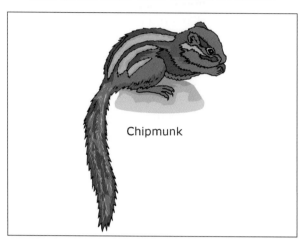

Chipmunk

There are eight chipmunk species in the Sierra Nevada mountain range, and most of them look pretty much alike. But eight different species of chipmunks scurrying around a picnic area will not be found. Nowhere in the Sierra do all eight species occur together. Each species tends strongly to occupy a specific habitat type, within an elevational range, and the overlap among them is minimal.

The eight chipmunk species of the Sierra Nevada represent but a few of the 15 species found in western North America, yet the whole of eastern North America makes do with but one species: the Eastern chipmunk. Why are there so many very similar chipmunks in the West? The presence of tall mountains interspersed with vast areas of arid desert and grassland makes the West ecologically far different from the East. The West affords much more opportunity for chipmunk populations to become geographically isolated from one another, a condition of species formation. Also, there are more extremes in western habitats. In the Sierra Nevada, high elevations are close to low elevations, at least in terms of mileage, but ecologically they are very different.

Most ecologists believe that ancient populations of chipmunks diverged genetically when isolated from one another by mountains and unfavorable ecological habitat. These scattered populations first evolved into races—adapted to the local ecological conditions—and then into species, reproductively isolated from one another. This period of evolution was relatively recent, as evidenced by the similar appearance of all the western chipmunk species.

Ecologists have studied the four chipmunk species that occur on the eastern slope of the Sierra and have learned just how these species interact while remaining separate, each occupying its own elevational zone. The sagebrush chipmunk is found at the lowest elevation, among the sagebrush. The yellow pine chipmunk is common in low to mid-elevations and open conifer forests, including piñon and ponderosa and Jeffrey pine forests. The lodgepole chipmunk is found at higher elevations, among the lodgepoles, firs, and high-elevation pines. The alpine chipmunk is higher still, venturing among the talus slopes, alpine meadows, and high-elevation pines and junipers. Obviously, the ranges of each species overlap. Why don't sagebrush chipmunks move into the pine zones? Why don't alpine chipmunks move to lower elevations and share the conifer forests with lodgepole chipmunks?

The answer, in one word, is aggression. Chipmunk species actively defend their ecological zones from encroachment by neighboring species. The yellow pine chipmunk is more aggressive than the sagebrush chipmunk, possibly because it is a bit larger. It successfully bullies its smaller evolutionary cousin, excluding it from the pine forests. Experiments have shown that the sagebrush chipmunk is physiologically able to live anywhere in the Sierra Nevada, from high alpine zones to the desert. The little creature is apparently restricted to the desert not because it is specialized to live only there but because that is the only habitat where none of the other chipmunk species can live. The fact that sagebrush chipmunks tolerate very warm temperatures makes them, and only them, able to live where they do. The sagebrush chipmunk essentially occupies its habitat by default. In one study, ecologists established that yellow pine chipmunks actively exclude sagebrush chipmunks from pine forests; the ecologists simply trapped all the yellow pine chipmunks in a section of forest and moved them out. Sagebrush chipmunks immediately moved in, but yellow pine chipmunks did not enter sagebrush desert when sagebrush chipmunks were removed.

The most aggressive of the four eastern-slope species is the lodgepole chipmunk, a feisty rodent indeed. It actively prevents alpine chipmunks from moving downslope, and yellow pine chipmunks from moving upslope. There is logic behind the lodgepole's aggressive demeanor. It lives in the cool, shaded conifer forests, and of the four species, it is the least able to tolerate heat stress. It is, in other words, the species of the strictest habitat needs: it simply must be in those shaded forests. However, if it shared its habitat with alpine and yellow pine chipmunks, either or both of these species might outcompete it, taking most of the available food. Such a competition could effectively eliminate lodgepole chipmunks from the habitat. Lodgepoles survive only by virtue of their aggression.

Directions: Now answer the questions.

PARAGRAPH 2

The eight chipmunk species of the Sierra Nevada represent but a few of the 15 species found in western North America, yet the whole of eastern North America makes do with but one species: the Eastern chipmunk. Why are there so many very similar chipmunks in the West? The presence of tall mountains interspersed with vast areas of arid desert and grassland makes the West ecologically far different from the East. The West affords much more opportunity for chipmunk populations to become geographically isolated from one another, a condition of species formation. Also, there are more extremes in western habitats. In the Sierra Nevada, high elevations are close to low elevations, at least in terms of mileage, but ecologically they are very different.

1. In paragraph 2, the author indicates that a large variety of chipmunk species exist in western North America because of

   Ⓐ a large migration of chipmunks from eastern North America in an earlier period

   Ⓑ the inability of chipmunks to adapt to the high mountainous regions of eastern North America

   Ⓒ the ecological variety and extremes of the West that caused chipmunks to become geographically isolated

   Ⓓ the absence of large human populations that discouraged species formation among chipmunks in the East

PARAGRAPH 3

Most ecologists believe that ancient populations of chipmunks **diverged** genetically when isolated from one another by mountains and unfavorable ecological habitat. These scattered populations first evolved into races—adapted to the local ecological conditions—and then into species, reproductively isolated from one another. This period of evolution was relatively recent, as evidenced by the similar appearance of all the western chipmunk species.

2. The word "**diverged**" in the passage is closest in meaning to

   Ⓐ declined

   Ⓑ competed

   Ⓒ progressed

   Ⓓ separated

PARAGRAPH 4

Ecologists have studied the four chipmunk species that occur on the eastern slope of the Sierra and have learned just how these species interact while remaining separate, each occupying its own elevational zone. The sagebrush chipmunk is found at the lowest elevation, among the sagebrush. The yellow pine chipmunk is common in low to mid-elevations and open conifer forests, including piñon and ponderosa and Jeffrey pine forests. The lodgepole chipmunk is found at higher elevations, among the lodgepoles, firs, and high-elevation pines. The alpine chipmunk is higher still, venturing among the talus slopes, alpine meadows, and high-elevation pines and junipers. Obviously, the ranges of each species overlap. Why don't sagebrush chipmunks move into the pine zones? Why don't alpine chipmunks move to lower elevations and share the conifer forests with lodgepole chipmunks?

3. Which of the sentences below best expresses the essential information in the highlighted sentence in paragraph 4? Incorrect choices change the meaning in important ways or leave out essential information.

   Ⓐ Ecologists studied how the geographic characteristics of the eastern slope of the Sierra influenced the social development of chipmunks.

   Ⓑ Ecologists learned exactly how chipmunk species separated from each other on the eastern slope of the Sierra relate to one another.

   Ⓒ Ecologists discovered that chipmunks of the eastern slope of the Sierra invade and occupy higher elevational zones when threatened by another species.

   Ⓓ Ecologists studied how individual chipmunks of the eastern slope of the Sierra avoid interacting with others of their species.

4. Where does paragraph 4 indicate that the yellow pine chipmunk can be found in relationship to the other species of the eastern slope of the Sierra?

   Ⓐ Below the sagebrush chipmunk
   Ⓑ Above the alpine chipmunk
   Ⓒ At the same elevation as the sagebrush chipmunk
   Ⓓ Below the lodgepole chipmunk

PARAGRAPH 5

The answer, in one word, is aggression. Chipmunk species actively defend their ecological zones from **encroachment** by neighboring species. The yellow pine chipmunk is more aggressive than the sagebrush chipmunk, possibly because it is a bit larger. It successfully bullies its smaller evolutionary cousin, excluding it from the pine forests. Experiments have shown that the sagebrush chipmunk is physiologically able to live anywhere in the Sierra Nevada, from high alpine zones to the desert. The little creature is apparently restricted to the desert not because it is specialized to live only there but because that is the only habitat where none of the other chipmunk species can live. The fact that sagebrush chipmunks tolerate very warm temperatures makes them, and only them, able to live where they do. The sagebrush chipmunk essentially occupies its habitat by default. In one study, ecologists established that yellow pine chipmunks actively exclude sagebrush chipmunks from pine forests; the ecologists simply trapped all the yellow pine chipmunks in a section of forest and moved them out. Sagebrush chipmunks immediately moved in, but yellow pine chipmunks did not enter sagebrush desert when sagebrush chipmunks were removed.

5. The word "**encroachment**" in the passage is closest in meaning to

   Ⓐ complete destruction
   Ⓑ gradual invasion
   Ⓒ excessive development
   Ⓓ substitution

6. Paragraph 5 mentions all of the following as true of the relationship of sagebrush chipmunks to their habitats EXCEPT:

Ⓐ Sagebrush chipmunks are able to survive in any habitat of the Sierra Nevada.

Ⓑ Sagebrush chipmunks occupy their habitat because of the absence of competition from other chipmunks.

Ⓒ Sagebrush chipmunks are better able to survive in hot temperatures than other species of chipmunks.

Ⓓ Sagebrush chipmunks spend the warm season at the higher elevations of the alpine zone.

7. Which of the following statements is supported by the results of the experiment described at the end of paragraph 5?

Ⓐ The habitat of the yellow pine chipmunk is a desirable one to other species, but the habitat of the sagebrush chipmunk is not.

Ⓑ It was more difficult to remove sagebrush chipmunks from their habitat than it was to remove yellow pine chipmunks from theirs.

Ⓒ Yellow pine chipmunks and sagebrush chipmunks require the same environmental conditions in their habitats.

Ⓓ The temperature of the habitat is not an important factor to either the yellow pine chipmunk or the sagebrush chipmunk.

PARAGRAPH 6

The most aggressive of the four eastern-slope species is the lodgepole chipmunk, a feisty rodent indeed. It actively prevents alpine chipmunks from moving downslope, and yellow pine chipmunks from moving upslope. There is logic behind the lodgepole's aggressive demeanor. It lives in the cool, shaded conifer forests, and of the four species, it is the least able to tolerate heat stress. It is, in other words, the species of the strictest habitat needs: it simply must be in those shaded forests. However, if it shared its habitat with alpine and yellow pine chipmunks, either or both of these species might outcompete it, taking most of the available food. Such a competition could effectively eliminate lodgepole chipmunks from the habitat. Lodgepoles survive only by virtue of their aggression.

8. According to paragraph 6, why is the lodgepole chipmunk so protective of its habitat from competing chipmunks?

Ⓐ It has specialized food requirements.

Ⓑ It cannot tolerate cold temperatures well.

Ⓒ It requires the shade provided by forest trees.

Ⓓ It prefers to be able to move between areas that are downslope and upslope.

P
A
R
A
G
R
A
P
H

4

Ecologists have studied the four chipmunk species that occur on the eastern slope of the Sierra and have learned just how these species interact while remaining separate, each occupying its own elevational zone. The sagebrush chipmunk is found at the lowest elevation, among the sagebrush. The yellow pine chipmunk is common in low to mid-elevations and open conifer forests, including piñon and ponderosa and Jeffrey pine forests. The lodgepole chipmunk is found at higher elevations, among the lodgepoles, firs, and high-elevation pines. The alpine chipmunk is higher still, venturing among the talus slopes, alpine meadows, and high-elevation pines and junipers. **(A)** Obviously, the ranges of each species overlap. **(B)** Why don't sagebrush chipmunks move into the pine zones? **(C)** Why don't alpine chipmunks move to lower elevations and share the conifer forests with lodgepole chipmunks? **(D)**

9. Look at the part of the passage that is displayed above. The letters **(A)**, **(B)**, **(C)**, and **(D)** indicate where the following sentence could be added.

   Yet each species remains within a fairly well-defined elevational zone.

   Where would the sentence best fit?

   Ⓐ Choice A
   Ⓑ Choice B
   Ⓒ Choice C
   Ⓓ Choice D

10. **Directions**: An introductory sentence for a brief summary of the passage is provided below. Complete the summary by selecting the THREE answer choices that express the most important ideas in the passage. Some sentences do not belong in the summary because they express ideas that are not presented in the passage or are minor ideas in the passage. **This question is worth 2 points.**

Write your answer choices in the spaces where they belong. You can either write the letter of your answer choice or you can copy the sentence.

> **A variety of chipmunk species inhabit western North America.**
>
> ●
>
> ●
>
> ●

Answer Choices

[A] Ecological variation of the Sierra Nevada resulted in the differentiation of chipmunk species.

[B] Only one species of chipmunk inhabits eastern North America.

[C] Although chipmunk species of the Sierra Nevada have the ability to live at various elevations, each species inhabits a specifically restricted one.

[D] Chipmunks aggressively defend their habitats from invasion by other species of chipmunks.

[E] Experimental studies indicate that sagebrush chipmunks live in the desert because of their physiological requirements.

[F] The most aggressive of the chipmunk species is the lodgepole chipmunk.

Directions: Read the passage. Then answer the questions. You have 18 minutes on average to answer the questions.

A MODEL OF URBAN EXPANSION

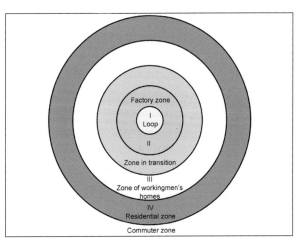

In the early twentieth century, the science of sociology found supporters in the United States and Canada partly because the cities there were growing so rapidly. It often appeared that North American cities would be unable to absorb all the newcomers arriving in such large numbers. Presociological thinkers like Frederick Law Olmsted, the founder of the movement to build parks and recreation areas in cities, and Jacob Riis, an advocate of slum reform, urged the nation's leaders to invest in improving the urban environment, building parks and beaches, and making better housing available to all. These reform efforts were greatly aided by sociologists who conducted empirical research on the social conditions in cities. In the early twentieth century, many sociologists lived in cities like Chicago that were characterized by rapid population growth and serious social problems. It seemed logical to use empirical research to construct theories about how cities grow and change in response to major social forces as well as more controlled urban planning.

The founders of the Chicago school of sociology, Robert Park and Ernest Burgess, attempted to develop a dynamic model of the city, one that would account not only for the expansion of cities in terms of population and territory but also for the patterns of settlement and land use within cities. They identified several factors that influence the physical form of cities. As Park stated, among them are "transportation and communication, tramways and telephones, newspapers and advertising, steel construction and elevators—all things, in fact, which tend to bring about at once a greater mobility and a greater concentration of the urban populations."

Park and Burgess based their model of urban growth on the concept of "natural areas"—that is, areas such as occupational suburbs or residential enclaves in which the population is relatively homogeneous and land is used in similar ways without deliberate planning. Park and Burgess saw urban expansion as occurring through a series of "invasions" of successive zones or areas surrounding the center of the city. For example, people from rural areas and other societies "invaded" areas where housing was inexpensive. Those areas tended to be close to the places where they worked. In turn, people who could afford better housing and the cost of commuting "invaded" areas farther from the business district.

Park and Burgess's model has come to be known as the "concentric-zone model" (represented by the figure). Because the model was originally based on studies of Chicago, its center is labeled "Loop," the term commonly applied to that city's central commercial zone. Surrounding the central zone is a "zone in transition," an area that is being invaded by business and light manufacturing. The third zone is inhabited by workers who do not want to live in the factory or business district but at the same time need to live reasonably close to where they work. The fourth or residential zone consists of upscale apartment buildings and single-family homes. And the outermost ring, outside the city limits, is the suburban or commuters' zone; its residents live within a 30- to 60-minute ride of the central business district.

Studies by Park, Burgess, and other Chicago-school sociologists showed how new groups of immigrants tended to be concentrated in separate areas within inner-city zones, where they sometimes experienced tension with other ethnic groups that had arrived earlier. Over time, however, each group was able to adjust to life in the city and to find a place for itself in the urban economy. Eventually many of the immigrants moved to unsegregated areas in outer zones; the areas they left behind were promptly occupied by new waves of immigrants.

The Park and Burgess model of growth in zones and natural areas of the city can still be used to describe patterns of growth in cities that were built around a central business district and that continue to attract large numbers of immigrants. But this model is biased toward the commercial and industrial cities of North America, which have tended to form around business centers rather than around palaces or cathedrals, as is often the case in some other parts of the world. Moreover, it fails to account for other patterns of urbanization, such as the rapid urbanization that occurs along commercial transportation corridors and the rise of nearby satellite cities.

Directions: Now answer the questions.

PARAGRAPH 1

In the early twentieth century, the science of sociology found supporters in the United States and Canada partly because the cities there were growing so rapidly. It often appeared that North American cities would be unable to absorb all the newcomers arriving in such large numbers. Presociological thinkers like Frederick Law Olmsted, the founder of the movement to build parks and recreation areas in cities, and Jacob Riis, an advocate of slum reform, urged the nation's leaders to invest in improving the urban environment, building parks and beaches, and making better housing available to all. These reform efforts were greatly aided by sociologists who conducted empirical research on the social conditions in cities. In the early twentieth century, many sociologists lived in cities like Chicago that were characterized by rapid population growth and serious social problems. It seemed logical to use empirical research to construct theories about how cities grow and change in response to major social forces as well as more controlled urban planning.

11. Which of the following can be inferred from paragraph 1 about what Olmsted and Riis had in common?

    Ⓐ Both constructed theories based on empirical research on cities.
    Ⓑ Both were among a large number of newcomers to North American cities.
    Ⓒ Both wanted to improve the conditions of life in cities.
    Ⓓ Both hoped to reduce the rapid growth of large cities.

12. Which of the following best states the relationship that Olmsted and Riis had to the study of sociology?

    Ⓐ Their goals were supported by the research conducted later by sociologists.
    Ⓑ Their approach led them to oppose empirical sociological studies.
    Ⓒ They had difficulty establishing that their work was as important as sociological research.
    Ⓓ They used evidence from sociological research to urge national leaders to invest in urban development.

PARAGRAPH 2

The founders of the Chicago school of sociology, Robert Park and Ernest Burgess, attempted to develop a dynamic model of the city, one that would account not only for the expansion of cities in terms of population and territory but also for the patterns of settlement and land use within cities. They identified several factors that influence the physical form of cities. As Park stated, among them are "transportation and communication, tramways and telephones, newspapers and advertising, steel construction and elevators—all things, in fact, which tend to bring about at once a greater mobility and a greater concentration of the urban populations."

13. Which of the sentences below best expresses the essential information in the highlighted sentence in paragraph 2? Incorrect choices change the meaning in important ways or leave out essential information.

    Ⓐ The Chicago school of sociology founded by Park and Burgess attempted to help the population of growing cities protect the land around them.
    Ⓑ The model that Park and Burgess created was intended to explain both why the population and area of a city like Chicago grew and in what way urban land was used or settled.
    Ⓒ The founders of the Chicago school of sociology wanted to make Chicago a dynamic model for how other cities should use and settle their land.
    Ⓓ Park and Burgess were concerned that cities like Chicago should follow a model of good land use as the population grew and settled new areas.

14. The author includes the statement by Robert Park in paragraph 2 in order to

    Ⓐ establish the specific topics about which Park and Burgess may have disagreed
    Ⓑ identify the aspects of Chicago's development that required careful planning
    Ⓒ specify some of the factors that contributed to the pattern of development of cities
    Ⓓ compare the definitions given by Park and Burgess for the physical form of cities

PARAGRAPH 3

Park and Burgess based their model of urban growth on the concept of "natural areas"—that is, areas such as occupational suburbs or residential enclaves in which the population is relatively homogeneous and land is used in similar ways without deliberate planning. Park and Burgess saw urban expansion as occurring through a series of "invasions" of successive zones or areas surrounding the center of the city. For example, people from rural areas and other societies "invaded" areas where housing was inexpensive. Those areas tended to be close to the places where they worked. In turn, people who could afford better housing and the cost of commuting "invaded" areas farther from the business district.

15. Paragraph 3 indicates that all of the following are true of "natural areas" as conceived by Park and Burgess EXCEPT:

   Ⓐ Use of the land in natural areas follows a consistent pattern but is generally unplanned.
   Ⓑ People living in natural areas tend to have much in common.
   Ⓒ Natural areas are usually protected from "invasion" by people in other areas.
   Ⓓ Natural areas are an important basic component of the model Park and Burgess developed.

PARAGRAPH 4

Park and Burgess's model has come to be known as the "concentric-zone model" (represented by the figure). Because the model was originally based on studies of Chicago, its center is labeled "Loop," the term commonly applied to that city's central commercial zone. Surrounding the central zone is a "zone in transition," an area that is being invaded by business and light manufacturing. The third zone is inhabited by workers who do not want to live in the factory or business district but at the same time need to live reasonably close to where they work. The fourth or residential zone consists of upscale apartment buildings and single-family homes. And the outermost ring, outside the city limits, is the suburban or commuters' zone; its residents live within a 30- to 60-minute ride of the central business district.

16. According to paragraph 4, why is the term "Loop" used in the concentric-zone model?

   Ⓐ It indicates the many connections between each of the zones in the model.
   Ⓑ It indicates that zones are often in transition and frequently changing.
   Ⓒ It reflects the fact that the model was created with the city of Chicago in mind.
   Ⓓ It emphasizes the fact that populations often returned to zones in which they used to live.

PARAGRAPH 5

Studies by Park, Burgess, and other Chicago-school sociologists showed how new groups of immigrants tended to be concentrated in separate areas within inner-city zones, where they sometimes experienced tension with other ethnic groups that had arrived earlier. Over time, however, each group was able to adjust to life in the city and to find a place for itself in the urban economy. Eventually many of the immigrants moved to unsegregated areas in outer zones; the areas they left behind were **promptly** occupied by new waves of immigrants.

17. The word "**promptly**" in the passage is closest in meaning to

 (A) quickly
 (B) usually
 (C) eventually
 (D) easily

PARAGRAPH 6

The Park and Burgess model of growth in zones and natural areas of the city can still be used to describe patterns of growth in cities that were built around a central business district and that continue to attract large numbers of immigrants. But this model is biased toward the commercial and industrial cities of North America, which have tended to form around business centers rather than around palaces or cathedrals, as is often the case in some other parts of the world. Moreover, it fails to account for other patterns of urbanization, such as the rapid urbanization that occurs along commercial transportation corridors and the rise of nearby satellite cities.

18. Paragraph 6 indicates which of the following about the application of the Park and Burgess model to modern North American cities?

 (A) It is especially useful for those cities that have been used as models for international development.
 (B) It remains useful in explaining the development of some urban areas but not all cities.
 (C) It can be applied equally well to cities with commercial centers and those with palaces and cathedrals at their center.
 (D) It is less applicable to modern cities because of changes in patterns of immigration.

P
A
R
A
G
R
A
P
H
S

5
&
6

Studies by Park, Burgess, and other Chicago-school sociologists showed how new groups of immigrants tended to be concentrated in separate areas within inner-city zones, where they sometimes experienced tension with other ethnic groups that had arrived earlier. Over time, however, each group was able to adjust to life in the city and to find a place for itself in the urban economy. **(A)** Eventually many of the immigrants moved to unsegregated areas in outer zones; the areas they left behind were promptly occupied by new waves of immigrants.

The Park and Burgess model of growth in zones and natural areas of the city can still be used to describe patterns of growth in cities that were built around a central business district and that continue to attract large numbers of immigrants. **(B)** But this model is biased toward the commercial and industrial cities of North America, which have tended to form around business centers rather than around palaces or cathedrals, as is often the case in some other parts of the world. **(C)** Moreover, it fails to account for other patterns of urbanization, such as the rapid urbanization that occurs along commercial transportation corridors and the rise of nearby satellite cities. **(D)**

19. Look at the part of the passage that is displayed above. The letters **(A)**, **(B)**, **(C)**, and **(D)** indicate where the following sentence could be added.

    Typical of this kind of urban growth is the steel-producing center of Gary, Indiana, outside of Chicago, which developed because massive heavy industry could not be located within the major urban center itself.

    Where would the sentence best fit?

    (A) Choice A
    (B) Choice B
    (C) Choice C
    (D) Choice D

20. **Directions**: An introductory sentence for a brief summary of the passage is provided here. Complete the summary by selecting the THREE answer choices that express the most important ideas in the passage. Some sentences do not belong in the summary because they express ideas that are not presented in the passage or are minor ideas in the passage. **This question is worth 2 points.**

Write your answer choices in the spaces where they belong. You can either write the letter of your answer choice or you can copy the sentence.

> **Two sociologists, Robert Park and Ernest Burgess, developed the "concentric-zone model" of how cities use land and grow.**
>
> ●
>
> ●
>
> ●

Answer Choices

A The model was developed to explain how the city of Chicago was developing around centrally located transportation and communication systems.

B The model arose out of concern for the quality of life in the rapidly growing cities of early twentieth-century America.

C The founders of the model did not believe in formal city planning and instead advocated growth through the expansion of so-called "natural areas."

D According to the model, a group new to the city tends to live together near the center and over time moves to outer areas that are more diverse ethnically and occupationally.

E The model is applicable to cities that grow by attracting large numbers of workers to centrally located businesses.

F The model predicts that eventually the inner city becomes so crowded that its residents move to new satellite cities outside the city limits.

LISTENING

In this section, you will be able to demonstrate your ability to understand conversations and lectures in English.

In the actual test, the section is divided into two separately timed parts. You will hear each conversation or lecture only one time. A clock will indicate how much time remains. The clock will count down only while you are answering questions, not while you are listening. You may take up to 16.5 minutes to answer the questions.

In this practice test, there is no time limit for answering questions.

You may take notes while you listen. You may use your notes to help you answer the questions. Your notes will not be scored.

Answer the questions based on what is stated or implied by the speakers.

In some questions, you will see this icon: 🎧 . This means that you will hear, but not see, part of the question.

In the actual test, you must answer each question. You cannot return to previous questions.

At the end of this practice test, you will find an answer key.

Directions: Listen to Track 70.

Directions: Now answer the questions.

1. What are the speakers mainly discussing?

   (A) Getting financial aid for college
   (B) Planning a student's course schedule for the next four years
   (C) Taking courses during the summer session
   (D) Differences in admissions requirements between Hooper University and two other schools

2. Why does the student want to take classes at City College?

   (A) Because Hooper University does not offer the classes he wants
   (B) Because City College classes cost less money than ones at Hooper University
   (C) So that he can take classes on the weekend
   (D) So that he can graduate from Hooper University early

3. Why will the man probably take only two courses?

   (A) Students are limited to two summer courses.
   (B) He can attend classes only on Saturday and Sunday.
   (C) His financial aid will pay for only two courses.
   (D) His summer job will keep him from taking more than two courses.

4. What will Ms. Brinker probably do for the man? *Select 2 answers.*

   [A] Give the man a student ID number
   [B] Give the man a financial aid form
   [C] Help the man figure out which classes to take
   [D] Help the man apply to Hooper University
   [E] Put the man's information into the City College admission system

5. Listen to Track 71.

   (A) The man waited too long to apply to City College.
   (B) The man should not attend Hooper University.
   (C) The man will be able to do what he wants to do.
   (D) The man is very unlucky.

Directions: Listen to Track 72.

World History

Directions: Now answer the questions.

6. What is the main purpose of the lecture?

    (A) To compare the study of world history to the study of United States history
    (B) To explain to the students their next assignment
    (C) To explain different approaches to the study of world history
    (D) To explain the origins of history as an academic discipline

7. Why does the professor mention the Western-Heritage Model used in her high school?

    (A) To explain why she prefers using the model
    (B) To emphasize that the model was widely used in the past
    (C) To correct an error in a student's description of the model
    (D) To compare high school history courses to college history courses

8. According to the professor, what is an advantage of the Different-Cultures Model?

    (A) It focuses on the history of the United States.
    (B) It is based upon the most widely researched theories.
    (C) It includes the history of a variety of cultural groups.
    (D) It makes thematic connections across different cultural groups.

9. What aspect of Islamic civilization will the professor likely discuss in the course?

    (A) A succession of Islamic rulers
    (B) The ancient origins of Islamic architecture
    (C) The isolation of European cultures from Islamic influence
    (D) Islamic elements in African cultures

10. Match each of the topics below with the type of world history course in which it would most likely be discussed.

    Write your answer choices in the spaces where they belong.

The Western-Heritage Model	The Different-Cultures Model	The Patterns-of-Change Model

Answer Choices

    [A] The contributions of Native American art to United States culture
    [B] The independent discovery of printing techniques in Asia and Europe
    [C] Ancient Roman foundations of the United States legal system

11. *Listen again to part of the lecture by playing Track 73.* 🎧 *Then answer the question.*

    What is the professor's attitude?

    (A) She doubts that the course will fulfill the students' expectations.
    (B) She hopes that the students selected the course because of their interest.
    (C) She is pleased that the course will fulfill the requirements.
    (D) She is worried that the students might not be familiar with the course requirements.

Directions: Listen to Track 74.

Directions: Now answer the questions.

12. Why does the man go to see the woman?

    (A) To ask her to talk to his professor about an exam

    (B) To get help completing an assignment

    (C) To get help understanding why he is having trouble in his classes

    (D) To ask her opinion about which class he should take

13. What does the man imply about his Spanish class?

    (A) He helps other students in the class.

    (B) He is doing well in the class.

    (C) He cannot complete all the assignments.

    (D) He needs to study more for the class.

14. What problem does the man have with his reading assignments?

    (A) He is not interested in what he reads.

    (B) He cannot memorize definitions of terms.

    (C) He is overwhelmed by the amount he has to read.

    (D) He has difficulty identifying what is important information.

15. Why does the woman tell the man about her own experience as a student?

    (A) To make him aware that other students have similar problems

    (B) To encourage him to spend more time studying at the library

    (C) To explain the importance of remembering details

    (D) To convince him to take a study-skills course

16. What recommendations does the woman make about what the man should do?
Select 2 answers.

    [A] Underline definitions in the text as he reads

    [B] Write a summary of what he reads

    [C] Read the text twice

    [D] Find additional texts on his own

Directions: Listen to Track 75.

Astronomy

nebulae

gamma-ray bursters

Directions: Now answer the questions.

17. What is the lecture mainly about?

   Ⓐ How astronomers found the correct interpretation for a certain observation
   Ⓑ How astronomers distinguish between two kinds of nebulae
   Ⓒ Various improvements to the telescope over the last 300 years
   Ⓓ An old problem in astronomy that remains unsolved

18. According to the lecture, how did distant galaxies appear to eighteenth-century astronomers?

   Ⓐ Like the moons of planets
   Ⓑ Like small clouds
   Ⓒ Like variable stars
   Ⓓ Like bright points of light

19. What could astronomers better estimate once they knew what nebulae really were?

   Ⓐ The diameter of variable stars
   Ⓑ The density of cosmic dust
   Ⓒ The size of the universe
   Ⓓ The average number of planets in a galaxy

20. According to the professor, what did a 1920s telescope allow astronomers to do for the first time?

   Ⓐ Study the moons of Jupiter
   Ⓑ Observe gamma-ray bursters
   Ⓒ Reject the dust theory of nebulae
   Ⓓ Prove that galaxies are surprisingly small

21. What did eighteenth-century astronomers have in common with astronomers today?

   Ⓐ They could not explain everything they detected with their instruments.
   Ⓑ They knew the correct distances of objects they could not identify.
   Ⓒ Their instruments were not powerful enough to detect spiral nebulae.
   Ⓓ They argued over the natural brightness of variable stars.

22. *Listen again to part of the lecture by playing Track 76.* 🎧 *Then answer the question.*

   What can be inferred about the student when she says this?

   Ⓐ She is certain about the correct answer.
   Ⓑ She is now aware that her original idea had a weakness.
   Ⓒ She is not convinced that the professor is right.
   Ⓓ She thinks that the professor misunderstood what she said earlier.

Directions: Listen to Track 77.

Art History

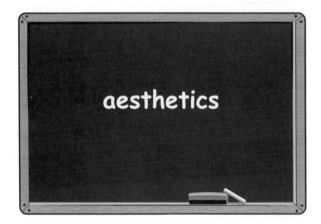

aesthetics

Directions: Now answer the questions.

23. What is the lecture mainly about?

    Ⓐ Various painting techniques
    Ⓑ Ways to determine the purpose of a piece of art
    Ⓒ How moral values are reflected in art
    Ⓓ How to evaluate a piece of art

24. According to the professor, what did ancient Greek philosophers value in a work of art?

    Ⓐ An accurate imitation of life
    Ⓑ An unusual perspective on life
    Ⓒ The expression of complex emotions
    Ⓓ The use of symbolism

25. Why does the professor talk about personal taste?

    Ⓐ To point out its importance in the evaluation of art
    Ⓑ To help students understand the meaning of aesthetics
    Ⓒ To show that personal taste and aesthetics are the same
    Ⓓ To help explain art from different cultures

26. Why does the professor mention wheels and spheres?

    Ⓐ To illustrate how movement can be expressed in a piece of art
    Ⓑ To demonstrate that objects are more important than colors in a piece of art
    Ⓒ To give an example of objects that have symbolic significance
    Ⓓ To explain why some objects rarely appear in works of art

27. The professor mentions four formal steps used in examining a piece of art. Place the steps in order from first to last.

Write your answer choices in the spaces where they belong. You can either write the letter of your answer choice or you can copy the sentence.

1	
2	
3	
4	

Answer Choices

A Give an opinion about the piece of art.
B Identify possible symbols.
C Describe the piece of art.
D Determine the artist's meaning.

28. *Listen to Track 78 to answer the question.*

What does the professor imply when he says this?

Ⓐ He will assign 12 pieces of art to evaluate.
Ⓑ He is organizing a class trip to the art museum.
Ⓒ It takes a lot of time to evaluate a piece of art.
Ⓓ Students will now be able to evaluate art quickly.

SPEAKING

In this section, you will be able to demonstrate your ability to speak about a variety of topics.

In the actual test, the Speaking section will last approximately 16 minutes. You will answer four questions by speaking into the microphone. You may take notes while you listen. You may use your notes to help you answer the questions. Your notes will not be scored. For each question, you will have time to prepare before giving your response. You should answer the questions as completely as possible in the time allowed.

For this practice test, you may want to use a personal recording device to record and play back your responses.

For each question, play the audio track listed and follow the directions to complete the task.

At the end of this practice test, you will find important points about each question.

1. You will now give your opinion about a familiar topic. After you hear the question, you should give yourself 15 seconds to prepare and 45 seconds to speak.

   Listen to Track 79.

   > Some people enjoy watching movies or television in their spare time. Others prefer reading books or magazines. State which you prefer and explain why.
   >
   > | Preparation Time: 15 seconds |
   > | :---: |
   > | Response Time: 45 seconds |

2. Now you will read a passage about a campus situation and then listen to a conversation about the same topic. You will then answer a question, using information from both the reading passage and the conversation. You should give yourself 30 seconds to prepare and 60 seconds to speak.

   Listen to Track 80.

Reading Time: 45 seconds

   Plans for Campus Gym

   The recreational services department will receive special funding from this year's budget to increase the number of exercise machines in the campus gym. The increase is in response to numerous student complaints regarding the insufficient number of machines available. Recreational services agrees that, due to an increase in university enrollment, more students are using the gym. They, therefore, welcomed the proposal, adding that it would encourage even more students to exercise and would help to promote a healthier lifestyle among students.

Listen to Track 81.

The woman expresses her opinion about the plan described in the announcement. Briefly summarize the plan. Then state her opinion about the plan and explain the reasons she gives for holding that opinion.

Preparation Time: 30 seconds
Response Time: 60 seconds

3. Now you will read a passage about an academic subject and then listen to a lecture on the same topic. You will then answer a question, using information from both the reading passage and the lecture. You should give yourself 30 seconds to prepare and 60 seconds to speak.

Listen to Track 82.

Reading Time: 50 seconds

Keystone Species

Within a habitat, each species depends on other species, and contributes to the overall stability of that ecosystem. However, some species do more than others by providing essential services. Without the influence of these key species, the habitat changes significantly. Scientists refer to these important players in an ecosystem as *keystone species*. When a keystone species disappears from its habitat, the habitat changes dramatically. Their disappearance can then trigger the loss of other species. As some species vanish, others move in or become more abundant. The new mix of species changes the habitat's appearance and character.

Listen to Track 83.

The professor gives examples of the effects of elephants on the African grasslands habitat. Using the examples from the talk, explain why elephants are considered a keystone species.

Preparation Time: 30 seconds
Response Time: 60 seconds

4. Now you will listen to a lecture. You will then be asked to summarize the lecture. You should give yourself 20 seconds to prepare and 60 seconds to speak.

Listen to Track 84.

Using the examples mentioned by the professor, describe two ways that writers create emphasis when writing dialogue.

Preparation Time: 20 seconds
Response Time: 60 seconds

WRITING

In this section, you will be able to demonstrate your ability to use writing to communicate in an academic environment. There will be two writing tasks.

At the end of this practice test, you will find topic notes for each question.

Turn the page to see the directions for the first writing task.

Writing Based on Reading and Listening

For this task, you will read a passage about an academic topic. Then you will listen to a lecture about the same topic. You may take notes while you listen.

In your response, provide a detailed summary of the lecture and explain how the lecture relates to the reading passage.

In the actual test, you will have 3 minutes to read the passage and 20 minutes to write your response. While you write, you will be able to see the reading passage. If you finish your response before time is up, you may go on to the second writing task.

Reading Time: 3 minutes

Soon technology will provide smart cars: cars that virtually drive themselves. A computer in the car determines the speed and route to the desired destination. The computer is in continuous contact with a global positioning system and other technologies that will provide extremely accurate information about the location of the car, other cars on the road, congestion, accidents, and so forth. The human driver will be little more than a passenger. Smart cars promise to make driving safer, quicker, and less expensive.

First of all, smart cars will prevent many accidents, thereby saving lives. The cars will be equipped with a variety of sensors that very accurately detect cars and other obstacles in their path, and they will have automatic programs that control braking and turning to avoid collisions. Given the hundreds of accidents that occur on highways daily, it is clear that humans do a poor job of avoiding accidents and that computer control would be a great improvement.

Second, with the wide use of smart cars, traffic problems will practically disappear. These computer-controlled cars can follow each other closely, even at high speeds. This ability will result in increased highway speeds. Today commuting by car can take hours a day. So the increased speed of smart cars will be a great benefit, welcomed by the many people who commute by car.

Finally, smart cars will bring a reduction in the costs of driving. Because smart cars are programmed to drive the most direct routes, car owners will have to spend less money on repairs and replacement parts. Expensive items such as brakes, tires, and transmissions will last much longer in smart cars than in other cars.

Listen to Track 85.

Directions: You have 20 minutes to plan and write your response. Your response will be judged on the basis of the quality of your writing and on how well your response presents the points in the lecture and their relationship to the reading passage. Typically, an effective response will contain a minimum of 150 words.

Listen to Track 86.

Response Time: 20 minutes

Question 1

Summarize the points made in the lecture, being sure to explain how they challenge specific points made in the reading passage.

_____

_____

_____

_____

_____

_____

_____

_____

_____

_____

Writing for an Academic Discussion

For this task, you will read an online discussion. A professor has posted a question about a topic, and some classmates have responded with their ideas.

In the actual test, you will have 10 minutes to write a response that contributes to the discussion.

Question 2

Your professor is teaching a class on child development. Write a post responding to the professor's question.

In your response, you should do the following.
- Express and support your opinion.
- Make a contribution to the discussion in your own words.

An effective response will contain at least 100 words.

Dr. Achebe

Next week, we'll begin discussing the effect of parental monitoring on child development. We'll start by looking specifically at parental monitoring of children's access to the Internet. Some parents believe that they need to closely watch and restrict their children's online activity. Do you agree with this approach? Do you think it is important for parents to monitor and limit their children's access to the Internet? Why or why not?

Claire

In my opinion, this kind of parental monitoring is essential. If parents are aware of what their children are doing online, they can help them avoid making mistakes. For example, they can intervene if they see their child has accidentally made a big purchase from an online retailer.

Paul

I respectfully disagree with Claire. Parental monitoring hinders a child's growth and learning. Yes, children can make mistakes online, but making mistakes is how they learn. If parents always step in to correct these mistakes, it prevents children from learning from the consequences of their actions.

Response Time: 10 minutes

Appendix

Speaking and Writing Scoring Rubrics

Appendix

이 부록에는 채점자가 말하기 및 쓰기 영역 답안을 채점할 때 활용하는 채점 기준이 모두 제시되어 있다. 말하기 영역 채점에 활용되는 두 가지 평가 기준과 쓰기 영역 채점에 활용되는 두 가지 평가 기준이 있다.

말하기 1번 문항은 독립형 말하기 평가 기준을 활용해 채점하고, 2~4번 문항은 통합형 채점 기준을 활용해 채점한다. 쓰기 1번 문항은 통합형 쓰기 평가 기준을 활용해 채점하고, 2번 문항은 학술 토론을 위한 쓰기 평가 기준을 활용해 채점한다.

아래 도표에는 점수를 부여할 때 반드시 고려하는 답변의 중요한 특징이 정리되어 있다.

영역	문항	평가 기준	채점 시 고려하는 주요 특징	
말하기	1	독립형 말하기	**전달력**	• 얼마나 명료한가? 훌륭한 답변은 유창하고 명료하며, 발음이 정확하고 속도와 억양이 자연스럽다. • 최고 수준의 답변에도 사소한 문제가 있을 수 있지만 청자가 알아듣기에 무리가 없다.
			언어 구사력	• 문법과 어휘를 얼마나 효과적으로 활용해 의견을 전달하는가? 훌륭한 답변은 기초적인 문장 구조와 더 복잡한 문장 구조를 모두 능숙하게 구사하며 적절한 어휘를 사용한다. • 최고 수준의 답변에도 일부 사소한 오류나 특정 패턴에서 반복되는 오류가 눈에 띄지만 의미가 흐려지지는 않는다.
			주제 전개	• 질문에 얼마나 충실하게 답변하는가? 그리고 얼마나 조리 있게 의견을 제시하는가? 훌륭한 답변은 개념 간 연관관계가 명확하고 이해하기 쉬우며 한 개념에서 다음 개념으로 넘어가는 흐름이 선명하고 이해하기 쉽다. 훌륭한 답변은 대체로 주어진 시간을 대부분 또는 전부 활용한다.

영역	문항	평가 기준	채점 시 고려하는 주요 특징	
말하기	2, 3, 4	통합형 말하기	전달력	• 얼마나 명료한가? 훌륭한 답변은 유창하고 명료하며, 발음이 정확하고 속도와 억양이 자연스럽다. • 최고 수준의 답변에도 사소한 문제가 있을 수 있지만 청자가 알아듣기에 무리가 없다.
			언어 구사력	• 문법과 어휘를 얼마나 효과적으로 활용해 의견을 전달하는가? 훌륭한 답변은 기초적인 문장 구조와 더 복잡한 문장 구조를 모두 능숙하게 구사하며 적절한 어휘를 사용한다. • 최고 수준의 답변에도 일부 사소한 오류나 특정 패턴에서 반복되는 오류가 눈에 띄지만 의미가 흐려지지는 않는다.
			주제 전개	• 질문에 얼마나 충실하게 답변하는가, 그리고 얼마나 조리 있게 의견을 제시하는가? 제시된 정보를 종합해 요약할 수 있는가? 훌륭한 답변은 개념 간 연관관계가 명확하고 이해하기 쉬우며 한 개념에서 다음 개념으로 넘어가는 흐름이 선명하고 이해하기 쉽다. 훌륭한 답변은 대체로 주어진 시간을 대부분 또는 전부 활용한다. • 최고 수준의 답변에도 세부 사항에서 부정확한 부분이나 관련 세부 내용에 사소한 누락이 있을 수 있다.
쓰기	1	통합형 쓰기	작문의 수준	• 훌륭한 답변은 구성이 짜임새 있으며, 문법과 어휘 사용이 적절하고 정확하다.
			내용의 완성도와 정확도	• 훌륭한 답변은 강의에서 중요한 정보를 선택해 읽기 지문에 있는 관련 정보와의 연관성을 조리 있고 정확하게 제시한다. • 최고 수준의 답변에도 가끔 언어 구사에 오류가 있을 수 있지만, 내용이나 내용 간 연결이 부정확하거나 모호하지는 않다.
쓰기	2	학술 토론을 위한 쓰기	작문의 수준	• 훌륭한 답변은 주제와 연관 있는 적절한 내용을 매우 명료하게 표현해 온라인 토론에 기여하며, 꾸준히 능숙한 언어 구사력을 발휘한다. • 최고 수준의 답변에도 어휘나 문법에서 사소한 오류가 있을 수 있지만, 의미 전달에 방해가 되지는 않는다.

TOEFL iBT® 말하기 채점 기준 — 독립형 과제

점수	총평	전달력	언어 구사력	주제 전개
4	과제의 요구사항을 충족하고 있다. 완성도에 결함이 있지만 기껏해야 사소한 정도에 그친다. 답변은 매우 이해하기 쉬우며 꾸준하고 조리 있게 담화를 이어 나간다. 이 수준의 답변에는 다음과 같은 특징이 모두 나타난다:	전반적으로 말하는 속도가 적절하다(유창한 표현). 발화가 명확하다. 발음이나 억양에 사소한 결함이 있을 수 있지만, 전반적인 내용을 이해하는 데는 무리가 없다.	문법과 어휘를 효과적으로 사용한다. 기초적이고 복잡한 문장 구조를 적절하고 능숙하게 구사하며, 내용을 떠올리자마자 자동으로 발화할 수 있다. 일부 사소한 오류나 특정 패턴에서 반복되는 오류가 눈에 띄지만 의미가 흐려지지는 않는다.	꾸준히 담화를 이어 나가며 과제를 충실하게 수행한다. 대체로 논지 전개가 충분하고 조리가 있으며 개념 간 연관관계가 명확하다(개념의 흐름이 명확하다).
3	과제를 적절히 수행하고 있지만 논지 전개에 미흡한 점이 보인다. 대체로 이해하기 쉽고 조리 있으며 표현이 어느 정도 유창하지만 개념 표현에서 결함이 눈에 띈다. 이 수준의 답변은 다음 중 최소 2가지 특징을 보인다:	발화가 대체로 명료하며, 표현도 어느 정도 유창하지만, 발음, 억양 또는 속도 조절에 사소한 어려움이 눈에 띄고 때로는 청자의 노력이 필요하다. 전반적인 내용을 이해하는 데는 크게 지장이 없다.	내용을 떠올리자마자 문법과 어휘를 거의 자동적이며 효과적으로 사용하고, 관련 개념을 상당히 조리 있게 표현한다. 일부 어휘나 문법 구조가 애매하거나 정확하지 않으며, 혹은 사용된 문장 구조의 범위에 다소 제약이 있을 수 있다. 이런 제약이 전반적인 유창함에 영향을 미치기도 하지만, 메시지 전달에 크게 방해가 되지는 않는다.	대체로 조리 있고 꾸준히 담화를 이어 나가며 적절한 개념 및 정보를 전달한다. 전반적인 논지 전개에는 다소 미흡한 점이 있으며, 대체로 정교함이나 구체성이 부족하다. 개념 간 연결고리가 즉각 선명하게 드러나지 않는 경우도 있다.
2	과제를 수행하지만 주제 전개가 미흡하다. 이해하기 쉽지만 전달력 및 전반적인 논리적 일관성에 문제가 있어 곳곳에서 의미가 흐려진다. 이 수준의 답변은 다음 중 적어도 두 가지 특징을 보인다:	대략적인 내용은 파악할 수 있지만, 발음이 불분명하고 억양이 어색하거나 리듬/속도가 들쑥날쑥해 청자가 노력을 기울여야 한다. 따라서 곳곳에서 의미가 흐려진다.	문법 및 어휘의 범위와 구사력에 한계가 있어 종종 의견을 충분히 표현하지 못한다. 대체로 기초적인 문장 구조만 제대로 사용하며 유창하게 말한다. 문장 구조와 어휘는 대체로 단순하거나 짧고 대강을 추리는 진술에 그치며 진술 간 연결이 단순하거나 명확하지 않다(나열, 접속사, 병치).	과제와 관련된 답변이지만, 제시된 개념의 수나 개념의 전개가 미흡하다. 대체로 기본적인 개념으로 표현에 정교함, 세부 사항과 뒷받침하는 근거 등이 부족하다. 때때로 관련된 요지가 모호하게 표현되거나 반복된다. 개념 간 연결이 불분명할 수 있다.
1	내용이 빈약하고 조리가 없거나 과제와 연관관계가 미약하며 대체로 알아듣기 어렵다. 이 수준의 답변은 다음 중 최소 두 가지 특징을 보인다:	발음, 강세, 억양에 어려움이 지속돼 청자는 상당한 노력이 필요하다. 말이 끊기거나 속도가 들쑥날쑥하고 단편적이며 전보문처럼 지나치게 간결하다. 자주 멈추고 머뭇거린다.	문법 및 어휘의 범위와 구사력이 부족해 개념과 개념 간 연관성을 표현하는 데 제약이 많다(또는 연관성을 표현하지 못한다). 낮은 수준의 일부 답변은 암기한 표현이나 틀에 박힌 표현에 크게 의존하기도 한다.	주제와 연관성이 떨어진다. 대체로 매우 기본적인 개념의 표현을 넘어서는 실질적인 내용이 부족하다. 화자는 꾸준히 담화를 이어가 과제를 완수할 수 없으며, 문항에 나온 어구를 반복하는 데 크게 의존한다.
0	화자가 답변을 시도하지 않거나 답변이 주제와 무관하다.			

TOEFL iBT® 말하기 채점 기준 — 통합형 과제

점수	총평	전달력	언어 구사력	주제 전개
4	완성도에 사소한 결함이 있지만 과제의 요구사항을 충족하고 있다. 답변은 매우 이해하기 쉬우며, 꾸준하고 조리 있게 담화를 이어 나간다. 이 수준의 답변에는 다음과 같은 특징이 모두 나타난다:	대체로 명료하고 유창하며 꾸준히 담화를 이어 나간다. 발음이나 억양에 사소한 결함이나 어려움이 있을 수 있다. 화자가 정보를 떠올리려고 할 때 때때로 속도가 달라지기도 한다. 전반적으로 아주 쉽게 이해할 수 있다.	기초적이고 복잡한 문법 구조를 능숙하게 구사해 적절한 개념을 조리 있고 효율적으로(내용을 떠올리자마자 자동적으로) 표현할 수 있다. 어휘 선택도 대체로 효과적이다. 일부 사소한 (또는 특정 패턴에서 반복되는) 오류나 부정확한 용법이 눈에 띄지만, 청자가 이해하는 데 노력이 필요하지는 않다 (또는 의미가 흐려지지는 않는다).	개념의 흐름이 명확하며 과제가 요구하는 관련 정보를 전달한다. 적절한 세부 사항이 포함되어 있지만, 사소한 오류나 누락이 있을 수 있다.
3	과제를 적절히 수행하고 있지만 논지 전개에 미흡한 점이 보인다. 대체로 이해하기 쉽고 조리 있으며 표현이 어느 정도 유창하지만 개념 표현에서 결함이 눈에 띈다. 이 수준의 답변은 다음 중 최소 2가지 특징을 보인다:	발화가 대체로 명료하며, 표현도 어느 정도 유창하지만, 발음, 억양 또는 속도 조절에 사소한 어려움이 보이며 때때로 청자의 노력이 필요할 수 있다. 그러나 전반적으로 쉽게 이해할 수 있다.	내용을 떠올리자마자 문법과 어휘를 거의 자동적이며 효과적으로 사용하고, 관련 개념을 상당히 조리 있게 표현한다. 일부 어휘나 문법 구조가 애매하거나 정확하지 않으며, 혹은 사용된 문장 구조의 범위에 다소 제약이 있을 수 있다. 그러나 이러한 제약 때문에 메시지 전달에 크게 방해가 되지는 않는다.	꾸준히 담화를 이어 나가며 과제에서 요구되는 적절한 정보를 전달한다. 그러나 내용 면에서 완성도와 정확도에 미흡한 점이 있고 구체성이 부족한 한편 개념의 흐름이 매끄럽지 않다.
2	과제와 연관된 답변이지만 적절한 정보가 빠져 있거나 부정확한 내용이 포함되어 있다. 이해하기 쉬운 부분이 있지만 때때로 명료성 및/또는 전반적인 논리적 일관성에 문제가 있어 의미가 흐려진다. 이 수준의 답변은 다음 중 적어도 두 가지 특징을 보인다:	때때로 발화가 명확하지만, 발음, 억양 또는 속도에 문제가 있어 청자는 상당한 노력을 기울여야 할 수 있다. 발화가 처음부터 끝까지 일관된 수준으로 유지되지 않을 수 있다. 명료성에 문제가 있어 일부에서 의미가 흐려지기도 한다.	어휘와 문법의 범위와 구사력에 한계가 있다. 복잡한 문장 구조를 일부 사용하지만 대체로 오류가 있다. 그 결과 적절한 개념이 제한적으로 또는 막연하게 표현되며 혹은 연결이 애매하거나 부정확하다. 내용을 떠올리자마자 자동으로 나오는 표현은 구절 수준에서만 뚜렷하게 드러난다.	관련 정보 일부를 전달하고 있지만 불완전하거나 부정확하다. 핵심 개념을 누락하거나 모호하게 언급하며 중요한 정보의 전개가 미흡하다는 면에서 불완전하다. 또한 제시된 자료의 핵심 개념을 오해하고 있다는 점에서 부정확하다. 대체로 표현된 개념 간에 연계성이나 논리적 일관성이 부족해 논의된 내용을 이해하려면 제시된 자료에 대한 사전 지식이 필요하다.
1	내용이 빈약하거나 논리적 일관성이 매우 부족하거나 과제와 연관관계가 미약하다. 대체로 알아듣기 어렵다. 이 수준의 답변은 다음 중 최소 두 가지 특징을 보인다:	발음, 강세, 억양에 어려움이 지속돼 청자는 상당한 노력이 필요하다. 말이 끊기거나 속도가 들쑥날쑥하고 단편적이며 전보문처럼 지나치게 간결하다. 자주 멈추고 머뭇거린다.	문법 및 어휘의 범위와 구사력이 부족해 개념과 개념 간 연관성을 표현하는 데 제약이 많다(또는 연관성을 표현하지 못한다). 매우 낮은 수준의 일부 답변은 고립된 어휘나 짧은 발언에 의존해 의견을 전달한다.	주제와 관련된 정보를 거의 제공하지 않는다. 표현된 개념이 부정확하거나 모호한 발언에 한정되며 반복(제시된 자료의 반복 포함)되는 경우가 많다
0	화자가 답변을 시도하지 않거나 답변이 주제와 무관하다.			

TOEFL iBT® 쓰기 채점 기준 — 통합형 과제

점수	총평
5	이 수준의 답변은 강의에서 중요한 정보를 정확하게 선택하고 이 정보를 읽기 지문에 제시된 관련 정보와 연계해 조리 있고 정확하게 제시한다. 구성이 짜임새 있으며 간혹 언어에 오류가 있지만 내용이나 연결이 부정확하거나 애매하게 제시되지는 않는다.
4	이 수준의 답변은 대체로 능숙하게 강의에서 중요한 정보를 선택하고 이 정보를 읽기 지문에 있는 관련 정보와 연계해 조리 있고 정확하게 제시하지만 사소한 누락, 부정확성, 모호성 또는 애매함이 드러난다. 사소한 언어 오류가 잦거나 눈에 띄고 혹은 이러한 용법과 문법 구조 때문에 때때로 명확성이나 개념 연계에 결함이 생기더라도 더 심각한 결과를 초래하지 않는다면 해당 점수를 받을 수 있다.
3	이 수준의 답변에는 강의의 중요한 정보가 포함되어 있으며 읽기 지문과 어떤 연관성이 있는지 전달하지만 다음 중 하나 이상에 해당한다: • 전반적인 답변은 분명 과제에 집중하고 있지만, 강의에서 제시된 논점과 읽기 지문이 밝히는 논점 사이의 연관성이 막연하고 포괄적이며 불명확하거나 다소 부정확하다. • 강의에서 제시된 중요한 논점 하나가 누락되었다. • 강의나 읽기 지문에 제시된 몇 가지 핵심 사항, 또는 둘 사이의 연계가 불완전하거나 부정확하며 혹은 애매할 수 있다. • 용법 및/또는 문법 오류가 더 빈번하거나 개념과 연관성을 전달할 때 모호한 표현 또는 애매한 의미로 이어질 수 있다.
2	이 수준의 답변에는 강의와 관련된 정보가 포함되어 있지만, 중요한 언어 문제가 드러나거나 강의 또는 강의와 읽기 지문 간 연관관계에서 중요한 개념을 누락하거나 부정확하게 제시한다. 이 수준의 답변은 다음 중 하나 또는 하나 이상에 해당한다: • 강의와 읽기 지문의 전반적인 연관관계를 현저히 잘못 전달하거나 완전히 누락한다. • 강의에서 제시된 중요한 논점들을 상당 부분 누락하거나 잘못 전달한다. • 개념이 연결되는 중요한 접점에서 연관관계나 의미를 현저히 모호하게 만드는 언어 오류나 표현이 포함된다. 또한 답변을 읽는 사람이 읽기 지문이나 강의에 아직 익숙하지 않다면 이러한 언어 오류나 표현 때문에 주요 개념에 대한 이해가 흐려질 수 있다.
1	이 수준의 답변은 다음 중 하나 또는 하나 이상에 해당한다: • 강의에서 의미 있거나 적절하고 일관된 내용을 거의 또는 전혀 제공하지 않는다. • 언어 수준이 매우 낮아 의미를 도출하기 어렵다.
0	이 수준의 답변은 읽기 지문에서 문장을 그대로 베끼고 주제를 무시하거나 주제와 관련이 없다. 혹은 영어가 아닌 언어로 작성되거나 키보드 입력 문자로 구성되거나 공백 상태이다.

TOEFL iBT® 쓰기 채점 기준 — 학술 토론을 위한 쓰기 과제

점수	총평
5	**충실하고 완성도 높은 답변** 주제에 적절한 내용을 매우 명료하게 표현해 온라인 토론에 기여하며, 꾸준히 능숙한 언어 구사력을 발휘한다. 전형적인 답변은 다음과 같은 특징을 보인다: • 적절하고 매우 정교한 설명, 예시 및/또는 세부 사항 • 다양한 문장 구조의 효과적인 사용과 정확한 어휘 및 관용 표현 선택 • 글쓴이가 유능해도 제한된 시간 내에 작문할 때 예상되는 오류(예: 흔한 오타나 철자 오류, there/their처럼 발음이 비슷하거나 같은 어휘를 혼동하는 오류) 외에는 어휘나 문법 오류가 거의 없다.
4	**대체로 완성도 있는 답변** 온라인 토론에 적절하게 기여하며, 능숙하게 언어를 구사해 글쓴이의 의견을 쉽게 이해할 수 있다. 전형적인 답변은 다음과 같은 특징을 보인다: • 적절하고 충분히 정교한 설명, 예시 및/또는 세부 사항 • 다양한 문장 구조와 적절한 어휘 선택 • 어휘나 문법 오류가 거의 없음
3	**부분적으로 완성도 있는 답변** 대체로 적절하고 이해 가능한 글로 온라인 토론에 기여하며, 일정 정도 능숙하게 언어를 구사한다. 전형적인 답변은 다음과 같은 특징을 보인다: • 설명, 예시 또는 세부 사항 일부가 누락되거나 불분명하며 관련 없는 부분이 있을 수 있음 • 일정 정도 다양한 문장 구조와 폭넓은 어휘 사용 • 문장 구조, 어휘 형태, 또는 관용어 사용에서 두드러지는 어휘 및 문법 오류가 있음
2	**대체로 완성도가 낮은 답변** 온라인 토론에 기여하려는 시도는 보이지만 언어 구사력의 로 글쓴이의 생각을 따라가기 어렵다. 전형적인 답변은 다음과 같은 특징을 보인다: • 개념이 충분히 설명되지 않거나 일부분만 연관성이 있음 • 구문 구조와 어휘의 범위가 제한됨 • 문장 구조, 어휘 형태 또는 용법의 오류 누적
1	**미흡한 답변** 온라인 토론에 효과적으로 기여하지 못하며, 언어 구사력의 한계로 의견을 제대로 표현하지 못한다. 전형적인 답변은 다음과 같은 특징을 보인다: • 과제 수행 의도가 보이는 어휘와 구절이 있지만, 일관된 개념이 거의 또는 전혀 없음 • 구문 구조와 어휘의 범위가 극히 제한됨 • 어휘 용법의 심각하고 빈번한 오류 • 독창적인 언어를 거의 구사하지 못하며 조리에 맞는 언어는 대부분 제시된 자료에서 차용됨
0	공백 상태, 주제를 무시하거나 영어가 아닌 언어로 작성되었으며 읽기 지문에서 문장을 전부 베끼거나 읽기 지문과 전혀 관련이 없는 내용, 또는 키보드를 임의로 두드린 문자로 구성되어 있다.

*toefl ibt.

Official
TOEFL
iBT® TESTS

Official TOEFL iBT® Tests

VOLUME 1 | 5TH EDITION

해설 및 정답

Mc Graw Hill   YBM

TOEFL is a registered trademark of Educational Testing Service.

Official
TOEFL
iBT® TESTS

VOLUME **1** 5TH EDITION

해설 및 정답

Contents

TOEFL iBT® Test 4

TOEFL iBT® Test 5

READING

DEER POPULATIONS OF THE PUGET SOUND

퓨젓사운드의 사슴 개체 수　　　　　　　　*p.16*

1. Two species of deer have been prevalent in the Puget Sound area of Washington state in the Pacific Northwest of the United States. The black-tailed deer, a lowland, west-side cousin of the mule deer of eastern Washington, is now the most common. The other species, the Columbian white-tailed deer, in earlier times was common in the open prairie country; it is now restricted to the low, marshy islands and flood plains along the lower Columbia River.

2. Nearly any kind of plant of the forest understory can be part of a deer's diet. Where the forest inhibits the growth of grass and other meadow plants, the black-tailed deer browses on huckleberry, salal, dogwood, and almost any other shrub or herb. But this is fair-weather feeding. What keeps the black-tailed deer alive in the harsher seasons of plant decay and dormancy? One compensation for not hibernating is the built-in urge to migrate. **(A)** Deer may move from high-elevation browse areas in summer down to the lowland areas in late fall. **(B)** Even with snow on the ground, the high bushy understory is exposed; also snow and wind bring down leafy branches of cedar, hemlock, red alder, and other arboreal fodder. **(C)**

3. The numbers of deer have fluctuated markedly since the entry of Europeans into Puget Sound country. **(D)** The early explorers and settlers told of abundant deer in the early 1800s and yet almost in the same breath bemoaned the lack of this succulent game animal. Famous explorers of the North American frontier, Lewis and Clark arrived at the mouth of the Columbia River on November 14, 1805, in nearly starved circumstances. They had experienced great difficulty finding game west of the Rockies and not until the second of December did they kill their first elk. To keep 40 people alive that winter, they consumed approximately 150 elk and 20 deer. And when game moved out of the lowlands in early spring, the expedition decided to return east rather than face possible starvation. Later on in the early years of the nineteenth century, when Fort Vancouver became the headquarters for the Hudson's Bay Company, deer populations continued to fluctuate. David Douglas, Scottish botanical explorer of the 1830s, found a disturbing change in the animal life around the fort during the period between his first visit in 1825 and his final contact with the fort in 1832. A recent Douglas biographer states: "The deer which once picturesquely dotted the meadows around the fort were gone [in 1832], hunted to extermination in order to protect the crops."

1. 미국 태평양 연안 북서부의 워싱턴 주에 있는 퓨젓사운드 지역에는 두 종의 사슴이 번성해왔다. 검은꼬리사슴은 워싱턴 주 동부에 서식하는 노새사슴의 사촌뻘로 워싱턴 주 서부의 저지대에 서식하며 현재 가장 흔한 종이다. 다른 한 종은 컬럼비아 흰꼬리사슴으로 광활한 대초원 지대에서 흔히 볼 수 있었으나 현재는 컬럼비아 강 하류를 따라 펼쳐진 습한 저지대 섬들과 범람원에만 국한되어 서식하고 있다.

2. 삼림 하층의 식물이라면 거의 모든 종류가 사슴 먹이의 일부가 될 수 있다. 삼림이 풀과 기타 목초지 식물의 생장을 막고 있는 곳이라면 검은꼬리사슴은 월귤나무, 살랄, 층층나무를 비롯한 거의 모든 종류의 관목과 풀을 뜯어먹는다. 그러나 이것은 계절이 좋을 때의 섭생이다. 식물이 시들고 휴면하는 척박한 계절에 검은꼬리사슴이 생존을 유지하도록 만드는 것은 무엇일까? 동면을 하지 않는 것에 대한 한 가지 보상은 내재된 이주 본능이다. 사슴은 고지대 목초지에서 여름을 보낸 후 늦가을이 되면 저지대로 내려올 수 있다. 땅이 눈으로 덮여도 하층 식생 중 키 큰 관목은 드러나고 눈과 바람이 삼나무, 솔송나무, 오리나무 등 먹잇감이 되는 수목의 잎 많은 나뭇가지를 떨구어 준다.

3. 유럽인들이 퓨젓사운드 지역으로 유입된 이래로 사슴 개체 수는 상당한 변동을 거듭했다. 초창기 개척자들과 정착민들은 1800년대 초반만 해도 사슴 수가 넘쳐난다고 말했으나 얼마 가지 않아 이 육즙 풍부한 사냥감이 부족하다며 한탄했다. 북미 변경의 유명한 탐험가들이었던 루이스와 클락은 거의 아사 상태에서 1805년 11월 14일 컬럼비아 강 상류에 도달했다. 이들은 로키산맥의 서쪽에서 사냥감을 발견하는 데 무척 어려움을 겪었고 12월 2일이 되어서야 처음으로 엘크 한 마리를 사냥할 수 있었다. 그해 겨울 동안 40명의 사람들이 생존을 위해 어림잡아 엘크 150마리와 사슴 20마리 정도를 먹었다. 그리고 초봄에 사냥감이 저지대에서 이동해 나가자 탐험대도 굶어 죽는 것보다는 낫다며 로키산맥 동쪽으로 되돌아가기로 결정했다. 이후 19세기 초반 포트밴쿠버에 허드슨베이컴퍼니 본사가 들어서자 사슴 개체 수는 변동을 거듭했다. 1830년대의 스코틀랜드 출신 식물 탐험가 데이비드 더글러스는 자신이 처음 방문했던 1825년과 마지막으로 방문했던 1832년 사이에 포트밴쿠버 주변 동물의 생태에 충격적인 변화가 생겼음을 발견했다. 최근 더글러스의 전기 작가는 이렇게 말한다. "한때 포트밴쿠버 주변 목초지를 그림처럼 수놓았던 사슴들이 [1832년에는] 사라졌다. 작물을 보호하느라 사냥한 탓에 몰살된 것이다."

4. Reduction in numbers of game should have boded ill for their survival in later times. A worsening of the plight of deer was to be expected as settlers encroached on the land, logging, burning, and clearing, eventually replacing a wilderness landscape with roads, cities, towns, and factories. No doubt the numbers of deer declined still further. Recall the fate of the Columbian white-tailed deer, now in a protected status. But for the black-tailed deer, human pressure has had just the opposite effect. Wildlife zoologist Helmut Buechner (1953), in reviewing the nature of biotic changes in Washington through recorded time, says that "since the early 1940s, the state has had more deer than at any other time in its history, the winter population fluctuating around approximately 320,000 deer (mule and black-tailed deer), which will yield about 65,000 of either sex and any age annually for an indefinite period."

5. The causes of this population rebound are consequences of other human actions. First, the major predators of deer—wolves, cougar, and lynx—have been greatly reduced in numbers. Second, conservation has been insured by limiting times for and types of hunting. But the most profound reason for the restoration of high population numbers has been the fate of the forests. Great tracts of lowland country deforested by logging, fire, or both have become ideal feeding grounds for deer. In addition to finding an increase of suitable browse, like huckleberry and vine maple, Arthur Einarsen, longtime game biologist in the Pacific Northwest, found quality of browse in the open areas to be substantially more nutritive. The protein content of shade-grown vegetation, for example, was much lower than that for plants grown in clearings.

4. 사냥감의 감소는 추후 사슴의 생존에 불길한 징조여야 마땅했다. 정착민들은 벌목, 화전, 개간 등을 하며 땅을 잠식해 들어왔으며, 종국에는 야생 경관이 있던 자리에 도로, 도시, 마을, 공장이 들어서면서 사슴의 곤경이 심해지리라 예견되었다. 분명 사슴의 수는 훨씬 줄었다. 이제는 보호종이 된 컬럼비아 흰꼬리사슴의 운명을 상기해 보라. 그러나 검은꼬리사슴의 경우에는 인간의 압력이 정반대의 결과를 낳았다. 야생동물학자인 헬무트 부케너(1953)는 기록된 대상기간에 워싱턴 지역에서 일어난 생물 변화의 속성을 연구하던 중 다음과 같이 말했다. "1940년대 초 이후 워싱턴 주에는 유사 이래 그 어느 때보다 많은 사슴이 서식했는데, 겨울철 개체 수만 하더라도 (노새사슴과 검은꼬리사슴을 합쳐) 약 32만 마리 선에서 증감했으며, 녀석들은 무기한 나이에 관계 없이 암수 합쳐 해마다 6만 5000마리 정도를 생산할 것이다".

5. 이런 사슴 개체 수의 반등은 인간의 다른 행위들에 따른 결과다. 첫째, 사슴의 주요 포식자인 늑대, 쿠거, 스라소니의 수가 대폭 감소했다. 둘째, 사냥 시간과 사냥감의 종류에 제한을 가해 보존이 보장되었다. 하지만 개체 수 복원의 가장 근본적인 원인은 바로 숲의 운명이었다. 벌목이나 화전 또는 두 행위 모두로 삼림이 없어진 넓은 면적의 저지대가 오히려 사슴에겐 이상적인 섭식 장소가 된 것이었다. 태평양 연안 북서부에서 오랫동안 사냥감 동물을 연구해온 생물학자 아서 아이나슨은 월귤나무, 덩굴단풍나무 등 알맞은 먹이가 증가했을 뿐만 아니라 개간지에서 자라는 풀의 영양가가 상당히 높아졌음을 알아냈다. 가령 음지에서 자라난 식물의 단백질 함량이 개간지에서 자란 식물보다 훨씬 낮았다.

어휘

1. prevalent 널리 퍼진, 번성한 mule deer 노새사슴 prairie 북미 대초원 marshy 늪지[습지]의, 눅눅한 flood plain 범람원 2. forest understory 삼림의 하층 식물 군락 inhibit 억제하다, 억누르다 browse on 풀을 뜯어먹다 huckleberry 월귤나무 salal 살랄(북미 서해안에 서식하며 흑자색 열매를 맺음) dogwood 층층나무 decay 부패, 쇠약 dormancy 휴면 compensation for A is B A에 대한 보상은 B hibernate 동면하다 built-in 내재된, 내장된 urge 충동, 본능 migrate 이동하다 be exposed 노출되다 cedar 삼나무, 향나무 hemlock 솔송나무 red alder 오리나무 arboreal 수목의 fodder 사료 3. fluctuate 변동을 거듭하다 markedly 두드러지게, 현저하게 explorer 탐험가, 개척자 in the same breath 숨도 쉬지 않고 연이어서, 곧 bemoan 신음하다, 개탄하다 succulent 살과 즙이 많은 game animal 사냥감 disturbing 마음을 불편하게 하는, 충격적인 contact 접촉, 방문 extermination 몰살, 멸종 4. bode ill for ~에게 나쁜 징조가 되다 plight 곤경, 역경 encroach on 잠식하다 logging 벌목 burning 화전 clearing 개간 replace A with B A를 B로 대체하다 wilderness landscape 야생 환경 no doubt 분명히, 의심의 여지 없이 pressure 압박, 고난 zoologist 동물학자 yield 생산하다 annually 해마다, 연간 indefinite 무기한의, 막연한 5. consequence 결과 predator 포식자, 약탈자 cougar 쿠거(북미에 서식하는 퓨마) lynx 스라소니 profound 깊은, 심오한 restoration 복원 tract 지역, 지대 deforest 삼림을 없애다 feeding ground 먹이를 섭취하는 곳, 섭식 장소 browse (소, 사슴 등이 먹는) 새싹, 어린 줄기 vine maple 덩굴단풍나무 game 사냥감 shade 음지, 그늘 vegetation 식생, 식물 clearing 빈터, 개간지

1. 첫 번째 단락에 따르면, 다음 중 퓨젓사운드의 흰꼬리사슴에 대한 설명으로 옳은 것은?

   Ⓐ 저지대와 습지에서 자생한다.

   Ⓑ 다른 종의 사슴보다 동부 워싱턴에 서식하는 노새사슴과 더 밀접한 근연관계에 있다.

   Ⓒ 탁 트인 대초원에 서식하던 검은꼬리사슴을 대체했다.

   Ⓓ 한때 살았던 특정 유형의 서식지에서 더 이상 살지 않는다.

어휘 native to ~ 원산[토종]인 replace 대체하다
     habitat 서식지

2. 두 번째 단락의 설명에서 겨울철 상황에 대해 추론할 수 있는 것은?

   Ⓐ 일부 사슴이 동면하게 만든다.

   Ⓑ 사슴이 고지대에서 먹이 구하기가 힘들어진다.

   Ⓒ 사슴이 하층 식물을 찾기가 더 쉬워진다.

   Ⓓ 사슴의 겨울철 이동을 막는다.

어휘 locate 위치를 찾아내다 prevent 막다, 방해하다

3. 세 번째 단락에서 글쓴이가 탐험가 루이스와 클락을 언급한 것은 다음 중 무엇을 설명하기 위한 것인가?

   Ⓐ 퓨젓사운드 지역내의 사슴 수는 시간의 흐름에 따라 변동했다.

   Ⓑ 퓨젓사운드 지역에 왔던 탐험가 대부분은 주로 사냥에 관심 있었다.

   Ⓒ 미국의 서부보다 동부에 사냥감이 더 많았다.

   Ⓓ 개인 탐험가들은 무역회사만큼 사냥감을 찾아내지 못했다.

어휘 vary (상황에 따라) 달라지다 trading company 무역회사

4. 세 번째 단락에 따르면, 1832년 데이비드 더글러스가 돌아왔을 때 포트밴쿠버는 어떻게 변모해 있었나?

   Ⓐ 포트밴쿠버는 허드슨베이컴퍼니의 본거지가 되어 있었다.

   Ⓑ 사슴이 포트밴쿠버 주변 목초지에 살기 시작했다.

   Ⓒ 포트밴쿠버 인근의 사슴이 몰살되었다.

   Ⓓ 포트밴쿠버 주변 지역의 곡물 수확량이 감소했다.

어휘 populate 거주하다 destroy (필요 없는 동물을) 죽이다

5. 글쓴이가 야생 경관의 변화를 언급하면서 독자들에게 "흰꼬리사슴의 운명"을 상기하라고 한 이유는?

   Ⓐ 서식지 파괴가 개체 수 감소로 귀결되었다는 주장을 뒷받침하기 위해

   Ⓑ 두 종의 사슴이 야생환경에 어떤 생물학적 변화를 초래했는지 비교하기 위해

   Ⓒ 인간 정착지에 성공적으로 적응한 사슴 한 종을 예로 들기 위해

   Ⓓ 일부 사슴 종은 보호종 지위를 부여 받아야 한다고 주장하기 위해

어휘 adapt to ~에 적응하다 status 지위, 신분

6. 네 번째 단락의 indefinite period와 의미상 가장 가까운 것은?

   Ⓐ 끝이 정해지지 않은

   Ⓑ 예상 시점에 시작하지 않은

   Ⓒ 잠시만 지속되는

   Ⓓ 중요성이 알려지지 않은 상태로 있는

7. 다음 중 사슴 개체 수와 관련하여 네 번째 단락의 정보가 입증하는 내용은 무엇인가?

   Ⓐ 사슴 개체 수는 1940년대에 정점에 도달한 이후 감소하기 시작했다.

   Ⓑ 정착민들의 활동은 이후 예기치 않은 방식으로 특정 사슴 종의 개체 수 증가에 기여했다.

   Ⓒ 건설을 위한 원시 토지 개간은 생물 변화를 초래했고, 검은꼬리사슴 개체 수는 그 변화로부터 결코 회복하지 못했다.

   Ⓓ 1940년대 이후 겨울철 사슴 개체 수는 여름철 개체 수보다 변동이 심했다.

어휘 reach highest point 정점에 도달하다
     unexpected 예상치 못한, 뜻밖의

8. 다음 중 다섯 번째 단락에서 음영으로 표시된 문장이 담고 있는 핵심 정보를 가장 잘 표현한 것은? 정답 외의 보기들은 의미가 상당히 왜곡되거나 필수적인 정보가 빠져 있다.

   Ⓐ 아서 아이나슨은 태평양 연안 북서부에 대해 오래 전부터 잘 알고 있었기 때문에 사슴에게 알맞은 풀이 늘어난 곳을 찾아낼 수 있었다.

   Ⓑ 아서 아이나슨은 삼림이 사라진 섭식 장소가 사슴에게 더 풍부하고 질 좋은 먹이를 제공했다는 사실을 알아냈다.

   Ⓒ 아서 아이나슨 같은 생물학자들은 사슴이 서식하기에 알맞은 적당한 먹이가 있는 개간지를 더 찾아내는 것이 중요하다고 생각한다.

   Ⓓ 아이나슨에 따르면, 월귤나무와 덩굴단풍나무는 태평양 연안 북서부의 개간지에 사는 사슴의 영양 상태를 언젠가는 개선할 수 있는 식물들이다.

어휘 provide A with B A에게 B를 제공하다
     nutrition 영양, 영양소

9. 위에 제시된 지문의 일부를 보시오. 지문에 표시된 **(A)**, **(B)**, **(C)**, **(D)** 중 하나에 다음 문장이 삽입될 수 있다.

There food is available and accessible throughout the winter.
(그곳에서는 겨울 내내 먹이를 구할 수 있다.)

이 문장이 들어갈 가장 적당한 위치는?

What keeps the black-tailed deer alive in the harsher seasons of plant decay and dormancy? One compensation for not hibernating is the built-in urge to migrate. **(A)** Deer may move from high-elevation browse areas in summer down to the lowland areas in late fall. **(B)** There food is available and accessible throughout the winter. Even with snow on the ground, the high bushy understory is exposed; also snow and wind bring down leafy branches of cedar, hemlock, red alder, and other arboreal fodder. **(C)**

The numbers of deer have fluctuated markedly since the entry of Europeans into Puget Sound country. **(D)** The early explorers and settlers told of abundant deer in the early 1800s and yet almost in the same breath bemoaned the lack of this succulent game animal.

Ⓐ (A)   Ⓑ (B)   Ⓒ (C)   Ⓓ (D)

어휘 accessible 접근[이용]할 수 있는, 구할 수 있는

10. 지문을 간단히 요약하기 위한 도입 문장이 아래에 제시되어 있다. 아래 보기들 중에서 지문의 가장 중요한 개념을 표현한 문장 3개를 골라 요약을 완성하라. 보기들 중에는 지문에 나오지 않았거나 중요하지 않은 개념이기 때문에 요약으로 적절치 않은 것들도 있다. 이 문제의 배점은 2점이다.

퓨젓사운드 지역의 사슴은 다양한 종류의 먹이를 섭취하고 먹이를 찾기 위해 계절 따라 이동한다.

Ⓐ 퓨젓사운드 지역의 사슴 종들간의 균형은 시대별로 변동했고, 현재 컬럼비아 흰꼬리사슴의 수가 다른 종의 수를 초월했다.

Ⓑ 퓨젓사운드 지역의 사슴은 이동하기 때문에, 특정 시점에 미국 서부에 서식 중인 사슴의 수를 정확히 집계하는 것은 과거와 마찬가지로 지금도 여전히 어렵다.

Ⓒ 사슴 개체 수는 자연 증감하지만 퓨젓사운드 지역의 초기 정착민들 때문에 당시 그 지역 사슴 개체 수 전반적으로 감소했다.

Ⓓ 미국 서부지역에 사람이 정착하면서 전체 사슴 개체 수가 영구적으로 감소하리라 예상되었음에도 불구하고, 특정 종의 사슴에게는 정반대 현상이 일어났다.

Ⓔ 장기적으로 보면 퓨젓사운드 지역의 검은꼬리사슴은 자연 포식자가 제거되고 삼림 벌채 지역 먹이의 양과 질이 개선되는 등 인간의 활동으로 수혜를 입었다.

Ⓕ 야생 생물학자들은 삼림이 손실되면 사슴이 영양 실조에 걸릴 가능성이 있다고 오랫동안 우려해왔다.

어휘 A outnumber B A의 수가 B의 수를 초월하다
elimination 제거
nutritional deficiency 영양 결핍, 영양 실조

유럽의 동굴 예술 *p.22*

1. The earliest discovered traces of art are beads and carvings, and then paintings, from sites dating back to the Upper Paleolithic period. We might expect that early artistic efforts would be crude, but the cave paintings of Spain and southern France show a marked degree of skill. So do the naturalistic paintings on slabs of stone excavated in southern Africa. Some of those slabs appear to have been painted as much as 28,000 years ago, which suggests that painting in Africa is as old as painting in Europe. But painting may be even older than that. The early Australians may have painted on the walls of rock shelters and cliff faces at least 30,000 years ago, and maybe as much as 60,000 years ago.

2. The researchers Peter Ucko and Andrée Rosenfeld identified three principal locations of paintings in the caves of western Europe: (1) in obviously inhabited rock shelters and cave entrances; (2) in galleries immediately off the inhabited areas of caves; and (3) in the inner reaches of caves, whose difficulty of access has been interpreted by some as a sign that magical-religious activities were performed there.

3. The subjects of the paintings are mostly animals. The paintings rest on bare walls, with no backdrops or environmental trappings. Perhaps, like many contemporary peoples, Upper Paleolithic men and women believed that the drawing of a human image could cause death or injury, and if that were indeed their belief, it might explain why human figures are rarely depicted in cave art. Another explanation for the focus on animals might be that these people sought to improve their luck at hunting. **(A)** This theory is suggested by evidence of chips in the painted figures, perhaps made by spears thrown at the drawings. **(B)** But if improving their hunting luck was the chief motivation for the paintings, it is difficult to explain why only a few show signs of having been speared. **(C)** Perhaps the paintings were inspired by the need to increase the supply of animals. Cave art seems to have reached a peak toward the end of the Upper Paleolithic period, when the herds of game were decreasing. **(D)**

4. The particular symbolic significance of the cave paintings in southwestern France is more explicitly revealed, perhaps, by the results of a study conducted by researchers Patricia Rice and Ann Paterson. The data they present suggest that the animals portrayed in the cave paintings were mostly the ones that the painters preferred for meat and for materials such as hides. For example, wild cattle (bovines) and horses are portrayed more often than we would expect by chance, probably because they were larger and heavier (meatier) than other animals in the environment. In addition, the paintings mostly portray animals that the painters may have feared the

1. 최초로 발견된 예술의 흔적들은 구슬, 조각, 그림들로 후기 구석기시대까지 거슬러 올라간다. 원시 예술은 투박할 것이라고 짐작하겠지만 스페인과 남부 프랑스의 동굴 벽화들은 상당한 정도의 기교를 드러낸다. 남아프리카에서 발굴된 돌판에 그린 자연에 대한 묘사 역시 마찬가지다. 어떤 돌판 그림들은 무려 2만 8000년 전에 그린 것으로 추정되는데, 이는 아프리카의 그림이 유럽의 회화들만큼이나 오래되었음을 시사한다. 그러나 그림의 역사는 그보다 훨씬 더 오래되었을 수 있다. 초기 호주 원주민들은 어쩌면 적어도 3만 년 전부터, 더 이르면 6만 년 전부터 동굴 은신처의 벽면과 절벽에 그림을 그리기 시작했을지도 모른다.

2. 연구자 피터 우코와 안드레 로젠펠드는 서유럽 동굴에서 벽화가 있는 3대 주요 지점을 알아냈다. 첫째는 사람이 거주한 것이 분명한 동굴 은신처 및 동굴 입구, 둘째는 동굴의 거주 지역과 바로 인접한 갱도, 셋째는 동굴 안쪽 깊숙한 지점으로, 접근이 어렵다는 점에서 일부 학자들은 이곳에서 주술 및 종교 활동이 거행된 증거로 해석하기도 한다.

3. 그림의 주제는 대부분 동물이다. 그림은 빈 벽에 그려져 있으며, 배경이나 주변 장식은 없다. 아마도 많은 현대인들처럼 후기 구석기 남자와 여자는 사람의 형상을 그리면 죽거나 다치게 될지도 모른다는 믿음이 있었을 지도 모르며, 실제로 그런 믿음이 있었다고 보면, 동굴 벽화에 사람 모습이 거의 묘사되지 않은 점이 설명된다. 동물 천착에 관한 또 다른 설은 당시 사람들이 사냥에서 운기 상승을 바랐다는 것이다. 그려진 형상에 나 있는 패인 자국이 증거로 제시되고 있으며, 그림을 향해 창을 던졌기 때문에 자국이 난 것으로 추정된다. 그러나 사냥에서 행운을 부르는 것이 주요 동기라고 한다면 그림에 난 창 자국이 왜 얼마 되지 않는지는 설명하기 힘들다. 동물 공급량을 늘려야 할 필요성이 그림의 영감으로 작용했을지도 모른다. 동굴 벽화는 후기 구석기 말기에 절정에 도달했던 것으로 보이며, 그때는 바로 사냥감이 감소하던 시기였다.

4. 특히 남서 프랑스 지방 동굴 벽화의 상징적 중요성은 연구자 패트리샤 라이스와 앤 패터슨이 수행한 연구 결과로 더욱 명확하게 드러난다. 이들이 제시한 자료에 따르면, 동굴 벽화에 묘사된 동물은 대부분 그것을 그린 사람이 고기나 가죽의 재료로 선호했던 동물이었다는 것이다. 예를 들면, (솟과 짐승인) 야생 들소와 말이 무심코 예상하는 것보다 더 많은 빈도로 그려졌는데, 아마도 당시 환경에서는 다른 동물보다 더 크고 무거웠기 (살이 더 많았기) 때문으로 추정된다. 또한 그림에는 덩치, 속도, 엄니나 뿔 같은 타고난 무기와 예측 불가능한 행태 때문에 그림을 그린 사람들이 가장 두려워했을 법한 동물들이 대부분 묘사되었다는 것이다. 즉, 사슴이나 순록보다는 매머드, 솟과 짐승, 말들이 더 많이 그려졌다. 따라서 이런 그림들은 후기 구석기 사람들의 경제에서

most because of their size, speed, natural weapons such as tusks and horns, and the unpredictability of their behavior. That is, mammoths, bovines, and horses are portrayed more often than deer and reindeer. Thus, the paintings are consistent with the idea that the art is related to the importance of hunting in the economy of Upper Paleolithic people. Consistent with this idea, according to the investigators, is the fact that the art of the cultural period that followed the Upper Paleolithic also seems to reflect how people got their food. But in that period, when getting food no longer depended on hunting large game animals (because they were becoming extinct), the art ceased to focus on portrayals of animals.

5. Upper Paleolithic art was not confined to cave paintings. Many shafts of spears and similar objects were decorated with figures of animals. The anthropologist Alexander Marshack has an interesting interpretation of some of the engravings made during the Upper Paleolithic. He believes that as far back as 30,000 B.C., hunters may have used a system of notation, engraved on bone and stone, to mark phases of the Moon. If this is true, it would mean that Upper Paleolithic people were capable of complex thought and were consciously aware of their environment. In addition to other artworks, figurines representing the human female in exaggerated form have also been found at Upper Paleolithic sites. It has been suggested that these figurines were an ideal type or an expression of a desire for fertility.

수렵의 중요성과 예술 간에 연관성이 있다는 생각과 일치한다. 이런 생각과 일맥상통하는 사실은, 연구자들에 따르면, 후기 구석기 다음에 왔던 문화 시대의 예술도 당시 사람들이 식량을 구했던 방식을 반영하는 듯하다는 점이다. 그러나 그 시대에는 식량을 구할 때 더 이상 거대한 사냥감 동물을 사냥하는 데 의존하지 않았으므로 (그런 동물들이 멸종되고 있었으므로) 예술의 대상이 더 이상 동물 묘사에 집중되지 않았다.

5. 후기 구석기 예술이 동굴 벽화에만 국한되는 것은 아니다. 많은 창 자루, 그리고 유사한 사물들이 동물의 모양으로 장식되었다. 인류학자 알렉산더 마르샥은 후기 구석기시대의 판화 일부에 대해 흥미로운 해석을 하고 있다. 그는 기원전 3만 년 경의 수렵인들은 월령을 표시하기 위해 뼈나 돌에 새기는 표기법을 사용했을 수도 있다고 생각한다. 이것이 사실이라면 후기 구석기인들은 복잡한 사고를 할 수 있었으며 주변 환경을 인지하고 있었다는 의미가 된다. 다른 예술품들과 더불어 여자를 과장된 형태로 묘사한 작은 조각상이 후기 구석기 유적지에서 함께 발견되었다. 이런 작은 조각상들은 이상형 또는 다산에 대한 열망을 표현한 것으로 추정된다.

어휘

1. date back to ~ 시점으로 거슬러 올라가다   Upper Paleolithic 후기 구석기   crude 투박한, 정교하지 않은   cave 동굴   marked 현저한, 뚜렷한   naturalistic 자연을 그린   slab 판, 조각   excavate 발굴하다, 파내다   **2.** principal 주요한   inhabit 거주하다   rock shelter 동굴 은신처, 얕은 동굴   galleries 회랑, 갱도   inner reaches 안쪽 깊은 곳   magical 주술적인   religious 종교적인   **3.** rest on ~에 놓여 있다   bare 헐벗은, 텅 빈   backdrop 배경   trappings 장식, 과시적인 요소   contemporary 동시대의   figure 모습, 형상   depict 묘사하다   chip (그릇이나 연장의) 이가 빠진 흔적, 흠   spear 창   inspire 영감을 주다   herd (동물) 떼, 무리   game 사냥감   **4.** explicitly 명확하게   reveal 드러내다   portray 그리다   prefer 선호하다   hide 가죽   bovine 솟과 짐승   meatier meaty(살이 많은)의 비교급   tusk 엄니   reindeer 순록   be consistent with ~와 일치하다   **5.** be confined to ~에 국한되다   shaft 손잡이, 자루   engraving 판화   notation 표기   engraved 조각된   phases 위상   be aware of ~을 인지하다   exaggerate 과장하다   figurine 작은 조각상   fertility 생식력, 다산

11. 첫 번째 단락의 marked와 의미상 가장 가까운 것은?

　Ⓐ 상당한

　Ⓑ 놀랄 만한

　Ⓒ 제한된

　Ⓓ 적절한

12. 다음 중 유럽 그림에 관하여 첫 번째 단락이 입증하는 내용은?

　Ⓐ 호주 그림보다 훨씬 오래되었다.

　Ⓑ 2만 8000년이나 되었다.

　Ⓒ 남아프리카 그림만큼 오래되지는 않았다.

　Ⓓ 3만 년보다 훨씬 더 오래 되었다.

13. 두 번째 단락에 따르면, 일부 연구자들이 특정 동굴 벽화가 주술 및 종교 활동과 관련 있다고 보는 이유는?

　Ⓐ 많은 사람들이 쉽게 볼 수 있는 곳에 그림이 있어서 많은 사람들이 주술 및 종교 활동에 참여할 수 있었다.

　Ⓑ 후기 구석기인들은 주술 및 종교 의식에 동물 그림을 사용하는 현대인들과 유사한 믿음을 갖고 있었다.

　Ⓒ 주술 및 종교 활동의 증거가 사람이 거주했던 동굴의 지점과 바로 인접한 갱도에서 발견되었다.

　Ⓓ 동굴 내에서 사람이 거주하던 지점에서 멀리 떨어진 도달하기 어려운 곳에서 그림이 발견되었다.

　어휘 share 공유하다　contemporary 현생의, 동시대의
　　　 hard-to-reach 도달하기 힘든

14. 세 번째 단락에 따르면, 학자들이 동물 그림에 자국이 난 이유를 무엇이라고 추정하는가?

　Ⓐ 후기 구석기 예술가들은 표식을 사용하여 그들이 본 동물들을 기록했다.

　Ⓑ 그림에 영감을 준 것은 사냥감 공급량을 늘리기 위한 필요성이었다.

　Ⓒ 예술가들은 동굴 벽의 거칠거칠한 부분을 제거했다.

　Ⓓ 후기 구석기인들은 그림을 이용해 사냥에서 행운을 부르고자 했다.

　어휘 mark 표식　remove 제거하다　rough (표면이) 거친

15. 글쓴이가 "후기 구석기 말기에 절정에 도달했던 것으로 보이며, 그 때는 바로 사냥감이 감소하던 시기였다."라고 언급한 이유는?

　Ⓐ 사냥감이 희소해지자 후기 구석기 예술에는 더 이상 동물이 포함되지 않았다고 주장하기 위해

　Ⓑ 그림의 목적이 사냥 동물의 공급량을 늘리기 위한 것이었다는 주장을 뒷받침하기 위해

　Ⓒ 후기 구석기 시기를 통틀어 동굴 예술의 수준이 계속 향상되었다는 점을 강조하기 위해

　Ⓓ 사냥감 감소와 후기 구석기의 종말 간에 직접적인 연관성이 있다는 것을 드러내기 위해

　어휘 cease 중단하다, 더 이상 ~하지 않다　scarce 희소한
　　　 connection 연관성

16. 네 번째 단락에 따르면, 다음 중 후기 구석기시대 수렵인들의 사슴과 순록에 대한 태도를 가장 잘 설명하는 것은?

　Ⓐ 사슴이나 순록을 말이나 매머드 같이 덩치 큰 사냥감만큼 두려워하지 않았다.

　Ⓑ 덩치와 속도 때문에 사슴이나 순록을 사냥하는 데 관심이 없었다.

　Ⓒ 다른 동물들보다 사슴이나 순록의 고기와 가죽을 선호했다.

　Ⓓ 뿔 같은 타고난 무기 때문에 사슴이나 순록을 피했다.

　어휘 fear 두려워하다　avoid 피하다

17. 네 번째 단락에 따르면, 후기 구석기 이후의 예술에서 나타난 뚜렷한 변화는?

　Ⓐ 거대 동물보다는 작은 동물들을 그리기 시작했다.

　Ⓑ 사람들이 식량을 구했던 방법을 더 이상 반영하지 않았다.

　Ⓒ 더 이상 동물 묘사가 주를 이루지 않게 되었다.

　Ⓓ 경제에서 수렵의 중요성을 드러내기 시작한다.

　어휘 obtain 얻다, 획득하다　consist of ~으로 구성되다
　　　 representation 묘사, 표현

18. 다섯 번째 단락에 따르면, 다음 중 후기 구석기인들이 복잡한 사고가 가능했고 주변 환경을 의식적으로 인식했다는 증거로 제시된 것은 무엇인가?

　Ⓐ 창의 손잡이와 다른 사물들에 동물 모양을 새겨 넣었다.

　Ⓑ 월령을 기록하기 위해 조각된 표식을 사용했을 수도 있다.

　Ⓒ 작은 조각상은 여자를 과장된 형태로 묘사했다.

　Ⓓ 작은 조각상을 통해 이상형을 묘사하거나 다산에 대한 열망을 표현했을 수도 있다.

　어휘 portray 묘사하다, 그리다

19. 위에 제시된 지문의 일부를 보시오. 지문에 표시된 **(A)**, **(B)**, **(C)**, **(D)** 중 하나에 다음 문장이 삽입될 수 있다.

Therefore, if the paintings were connected with hunting, some other explanation is needed.
(그러므로 그림이 사냥과 관련 있다면 다른 설명이 필요하다.)

이 문장이 들어갈 가장 적당한 위치는?

The subjects of the paintings are mostly animals. The paintings rest on bare walls, with no backdrops or environmental trappings. Perhaps, like many contemporary peoples, Upper Paleolithic men and women believed that the drawing of a human image could cause death or injury, and if that were indeed their belief, it might explain why human figures are rarely depicted in cave art. Another explanation for the focus on animals might be that these people sought to improve their luck at hunting. **(A)** This theory is suggested by evidence of chips in the painted figures, perhaps made by spears thrown at the drawings. **(B)** But if improving their hunting luck was the chief motivation for the paintings, it is difficult to explain why only a few show signs of having been speared. **(C)** Therefore, if the paintings were connected with hunting, some other explanation is needed. Perhaps the paintings were inspired by the need to increase the supply of animals. Cave art seems to have reached a peak toward the end of the Upper Paleolithic period, when the herds of game were decreasing. **(D)**

Ⓐ (A)　　Ⓑ (B)　　Ⓒ (C)　　Ⓓ (D)

어휘 be connected with ~와 관련된

20. 지문을 간단히 요약하기 위한 도입 문장이 아래에 제시되어 있다. 아래 보기들 중에서 지문의 가장 중요한 개념을 표현한 문장 3개를 골라 요약을 완성하라. 보기들 중에는 지문에 나오지 않거나 중요하지 않은 개념이기 때문에 요약문으로 적절치 않은 것들도 있다. 이 문제의 배점은 2점이다.

서유럽의 후기 구석기 동굴 벽화는 인류 최초의 예술적 시도에 속한다.

Ⓐ 연구자들은 동물이 동굴 벽화에서 가장 흔한 주제였다는 사실에 대해 몇 가지 다른 설명을 제시했다.

Ⓑ 동굴 벽화는 동물들이 보통 발견되는 자연 환경에 대한 묘사 없이 동물을 그리는 것에만 집중하고 있다.

Ⓒ 후기 구석기 이후 문화 시대의 예술에는 더 이상 거대 사냥감 동물이 묘사되지 않고 그 시대 사람들이 사냥하기 선호했던 종류의 동물이 집중적으로 등장했다.

Ⓓ 일부 연구자들은 동굴 벽화는 주로 후기 구석기인들에게 고기와 재료를 제공했던 거대 동물을 묘사했다고 생각한다.

Ⓔ 일부 연구자들은 스페인, 남아프리카, 호주에서 발견된 그림보다 프랑스에서 발견된 그림이 상징적 중요성에 대한 더 분명한 증거를 제공한다고 생각한다.

Ⓕ 후기 구석기인들은 동굴 벽화뿐만 아니라 여러 가지 예술품을 남겼는데, 그중 하나는 복잡한 사고력에 대한 증거로 간주된다.

어휘 depict 그리다, 묘사하다　significance 중요성

LISTENING

Questions 1~5

N Narrator **L** Librarian **S** Student

Script T-1

N Listen to a conversation between a student and a librarian.

L Can I help you?

S Yeah, I need to find a review. It's for my English class. We have to find reviews of the play we're reading. But they have to be from when the play was first performed—so I need to know when that was … and I suppose I should start with newspaper reviews …

L Contemporary reviews.

S Sorry?

L You want contemporary reviews. What's the name of the play?

S It's *Happy Strangers*. It was written in 1962 and we're supposed to write about its influence on American theater— show why it's been so important.

L Well, that certainly explains why your professor wants you to read some of those old reviews. The critics really tore the play to pieces when it opened. It was just so controversial— nobody'd ever seen anything like it on the stage.

S Really? It was that big a deal?

L Oh sure. Of course, the critics' reaction made some people kinda curious about it; they wanted to see what was causing all the fuss. In fact, we were on vacation in New York—I had to be, oh around sixteen or so—and my parents took me to see it. That would've been about 1965.

S So that was the year it premiered? Great! But … newspapers from back then aren't online, so how do I …

L Well, we have copies of old newspapers in the basement, and all the *major* papers publish reference guides to their articles, reviews, etc. You'll find *them* in the reference stacks in back. But I'd start with 1964. I think the play'd been running for a little while when I saw it.

S Oh, how'd you like it? I mean it's just two characters onstage hanging around and basically doing nothing.

L Well, I was impressed: the actors were famous and, besides, it was my first time in a *real* theater. But you're right—it was definitely different from any plays that we'd read in high school. Of course, in a small town, the assignments are pretty traditional.

S I've only read it, but it doesn't seem like it'd be much fun to watch. The story doesn't progress in a, in any sort of logical manner. It doesn't have any real ending either. It just stops. Honestly, y'know, I thought it was kinda slow and boring.

L Well, I guess you might think that, but when I saw it back then it was anything but boring! Some parts were really

N 학생과 사서의 대화를 들으시오.

L 뭘 도와드릴까요?

S 예, 비평을 하나 찾아야 하는데요, 영문학 수업 때문이에요. 현재 읽고 있는 희곡에 대한 비평을 찾아야 합니다. 그런데 이 연극 초연 당시에 발표된 것이어야 해서, 그게 언제인지를 알아야 하는데, 신문에 실렸던 것들부터 찾아봐야 하나….

L 당대 비평 말이군요.

S 예?

L 지금 학생이 찾는 게 당대 비평이에요. 희곡 제목이 뭔가요?

S 〈행복한 이방인들〉이에요. 1962년도 작품이고, 이 작품이 미국 연극에 미친 영향, 즉 이 작품이 왜 그토록 중요한지에 대해 써야 합니다.

L 아하, 교수님이 왜 과거 비평을 읽으라고 하시는지 확실히 알겠네요. 이 작품이 공개되자 비평가들이 실로 혹평을 쏟아냈죠. 엄청난 논란을 일으켰어요. 누구도 무대에서 본 적 없는 그런 연극이었죠.

S 정말이요? 그렇게 대단했단 말이죠?

L 그럼요. 물론 일부는 비평가들의 반응 때문에 호기심이 생기기도 했죠. 대체 왜 그렇게 난리인지 보고 싶었던 거죠. 사실, 당시 우리 가족은 뉴욕에 휴가를 갔는데, 제가 열여섯쯤이었을 텐데, 부모님께서 절 데리고 가 주셔서 그 연극을 봤어요. 아마 1965년쯤 될 겁니다.

S 그해에 초연되었다는 말씀인 거죠? 잘됐다! 그런데, 당시 신문은 인터넷 검색이 안 될 텐데 어쩌죠.

L 음, 옛날 신문들은 지하에 보관하고 있고, 주요 신문들은 논설, 평론 등에 대한 색인을 발간합니다. 뒤쪽 색인대에 보면 있어요. 1964년도부터 검색하는 게 나을 거예요. 제가 봤을 때만 해도 벌써 공연한지 어느 정도 되었으니까요.

S 참, 연극은 어땠나요? 등장인물은 둘뿐이고 무대에서 딱히 하는 일 없이 어슬렁거린다면서요?

L 저는 감동적이었어요. 배우들도 유명했고 실제 극장에 가 본 것도 처음이었으니까요. 하지만 학생 말이 맞긴 해요. 고등학교에서 읽었던 희곡들과는 전혀 딴판이었죠. 물론 소도시에서는 과제들이 꽤 인습적이죠.

S 저는 아직 읽기만 했지만 관람하기에 그다지 재미있을 것 같진 않아요. 논리적으로 따지면 이야기가 도무지 진전이 없어요. 제대로 된 결말도 없고요. 그냥 난데없이 중단돼요. 솔직히 좀 더디고 지루했어요.

L 아마 그랬을 거예요. 하지만 당시 극장에서 관람했을 때 난 전혀 지루하지 않았어요. 어떤 대목은 정말 웃겼고,

funny—but I remember crying, too. But I'm not sure just reading it … You know, they've done this play at least once on campus. I'm sure there's a tape of the play in our video library. You might want to borrow it.

S   That's a good idea. I'll have a better idea of what I *really* think of it—before I read those reviews.

L   I'm sure you'll be surprised that anyone ever found it radical— but you'll see why it's still powerful—dramatically speaking.

S   Well, there must be *something* about it or the professor wouldn't have assigned it. I'm sure I'll figure it out.

또 울었던 기억도 나요. 그냥 읽는 것만으로는 글쎄요 … 저기 말이죠, 이 캠퍼스에서 한 번 정도는 공연했을 거예요. 비디오 자료실에 분명 실황 테이프가 있을 겁니다. 한번 빌려 보세요.

S   그럼 좋겠네요. 비평을 읽기 전에 직접 보면 제 느낌도 잘 알 수 있을 것 같아요.

L   분명 대체 누가 그걸 보고 급진적이라고 했을까 의아할 테지만, 그럼에도 불구하고 그 작품이 강렬한 이유를 알게 될 거예요. 극적으로 말하자면 말이죠.

S   분명 뭔가 있겠죠, 그렇지 않다면 교수님께서 과제로 정하지 않으셨겠죠. 그게 뭔지 알아낼 수 있을 거예요.

어휘

review 비평   contemporary 당대의   tear ~ to pieces ~을 혹평하다   controversial 논란이 많은   fuss 난리, 야단   premiere (연극) 초연하다, (영화) 개봉하다   reference guide 색인   hang around 어슬렁거리다, 배회하다   assignment 과제, 숙제   radical 급진적인   dramatically speaking 극적으로 말하자면

---

1.   남자가 여자의 도움이 필요한 이유는? 두 개의 답을 고르시오.

   A   필요한 비평의 발행일을 몰라서
   B   도서관에서 연극 실황 테이프 모음집이 비치된 위치를 몰라서
   C   현재 연극이 어디에서 상연되고 있는시 일아볼 방법을 몰라서
   D   어떤 신문을 찾아봐야 하는지 몰라서

   어휘 publication 발행, 출판   perform 상연[공연]하다
         determine 결정하다

2.   희곡 〈행복한 이방인들〉에 대한 평단의 반응에 대해 여자가 암시하는 것은?

   A   부정적인 평단의 반응으로 초연 이후 내용이 수정되었다.
   B   대학생들 사이에 늘 높은 인기를 누렸다.
   C   극에 대한 반응이 과거보다 현재에 더 긍정적이다.
   D   비평가들이 좋아한 적이 없어 요즘은 거의 공연되지 않는다.

   어휘 critical 비평의, 평단의

3.   여자가 어렸을 때 〈행복한 이방인들〉을 관람한 경험에 대해 어떻게 이야기하는가? 두 개의 답을 고르시오.

   A   전문적으로 공연되는 연극 관람은 처음이었다.
   B   부모는 보고 싶어하지 않았지만 관람했다.
   C   공연이 너무 전통적이어서 놀랐다.
   D   연극을 보며 다양한 감정을 느꼈다.

   어휘 professionally 전문적으로
         against the wishes of ~의 바람을 거스르는

4.   현재 과제에 대한 남자의 태도는?

   A   필요한 자료를 찾을 수 있을지 확신이 없다.
   B   작품을 읽는 것보다는 직접 공연하는 것이 덜 지루하리라 생각한다.
   C   당대 비평보다는 자신의 평이 더욱 객관적이리라 생각한다.
   D   자신이 조사하고 있는 작품의 진가를 알게 되리라 낙관한다.

   어휘 objective 객관적인   optimistic 낙관적인
         appreciate (작품) 감상하다, 진가를 인정하다
         research 조사하다, 연구하다

5.   대화의 일부를 다시 듣고 질문에 답하라.

 T-2

   S   I suppose I should start with newspaper reviews …
   L   Contemporary reviews.
   S   Sorry?
   L   You want contemporary reviews. What's the name of the play?

   N   *Why does the woman say this:*
   L   Contemporary reviews.

   A   남자에게 요청하는 바를 명확히 하라고 부탁하기 위해
   B   남자의 요청을 더 정확히 일러주기 위해
   C   남자의 말을 제대로 들었는지 확인하기 위해
   D   남자의 실수를 정정하기 위해

   어휘 clarify 명확히 하다   precisely 정확하게

Questions 6~11

p.32

N Narrator P Professor M Male Student F Female Student

Script T-3

N Listen to part of a lecture in a biology class. The class is discussing animal behavior.

P OK, the next kind of animal behavior I want to talk about might be familiar to you. You may have seen, for example, a bird that's in the middle of a mating ritual. And, and suddenly it stops and preens—you know, it takes a few moments to straighten its feathers—and then returns to the mating ritual. This kind of behavior—this doing something that seems completely out of place—is what we call a displacement activity.

Displacement activities are activities that animals engage in when they have conflicting drives—if, if we take our example from a minute ago—if the bird is afraid of its mate, it's conflicted, it wants to mate, but it's also afraid and wants to run away, so instead it starts grooming itself. So the displacement activity, the, the grooming, the straightening of its feathers seems to be an irrelevant behavior.

So what do you think another example of a displacement activity might be?

M How about an animal that, um, instead of fighting its enemy or running away, it attacks a plant or a bush?

P That's a really good suggestion, Carl, but *that's* called redirecting. The animal is *redirecting* its behavior to another object, in this case, the plant or the bush. But that's not an irrelevant or inappropriate behavior—the behavior makes sense—it's appropriate under the circumstances, but what doesn't make sense is the *object* the behavior's directed towards. OK, who else? Carol?

F I think I read in another class about an experiment, um, where an object that the animal was afraid of was put next to its food—next to the animal's food—and the animal, it was conflicted between confronting the object, and eating the food, so instead it just fell asleep. Like that?

P That's *exactly* what I mean. Displacement occurs because the animal's got two conflicting drives, two competing urges, in this case, fear and hunger—and what happens is they *inhibit* each other—they cancel each other out in a way, and a third, seemingly *irrelevant* behavior surfaces ... through a process that we call disinhibition.

Now, in disinhibition, the basic idea is that two drives that seem to inhibit, to hold back a third drive, well, well, they get in the way of each other in a, in a conflict situation, and somehow lose control, lose their inhibiting effect on that third behavior ... wh-which means that the third drive surfaces ...

N 생물학 강의의 일부를 들으시오. 학급은 동물 행동에 대해 논의하고 있다.

P 이제 설명하려는 동물 행동은 아마 여러분들도 익히 알고 있을지 모르겠습니다. 예를 들면, 짝짓기 의식이 한창인 새를 본 적이 있을 겁니다. 그런데 새가 갑자기 짝짓기 의식을 멈추고는 부리로 깃털을 다듬습니다. 잠시 깃털을 고르고는 다시 짝짓기 의식으로 돌아가는 겁니다. 이런 유형의 행위, 즉 상황과 전혀 동떨어진 어떤 일을 하는 것을 소위 '전위활동(轉位活動)'이라고 합니다.

전위활동이란 상충되는 욕구들이 있을 때 하는 행동으로, 좀 전 예로 다시 돌아가죠. 새가 짝짓기 상대를 두려워한다면, 갈등하게 되는 거죠. 짝짓기는 하고 싶은데 두렵기도 해서 도망치고 싶은 겁니다. 그래서 대신 깃털을 다듬기 시작하는 거죠. 따라서 이런 전위활동, 몸단장, 깃털 고르는 행동은 생뚱맞은 행동처럼 보이죠.

전위활동의 다른 예로는 어떤 것이 있을까요?

M 어, 동물이 적과 싸우거나 도망치는 대신 나무나 덤불을 공격하는 건 어떤가요?

P 아주 훌륭한 추측인데요, 칼, 그건 전환반응이라고 해요. 동물은 행위를 다른 대상으로 전환하는데, 방금 그 상황에서는 나무나 덤불이죠. 하지만 무관하거나 부적절한 행동은 아니에요. 그 행위는 납득이 가죠. 그런 상황에선 그럴 수도 있으니까. 다만 이해가 안 되는 부분은 하필 그 대상으로 행동의 방향을 수정했느냐 하는 것이죠. 그래요, 누구 또 얘기할 사람? 캐롤?

F 다른 수업시간에 어떤 실험에 대해 읽은 적이 있어요. 한 동물이 무서워하는 것을 먹이 옆에 놓아두면, 녀석은 그 대상과 맞설지 먹이를 먹을지 갈등하다 그냥 잠들어버리던데요. 이런 거 아닌가요?

P 바로 그거죠. 동물은 상충되는 두 가지 욕구, 즉 두 가지 다투는 충동을 갖고 있는 거죠. 이 경우는 두려움과 배고픔이죠. 이 상반된 욕구들이 서로 억제하다가 어쩌다 상쇄하게 되면, 겉보기에 생뚱맞은 제3의 행동이 부상합니다. 이른바 '탈억제(脫抑制)'라는 과정을 통해서죠.

탈억제에서 기본 개념은 두 가지 욕구가 제 3의 욕구를 억제하고 억누르다가, 그러니까, 갈등 상황에서 서로 방해하는 겁니다. 그런데 어쩌다 통제력을 상실하면, 제 3의 행동에 대한 억제 효과를 상실하면 제 3의 욕구가 부상하게 되고, 동물의 행동을 통해 발현됩니다.

전위활동에는 먹기, 마시기, 몸단장, 심지어 수면까지도

it-it's expressed in the animal's behavior.

Now, these displacement activities can include feeding, drinking, grooming, even sleeping. These are what we call "comfort behaviors." So why do you think displacement activities are so often comfort behaviors, such as grooming?

M Maybe because it's easy for them to do—I mean, grooming is like one of the most accessible things an animal can do—it's something they do all the time, and they have the–the *stimulus* right there, on the outside of their bodies in order to do the grooming—or if food is right in front of them. Basically, they don't have to think very much about those behaviors.

F Professor, isn't it possible that animals groom because they've gotten messed up a little from fighting or mating? I mean, if a bird's feathers get ruffled, or an animal's fur— maybe it's not so strange for them to stop and tidy themselves up at that point.

P That's another possible reason, although it doesn't necessarily explain other behaviors such as eating, drinking, or sleeping. What's interesting is that studies have been done that suggest that the animal's *environment* may play a part in determining what kind of behavior it displays. For example, there's a bird—the wood thrush, anyway when the wood thrush is in an attack-escape conflict—that is, it's caught between the two urges to escape from or to attack an enemy—if it's sitting on a horizontal branch, it'll wipe its beak on its perch. If it's sitting on a vertical branch, it'll groom its breast feathers. The immediate environment of the bird—its immediate, um, its relationship to its immediate environment seems to play a part in which behavior it will display.

포함됩니다. 이를 일컬어 '위안 행동'이라 합니다. 그렇다면, 왜 전위활동이 아주 빈번하게 몸단장 같은 위안 행동으로 발현되는 걸까요?

M 쉽게 할 수 있기 때문이겠죠. 몸단장은 동물이 가장 쉽게 할 수 있는 행동, 즉 늘 하는 행위인데, 하필 바로 거기에, 그러니까 몸 외부에 자극을 받는 거죠. 아니면 음식이 바로 눈앞에 있기 때문일 수도 있고요. 기본적으로 많이 생각할 필요가 없는 행동들이죠.

F 교수님, 혹시 싸움이나 짝짓기를 하느라 지저분해져서 몸단장을 하는 건 아닐까요? 그러니까 새의 깃털이나 동물의 털이 헝클어진다면 그 자리에서 하던 행동을 멈추고 몸단장하는 건 그다지 이상하지 않은데요.

P 그것도 가능한 추리네요. 먹기, 마시기, 잠자기 같은 행동까지 설명하진 못하지만. 흥미로운 점은, 동물의 환경이 행동을 결정 짓는 한 요소가 될 수 있다는 점을 시사한 연구가 있었습니다. 예를 들어, 새 한 마리, 개똥지빠귀가 있습니다. 녀석이 공격-도피 갈등을 겪을 때, 즉 도망갈 것인지, 적을 공격할 것인지 두 가지 욕구 사이에서 갈등할 때 만약 녀석이 수평으로 뻗은 가지에 앉아 있다면 횃대에 부리를 닦을 겁니다. 만약 수직으로 뻗은 가지에 앉아 있으면 가슴 털을 고를 겁니다. 새가 당면한 환경, 즉 바로 곁에 있는 환경과의 관계가 새가 표출하는 행동을 유발하는 요인 중 하나로 보입니다.

어휘
....
mating 짝짓기, 교미   ritual 의식   preen (새가) 부리로 깃털을 다듬다   displacement activity 전위활동(어떤 자극 때문에 상황에 맞지 않은 행동을 하는 것)
out of place 상황에 맞지 않은, 생뚱맞은   engage in ~에 관여[참여]하다, ~에 종사하다   conflicting 상충하는   drive 충동, 욕구   groom (털을) 다듬다,
반듯하게 손질하다   irrelevant 무관한, 부적절한   redirecting 전환반응(행위를 다른 대상으로 전환하는 것)   inappropriate 부적절한   make sense 말이 되
다, 이해되다   under the circumstances 그런 상황에서   confronting 맞서다, 대면하다   occur 발생하다   competing 경쟁하는, 다투는   inhibit 억제
하다   surface 부상하다, 표면 위로 떠오르다   disinhibition 탈억제(외부 자극에 일시적으로 억제를 상실하는 현상)   hold back 억누르다   get in the way
of ~에 방해되다   accessible 접할[구할] 수 있는   stimulus 자극   mess up 망치다, 엉망으로 만들다   ruffle 헝클다   tidy oneself up 매무새를 다듬다,
단장하다   wood thrush 개똥지빠귀   attack 공격   escape 도피, 탈출   be caught between ~ 사이에서 갈등하다   horizontal 수평의   beak 부리
perch 횃대, 높은 자리   vertical 수직의   immediate 바로 가까이에 있는, 당면한   display 표출하다

6. 이 강의의 주제는 무엇인가?

    Ⓐ 동물의 이상 행동을 관찰하는 방법들
    Ⓑ 새가 짝짓기 상대를 유혹하는 방법에 관한 이론
    Ⓒ 상충된 욕구가 있을 때 동물이 행동하는 방식들
    Ⓓ 동물 행동을 분류하는 기준들

어휘 method 방법, 방법론 criteria 기준 classify 분류하다

7. 아래 행동들이 전위활동을 설명하는지 여부를 해당 칸에 표시하시오.

	예	아니오
동물이 적 대신 땅을 공격한다.		✓
동물이 짝짓기 의식 도중에 잠든다.	✓	
동물이 적과 마주쳤을 때 먹이를 먹는다.	✓	
동물이 몸단장을 한 후 물을 마신다.		✓

어휘 be confronted by ~과 마주치다

8. 탈억제에 대하여 교수가 설명하는 것은?

    Ⓐ 전위활동의 발생을 막을 수 있다.
    Ⓑ 동물이 동시에 여러 가지 욕구에 따라 행동하도록 만들 수 있다.
    Ⓒ 많은 유형의 전위활동을 설명하는 데 유용하지 않다.
    Ⓓ 겉보기에 무관한 행동이 나타나는 원인이다.

어휘 act on ~에 따라 행동하다
    be responsible for ~의 원인이다

9. 강의에 따르면, 전위활동이 종종 몸단장 행위로 발현되는 한 가지 가능한 이유는?

    Ⓐ 몸단장은 적이나 포식자를 혼란스럽게 할 수 있다.
    Ⓑ 몸단장은 편하고 쉽게 할 수 있는 행위다.
    Ⓒ 몸단장은 먹고 마시기 전에 종종 일어난다.
    Ⓓ 몸단장은 공통적인 사회적 행동이다.

어휘 common 공통의, 흔한

10. 교수가 개똥지빠귀를 언급하는 이유는?

    Ⓐ 다른 동물 종이 하는 전위활동과 대조하기 위해
    Ⓑ 일부 동물은 몸단장 이외의 전위활동을 보인다는 것을 설명하기 위해
    Ⓒ 전위활동이 어떻게 환경의 영향을 받는지 적시하기 위해
    Ⓓ 전위활동을 보이지 않는 동물의 예를 들기 위해

어휘 contrast A with B A와 B를 대조하다

11. 강의의 일부를 다시 듣고 질문에 답하라.

 T-4

> **P** So what do you think another example of a displacement activity might be?
>
> **M** How about an animal that, uh, instead of fighting its enemy or running away, it attacks a plant or a bush?
>
> **P** That's a really good suggestion, Carl, but that's called redirecting.
>
> **N** *What does the professor mean when she says this:*
>
> **P** That's a really good suggestion, Carl, but that's called redirecting.

    Ⓐ 전환반응에 대해 학생들이 많이 알고 있다는 것에 감탄해서
    Ⓑ 강의의 다음 부분으로 넘어가야 할 시점이라고 생각해서
    Ⓒ 학생의 답변이 전위활동의 예가 아니라서
    Ⓓ 학생이 이후 토론할 다른 동물 행동을 제안해야 하므로

어휘 move on to ~로 넘어가다

Questions 12~17

p.34

N Narrator **P** Professor

Script   T-5

N Listen to part of a lecture in a literature class.

P All right, so let me close today's class with some thoughts to keep in mind while you're doing tonight's assignment. You'll be reading one of Ralph Waldo Emerson's best-known essays, "Self-Reliance," and comparing it with his poems and other works. I think this essay has the potential to be quite meaningful for all of you — as young people who probably wonder about things like truth, and where your lives are going … all sorts of profound questions.

Knowing something about Emerson's philosophies will help you when you read "Self-Reliance." And basically, one of the main beliefs that he had, was about *truth*. Not that it's something that we can be taught … Emerson says it's found within ourselves.

So this truth … the idea that it's in each one of us … is one of the first points that you'll see Emerson making in this essay. It's a bit abstract, but he's very into, ah, into each person believing his or her own thought. Believing in yourself, the thought or conviction that's true for you.

But actually, he ties that in with a sort of universal truth, something that everyone knows but doesn't realize they know. Most of us aren't in touch with ourselves, in a way, so we just aren't *capable* of recognizing profound truths. It takes geniuses … people like, say, Shakespeare, who are unique because when they have a glimpse of this truth — this universal truth — they pay attention to it and express it, and don't just dismiss it like most people do.

So, Emerson is really into each individual believing in, and trusting, him- or herself. You'll see that he writes about … well, first, conformity. He *criticizes* the people of his time, for abandoning their own minds and their own wills for the sake of conformity and consistency. They try to fit in with the rest of the world, even though it's at odds with their beliefs and their identities. Therefore, it's best to be a *nonconformist* — to do your own thing, not worrying about what other people think. That's an important point — he really drives this argument home throughout the essay.

When you're reading I want you to think about that, and why that kind of thought would be relevant to the readers of his time. Remember, this is 1838. Self-reliance was a novel idea at the time, and United States citizens were less secure about themselves as individuals and as Americans. The country as a whole was trying to define itself. Emerson wanted to give people something to really think about. Help them find their

N 문학 강의의 일부를 들으시오.

P 좋아요, 여러분이 오늘 저녁에 과제를 할 때 유의할 몇 가지를 말하면서 오늘 수업을 마칠까 합니다. 여러분은 랄프 왈도 에머슨의 가장 유명한 산문인 〈자립〉을 읽고 그의 시나 다른 작품들과 비교하게 될 겁니다. 이 산문은 여러분에게 상당히 의미 있는 작품이 될 잠재력이 있습니다. 젊은이라면 진리란 무엇인가, 내 삶은 어디로 가고 있는가 등 온갖 종류의 심오한 질문들에 대해 고민하니까요.

에머슨의 철학을 좀 알면 〈자립〉을 읽을 때 도움이 될 겁니다. 기본적으로 에머슨의 주요 신념들 중 하나가 바로 진리에 대한 것입니다. 진리란 배워서 깨닫는 것이 아니라 내면에서 발견되는 거라고 에머슨은 말하죠.

따라서 진리가 우리 각자의 내면에 있다는 생각은 에머슨이 이 글에서 가장 먼저 주장하는 논지 중 하나입니다. 다소 추상적이기는 하지만 그는 모든 이가 각자의 생각을 믿어야 한다는 것에 깊이 천착하고 있습니다. 자기 자신, 자신에게 맞는 생각이나 신념을 믿어야 한다는 거죠.

하지만 사실 그는 이를 일종의 보편적 진리로 보았습니다. 모두가 알고 있지만 알고 있다고 자각하지 못하는 어떤 것 말이죠. 우리들 대부분은 어떻게 보면 자기 자신과 소통하고 있지 않아 심오한 진리를 깨달을 수 없습니다. 천재성이 요구되죠. 이를테면 셰익스피어 같은 인물들은 이러한 진리, 즉 보편적 진리를 어렴풋이 보면 여느 사람들처럼 그냥 무시하지 않고 거기에 주목하고 표현해 내기 때문에 독보적이죠.

고로, 에머슨은 각자 자신을 믿는 것, 신뢰하는 것에 천착했죠. 그는 먼저 순응에 대해 쓰고 있습니다. 그는 동시대 사람들이 순응과 일관성을 위해 자신만의 생각과 뜻을 버린다고 비판합니다. 자신의 신념, 정체성과 맞지 않는데도 자신을 세상에 맞추려 애쓴다는 거죠. 고로, '이단자'가 되는 것, 즉 남들이 어떻게 생각할지 신경 쓰지 않고 자신이 가장 좋아하는 일을 하는 게 최선이라는 겁니다. 이게 핵심인데요, 그는 글 전반에 걸쳐 이 주장을 설파합니다.

과제물을 읽으면서 이 점을 생각해 보고 이런 사고가 에머슨 당대 독자들에게 왜 유의미했을지 한번 생각해 보기 바랍니다. 그때는 1838년임을 상기합시다. 당시로서 자립은 새로운 개념이었고 미국인들은 개인으로서, 또 미국인으로서 스스로에 대해 자신감이 부족했습니다. 나라 전체가 정체성을 찾아 나가던 시기였죠. 에머슨은 사람들이 정말 생각해 봐야 할 무언가를 제시하고자 했어

own way and, ah, what it meant to *be* who they were.

So, that's something that I think is definitely as relevant today as it was then … probably, uh … especially among young adults like yourselves. You know, uh, college being a time to sort of really think about who you are and where you're going.

Now, we already said that Emerson really emphasized nonconformity, right? As a way to sort of not lose your own self and identity in the world? To have your own truth and not be afraid to listen to it? Well, he takes it a step *further*. Not conforming also means, ah, not conforming with *yourself*, or your past. What does *that* mean? Well, if you've always been a certain way, or done a certain thing, but it's not working for you anymore, or you're not content—Emerson says that it'd be foolish to be consistent even with our own past. Focus on the future, he says: that's what matters more. Inconsistency is good! He talks about a ship's voyage—and this is one of the most famous bits of the essay—how the best voyage is made up of zigzag lines. Up close, it seems a little all over the place, but from farther away the true path shows, and in the end it justifies all the turns along the way.

So, don't worry if you're not sure where you're headed or what your long-term goals are—stay true to yourself and it'll make sense in the end. I mean, *I* can attest to that. Before I was a literature professor, I was an accountant. Before that, I was a newspaper reporter. My life has taken some pretty interesting turns, and here I am, very happy with my experiences and where they've brought me. If you rely on yourself and trust your own talents, your own interests, don't worry. Your path will make sense in the end.

요. 사람들이 자신만의 길을 찾고, 본래 모습을 간직하는 게 어떤 의미인지 찾도록 도와주려 했죠.

저는 바로 이점이 그때 못지않게 오늘날에도 유의미하다고 봅니다. 특히, 여러분 같은 젊은이들에게. 대학 시절에는 나는 누구인지, 어디로 가고 있는지 진지하게 고민하니까요.

에머슨이 비순응을 아주 강조했다는 건 이미 말했죠? 세상에서 나의 고유한 자아와 정체성을 잃지 않는 한 가지 방법이죠? 나 자신만의 진리를 간직하고 두려움 없이 진리의 소리를 듣는 방법이고요? 에머슨은 여기서 한걸음 더 나아갑니다. 비순응이란 자기 자신, 자신의 과거와도 순응하지 않는 것입니다. 대체 무슨 소리일까요? 항상 어떤 방식을 고수해왔거나 어떤 일을 해왔는데, 이 방식이 더 이상 먹히지 않거나 만족스럽지 않다고 가정합시다. 에머슨은 심지어 자신의 과거에서 벗어나지 않는 것조차 어리석다고 말합니다. 그는 미래에 초점을 맞추는 것이 더 중요하다고 말합니다. 일관성이 없다는 건 바람직한 일입니다! 그는 배의 항해에 대해 말하죠, 이 산문에서 가장 유명한 대목인데요, 갈지자를 그리며 가는 것이 어째서 최고의 항해인지 말합니다. 가까이에서 보면 두서없이 엉망으로 보이지만, 멀리 떨어져서 보면 진짜 길이 보이며 종국에는 그동안 왜 그렇게 돌아왔는지 알게 된다는 겁니다.

그러니 자신이 어디로 가고 있는지 또는 장기적인 목표가 무엇인지 아리송해도 고민하지 마세요. 자신에게 충실하면 결국 이해가 될 겁니다. 제가 증언합니다. 저는 문학교수가 되기 전에 회계사였습니다. 그전에는 신문기자였죠. 제 인생은 꽤나 흥미로운 경로를 돌아서 이 자리까지 왔고, 과거의 경험, 그리고 과거의 경험이 데려다 준 지금의 자리에 만족합니다. 자신을 믿고 자신의 재능과 흥미를 믿는다면 걱정 마세요. 결국 걸어온 길을 이해할 수 있을 겁니다.

어휘

self-reliance 자립 profound 심오한 abstract 추상적인 be into ~에 천착하다, 몰두하다 conviction 신념 true for ~에 해당하는 tie A in with B A와 B를 일치시키다 capable of ~할 수 있는, ~이 가능한 genius 천재성 have a glimpse of ~을 어렴풋이[흘깃] 보다 dismiss 간과하다, 무시하다 conformity 순응 abandon 버리다, 포기하다 will 의지 for the sake of ~을 위해서, ~ 때문에 consistency 일관성 fit in with ~과 어울리다 at odds with ~과 맞지 않다, 상충하다 identity 정체성 nonconformist 이단자, 관행을 따르지 않는 사람 drive home (주장 따위를) 납득시키다, 설파하다 novel idea 새로운 발상[개념] conform with ~을 따르다, ~에 순응하다 work for (어떤 방법이) 먹히다, 통하다 be consistent with ~와 일치하다, 조화를 이루다 inconsistency 불일치, 모순 zigzag 지그재그, 갈지자 justify 합리화하다, 입증하다 attest to ~을 증명하다

12. 이 강의의 주요 목적은 무엇인가?

  ⒜ 에머슨의 산문과 시의 유사점 지적하기
  Ⓑ 에머슨 산문을 읽기 전 학생들 준비시키기
  Ⓒ 보편적 진리에 대한 에머슨의 개념과 타 작가들의 개념 비교하기
  Ⓓ 초기 미국 사회가 에머슨의 작품에 미친 영향 보여주기

13. 에머슨이 당대 사람들을 비판했던 이유는?

  ⒜ 보편적 진리에 대한 인식을 거부해서
  Ⓑ 특정 작가들의 천재성을 인정하지 않아서
  Ⓒ 신념이 확실히 정립되지 않아서
  Ⓓ 순응하는 것에만 몰두해서

  어휘 well-defined (개념 등이) 제대로 정립된

14. 과거에 대한 에머슨의 견해는?

  ⒜ 한 사람의 현재 행동을 이끌어야 한다.
  Ⓑ 면밀하게 검토되어야 한다.
  Ⓒ 미래만큼 중요하지 않다.
  Ⓓ 명확성과 보편적 진리가 없다.

  어휘 examine 조사하다, 검토하다   clarity 명확성

15. 교수가 배의 항로를 언급하면서 말하려는 논지는?

  ⒜ 사람들은 참된 길을 시야에서 놓치기 쉽다.
  Ⓑ 사람들 대부분은 자신에게 가상 좋은 길을 판단할 능력이 없다.
  Ⓒ 목적지에 도달하고 나서야 그동안 지나온 길이 뚜렷하게 보인다.
  Ⓓ 어떤 길을 택할지 결정하기 전에 목표부터 정해야 한다.

  어휘 lose sight of ~을 시야에서 놓치다
       reach destination 목적지에 도착하다

16. 문학 교수가 되기 전 실제 경험담을 이야기하면서 교수가 암시하는 것은? 두 개의 답을 고르시오.

  Ⓐ 자신의 결정에 따른 결과를 고려하지 않았다.
  Ⓑ 처음부터 문학 교수가 되려고 계획한 것은 아니었다.
  Ⓒ 언제나 일관되게 행동하려고 노력했다.
  Ⓓ 자신과 자신의 결정을 믿었다.

  어휘 recount 술회하다, 이야기하다   consequence 결과
       act consistently 일관되게 행동하다

17. 강의의 일부를 다시 듣고 질문에 답하라.

 T-6

> P Remember, this is 1838. Self-reliance was a novel idea at the time, and United States citizens were less secure about themselves as individuals and as Americans.
>
> N *Why does the professor say this:*
> P Remember, this is 1838.

  ⒜ 미국 시민들이 그동안 그다지 변하지 않았다는 점을 시사하려고
  Ⓑ 학생들이 이 시기에 관한 더 상세한 정보를 찾도록 하려고
  Ⓒ 에머슨의 글이 일부 타당성을 상실한 이유를 설명하려고
  Ⓓ 설명하려는 개념에 대한 배경 지식을 제공하려고

  어휘 relevance 타당성

N Narrator   P Professor   S Student

Script T-7

N   Listen to a conversation between a student and a professor.

P   Hey Jane. You look like you're in a hurry ...

S   Yeah, things're a little crazy.

P   Oh, yeah? What's going on?

S   Oh, it's nothing ... Well, since it's your class ... I guess it's OK ... it's, it's just that I'm having trouble with my group project.

P   Ah, yes. Due next week. What's your group doing again?

S   It's about United States Supreme Court decisions. We're looking at the impact of recent cases on property rights, municipal land use cases, zoning disputes ...

P   Right, OK ... And it's not going well?

S   Not really. I'm worried about the other two people in my group. They're just sitting back, not really doing their fair share of the work, and waiting for an A. It's kinda stressing me out, because we're getting close to the deadline and I feel like I'm doing everything for this project ...

P   Ah, the good ole "free-rider" problem.

S   Free rider?

P   Oh, it's just a term that describes this situation: when people in a group seek to get the benefits of being in the group without contributing to the work ... Anyway, what exactly do you mean when you say they just sit back? I mean, they've been filing their weekly progress reports with me ...

S   Yes, but I feel like I'm doing 90 percent of the work. I hate to sound so negative here, but honestly, they're taking credit for things they shouldn't be taking credit for. Like last week in the library, we decided to split up the research into three parts, and then each of us was supposed to find sources in the library for our parts. I went off to the stacks and found some really good material for my part, but when I got back to our table they were just goofing off and talking. So I went and got material for their sections as well.

P   Hmm, you know you shouldn't do that.

S   I know, but I didn't want to risk the project going down the drain.

P   I know Theresa and Kevin, I've had both of them in other courses ... so I'm familiar with their work, and their work habits.

S   I know, me too, and that's why this has really surprised me.

P   Do you ... does your group like your topic?

S   Well, I think we'd all rather focus on cases that deal with personal liberties—questions about freedom of speech, things like that—but I chose property rights ...

N   학생과 교수의 대화를 들으시오.

P   제인, 어딜 그리 급히 가나?

S   예, 좀 정신이 없네요.

P   그래? 무슨 일이지?

S   별건 아니고요. 하긴, 교수님 과목이니까 괜찮을지도 모르겠네요. 그러니까, 그게, 조별 과제 때문에 좀 힘들어서요.

P   아, 그래, 다음 주 마감이지. 자네 조는 뭘 한다고 했더라?

S   미국 대법원 판례에 관한 거예요. 최근 판례들이 재산권, 도시 용지 사용 사건, 용도지역 설정을 둘러싼 분쟁 등에 미친 영향을 살펴보고 있어요.

P   그렇지, 근데 잘 안 되고 있나?

S   예, 조원 둘 때문에 고민이에요. 마땅히 해야 할 몫은 하지도 않고 뒷짐 지고 A학점만 기다리고 있다니까요. 마감은 다가오는데 제가 모든 걸 도맡아 하는 것 같아서 속이 타네요.

P   그 유명한 '무임승차자' 문제로군.

S   무임승차자라고요?

P   한 집단에 속한 사람들이 기여하는 것 없이 집단에 속한 잇속만 차리려 하는 상황을 표현하는 용어지. 그나저나, 조원들이 손 놓고 앉아 있다는 게 대체 무슨 말인가? 내게 매주마다 진도 보고서를 제출해왔는데 무슨 소리지?

S   그렇죠, 하지만 과제의 90%는 제가 하고 있는 것 같아요. 너무 부정적으로 말씀드리긴 싫지만, 솔직히 하는 일 없이 공을 차지하고 있어요. 지난주 도서관에서만 해도 그래요. 자료 검색을 세 부분으로 나눠서 도서관에서 각자 맡은 자료를 찾기로 했죠. 서가로 가서 제가 담당한 부분에 대해 정말 좋은 자료를 찾아냈어요. 그런데 자리로 돌아와 보니 그냥 빈둥거리며 수다만 떨고 있더라고요. 그래서 제가 되돌아가 걔들 것까지 다 찾아왔지 뭐예요.

P   흠, 그러지 말았어야지.

S   알죠, 하지만 과제를 망치게 놔둘 순 없어서요.

P   내가 테레사와 케빈을 잘 아는데, 다른 수업이지만 내 수업을 수강했거든. 그래서 그 친구들 어떻게 하는지, 행태를 아는데 말이야.

S   저도요, 그래서 더 놀랍다니까요.

P   자네, 아니 자네 조는 주제를 맘에 들어 하나?

S   글쎄요, 우리 모두 개인의 자유를 다룬 판례 위주로 하고 싶어했죠. 표현의 자유 같은 문제요. 하지만 제가 재

P   You chose the topic?

S   Yeah, I thought it would be good for us, all of us, to try something new.

P   Maybe that's part of the problem—maybe Theresa and Kevin aren't that excited about the topic—and since you picked it … Have you thought … talked to them at all about picking a different topic?

S   But, we've already got all the sources. And it's due next week. We don't have time to start from scratch.

P   OK, well, I'll let you go 'cause I know you're so busy. But you might … consider talking to your group about your topic choice …

S   I'll think about it. Gotta run. See you in class.

산권을 선택했어요.

P   자네가 그 주제를 택했다고?

S   그게 모두에게 좋을 것 같아서요, 새로운 걸 시도하는 거요.

P   그게 문제인 거 같은데, 테레사와 케빈이 그 주제에 별 흥미를 못 느끼는 지도 몰라, 자네가 고른 거니까. 생각해 봤나? 얘기해 봤나? 다른 주제로 바꿔 보자고.

S   하지만 벌써 자료를 다 찾아놨는데요. 마감도 다음 주고요. 처음부터 다시 시작할 시간이 없어요.

P   그래, 바쁠 테니 더 이상 붙잡지 않겠네. 하지만 주제 선정에 대해 조원들과 한번 얘기해 보는 게 좋을 거 같네.

S   생각해 보겠습니다. 이만 가 봐야 해서요. 수업시간에 뵙겠습니다.

어휘

due (언제까지) 예정된, 마감인   property 재산   municipal land 도시 용지   zoning disputes (도시계획) 용도지역 설정을 둘러싼 분쟁   sit back 수수방관하다   fair share 응분의 몫   stress somebody out 초조하게 만들다, 지치게 만들다   good ole(old) (애정 또는 비아냥) 옛날 옛적의, 그리운, 유명한   free-rider 무임승차자   file A with B B에게 A를 제출하다, 신고하다   take credit for ~에 대한 공을 차지하다   goof off 빈둥거리다   risk 위험을 무릅쓰다   go down the drain 헛수고로 돌아가다, 물거품이 되다   liberty 자유   freedom of speech 표현의 자유   property right 재산권   start from scratch 처음부터 다시 시작하다

18. 주로 무엇에 관한 대화인가?

   Ⓐ 프로젝트 관련 적절한 자료를 찾는 방법
   Ⓑ 여자가 프로젝트 수행에 어려움을 겪는 이유
   Ⓒ 교수가 조별 과제를 평가할 때 사용하는 기준
   Ⓓ 조별 과제 수행에 필요한 요령을 개발하는 방법

   어휘 criteria 기준   evaluate 평가하다

19. 교수가 '무임승차자' 문제를 언급하는 이유는?

   Ⓐ 수업시간에 설명한 개념을 복습하기 위해
   Ⓑ 학생에게 문제 해결 방안을 주려고
   Ⓒ 학생이 당면한 문제를 명확히 말하고자
   Ⓓ 조별 과제 수행의 장점을 설명하려고

   어휘 review 복습하다   clarify 명확히 하다

20. 여자가 속한 조의 다른 학생들에 대한 교수의 의견은?

   Ⓐ 자신들이 하지 않은 부분에 대해 공을 인정 받으려고 한다.
   Ⓑ 이전에 수강했던 자신의 수업에서 성적이 좋지 않았다.
   Ⓒ 단체 과제를 할 때 더 의욕적이다.
   Ⓓ 주제에 관심이 있을 때 열심히 한다.

   어휘 perform well 잘하다, (성적 등이) 좋다

21. 여자가 재산권을 주제로 선정한 이유는?

   Ⓐ 교수가 그 주제를 권해서
   Ⓑ 그 주제에 대한 참고 자료를 이미 많이 갖고 있어서
   Ⓒ 뭔가 새로운 것을 배워보고 싶어
   Ⓓ 학교 도서관에서 자료 조사하기가 쉬워서

   어휘 recommend 권고하다   reference 참고, 참조

22. 교수는 조별 과제 수행 과정에서 여자가 어떤 실수를 했다고 암시하는가? 두 개의 답을 고르시오.

   Ⓐ 조원들 자료를 대신 찾아준 것
   Ⓑ 주간 진도 보고서를 작성한 것
   Ⓒ 프로젝트 마감 일에 신경 쓰지 못한 것
   Ⓓ 주제 선정에 조원들을 참여시키지 않은 것

   어휘 work on a project 프로젝트를 추진하다
        involve 참여시키다

Questions 23~28

p.38

N Narrator   **P** Professor   **M** Male Student   **F** Female Student

Script T-8

N Listen to part of a discussion in a United States government class.

P OK, last time we were talking about government support for the arts. Who can sum up some of the main points? Frank?

M Well, I guess there wasn't *really* any, you know, *official* government support for the arts until the twentieth century. But the first attempt the United States government made to, you know, to support the arts was the Federal Art Project.

P Right. So, what can you say about the project?

M Um, it was started during the Depression, um, in the 1930s, to employ out-of-work artists.

P So was it successful? Janet? What do you say?

F Yeah, sure, it was successful—I mean, for one thing, the project established a lot of, like, community art centers and, uh, galleries in places like rural areas where people hadn't really had access to the arts.

P Right.

M Yeah, but didn't the government end up wasting a lot of money for art that wasn't even very good?

P Uh, some people might say that, but wasn't the primary objective of the Federal Art Project to provide jobs?

M That's true. I mean, it did provide jobs for thousands of unemployed artists.

P Right, but then, when the United States became involved in the Second World War, unemployment was down, and it seemed that these programs weren't really necessary any longer.
So, moving on … we don't actually see any govern—er, well, any *real* government involvement in the arts *again* until the early 1960s, when President Kennedy and other politicians started to push for major funding to support and promote the arts. It was felt by a number of politicians that, well, that the government had a *responsibility* to … uh, support the arts as sort of, oh what can we say, the soul, or *spirit* of the country. The idea was that there'd be a federal *subsidy*, uh, financial *assistance* to artists and artistic or cultural institutions. And for just those reasons, in 1965, the National Endowment for the Arts was created.
So, it was through the NEA, the National Endowment for the Arts, um, that the arts would develop, would be *promoted* throughout the nation. And then, individual states throughout the country started to establish their *own* state arts councils to help support the arts. There was kind of a cultural explosion—and by the mid-1970s, by 1974, I think, all 50

N 미국 정부에 대한 수업 중 토론의 일부를 들으시오.

P 지난 시간에는 정부의 예술 지원에 대해 이야기했습니다. 자, 누가 요점 정리해 볼 사람? 프랭크?

M 예, 20세기 이전까지는 공식적인 정부 지원은 사실상 없었던 것 같습니다. 그러나 예술 지원을 위한 미국 정부의 첫 번째 시도는 '연방예술사업'이었습니다.

P 그렇죠, 그 사업에 대해서도 설명해 보겠어요?

M 어, 대공황기인 1930년대에 일자리를 잃은 예술가들을 고용하기 위해 시작되었죠.

P 사업은 성공적이었나요? 재닛? 말해 볼래요?

F 예, 물론 성공적이었습니다. 일례로 평소에 예술을 접하기 힘든 지방 소도시 지역에 지역문화센터와 전시관 등이 많이 건립되었습니다.

P 맞아요.

M 하지만 결국 그저 그런 졸작들에 정부가 거금을 낭비한 건 아닌가요?

P 그렇게 생각할 사람도 있겠지만 연방예술사업의 주된 목적은 고용 창출 아니었나요?

M 그렇습니다. 실직한 수많은 예술가들에게 일자리를 제공하긴 했으니까요.

P 네, 그러다 미국이 제2차 세계대전에 참전하게 되어 실업률이 내려가자 이런 사업들이 더 이상 필요 없어졌죠. 그럼 진도를 나가 볼까요, 이후 어떤 정부도, 실제로 예술에 관여한 정부가 없다가 1960년대 초 케네디 대통령과 정치인들이 예술을 지원하고 진흥하기 위한 상당 규모의 기금 조성을 추진하기 시작했습니다. 정치계 일각에서 자각이 생긴 거죠. 정부는 국가의 혼, 또는 얼이라고 할 수 있는 예술을 지원할 책임이 있다는 것을 깨달은 거죠. 예술인 및 문화 예술 관련 기관들에 대한 연방 보조금, 즉 재정적 지원을 제공한다는 생각이었죠. 바로 그런 취지에서 1965년 '국가예술기금(NEA)'이 탄생했습니다.
이리하여 NEA, 즉 국가예술기금을 통해 예술이 발전하기 시작했고 전국적으로 홍보되었습니다. 그러다 미국 전역에 걸쳐 주정부들이 자체적으로 예술위원회를 설치하여 예술을 지원하기 시작했어요. 그때부터 문화예술사업이 폭발적으로 증가하게 되었고, 1970년대 중반, 그러니까 1974년도까지 제 생각엔 50개 주정부 모두가 산하에 예술사업 기관인 주정부 차원의 예술위원회를 설치하고 연방정부, 기업, 예술가, 공연 등과 연계해 사업을 추진했습니다.

states had their own arts agencies, their own state arts councils that worked with the federal government, with corporations, artists, performers, you name it.

M Did you just say corporations? How were they involved?

P Well, you see, corporations aren't always altruistic, they might not support the arts unless … well, unless the government made it attractive for them to do so, by offering corporations tax incentives to support the arts—that is by letting corporations pay less in taxes if they were patrons of the arts. Uh, the Kennedy Center in Washington, D.C., you may, maybe you've been there, or Lincoln Center in New York. Both of these were built with substantial financial support from corporations. And the Kennedy and Lincoln Centers aren't the only examples—many of your cultural establishments in the United States will have a plaque somewhere acknowledging the support, the money, they've received from whatever corporation. Yes, Janet?

F But aren't there a lot of people who don't think it's the government's role to support the arts?

P Well, as a matter of fact, a lot of politicians who did not believe in government support for the arts, they wanted to do away with the agency entirely for that very reason—to get rid of governmental support—but they only succeeded in taking away about half the annual budget. And as far as the public goes … well, there are about as many individuals who disagree with government support as there are those who agree—in fact, with artists in particular, you have lots of artists who support—and who have benefitted from—this agency, although it seems that just as many artists oppose a government agency being involved in the arts for many different reasons—reasons like they don't want the government to control what they create. In other words … the arguments both for and against government funding of the arts are as many and, and as varied as the individual styles of the artists who hold them.

M 기업이라고 하셨나요? 기업들이 어떤 식으로 관여했나요?

P 기업이 항상 이타적이진 않죠. 아마도 예술 지원에 대한 법인세 혜택을 제공하는 정부의 유인책이 없었더라면 그러니까, 예술을 후원하는 기업에게 법인세를 감면해 주지 않았더라면 기업의 예술 지원은 없었을지도 몰라요. 워싱턴 DC에 있는 케네디센터, 아마 가 본 적 있을 거예요, 뉴욕에 있는 링컨센터, 모두 기업의 상당한 재정 지원으로 건립되었죠. 케네디센터, 링컨센터만 지원을 받은 게 아닙니다. 미국에 있는 수많은 문화 관련 시설에 가 보면 어딘가에는 어떤 기업으로부터 받은 지원이나 후원금에 대한 명판이 걸려 있을 겁니다. 재닛?

F 하지만 예술 지원이 정부의 역할은 아니라고 생각하는 사람들도 많지 않나요?

P 사실 예술 지원은 정부의 몫이 아니라고 생각하는 정치인들도 많고, 바로 그런 이유로 문화예술 관련 기관을 폐지하려고, 즉 정부 지원을 없애고 싶어합니다. 하지만 연간 예산의 절반 정도 밖에 삭감하지 못했어요. 국민들은 어떻게 볼까요. 정부의 예술 지원에 대해서 찬성하는 사람들만큼이나 반대하는 사람들도 많아요. 사실, 많은 예술가들, 특히 이런 기관의 혜택을 받아 본 예술가들은 그런 단체를 지지합니다. 그러나 여러 가지 이유에서 정부가 문화예술에 관여하는 것에 반대하는 예술가들 역시 많습니다. 정부가 창작 행위를 통제하는 것을 원치 않기 때문이죠. 다시 말해, 정부의 예술진흥기금에 대한 찬반 양론은 예술가들의 독자적인 예술 양식만큼이나 많고도 다양합니다.

어휘

endowment 기금 sum up 요약 정리하다 federal 연방정부의 the Depression 대공황(1929년 10월 미국에서 시작된 극심한 불황) out-of-work 일자리를 잃은 rural area 지방 소도시 access to ~을 접할 기회 end up -ing 결국 ~하는 결과를 초래하다 involvement in ~에 관여, 참여 push for ~을 추진하다 promote 진흥하다, 홍보하다 subsidy 보조금, 지원금 financial assistance 재정적 지원 endowment 기금 council 위원회, 협의회 agency 정부기관, 정부조직 you name it 기타 등등 altruistic 이타적인 corporation tax 법인세 incentive 혜택, 장려 patron 후원자 plaque 명판 acknowledge 인정하다 do away with ~을 없애다, 폐지하다 take away 빼앗다

23. 토론의 주된 내용은 무엇인가?

   Ⓐ 미국 정부가 예술을 지원하면 안 되는 이유

   Ⓑ 미국 정부의 예술 지원 역사

   Ⓒ 각종 정부 후원 예술 프로그램들의 장단점

   Ⓓ 정부가 예술가들을 지원할 수 있는 다양한 방법들

어휘 strengths and weaknesses 장단점
      sponsored 후원을 받는

24. 토론에 따르면, 어떤 두 가지 측면에서 연방예술사업이 성공적이었는가? 두 개의 답을 고르시오.

   Ⓐ 미술 학교에 대한 기준을 정립했다.

   Ⓑ 많은 예술가들에게 일자리를 제공했다.

   Ⓒ 뛰어난 예술가를 많이 배출했다.

   Ⓓ 많은 사람들에게 예술을 접할 수 있는 기회를 제공했다.

어휘 produce 배출하다

25. 이 수업에서는 미국 정부의 예술 지원과 관련한 주요 사건들이 논의되고 있다. 이 사건들을 연대순으로 나열하라.

1. 정부는 예술에 대한 공식적 후원을 제공하지 않았다.
2. C
3. D
4 A
5. B

   Ⓐ 미국의 전체 50개 주 산하에 예술위원회가 설치되었다.

   Ⓑ 연방정부의 예술지원 예산이 반으로 삭감되었다.

   Ⓒ 연방예술사업은 실업률 감소에 기여했다.

   Ⓓ 국가예술기금이 설치되었다.

26. 교수가 케네디센터와 링컨센터를 언급한 이유는?

   Ⓐ 기업 후원의 혜택을 입은 기관에 대한 예를 들기 위해

   Ⓑ 일부 예술가들이 문화센터 건립에 반대하는 이유를 설명하려고

   Ⓒ 두 센터가 예술을 지원했던 대통령의 이름을 따서 명명된 경위를 설명하려고

   Ⓓ 대공황기에 정부가 건립한 두 문화센터의 이름을 밝히려고

어휘 institution 기관, 단체   cultural center 문화센터

27. 정부의 문화예술 지원에 대한 예술가들의 의견에 관해 교수가 설명하는 것은?

   Ⓐ 예술가들 대부분은 정부가 더 많은 예술 지원 기금을 제공해야 한다고 생각한다.

   Ⓑ 예술가들 대부분은 정부가 예술을 지원하는 방식에 대해 찬성한다.

   Ⓒ 정부가 예술을 지원해야 하는지에 대해 예술가들 사이에도 이견이 있다.

   Ⓓ 예술가들조차도 정부의 예술 지원을 폄하한다.

어휘 approve of ~에 찬성하다, ~을 승인하다
      have a low opinion of ~을 폄하하다, 얕보다

28. 강의를 일부를 다시 듣고 질문에 답하라.

 T-9

> M Yeah, but didn't the government end up wasting a lot of money for art that wasn't even very good?
>
> P Uh, *some* people might say that, but wasn't the *primary* objective of the Federal Art Project to *provide jobs*?
>
> N *What does the professor imply when she says this:*
>
> P Uh, *some* people might say that, but wasn't the *primary* objective of the Federal Art Project to *provide jobs*?

   Ⓐ 다른 학생들이 남자의 발언을 평가해야 한다.

   Ⓑ 대부분의 사람들이 남자의 의견에 동의할 것이다.

   Ⓒ 정부 지원을 받은 작품은 대개 수준이 높다.

   Ⓓ 정부의 예술지원 사업은 돈 낭비가 아니었다.

어휘 remark 발언   artwork 예술작품

SPEAKING

Question 1

Narrator T-10

Many universities now offer academic courses over the Internet. However, some people still prefer learning in traditional classrooms. Which do you think is better? Explain why.

요즘 많은 대학들이 인터넷 강좌를 제공하고 있다. 하지만 여전히 전통적인 강의실 수업을 선호하는 사람들이 있다. 둘 중 어느 쪽이 더 나은지 밝히고 이유를 설명하시오.

준비 시간 : 15초
답변 시간 : 45초

중요 포인트

우선 인터넷 강의와 강의실 수업 중 무엇을 선호하는지 명확히 밝힌 다음 그 이유를 설명해야 한다. 만일 인터넷 등 온라인 매체를 통한 수강이 더 효율적이라고 생각한다면 "Internet or online courses are more effective because a student can study at anytime from anywhere." ("인터넷 또는 온라인 강좌는 언제 어디서든 수강할 수 있기 때문에 더 효율적이다.")라고 이유를 들 수 있다.

여기서 더 나아가 실제 경험담을 첨언할 수도 있다. 예를 들어 "I learn best in the evenings and so online courses allow me to learn when I am best able to concentrate, whereas in a traditional classroom, I have to concentrate at a particular time." (나는 밤에 공부가 잘되는데 교실 수업의 경우 억지로 집중해야 하는 특정 시간에 출석해야 하지만 온라인 강좌는 가장 집중력이 높은 시간에 배울 수 있어 좋다.")라고 풀어나갈 수 있다.

강의실 수업을 선호하는 경우 강의실 학습의 효과적 요소를 예로 든다. 대면 수업의 중요성을 강조하면서 이것이 학습에 어떻게 긍정적으로 작용할 수 있는지 설명해 보자.

Question 2

Narrator T-11

The computer department is considering making a scheduling change. You will have 45 seconds to read an article in the campus newspaper about the change. Begin reading now.

컴퓨터학과는 일정 변경을 고려하고 있다. 일정 변경과 관련한 대학 신문의 기사를 45초간 읽으시오. 지금 읽으시오.

Evening Computer Classes May Be Added

The computer department is considering offering evening classes in the fall. The proposal to add the classes is a response to student complaints that daytime computer classes have become increasingly overcrowded and there are no longer enough computers available. The department has decided that despite some added expense, the most cost-effective way of addressing this problem is by adding computer classes in the evening. It is hoped that this change will decrease the number of students enrolled in day classes and thus guarantee individual access to computers for all students in computer classes.

컴퓨터 야간 강좌 추가 예정

컴퓨터학과는 가을에 야간 강좌 개설을 검토하고 있다. 강좌 추가 제안은 주간 컴퓨터 강좌에 점점 수강생이 많이 몰려 컴퓨터가 모자란다는 학생들의 불만에 대한 대응책으로 마련된 것이다. 컴퓨터학과는 비용 증가에도 불구하고 가장 비용효율적인 문제 해결 방안은 야간 강좌 개설이라고 판단했다. 이번 변화로 주간 강좌 수강 인원이 줄어서 컴퓨터 수업 수강자 전원에게 각각 컴퓨터가 확실히 배정되기를 바란다.

어휘

department 학과, 부서   overcrowded 너무 붐비다   cost-effective 비용효율적인   address (문제) 해결하다, 다루다   guarantee 확실하게 하다, 보장하다   individual 각각의

Narrator T-12

Now listen to two students discussing the article.

신문 기사에 대한 두 학생의 대화를 들으시오.

(Script)

M I just don't think this will work.

F Why not?

M Because it's not gonna solve the problem. Students are busy at night … I mean, we have jobs, families, clubs, social events. Most of us already have something to do every single night of the week.

F I see your point. I sure couldn't fit anything into my schedule during the week—I've got swimming practice most nights.

M Right. And as far as expense goes, I think they're going about it the wrong way. I mean, it costs money to hire more teachers and keep the academic building open later. Which is a lot more expensive than just simply buying more computers.

F More computers?

M That's right. Computer prices have come way down the past few years, so the department won't have to spend as much now as they did in the past. Besides, the computer department classrooms, you know, the rooms themselves, they're actually very big … there's plenty of space to add more computers.

M 이거 잘 안 될 걸.

F 왜?

M 문제가 해결될 리 없으니까. 애들은 밤에 바빠. 일도 해야지, 가족과 시간도 보내야지, 동호회 활동에 모임도 있고 주중에는 대부분 매일 저녁마다 할 일이 있단 말이지.

F 그건 그래. 나만 해도 주중에 다른 일정을 끼워 넣을 수가 없거든. 저녁엔 대부분 수영 연습을 해서 말이야.

M 그렇지. 비용을 따져 봐도 잘못 생각하는 거 같아. 강사를 더 쓰고 강의동도 늦게까지 열어 놓으려면 비용이 꽤 들거야. 컴퓨터 몇 대 더 구입하는 것보다 훨씬 돈이 많이 들 텐데.

F 컴퓨터를 더?

M 그래, 최근 몇 년 사이에 컴퓨터 가격이 상당히 내려가서 예전처럼 돈을 많이 쓰지 않아도 될거야. 게다가 컴퓨터 학과 강의실은 워낙 커서 컴퓨터 더 들여 놓을 공간이 충분해.

어휘

work 효과가 있다   **social event** 사교 모임   **see one's point** 상대방의 의도를 알아듣다   **as far as ~ goes** ~라는 측면에서   **go about it** 접근하다, 다루다

Narrator

The man expresses his opinion about the proposal described in the article. Briefly summarize the proposal. Then state his opinion about the proposal and explain the reasons he gives for holding that opinion.

남자가 신문 기사에 실린 제안에 대한 의견을 말하고 있다. 제안을 간략히 요약한 다음, 남자의 의견이 무엇이며 그런 입장을 취하는 이유를 설명하시오.

준비 시간 : 30초
답변 시간 : 60초

중요 포인트

먼저 지시문대로 컴퓨터학과에서 야간 강좌를 개설하려 한다는 제안을 요약해야 한다. 그리고 왜 그런 제안을 하는지에 대한 요약(낮 시간대 강좌의 붐빔 현상)도 덧붙일 수 있다. 하지만 제안의 요약에 많은 시간을 할애해서는 안 된다. 그렇게 되면, 남학생이 제안에 반대하는 이유를 말할 시간이 모자라게 된다. 이런 유형의 질문에는 최소한의 요약만이 필요하다.

제안을 요약한 후 야간 강좌 개설에 대한 남학생의 의견을 말하면 되는데, 남학생은 학교의 제안에 반대하고 있다. 그렇다면 남학생이 반대하는 두 가지 이유를 설명하면 된다. 답변의 완성도를 높이기 위해 대화에서 얻은 정보와 독해 지문에서 나온 내용의 연결 고리를 맞추어야 한다.

먼저, 남학생은 학생들 대부분이 저녁에 시간이 없기 때문에 야간 수업 개설이 해결책이 아니라고 생각한다. 아르바이트, 모임 등 학생들이 저녁에 시간이 없는 이유를 덧붙여도 된다.

둘째로 야간 강좌를 개설하면 개설 비용이 많이 들어 비용을 절감할 수 없다는 남학생의 두 번째 반대 의견을 말하고, 그 근거로 강사비보다 컴퓨터 구입 비용이 더 저렴하다, 강의실을 늦게까지 개방하는 비용이 만만찮다, 강의실이 넓어 컴퓨터 몇 대를 더 수용할 여유 공간이 있다, 컴퓨터 값이 많이 저렴해졌다는 등의 이유를 첨언한다.

Narrator T-13

Now read a passage from a psychology textbook. You have 45 seconds to read the passage. Begin reading now.

심리학 교재에서 발췌한 지문을 45초 동안 읽으시오. 지금 읽으시오.

Verbal and Nonverbal Communication

When we speak with other people face-to-face, the nonverbal signals we give—our facial expressions, hand gestures, body movements, and tone of voice—often communicate as much as, or more than, the words we utter. When our nonverbal signals, which we often produce unconsciously, agree with our verbal message, the verbal message is enhanced and supported, made more convincing. But when they conflict with the verbal message, we may be communicating an entirely different and more accurate message than what we intend.

언어적 의사소통과 비언어적 의사소통

다른 사람들과 대면하여 이야기할 때, 우리가 보내는 비언어적 신호, 즉 얼굴 표정, 손짓, 몸의 움직임, 목소리 톤은 종종 입 밖에 내는 단어만큼이나 많은 혹은 그 이상의 의미를 전달한다. 우리의 비언어적 신호, 이는 종종 우리가 무의식적으로 만드는 것인데, 이것이 언어적 메시지와 일치할 때 언어적 메시지는 강화되고 뒷받침되며 설득력이 높아진다. 그러나 비언어적 신호가 언어적 메시지와 상충할 경우 의도와 전혀 다르고 더 정확한 메시지를 전달하게 될 수도 있다.

어휘

verbal 언어적   nonverbal 비언어적   face-to-face 대면으로, 얼굴을 직접 마주보고   utter 입 밖에 내다, 발설하다   unconsciously 무의식적으로   enhance 강화하다, 끌어올리다   convincing 설득력이 있는, 그럴싸한

Narrator T-14

Now listen to part of a lecture on this topic in a psychology course.

이 주제에 관한 심리학 강의의 일부를 들으시오.

Script

P   Last month my favorite uncle paid me a surprise visit. I hadn't seen him in many years ... The doorbell rang, I opened the door, and there was Uncle Pete. Now, I'm sure when I saw him I said something like: "Uncle Pete! What a surprise! How nice to see you!" Anyway, my wife was standing next to me and according to her—I wasn't really aware of this—my eyes got really wide and I broke into a huge big smile. She said I was actually jumping up and down, like a little boy. Well, anyway, later that evening Uncle Pete told me how very, very good he felt when he saw how happy I was to see him.

But compare that with this: my daughter ... she's six ... We were building a birdhouse together last week. And I was showing her how to use a hammer and nail. And of course, stupid me, I wasn't being very careful and I smashed my thumb with the hammer. Boy, did it hurt! I almost felt like screaming, but I didn't want to upset my daughter, so I said, "Don't worry, honey. It's nothing." Meanwhile, I was shaking my hand, as if that would stop my thumb from hurting, and my face was contorted in pain. My voice was trembling too. So even though I told my daughter I was OK, I'm sure she didn't believe me. Because she kept asking me if I was OK.

P   지난 달 제가 제일 좋아하는 삼촌께서 깜짝 방문하셨어요. 뵌 지 여러 해 되었죠. 초인종이 울려 나가 보았더니 글쎄 피트 삼촌이 있었어요. 저는 삼촌을 보자 대충 이렇게 말했던 것 같아요. "피트 삼촌! 웬일이세요! 이렇게 뵙게 되어서 정말 반가워요." 아무튼 그때 아내가 제 옆에 서 있었는데 아내 말에 따르면, 저는 전혀 의식하지 못했지만, 제 눈이 휘둥그렇게 되더니 갑자기 활짝 웃더라는 겁니다. 아내 말로는 제가 마치 어린 아이처럼 폴짝폴짝 뛰었다고 해요. 어쨌든 그날 저녁 피트 삼촌은 제가 그렇게 좋아하는 모습을 보니 정말 기분이 좋았다고 말씀하셨죠.

이제 다음 상황과 비교해 보세요. 제겐 여섯 살 난 딸이 있죠. 지난 주 우린 새집을 함께 지었는데 제가 아이에게 망치와 못 쓰는 법을 가르쳐 주고 있었어요. 물론 멍청하게도 저는 부주의한 나머지 망치로 제 엄지를 내리쳤답니다. 정말 아팠죠! 비명을 지르고 싶었지만 딸이 속상해할까 봐 이렇게 말했어요. "괜찮아, 아무것도 아냐." 말은 그렇게 했지만 저는 손을 털었어요. 그렇게 하면 엄지 통증이 없어지기라도 하는 냥 말이죠. 그리고 얼굴은 고통으로 일그러져 있었죠. 목소리도 떨리고 있었고요. 그래서 제가 괜찮다고 말했지만 딸 아이는 제 말을 믿지 않은 게 분명해요. 괜찮으냐고 계속 물었으니까요.

어휘

surprise visit 깜짝 방문   break into (웃음, 울음 등을) 갑자기 터뜨리다
smash 후려치다   scream 비명을 지르다   contort 일그러뜨리다
tremble 떨리다

Narrator

Explain how the examples from the professor's lecture illustrate the relationship between verbal and nonverbal communication.

강의에서 교수가 말하고 있는 예시들이 언어적 의사소통과 비언어적 의사소통 간의 관계를 어떻게 예증하는지 설명하시오.

준비 시간 : 30초
답변 시간 : 60초

중요 포인트

우선 언어적 의사소통과 비언어적 의사소통이 어떠한 관계인지 밝히고 교수가 강의에서 언급한 예시가 독해 지문의 내용을 어떻게 뒷받침하는지를 설명한다. 강의에서 나온 적절한 예와 논지를 활용해야 하며, 강의에 나오지 않은 내용을 언급하면 안 된다.

답변 서두에서 독해 지문의 내용을 간략히 요약하는 것이 좋다. 언어적 의사소통과 비언어적 의사소통에 대한 정의를 내리자. 때로는 손짓, 몸짓이 말만큼 효과적으로 의사를 전달한다는 설명으로 풀어도 좋다. 비언어적 신호로 전달되는 메시지가 언어로 전달되는 메시지와 부합할 수도 혹은 상충할 수도 있다는 점을 언급할 수도 있다.

이어서 교수가 말한 예가 독해 지문의 일반적 개념에 어떻게 부합하는지 설명한다. 첫 번째로, 교수가 삼촌을 오랜만에 만났을 때 활짝 웃었던지 펄쩍펄쩍 뛰었다던지 등 좋은 기분을 나타내는 비언어적 행동이 교수가 전하고자 하는 의사와 합치했다는 것을 설명하자. 또한 그런 행동으로 삼촌의 기분이 좋아졌다는 내용을 함께 언급해도 된다.

그리고 두 번째 예를 든다. 이 두 번째 사례에서 교수는 망치로 손을 때렸으나 딸을 안심시키려고 걱정하지 말라고 했다. 그러나 말과 행동이 일치하지 못했다. 즉 통증으로 손을 떨었고 목소리 또한 떨렸기 때문에 딸이 교수의 언어적 메시지를 믿지 않았다. 바로 비언어적 메시지가 더 정확했던 경우다.

강의나 독해 지문의 내용을 모두 반복할 시간 여유가 없으며 또한 그렇게 해서도 안 된다. 강의와 독해 지문의 요점을 적절히 취합하여 답을 완성하기만 하면 된다.

Question 4

p.44

Narrator T-15

Listen to part of a talk in an art appreciation class.

미술 감상에 대한 강의의 일부를 들으시오.

Script

P   In order for art to communicate—to appeal to the emotions or the intellect—it has to combine various *visual elements* to express meaning ... or emotion. It's really the visual components of the work—things like color, texture, shape, lines—and how these elements work together that tell *us* something about the work. Artists combine and manipulate these visual elements to express a message or to create a mood.

Think about how a painter might use *color*, for example. You all know from experience that different colors appeal in different ways to the senses and can convey different meanings. An artist chooses certain colors to evoke a particular mood and make powerful statements. The color red, for example, is a strong color and can conjure up strong emotions ... such as extreme joy, or excitement ... or even anger. Blue, on the other hand, is considered a cool color. Blue colors tend to have a calming effect on viewers.

Another visual element important to art is texture. By texture, I mean the surface quality or "feel" of the work ... its smoothness, or roughness, or softness. ... Now, of course, in some types of art, the texture is physical—it can actually be touched by the fingers. But in painting, for example, texture can be visual. The way an artist paints certain areas of a painting can create the illusion of texture ... an object's smoothness, or roughness, or softness. A rough texture can evoke stronger emotions and strength while a smooth texture is more calming and less emotional.

As I said earlier, artists often combine elements to convey a message about the work. Take a painting that, say, uses a lot of strong colors like reds and oranges and … and uses brushstrokes that are broad—wide, sweeping brushstrokes that suggest a rough texture. Well, these elements together can convey a wilder, more chaotic emotion in the viewer than, more than in, say … a painting with tiny, smooth brushstrokes and soft or pale colors. Artists use these visual effects and the senses they arouse to give meaning to their work.

P 미술이 소통하려면, 즉 감성이나 지성에 호소하려면 의미나 감정을 표현할 수 있는 다양한 시각적 요소들을 결합해야 합니다. 작품의 시각적 구성요소, 즉 색, 질감, 형태, 선 같은 시각적 구성요소들, 그리고 이것들이 어우러져 함께 작용하는 방식이 작품에 대한 얘기를 들려주는 거죠. 화가들은 이런 시각적 요소들을 결합하고 조작해 메시지를 표현하거나 분위기를 만들어냅니다.

예를 들어 화가가 어떤 식으로 색을 사용하는지 생각해 봅시다. 여러분도 경험을 통해 알 거예요, 색깔마다 감각에 호소하는 방식이 달라서 각기 다른 의미를 전달하죠. 화가는 어떤 특정한 기분을 불러일으켜 강력한 표현을 전달하고자 특정 색들을 선택합니다. 예를 들어, 빨강은 강렬한 색으로 극심한 기쁨이나 흥분 또는 분노 같은 격한 감정을 불러일으키죠. 반면 파랑은 차분한 색으로 간주되죠. 청색 계통은 보는 사람의 감정을 진정시키는 효과가 있어요.

미술에서 중요한 또 다른 시각적 요소는 질감입니다. 여기서 질감이라는 것은 표면의 질감이나 작품이 주는 '촉감'을 말합니다. 매끄러움, 거칠거칠함, 부드러움 등등. 물론 미술 유형에 따라 질감을 직접 신체로 느낄 수 있죠, 손끝으로 만져볼 수 있으니까요. 하지만 회화의 경우 질감은 시각적일 수 있죠. 작가가 화폭의 특정 영역들을 그려낸 방식에 따라 질감에 대한 착시가 일어납니다. 사물이 매끄러워 보이기도 하고, 거칠게 보이기도 하고, 부드럽게 보이기도 하는 거죠. 거친 질감은 더 강렬한 감정이나 힘을 불러일으키는 반면 매끄러운 질감은 더 차분하고 감정을 덜 자극하죠.

앞에서 말했듯이 화가들은 작품의 메시지를 전달하기 위해 종종 여러 요소들을 결합합니다. 회화의 예를 들면, 빨강, 주홍 같은 강렬한 색상을 쓰고, 붓놀림을 넓게 해서, 넓게 쓸어내리면 거친 질감이 표현되죠. 이런 요소들이 어우러져 보는 사람에게는 부드럽고 옅은 색으로 작고 부드러운 붓놀림으로 그린 경우보다는 더 거칠고, 혼란스러운 감정을 전달하게 됩니다.

어휘

art appreciation 미술 감상 appeal to ~에게 호소하다 emotion 감성, 감정 intellect 지성, 이성 visual 시각의 component 구성요소 texture 질감 manipulate 조작하다, 다루다 convey meaning 의미를 전달하다 evoke(=conjure up) ~을 불러일으키다 extreme 극단적인, 극심한 calming effect 진정 효과 viewer 보는 사람, 감상자 illusion 환상, 착시 brushstroke 붓놀림, 필법 sweeping 쓸어내리는 chaotic 혼란스러운, 무질서한 pale 옅은, 희미한 arouse (감정, 태도를) 불러일으키다

Narrator

Using points and examples from the lecture, explain the importance of visual elements in painting.

강의에 제시된 논지와 예시를 사용해 회화에서 시각적 요소의 중요성을 설명하시오.

준비 시간 : 20초
답변 시간 : 60초

중요 포인트

반드시 들은 강의 내용에 나온 논지와 예시만을 활용해 대답해야 한다. 답을 시작할 때 시각적 요소가 회화의 의미를 전달하거나 감성을 표현하는 기제로 작용한다는 주제에 대해 간략히 언급해야 한다. 그러고 나서 교수가 근거로 제시한 여러 논점을 설명한다. 가령, 색감이 감정을 유발할 수 있는데 빨강은 분노를 일으키고, 청색은 마음을 차분하게 가라앉힌다는 등의 예를 덧붙인다. 그런 다음 물리적 질감과 시각적 질감이 있을 수 있는데 부드러운 질감에는 진정효과가 있다는 식으로 예를 든다. 또한 작품의 메시지 전달을 위해 화가들이 여러 요소들을 결합하기도 한다고 언급하면서 빨강에 거친 필법이 결합되면 혼돈과 격한 감정이 표현된다고 예를 들 수 있다.

WRITING

Writing Based on Reading and Listening

p.46

Endotherms are animals such as modern birds and mammals that keep their body temperatures constant. For instance, humans are endotherms and maintain an internal temperature of 37°C, no matter whether the environment is warm or cold. Because dinosaurs were reptiles, and modern reptiles are not endotherms, it was long assumed that dinosaurs were not endotherms. However, dinosaurs differ in many ways from modern reptiles, and there is now considerable evidence that dinosaurs were, in fact, endotherms.

Polar dinosaurs

One reason for believing that dinosaurs were endotherms is that dinosaur fossils have been discovered in polar regions. Only animals that can maintain a temperature well above that of the surrounding environment could be active in such cold climates.

Leg position and movement

There is a connection between endothermy and the position and movement of the legs. The physiology of endothermy allows sustained physical activity, such as running. But running is efficient only if an animal's legs are positioned underneath its body, not at the body's side, as they are for crocodiles and many lizards. The legs of all modern endotherms are underneath the body, and so were the legs of dinosaurs. This strongly suggests that dinosaurs were endotherms.

Haversian canals

There is also a connection between endothermy and bone structure. The bones of endotherms usually include structures called Haversian canals. These canals house nerves and blood vessels that allow the living animal to grow quickly, and rapid body growth is in fact a characteristic of endothermy. The presence of Haversian canals in bone is a strong indicator that the animal is an endotherm, and fossilized bones of dinosaurs are usually dense with Haversian canals.

온혈동물은 현생 조류, 포유류처럼 체온을 일정하게 유지하는 동물이다. 예를 들어, 인간은 온혈동물로 주변이 따뜻하건 춥건 체온을 섭씨 37도로 유지한다. 공룡은 파충류고, 현생 파충류는 온혈동물이 아니므로 오랫동안 공룡은 온혈동물이 아니라고 추정했다. 그러나 공룡은 여러 가지 면에서 현생 파충류와 다르고, 공룡이 사실은 온혈동물이었다는 중요한 증거가 현재 있다.

극지방 공룡

공룡이 온혈동물이었다고 믿는 한 가지 이유는 공룡의 화석이 극지방에서 발견되고 있다는 점이다. 주변 환경의 온도보다 훨씬 높은 체온을 유지할 수 있는 동물만이 그렇게 추운 기후에서도 활동할 수 있다.

다리의 위치와 움직임

내온성과 다리의 위치 및 움직임 간에는 연관관계가 있다. 내온성의 생리학은 달리기 같은 지속적인 신체 활동을 가능하게 한다. 그러나 동물의 다리가 악어나 많은 도마뱀처럼 몸 측면에 붙어 있지 않고 몸 밑에 있어야만 달리는 동작이 효율적이다. 모든 현생 항온동물들의 다리는 몸 밑에 붙어 있고 공룡의 다리도 마찬가지였다. 이는 공룡이 온혈동물이었음을 강력하게 시사한다.

하버스관

내온성과 뼈의 구조 간에도 연관관계가 있다. 온혈동물의 뼈에는 대개 하버스관이라고 하는 조직이 포함되어 있다. 이들 관에는 살아 있는 동물을 빠르게 성장시키는 신경과 혈관이 들어 있는데, 빠른 성장은 사실 내온성의 특징이다. 뼛속에 하버스관이 있다는 것은 그 동물이 온혈동물이라는 강력한 표시이며 화석화된 공룡의 뼈에는 대개 하버스관이 빽빽하게 들어 있다.

어휘

endotherm 온혈동물   mammal 포유류   constant 일정한   reptile 파충류   assume 추정하다   considerable 상당한, 중요한   polar dinosaur 극지방 공룡   physiology 생리학   sustained 지속되는   Haversian canal 하버스관(뼛속의 모세혈관)   nerve 신경   blood vessel 혈관   indicator 표지, 표식   fossilized 화석화된   dense with ~으로 빽빽한

Narrator 🎧 T-16

Now listen to part of a lecture on the topic you just read about.

방금 읽은 주제에 관한 강의의 일부를 들으시오

Script

P Many scientists have problems with the arguments you read in the passage. They don't think those arguments prove that dinosaurs were endotherms. Take the polar dinosaur argument. When dinosaurs lived, even the polar regions where dinosaur fossils have been found were much warmer than today—warm enough during part of the year for animals that were not endotherms to live. And during the months when the polar regions were cold, the so-called polar dinosaurs could have migrated to warmer areas or hibernated like many modern reptiles do. So the presence of dinosaur fossils in polar regions doesn't prove the dinosaurs were endotherms.

Well, what about the fact that dinosaurs had their legs placed under their bodies, not out to the side, like a crocodile's? That doesn't necessarily mean dinosaurs were high-energy endotherms built for running. There's another explanation for having legs under the body: this body structure supports more weight. So with the legs under their bodies, dinosaurs could grow to a very large size. Being large had advantages for dinosaurs, so we don't need the idea of endothermy and running to explain why dinosaurs evolved to have their legs under their bodies.

OK, so how about bone structure? Many dinosaur bones do have Haversian canals, that's true, but dinosaur bones also have growth rings. Growth rings are a thickening of the bone that indicates periods of time when the dinosaurs weren't rapidly growing. These growth rings are evidence that dinosaurs stopped growing or grew more slowly during cooler periods. This pattern of periodic growth—ya know, rapid growth followed by no growth or slow growth and then rapid growth again—is characteristic of animals that are not endotherms. Animals that maintain a constant body temperature year round, as true endotherms do, grow rapidly even when the environment becomes cool.

P 많은 과학자들은 여러분이 방금 읽은 지문에 제기된 주장에 동의하지 않습니다. 그러한 주장들이 공룡이 온혈동물임을 입증하지 못한다고 생각하죠.

극지방 공룡에 대한 주장을 봅시다. 공룡이 살았을 당시엔 공룡 화석이 발견되었던 극지방도 요즘보다 훨씬 따뜻했습니다. 연중 어떤 기간에는 변온동물이 살 수 있었어요. 그리고 몇 달 동안 극지방이 추울 때면 소위 극지방 공룡들은 따뜻한 지역으로 이동하거나 많은 현생 파충류처럼 동면했을 수도 있죠. 따라서 극지방에 존재하는 공룡 화석이 공룡이 온혈동물임을 입증하지는 못합니다.

그렇다면 공룡의 다리가 악어처럼 측면으로 나와 있지 않고 몸 밑에 있다는 건 어떨까요? 그렇다고 해서 반드시 공룡이 달리기를 할 수 있는 몸 구조를 가진 고에너지 온혈동물이라고 할 순 없습니다. 다리가 몸 밑에 있는 이유를 설명하는 또 다른 가설이 있습니다. 이런 몸 구조가 많은 무게를 지탱한다는 겁니다. 따라서 다리가 몸 밑에 있어 공룡은 그렇게 몸집이 커질 수 있었습니다. 몸집이 크면 공룡에게 유리했고, 따라서 내온성 또는 달리기 위한 몸 구조는 공룡의 다리가 몸 밑에 붙도록 진화한 이유를 설명하는 데 반드시 필요한 개념은 아닙니다.

좋아요, 그렇다면 뼈의 구조는 어떨까요? 많은 공룡 뼈에 하버스관이 있는 건 사실입니다. 하지만 공룡 뼈에는 나이테도 있습니다. 나이테는 뼈가 굵어지는 것, 즉 공룡이 급격히 성장하지 않는 시기를 표시합니다. 이런 나이테는 공룡이 추운 기간 동안 성장을 멈추었거나 느리게 성장했다는 증거죠. 이런 주기적 성장 패턴, 즉 급성장, 정체 또는 저성장 그리고 다시 급성장을 반복하는 것은 변온동물의 특징입니다. 진정한 온혈동물이 그렇듯 연중 일정한 체온을 유지하는 동물들은 주변 환경이 추워져도 급속히 성장합니다.

어휘

migrate 이동[이주]하다 **hibernate** 동면하다 **presence** 존재 **not necessarily mean** 반드시 ~라는 뜻은 아니다 **high-energy endotherm** 고에너지 온혈동물 **support** 지탱하다 **endothermy** 내온성(동물의 체온이 체내에서 발생하는 대사열로 유지되는 성질) **evolve** 진화하다 **growth ring** 나이테 **thickening** 두꺼워짐 **indicate** 뜻하다, 시사하다 **periodic** 주기적인

Narrator T-17

Question 1

Summarize the points made in the lecture, being sure to explain how they challenge the specific points made in the reading passage.

방금 들은 강의의 논점들을 요약하되 이 논점들이 독해 지문의 구체적 논점들을 어떻게 반박하고 있는지 설명하시오.

해설

강의에서 중요한 점은 교수가 공룡이 온혈동물이었다는 독해 지문에 동의하지 않는 것이다. 즉, 공룡이 극지방에 살았고, 공룡의 다리는 몸체 아래에 붙어 있고 공룡의 뼈에는 하버스관이라는 구조가 있다는 점에 대해 교수는 회의적인 견해를 갖고 있다. 답변 시 교수가 지문에 제시된 근거만으로는 공룡이 온혈동물이었다고 할 수 없다고 말한 이유를 설명해야 한다. 높은 점수를 받으려면 지문의 요점에 대한 교수의 반론을 언급해야 한다. 정확한 문장 구조와 어휘력을 구사하여 표에 들어 있는 세 가지 요점 모두를 명확하게 설명해야만 5점을 받을 수 있다.

지문의 주요 내용	지문과 대조되는 강의 내용	지문의 주요 내용	지문과 대조되는 강의 내용
The presence of dinosaur fossils in the polar regions indicates that dinosaurs were able to survive in very cold climates and therefore must have been endotherms.	When dinosaurs lived, the polar regions were much warmer than they are today, so even animals that were not endotherms could have survived there for at least part of the year. Furthermore, polar dinosaurs could have migrated or hibernated during the months when the temperatures were the coldest.	Dinosaurs' bones contained Haversian canals, structures that allow for fast bone growth and, again, are typical of endotherms.	Despite containing Haversian canals, dinosaur bones also had features one would expect to see in animals that are not endotherms. In particular, dinosaur bones contained growth rings, which indicate periods of slow growth alternating with periods of fast growth. Such an uneven pattern of growth is typical of animals that are not endotherms.
Dinosaurs' legs were positioned underneath their bodies. Such leg positioning allows for running and similar physical activities typical of endotherms.	The positioning of dinosaurs' legs underneath their bodies may have served a function unrelated to running and similar activities. The positioning of legs underneath the body may have evolved to support the great body weight of many dinosaurs.		

Question 2

Your professor is teaching a class on sociology. Write a post responding to the professor's question.

In your response, you should do the following.

- Express and support your opinion.
- Make a contribution to the discussion in your own words.

An effective response will contain at least 100 words.

Dr. Achebe

Recently economic and technological changes have made it possible for some people to give up the idea of a "home" as a city or town where one resides for many years, thus becoming more nomadic—living and working from place to place, without ever "settling down" in one location. For those with the means to accomplish it, this lifestyle might be very fulfilling or liberating, but there must be disadvantages as well. What do you think those disadvantages are?

Claire

I think this is a romantic idea that is only realistic for younger people. As people age, they need more and more support. For example, it is helpful for them to have a regular doctor who knows their medical history. That sort of support can't happen if you're always moving.

Kelly

Being a modern nomad seems appealing, but how empowering is it? The disadvantage to this lifestyle is that you will likely feel like a foreigner in the places you spend your time, and that can be an obstacle to your success. Only at "home," where you feel culturally connected to other people within familiar surroundings, can you really thrive.

교수가 사회학 강의를 진행하고 있다. 교수의 질문에 답하는 게시글을 작성하시오.

답변은 다음 조건을 충족해야 한다.

– 의견을 표명하고 뒷받침하는 근거를 제시한다.
– 독자적인 표현과 관점으로 토론에 기여한다.
어느 정도 완성도를 갖추려면 최소 100단어 이상이어야 한다.

Dr. Achebe

최근 경제적, 기술적 변화들로 일부 사람들은 오래 거주하는 도시 혹은 마을로서 '집'의 개념을 포기하고 유목민처럼 사는 게 가능합니다. 결코 한 장소에 '정착'하지 않고 여기저기 이동하며 살고 일하죠. 이런 생활방식을 실현할 수 있는 수단을 가진 사람이라면 이런 생활이 무척 만족스럽거나 자유롭겠지만, 분명 단점도 있을 겁니다. 단점이 무엇이라고 생각하나요?

Claire

젊은 사람들에게나 가능하지, 낭만적인 생각 같아요. 나이 들수록 보살핌이 더욱 필요하죠. 예를 들어 자신의 병력 정보를 아는 주치의가 있으면 도움이 돼요. 그런데 늘 옮겨 다니면 이런 보살핌을 받을 수 없어요.

Kelly

현대판 유목민이라니 솔깃하지만, 얼마나 힘이 될까요? 이 생활방식의 단점은 지내는 장소에서 이방인이 된 듯한 기분이 든다는 점인데, 이런 느낌은 성공에 걸림돌이 될 수 있죠. 사람은 '집'에 있을 때 진정으로 성장하죠. 그러니까 익숙한 환경 속에서 다른 사람들과 문화적으로 연결되어 있다고 느껴야 해요.

해설
현대판 유목 생활의 잠재적 단점에 관한 토론이다. 고득점을 받으려면 이러한 토론에 기여하는 논지를 펼치며 답변해야 한다. 어느 정도 완성도를 갖추려면 최소 100단어 이상이어야 한다.

한 토론 참여자는 떠도는 생활이 젊은 층에게는 만족감을 줄 수 있지만, 나이 든 사람에게는 이런 생활방식이 문제가 될 수 있다고 주장한다. 나이 든 사람은 현대판 유목 생활에서 누릴 수 없는 안정과 보살핌을 소중히 여기기 때문이다. 또 다른 토론 참여자는 잦은 이동으로 소속감을 느끼지 못하는 것이 이런 생활방식의 중요한 단점이라고 주장한다. 답변 시 이미 서술된 개념을 포착해 더 상세히 논지를 전개해도 좋고 전혀 새로운 개념을 선보여도 좋다. 예를 들어 잠재적인 단점으로 한 장소에서 다른 장소로 이동하는 비용이나 끊임없이 이동하면 친구를 오래 사귀기 어렵다는 점을 지적할 수 있다.

반드시 자신의 의견을 뒷받침하는 탄탄한 근거와 예시를 제시하고 명확하게 표현해야 한다. 답안이 온라인 게시물 형태로 나타나므로 여러 단락으로 나누어 구성할 필요는 없다. 하지만 개념 간 연관성이 밀접하며 조리 있고 명료해야 한다. 채점은 '학술 토론을 위한 글쓰기 평가 기준(Appendix 참조)'을 토대로 이루어진다.

READING

MINERALS AND PLANTS

미네랄과 식물   *p.54*

1. Research has shown that certain minerals are required by plants for normal growth and development. The soil is the source of these minerals, which are absorbed by the plant with the water from the soil. Even nitrogen, which is a gas in its elemental state, is normally absorbed from the soil as nitrate ions. Some soils are notoriously deficient in micro nutrients and are therefore unable to support most plant life. So-called serpentine soils, for example, are deficient in calcium, and only plants able to tolerate low levels of this mineral can survive. In modern agriculture, mineral depletion of soils is a major concern, since harvesting crops interrupts the recycling of nutrients back to the soil.

2. Mineral deficiencies can often be detected by specific symptoms such as chlorosis (loss of chlorophyll resulting in yellow or white leaf tissue), necrosis (isolated dead patches), anthocyanin formation (development of deep red pigmentation of leaves or stem), stunted growth, and development of woody tissue in an herbaceous plant. Soils are most commonly deficient in nitrogen and phosphorus. Nitrogen-deficient plants exhibit many of the symptoms just described. Leaves develop chlorosis; stems are short and slender; and anthocyanin discoloration occurs on stems, petioles, and lower leaf surfaces. Phosphorus-deficient plants are often stunted, with leaves turning a characteristic dark green, often with the accumulation of anthocyanin. Typically, older leaves are affected first as the phosphorus is mobilized to young growing tissue. Iron deficiency is characterized by chlorosis between veins in young leaves.

3. Much of the research on nutrient deficiencies is based on growing plants hydroponically, that is, in soilless liquid nutrient solutions. This technique allows researchers to create solutions that selectively omit certain nutrients and then observe the resulting effects on the plants. Hydroponics has applications beyond basic research, since it facilitates the growing of greenhouse vegetables during winter. Aeroponics, a technique in which plants are suspended and the roots misted with a nutrient solution, is another method for growing plants without soil.

4. While mineral deficiencies can limit the growth of plants, an overabundance of certain minerals can be toxic and can also limit growth. Saline soils, which have high concentrations of sodium chloride and other salts, limit plant growth, and research continues to focus on developing salt-tolerant varieties of agricultural crops. Research has focused on the

1. 식물의 정상적인 성장과 발달을 위해 특정 미네랄이 필요하다는 연구 결과가 있다. 토양은 이러한 미네랄의 공급원이며, 식물은 이러한 미네랄을 물과 함께 토양으로부터 흡수한다. 질소조차도 자연 상태에서는 기체로 존재하지만 보통은 질소 이온의 형태로 토양으로부터 흡수된다. 일부 토양은 미량 영양소가 심각하게 결핍되어 있어 대부분 식물의 생장을 지탱하지 못한다. 예를 들어, 소위 사문암(蛇紋巖) 토양은 칼슘이 부족해서 저 칼슘 상태를 견뎌낼 수 있는 식물만이 생존할 수 있다. 현대 농업에서 토양의 미네랄 고갈이 주요한 우려사항이 되고 있는데, 작물 수확으로 양분이 토양으로 되돌아가는 순환이 단절되기 때문이다.

2. 미네랄 결핍은 특정 증상들로 감지할 수 있다. 백화현상(엽록소 손실로 황엽 또는 백엽 조직이 되는 현상), 괴사(고립된 채 죽어 있는 조직), 안토시아닌 변색 형성(잎이나 줄기에 진한 붉은 색소 부위 생성), 왜소 생장, 초본 식물에서 목질 조직이 생성되는 것 같은 증상들이다. 토양에서 가장 흔히 부족한 것은 질소나 인이다. 질소가 결핍된 식물들은 앞에서 설명한 많은 증상들을 보인다. 잎에는 백화현상이 나타나고, 줄기는 짧고 가늘며, 안토시아닌 변색이 줄기, 잎자루, 아래쪽 잎 표면에 나타난다. 인이 결핍된 식물들은 종종 왜소하고, 잎은 특유의 어두운 녹색으로 변색되며, 때로는 안토시아닌 색소가 누적된다. 인이 어린 성장 조직에 먼저 모이기 때문에 대개는 오래된 잎들이 먼저 영향을 받게 된다. 철 결핍은 어린 잎의 잎맥들 사이에서 백화현상이라는 특징으로 나타난다.

3. 영양소 결핍에 대한 많은 연구는 수경법, 즉 액체 영양소 용액으로 토양 없이 식물을 재배하는 것에 기반하고 있다. 이런 기법으로 연구자는 특정 영양소를 선택적으로 제외한 용액을 이용해 식물이 받는 영향을 관찰할 수 있다. 수경 재배는 기초 연구 수준을 뛰어넘는 응용 기술로 겨울철 온실 재배 채소의 성장을 촉진한다. 공중재배법은 식물을 매달아 두고 뿌리에 영양소 용액을 분무해 키우는 기술로 토양 없이 식물을 재배하는 또 다른 방법이다.

4. 미네랄 결핍은 식물의 성장을 제한할 수 있는 반면, 특정 미네랄의 과잉도 독이 될 수 있고 성장도 방해할 수 있다. 염화나트륨 및 기타 염분을 고농도로 함유한 염류토양은 식물 성장을 방해하므로 다양한 내염 작물을 개발하는 데 연구가 지속적으로 집중되고 있다. 납, 카드뮴, 수은, 알루미늄 같은 중금속의 독성 작용에 대한 집중적인 연구도 계속되었다. 그러나 필수 원소인 구리 및 아연조차도 고농도일 경우 역시 독성을 띨 수 있다. 대부분의 식물은 이러한 토양에서 생존할 수 없지만, 특정 식물은 높은 수치의 미네랄 함유량을 견딜 수 있는 능력이 있다.

toxic effects of heavy metals such as lead, cadmium, mercury, and aluminum; however, even copper and zinc, which are essential elements, can become toxic in high concentrations. Although most plants cannot survive in these soils, certain plants have the ability to tolerate high levels of these minerals.

5. Scientists have known for some time that certain plants, called hyperaccumulators, can concentrate minerals at levels a hundredfold or greater than normal. (A) A survey of known hyperaccumulators identified that 75 percent of them amassed nickel; cobalt, copper, zinc, manganese, lead, and cadmium are other minerals of choice. (B) Hyperaccumulators run the entire range of the plant world. (C) They may be herbs, shrubs, or trees. (D) Many members of the mustard family, spurge family, legume family, and grass family are top hyperaccumulators. Many are found in tropical and subtropical areas of the world, where accumulation of high concentrations of metals may afford some protection against plant-eating insects and microbial pathogens.

6. Only recently have investigators considered using these plants to clean up soil and waste sites that have been contaminated by toxic levels of heavy metals—an environmentally friendly approach known as phytoremediation. This scenario begins with the planting of hyperaccumulating species in the target area, such as an abandoned mine or an irrigation pond contaminated by runoff. Toxic minerals would first be absorbed by roots but later relocated to the stem and leaves. A harvest of the shoots would remove the toxic compounds off site to be burned or composted to recover the metal for industrial uses. After several years of cultivation and harvest, the site would be restored at a cost much lower than the price of excavation and reburial, the standard practice for remediation of contaminated soils. For example, in field trials, the plant alpine pennycress removed zinc and cadmium from soils near a zinc smelter, and Indian mustard, native to Pakistan and India, has been effective in reducing levels of selenium salts by 50 percent in contaminated soils.

5. 과학자들이 과축적제라고 부르는 식물을 알게 된 것은 꽤 오래전이다. 이 식물은 보통 수준보다 100배 이상의 미네랄을 축적할 수 있다. 알려진 과축적제에 대한 조사에 따르면, 75% 정도가 니켈을 축적하고 있으며, 코발트, 구리, 아연, 망간, 납, 카드뮴 등 기타 미네랄도 축적하고 있다. 과축적제는 식물군 전체에 분포하고 있다. 풀, 관목, 혹은 수목도 과축적제에 해당할 수 있다. 배춧과, 등대풀과, 콩과, 벼과 식물의 다수가 최고의 과축적제다. 과축적제들은 열대와 아열대 지역에서 많이 발견되는데, 고농도로 축적된 금속 성분은 식물을 갉아먹는 곤충과 병원성 미생물로부터 어느 정도 보호막을 제공할 수 있다.

6. 최근에야 비로소 연구자들은 중독 수준으로 중금속에 오염된 토양이나 폐기장 정화 작업에 과축적제 식물을 활용하는 방안을 검토했는데, 이것이 바로 식물환경복원이라고 하는 환경친화적 접근법이다. 이 계획의 시작은 유출로 오염된 관개용 못이나 폐광 같은 목표 지역에 과축적제 식물종을 심는 것이다. 독성 미네랄은 뿌리에 먼저 흡수되었다가 나중에 줄기나 잎으로 이동한다. 새순이 올라오면 뽑아버려 토양 속 독성 화합물을 제거하며, 뽑은 것들을 모아서 태우거나 퇴비로 만들어 산업용 금속을 회수한다. 이런 식으로 수년간 경작과 수확을 반복하면 오염된 토양을 복원하는 일반적인 방법인 터 파기 후 재매립하는 것보다 훨씬 저렴한 비용으로 오염지대가 복원된다. 실례로, 현장 실험에서 고산 말냉이는 아연 제련소 인근 토양의 아연과 카드뮴을 제거했으며, 파키스탄과 인도가 원산지인 갓은 오염 토양에서 셀레늄염 수준을 50퍼센트나 줄이는 효과를 보였다.

어휘

1. mineral 미네랄, 무기질 nitrogen 질소 elemental state 자연 상태 nitrate ion 질산염이온 deficient 부족한, 결핍된 micro nutrients 미량 영양소 serpentine 사문암 calcium 칼슘 depletion 고갈, 소모 2. chlorosis 백화현상 necrosis 괴사 anthocyanin 안토시아닌 pigmentation 색소, 색소 침착 stunted 왜소한 herbaceous 초본 식물의 phosphorus 인 slender 가느다란 discoloration 변색 petiole 잎자루 characteristic 특유의 accumulation 축적, 누적 affect 영향을 주다 mobilize 모이다, 집결하다 vein 잎맥 3. hydroponically 수경 재배로 solutions 용액 omit 제외하다 application 응용, 적용 facilitate 용이하게 하다, 촉진하다 aeroponics 공중재배법, 분무수경 suspend 걸어 두다 mist 분무하다 4. overabundance 과잉 saline soil 염류토양 sodium chloride 염화나트륨 salt-tolerant 내염성의 cadmium 카드뮴 mercury 수은 copper 구리 zinc 아연 5. hyperaccumulator 과축적제 amass 축적하다 run the range 범위에 분포하다 herbs 풀 shrub 관목 mustard family 배춧과 spurge family 등대풀과 legume family 콩과 grass family 벼과 subtropical 아열대의 afford 제공하다 pathogen 병원균, 병원체 microbial pathogen 병원성 미생물 6. contaminated 오염된 toxic 독성의 heavy metal 중금속 phytoremediation 식물환경복원 shoot (식물의) 순, 새싹 compound (화학) 화합물 compost 퇴비로 만들다, 비료를 주다 cultivation 경작 restore 복원하다, 회수하다 excavation 채굴, 터 파기 reburial 재매립 alpine 고산 지대의 pennycress 말냉이 smelter 제련소, 용광로 Indian mustard 갓 selenium salt 셀레늄염

1. 첫 번째 단락에 따르면, 사문암 토양에서 자랄 수 있는 식물에 대한 사실로 맞는 것은?

   Ⓐ 미량 영양소를 매우 잘 흡수한다.
   Ⓑ 대부분의 식물보다 훨씬 적은 양의 칼슘이 필요하다.
   Ⓒ 자연 상태의 질소를 흡수할 수 있다.
   Ⓓ 대표적인 식용 작물이다.

   어휘 absorb 흡수하다
        typically 전형적으로, 대표적으로

2. 두 번째 단락에 따르면, 다음 중 인 결핍 식물에는 나타나지만 질소나 철 결핍 식물에서 나타나지 않는 증상은?

   Ⓐ 잎의 백화현상
   Ⓑ 잎 색소가 어두운 녹색으로 변색됨
   Ⓒ 줄기의 짧고 왜소한 외관
   Ⓓ 잎이나 줄기의 적색 색소 침착

   어휘 shade 색조

3. 두 번째 단락에 따르면, 철 결핍 증상 가운데 어린 잎에 나타나는 것은?

   Ⓐ 잎맥 사이의 진한 적색 변색
   Ⓑ 잎맥 사이의 백색 또는 황색 조직
   Ⓒ 잎맥 사이의 괴사 부분
   Ⓓ 특유의 어두운 녹색 잎맥

   어휘 deep 색깔이 짙은   characteristic 특유의, 특징적인

4. 세 번째 단락의 facilitates와 의미상 가장 가까운 것은?

   Ⓐ 늦추다
   Ⓑ 영향을 미치다
   Ⓒ 쉽게 만들다
   Ⓓ 집중하다

5. 세 번째 단락에 따르면, 식물의 영양소 결핍에 대한 연구에서 수경 재배법의 이점은 무엇인가?

   Ⓐ 연구자가 식물이 흡수하는 영양소를 통제할 수 있다.
   Ⓑ 많은 수의 식물이 성장하는 것을 동시에 관찰할 수 있다.
   Ⓒ 식물의 뿌리를 직접적으로 관찰할 수 있다.
   Ⓓ 식물에 영양소 용액을 계속 분무할 필요가 없다.

   어휘 simultaneously 동시에

6. 글쓴이가 herbs, shrubs, trees를 언급한 이유는?

   Ⓐ 높은 수치의 유해 미네랄을 견딜 수 없는 식물 종류를 예시하기 위해
   Ⓑ 왜 그렇게 많은 식물들이 과축적제인지 보여주기 위해
   Ⓒ 과축적제가 왜 그렇게 많은 장소에서 발견되는지 설명하려고
   Ⓓ 과축적제가 광범위한 식물군에서 나타난다는 점을 강조하기 위해

   어휘 harmful 유해한   emphasize 강조하다

7. 다음 중 여섯 번째 단락에서 음영으로 표시된 문장이 담고 있는 핵심 정보를 가장 잘 표현한 것은? 정답 외의 보기들은 의미가 상당히 왜곡되거나 필수적인 정보가 빠져 있다.

   Ⓐ 식물환경복원을 고려하기 전에, 목표 지역에서 서식하는 과축적제 식물의 종류를 먼저 파악해야 한다.
   Ⓑ 조사는 오염의 정도를 판단하기 위해 목표 지역 내 독소오염지대에 대한 평가로 시작된다.
   Ⓒ 식물환경복원의 첫 단계는 정화 대상 지역에 과축적제 식물을 심는 것이다.
   Ⓓ 목표 지역에 과축적제 식물 종을 심어 광산과 관개용 못의 오염을 막을 수 있다.

   어휘 local to 현지에서 자라는   clean up 정화

8. 여섯 번째 단락에서 일반적인 오염 토양 복원법 대비 식물환경복원에 대해 추론할 수 있는 것은?

   Ⓐ 제거된 미네랄을 산업용으로 사용하는 것을 허용하지 않는다.
   Ⓑ 더 빨리 시행할 수 있다.
   Ⓒ 일반적인 방법만큼 환경친화적이다.
   Ⓓ 단기간 내 사용해야 하는 토양에는 적합하지 않다.

   어휘 remediation 복원   implement 시행하다

9. 위에 제시된 지문의 일부를 보시오. 지문에 표시된 **(A)**, **(B)**, **(C)**, **(D)** 중 하나에 다음 문장이 삽입될 수 있다.

Certain minerals are more likely to be accumulated in large quantities than others.
(특정 미네랄은 다른 미네랄에 비해 다량 축적되기 쉽다.)

이 문장이 들어갈 가장 적당한 위치는?

Scientists have known for some time that certain plants, called hyperaccumulators, can concentrate minerals at levels a hundredfold or greater than normal. **(A)** Certain minerals are more likely to be accumulated in large quantities than others. A survey of known hyperaccumulators identified that 75 percent of them amassed nickel; cobalt, copper, zinc, manganese, lead, and cadmium are other minerals of choice. **(B)** Hyperaccumulators run the entire range of the plant world. **(C)** They may be herbs, shrubs, or trees. **(D)** Many members of the mustard family, spurge family, legume family, and grass family are top hyperaccumulators. Many are found in tropical and subtropical areas of the world, where accumulation of high concentrations of metals may afford some protection against plant-eating insects and microbial pathogens.

Ⓐ (A)　　　Ⓑ (B)　　　Ⓒ (C)　　　Ⓓ (D)

10. 지문을 간단히 요약하기 위한 도입 문장이 아래에 제시되어 있다. 아래 보기들 중에서 지문의 가장 중요한 개념을 표현한 문장 3개를 골라 요약을 완성하라. 보기들 중에는 지문에 나오지 않았거나 중요하지 않은 개념이기 때문에 요약문으로 적절치 않은 것들도 있다. 이 문제의 배점은 2점이다.

식물은 정상적인 성장과 발달을 위해 토양에서 특정 미네랄을 적당량 흡수해야 한다.

Ⓐ 일부 식물은 특정 미네랄의 수치가 비교적 낮아도 생존할 수 있지만, 그런 식물들은 황폐한 토양에 영양소를 돌려보내는 데는 쓸모가 없다.

Ⓑ 식물은 충분한 양의 필수 미네랄을 흡수하지 못하면, 특유의 기형이 발생한다.

Ⓒ 많은 식물의 경우 미네랄 결핍은 뿌리에 영양액을 분무하거나 흙 없는 배양액으로 옮겨서 치유할 수 있다.

Ⓓ 염분, 기타 미네랄, 중금속은 미량이면 이로울 수도 있으나 다량 축적되면 식물에 유해할 수 있다.

Ⓔ 고농도의 염화나트륨 및 기타 염들은 대부분 식물의 생장을 방해하므로 내염성 농작물을 개발하기 위한 많은 연구들이 진행되었다.

Ⓕ 일부 식물은 특정 미네랄을 극히 높은 수준까지 축적할 수 있으므로 그 특정 미네랄이 독성 수준까지 오염된 토양을 정화하는 데 사용될 수 있다.

어휘 adequate 적당한　of little use 쓸모 없는
abnormality 기형, 이상　beneficial 이로운

THE ORIGIN OF THE PACIFIC
ISLAND PEOPLE

1. The greater Pacific region, traditionally called Oceania, consists of three cultural areas: Melanesia, Micronesia, and Polynesia. Melanesia, in the southwest Pacific, contains the large islands of New Guinea, the Solomons, Vanuatu, and New Caledonia. Micronesia, the area north of Melanesia, consists primarily of small scattered islands. Polynesia is the central Pacific area in the great triangle defined by Hawaii, Easter Island, and New Zealand. Before the arrival of Europeans, the islands in the two largest cultural areas, Polynesia and Micronesia, together contained a population estimated at 700,000.

2. Speculation on the origin of these Pacific islanders began as soon as outsiders encountered them; in the absence of solid linguistic, archaeological, and biological data, many fanciful and mutually exclusive theories were devised. Pacific islanders were variously thought to have come from North America, South America, Egypt, Israel, and India, as well as Southeast Asia. (A) Many older theories implicitly deprecated the navigational abilities and overall cultural creativity of the Pacific islanders. (B) For example, British anthropologists G. Elliot Smith and W. J. Perry assumed that only Egyptians would have been skilled enough to navigate and colonize the Pacific. (C) They speculated that the Egyptians even crossed the Pacific to found the great civilizations of the New World (North and South America). (D) In 1947 Norwegian adventurer Thor Heyerdahl drifted on a balsa-log raft westward with the winds and currents across the Pacific from South America to prove his theory that Pacific islanders were Native Americans (also called American Indians). Later Heyerdahl suggested that the Pacific was peopled by three migrations: by Native Americans from the Pacific Northwest of North America drifting to Hawaii, by Peruvians drifting to Easter Island, and by Melanesians. In 1969 he crossed the Atlantic in an Egyptian-style reed boat to prove Egyptian influences in the Americas. Contrary to these theorists, the overwhelming evidence of physical anthropology, linguistics, and archaeology shows that the Pacific islanders came from Southeast Asia and were skilled enough as navigators to sail against the prevailing winds and currents.

3. The basic cultural requirements for the successful colonization of the Pacific islands include the appropriate boat-building, sailing, and navigation skills to get to the islands in the first place; domesticated plants and gardening skills suited to often marginal conditions; and a varied inventory of fishing implements and techniques. It is now generally believed that these prerequisites originated with peoples speaking Austronesian languages (a group of several hundred related

1. 태평양 지역의 대부분은 전통적으로 오세아니아라고 부르며, 멜라네시아, 미크로네시아, 폴리네시아라는 세 가지 문화 지역으로 구성된다. 남서태평양에 위치한 멜라네시아는 뉴기니, 솔로몬 제도, 바나투, 뉴칼레도니아 같은 큰 섬들을 포함한다. 미크로네시아는 멜라네시아의 북쪽에 위치하며 주로 산재된 작은 섬들로 구성되어 있다. 폴리네시아는 센트럴퍼시픽 지역으로 하와이, 이스터 섬, 뉴질랜드를 연결하는 큰 삼각지대로 둘러싸여 있다. 유럽인들이 도착하기 전에는 2대 문화 지역인 폴리네시아와 미크로네시아 지역에 약 70만 명이 거주했다.

2. 태평양 섬 주민들의 기원에 대한 추측은 외지인들이 이들과 마주치자마자 시작되었다. 확실한 언어학적, 고고학적, 생물학적 자료가 없는 가운데 공상적이고 상호 배타적인 가설들이 다수 고안되었다. 태평양 섬 주민들이 동남아시아뿐만 아니라 북미, 남미, 이집트, 이스라엘, 인도 등 각지에서 유래했다고 본 것이다. 다수의 옛 가설들은 태평양 섬 주민들의 항해술과 전반적인 문화적 창의력을 암묵적으로 인정하지 않았다. 예를 들어, 영국의 인류학자 G. 엘리어트 스미스와 W. J. 페리는 이집트인만이 태평양을 항해해 식민지를 건설할 능력이 있었을 것이라고 추정했다. 두 사람은 심지어 이집트인들이 태평양을 건너와 신세계(북미와 남미)의 위대한 문명을 창건했다고 추측했다. 1947년 노르웨이인 탐험가 토르 헤위에르달은 발사통나무 뗏목을 타고 남미에서 출발해 바람과 해류를 타고 태평양을 건너 서쪽으로 항해했는데, 태평양 섬 주민들은 아메리카 원주민(즉, 아메리카 인디언)이라는 자신의 이론을 증명하기 위해서였다. 이후 헤위에르달은 3대 이주 사건으로 태평양 지역에 인구가 유입되었다는 설을 제시했다. 즉, 아메리카 원주민들이 북미 태평양 북서부에서 하와이로 이주했고, 페루인들이 이스터 섬으로 표류해 들어왔고, 멜라네시아인들이 이주해왔다는 것이다. 1969년 그는 이집트식 갈대 배를 타고 대서양을 건너 아메리카 대륙이 이집트 문명의 영향을 받았음을 증명하려 했다. 이런 가설들과는 반대로, 형질인류학, 언어학, 고고학의 압도적 증거들은 태평양 섬 주민들은 동남아시아 출신으로 우세풍과 탁월 해류를 거슬러 항해할 수 있을 만큼 노련한 항해자들이었음을 시사한다.

3. 태평양 섬을 성공적으로 식민지화하기 위한 기본적인 문화적 요건은 일단 섬까지 가기 위한 적절한 배 건조술, 항법 및 항해술이다. 때로는 한계 상황에 적합한 재배 작물 및 원예 기술도 필요하며, 갖가지 낚시 도구 및 기술도 포함된다. 이런 선결 요건들은 (수백 개의 관련어로 구성된 언어 집단인) 오스트로네시아어를 쓰는 민족들에게서 유래했으며 기원전 5000년경에 동남아시아에서 출현하기 시작했다고 보는 것이 현재 일반적인 견해다. 당시 문화를 고고학과 언어학으

languages) and began to emerge in Southeast Asia by about 5000 B.C.E. The culture of that time, based on archaeology and linguistic reconstruction, is assumed to have had a broad inventory of cultivated plants including taro, yams, banana, sugarcane, breadfruit, coconut, sago, and rice. Just as important, the culture also possessed the basic foundation for an effective maritime adaptation, including outrigger canoes and a variety of fishing techniques that could be effective for overseas voyaging.

4. Contrary to the arguments of some that much of the Pacific was settled by Polynesians accidentally marooned after being lost and adrift, it seems reasonable that this feat was accomplished by deliberate colonization expeditions that set out fully stocked with food and domesticated plants and animals. Detailed studies of the winds and currents using computer simulations suggest that drifting canoes would have been a most unlikely means of colonizing the Pacific. These expeditions were likely driven by population growth and political dynamics on the home islands, as well as the challenge and excitement of exploring unknown waters. Because all Polynesians, Micronesians, and many Melanesians speak Austronesian languages and grow crops derived from Southeast Asia, all these peoples most certainly derived from that region and not the New World or elsewhere. The undisputed pre-Columbian presence in Oceania of the sweet potato, which is a New World domesticate, has sometimes been used to support Heyerdahl's "American Indians in the Pacific" theories. However, this is one plant out of a long list of Southeast Asian domesticates. As Patrick Kirch, an American anthropologist, points out, rather than being brought by rafting South Americans, sweet potatoes might just have easily been brought back by returning Polynesian navigators who could have reached the west coast of South America.

로 재건하면, 토란, 참마, 바나나, 사탕수수, 빵나무, 코코넛, 사고, 쌀 등 다양한 재배 작물을 확보하고 있었다고 추정된다. 뿐만 아니라 이 문화는 해양 환경에 효과적으로 적응할 수 있는 기본 토대, 가령 먼바다 항해에 효과적인 아우트리거 카누와 다양한 낚시 기술 등을 보유하고 있었다는 점 역시 중요하다.

4. 방향을 잃고 표류하다 우연히 무인도에 고립된 폴리네시아인들이 태평양의 많은 지역에 정착했다는 일부의 주장과는 반대로, 식량, 재배 작물, 가축을 가득 싣고 식민지 건설을 위해 의도적으로 출항한 탐험대가 이룬 결과라는 주장이 타당해 보인다. 컴퓨터 모의실험을 통한 바람과 해류에 대한 상세 연구에 따르면, 카누 항해는 태평양 지역을 식민지화하기에는 가장 신빙성이 낮은 방법으로 보인다. 탐험대가 출항한 것은 미지의 바다를 탐험하려는 도전 정신과 흥미뿐만 아니라 고향 섬의 인구 증가와 정치적 역학관계에 기인했을 가능성이 있다. 폴리네시아인들, 미크로네시아인들 모두와 멜라네시아인들 다수가 오스트로네시아어를 사용하고 있고 동남아시아에서 유래된 작물을 경작하고 있으므로 그들 모두는 신대륙이나 타 지역이 아니라 바로 동남아시아 지역에서 유래했음이 거의 확실하다. 신대륙의 작물 중 하나인 고구마가 콜럼버스가 미 대륙을 발견하기 이전부터 오세아니아에 분명히 존재했다는 것은 헤위에르달의 "아메리카 인디언의 태평양 유입설"을 뒷받침하는 근거로 종종 이용되었다. 그러나, 고구마는 동남아시아인들이 재배하는 수많은 작물 중 하나다. 미국 인류학자 패트릭 키르히가 지적하듯 뗏목으로 항해하던 남미인들이 고구마를 들여왔다기보다 남미 서해안까지 도달했던 폴리네시아인 항해자들이 돌아오면서 그곳에서 고구마를 갖고 나왔을 가능성이 있다.

어휘

1. scattered 산재된 contain 포함하다, 수용하다 estimated at ~ 정도로 추산되는 2. speculation 추측 islander 섬 주민 encounter 마주치다 solid 확실한 linguistic 언어학의 archaeological 고고학의 biological 생물학의 fanciful 공상적인 mutually exclusive 상호 배타적인 devise 고안하다 implicitly 암시적으로 deprecate 반대하다 navigational 항해의 anthropologist 인류학자 colonize 식민지화하다 speculate 추측하다 found 설립하다 civilization 문명 drift 표류하다 balsa-log raft 발사통나무 뗏목 current 해류 people (사람이) 살다, 점유하다 migration 이주 reed boat 갈대 배 overwhelming 압도적인 physical anthropology 형질인류학, 자연인류학 prevailing wind 우세풍 3. navigation 항해 in the first place 우선 domesticate 재배하다, 길들이다, (동물을) 가축으로 만들다 gardening 원예 marginal condition 한계 상황 implements 도구 prerequisite 선결 요건, 전제 조건 originate 유래하다 Austronesian 오스트로네시아의 emerge 출현하다 taro 토란 yam 참마 sugarcane 사탕수수 breadfruit 빵나무 sago 사고야자 maritime 해양의 adaptation 적응 outrigger canoe 아우트리거 카누 overseas voyaging 먼바다 항해 4. contrary to ~와 대조적으로 maroon 섬에 버리다, 고립시키다 adrift 표류하는 feat 위업 deliberate 의도적인 colonization 식민지 건설, 식민지화 expedition 원정, 탐험 domesticate 사육[재배]하다 simulation 모의실험 dynamics 역학, 역동성 derive from ~에서 유래하다, 파생하다 undisputed 반박의 여지가 없는 pre-Columbian 콜럼버스의 미 대륙 발견 이전의

11. 가설들이 "상호 배타적"이라고 말한 의도는?

 Ⓐ 가설 중 하나가 사실이라면 나머지 모든 가설들은 반드시 거짓
  이다.

 Ⓑ 가설들간의 차이는 중요하지 않다.

 Ⓒ 가설들을 종합하면 모든 가능성을 포괄한다.

 Ⓓ 가설들이 상호 보완적이다.

 어휘 taken together 합쳐보면, 종합하면 cover 포괄하다

12. 두 번째 단락에 따르면, 다음 중 일부 초기 연구자들이 태평양 섬
 주민들이 이집트에서 왔다고 믿게 된 근거는?

 Ⓐ 이집트인들이 다른 위대한 문명을 창건했다고 알려져 있다.

 Ⓑ 다른 지역에서 온 항해자들은 대양을 건너는 데 필요한 기술이
  없다고 믿었다.

 Ⓒ 언어학적, 고고학적, 생물학적 자료들이 태평양 군도와 이집트
  를 연결하고 있다.

 Ⓓ 이집트의 기록은 아메리카 대륙뿐만 아니라 태평양을 식민지
  화했다고 주장했다.

 어휘 account 설명, 기록 claim responsibility 책임을 인정하다,
  자신의 소행이라고 주장하다

13. 세 번째 단락의 implements와 의미상 가장 가까운 것은?

 Ⓐ 기술

 Ⓑ 도구

 Ⓒ 기회

 Ⓓ 관습

14. 세 번째 단락에서 태평양 섬들을 성공적으로 식민지화하기 위한
 요건으로 언급되지 않은 것은?

 Ⓐ 다양한 오스트로네시아 계열 언어에 대한 지식

 Ⓑ 다양한 낚시 기술

 Ⓒ 항해술

 Ⓓ 작물 재배 지식

 어휘 a variety of(= various) 다양한, 여러 가지의

15. 세 번째 단락에서 글쓴이가 기원전 5000년경 동남아시아인들이 사
 용했던 배와 재배 작물의 종류에 대해 설명한 이유는?

 Ⓐ 초기 오스트로네시아 민족들에게 농업과 어업이 갖는 상대적
  중요성을 평가하기 위해

 Ⓑ 고대의 생활에 관한 세세한 사항을 발견하는 데 고고학 및 언
  어학적 방법론이 효과적임을 예증하기 위해

 Ⓒ 아시아 대륙의 생활 여건과 태평양 섬의 생활 여건을 대조하기
  위해

 Ⓓ 이 지역 민족들이 태평양 섬까지 건너가서 생존하는 데 필요한
  기술과 자원을 보유하고 있었음을 입증하기 위해

 어휘 relative 상대적인 living conditions 생활 여건
  resources 자원

16. 다음 중 네 번째 단락에서 음영으로 표시된 문장이 담고 있는 핵심
 정보를 가장 잘 표현한 것은? 정답 외의 보기들은 의미가 상당히
 왜곡되거나 필수적인 정보가 빠져 있다.

 Ⓐ 일각에서는 무역상들이 가축과 재배 작물을 운반하다 표류해
  태평양에 정착했다고 주장한다.

 Ⓑ 폴리네시아 원 정착민들은 섬에 고립되었다가, 이후에 치밀하
  게 준비된 식민지 탐험대와 합류했을 수도 있다.

 Ⓒ 식민지 탐험대가 자원을 완전히 비축한 상태로 출정했다고 보
  는 것이 합리적이겠지만 이에 대한 반박 증거들도 많다.

 Ⓓ 태평양 섬에 정착한 것은, 일부 주장처럼 우연이 아니라 의도
  적이고 계획적이었을 것이다.

 어휘 contradict 반박하다, 부정하다 intentional 의도적인

17. 네 번째 단락에 따르면, 다음 중 한 집단이 태평양 군도를 식민지화
 하려 했던 이유에 대한 설명이 아닌 것은?

 Ⓐ 인구가 증가하면서 추가 영토가 필요했다.

 Ⓑ 바람과 해류 덕분에 태평양 섬에 도달하기 쉬웠다.

 Ⓒ 모국의 정치적 상황이 이민을 원하도록 만들었다.

 Ⓓ 그들은 탐험을 도전적이고 신나는 일로 여겼다.

 어휘 territory 영토 emigration 이주, 이민
  desirable 바람직한, 호감 가는 exploration 탐험

18. 글쓴이가 패트릭 키르히의 견해를 언급한 이유는?

 Ⓐ 아메리카 인디언이 오세아니아로 이동했다는 헤위에르달의 가
  설에 유리한 증거를 제시하기 위해

 Ⓑ 태평양 군도 주민들이 세계 각지에서 재배되는 작물에 친숙했
  다는 점을 강조하기 위해

 Ⓒ 헤위에르달의 가설에 대한 추정적 증거가 다르게 설명될 수 있
  음을 시사하기 위해

 Ⓓ 동일한 작물의 일부는 남미와 오세아니아 모두에서 경작되었
  다는 것을 명시하기 위해

 어휘 familiarity 익숙함, 친숙함

19. 위에 제시된 지문의 일부를 보시오. 지문에 표시된 **(A)**, **(B)**, **(C)**, **(D)** 중 하나에 다음 문장이 삽입될 수 있다.

Later theories concentrated on journeys in the other direction.
(이후의 가설들은 다른 방향으로의 여정에 주목했다.)

이 문장이 들어갈 가장 적당한 위치는?

Speculation on the origin of these Pacific islanders began as soon as outsiders encountered them; in the absence of solid linguistic, archaeological, and biological data, many fanciful and mutually exclusive theories were devised. Pacific islanders were variously thought to have come from North America, South America, Egypt, Israel, and India, as well as Southeast Asia. **(A)** Many older theories implicitly deprecated the navigational abilities and overall cultural creativity of the Pacific islanders. **(B)** For example, British anthropologists G. Elliot Smith and W. J. Perry assumed that only Egyptians would have been skilled enough to navigate and colonize the Pacific. **(C)** They speculated that the Egyptians even crossed the Pacific to found the great civilizations of the New World (North and South America). **(D)** Later theories concentrated on journeys in the other direction. In 1947 Norwegian adventurer Thor Heyerdahl drifted on a balsa-log raft westward with the winds and currents across the Pacific from South America to prove his theory that Pacific islanders were Native Americans (also called American Indians). Later Heyerdahl suggested that the Pacific was peopled by three migrations; by Native Americans from Pacific Northwest of North America drifting to Hawaii, by Peruvians drifting to Easter Island, and by Melanesians. In 1969 he crossed the Atlantic in an Egyptian-style reed boat to prove Egyptian influences in the Americas. Contrary to these theorists, the overwhelming evidence of physical anthropology, linguistics, and archaeology shows that the Pacific islanders came from Southeast Asia and were skilled enough as navigators to sail against the prevailing winds and currents.

Ⓐ (A)　　Ⓑ (B)　　Ⓒ (C)　　Ⓓ (D)

어휘 concentrate on ~에 집중하다, 주목하다

20. 지문을 간단히 요약하기 위한 도입 문장이 아래에 제시되어 있다. 아래 보기들 중에서 지문의 가장 중요한 개념을 표현한 문장 3개를 골라 요약을 완성하라. 보기들 중에는 지문에 나오지 않았거나 중요하지 않은 개념이기 때문에 요약문으로 적절치 않은 것들도 있다. 이 문제의 배점은 2점이다.

멜라네시아, 미크로네시아, 폴리네시아가 합쳐 태평양 군도, 혹은 오세아니아로 표현되는 지역을 구성한다.

Ⓐ 태평양 군도에 어떻게 최초 거주자가 왔는지에 대한 가설이 다수 제시되었는데, 이 중 북미인과 남미인이 대양을 건너 단순히 표류했다는 설도 있다.

Ⓑ 태평양 군도의 초기 정복자들은 아마도 농경사회 출신이었겠지만, 어업 기반 경제를 택할 수 밖에 없었다.

Ⓒ 새로운 증거에 따르면, 태평양 군도 주민들은 고립 생활보다는 동남아시아인들과 무역 및 사회적 교류에 참여했다.

Ⓓ 태평양의 바람과 해류에 대한 컴퓨터 모의실험 결과 태평양 군도에 도달하는 것이 과거에 생각했던 것보다 훨씬 쉬웠다.

Ⓔ 식민지 건설 과정은 상당한 기술, 결단, 계획을 요하며, 우연히 일어날 수 없었다는 것이 지금의 견해다.

Ⓕ 언어학 및 고고학적 증거를 통해 인류학자들은 최초의 태평양 군도 거주자는 동남아시아에서 온 오스트로네시아인이라고 판단했다.

어휘 colonizer 식민지 개척자, 이주자
agriculture-based society 농경사회　adopt 채택하다
engage in ~에 참여하다

LISTENING

Questions 1~5

p.68

N Narrator   **S** Student   **C** Counselor

Script   T-18

N Listen to a conversation between a student and a counselor at the university counseling center.

S Hi, thanks for seeing me on such short notice.

C No problem. How can I help?

S Well, I think I might've made a mistake coming to this school.

C What makes you say that?

S I'm a little overwhelmed by the size of this place. I come from a small town. There were only 75 of us in my high school graduating class. Everyone knew everyone; we all grew up together.

C So it's a bit of a culture shock for you, being one of 15,000 students on a big campus in an unfamiliar city.

S *That's* an understatement. I just can't get comfortable in class, or in the dorms, you know, socially.

C Hmm, well—let's start with your academics. Tell me about your classes.

S I'm taking mostly introductory courses, and some are taught in these huge lecture halls.

C And you're having trouble keeping pace with the material?

S No, in fact, I got an A on my first economics paper. It's just that, it's so impersonal. I'm not used to it.

C Are all your classes impersonal?

S Nah … It's just that, for example, in sociology yesterday, the professor asked a question. So I raised my hand … several of us raised our hands … and I kept my hand up because I did the reading and knew the answer. But the professor just answered his own question and continued with the lecture.

C Well, in a big room, it's possible he didn't notice you. Maybe he was trying to save time. In either case, I wouldn't take it personally.

S I suppose. But I just don't know how to, you know, *distinguish* myself.

C Why not stop by his office during office hours?

S That wouldn't seem right, y'know … taking time from other students who need help.

C Don't say that. That's what office hours are for. There's no reason you couldn't pop in to say hi, to, uh, to make yourself known. If you're learning a lot in class, let the professor know. Wouldn't *you* appreciate positive feedback if *you* were a professor?

S You're right. That's a good idea.

C OK, uh, let's turn to your social life. How's it going in the dorms?

N 대학 상담실에서 학생과 상담 교수가 나누는 대화를 들으시오.

S 안녕하세요, 급하게 연락 드렸는데 만나 주셔서 감사해요.

C 괜찮아요. 뭘 도와 드릴까요?

S 이 학교에 진학한 게 실수 아닌가 해서요.

C 왜 그렇게 생각하죠?

S 이곳 규모에 좀 위축되네요. 전 소도시 출신입니다. 제가 다니던 고등학교 졸업반 학생수는 75명뿐이었어요. 모두가 서로 알았죠. 어릴 때부터 같이 자란 사이니까요.

C 문화 충격이겠네요. 전교생 1만 5000명에, 큰 캠퍼스에, 낯선 도시에.

S 그 정도가 아니에요. 강의실이고 기숙사고 편하지가 않아요. 그러니까 어울리지 못한다는 느낌이 들어요.

C 그래요. 그럼 학업부터 먼저 점검해 봅시다. 강의 얘기를 해 봐요.

S 대부분 개론 수업을 듣고 있고요, 어떤 강의는 대형 강의동에서 듣고요.

C 교재 따라가는 데 문제가 있나요?

S 아뇨, 사실 처음 낸 경제학 리포트는 A를 받았어요. 근데 그냥 참 비인간적이에요. 적응이 안 되네요.

C 모든 강의가 다 그런가요?

S 그렇진 않지만, 그런 거 있잖아요. 어제 사회학 강의에서 교수님이 질문을 하시길래 손을 들었죠. 학생들 몇이 더 손을 들었고요. 전 과제물을 읽어왔기 때문에 답을 알고 있어서 계속 손을 들고 있었어요. 그런데 교수님이 자문자답하시더니 강의를 계속하시는 거예요.

C 글쎄요, 대형 강의실에서는 교수님이 학생을 못 봤을 수도 있어요. 시간을 아끼려고 그랬을 수도 있고요. 여하간 저라면 상처 받진 않겠어요.

S 그랬겠지요. 하지만 어떻게 하면 제가 두각을 나타낼 수 있을까요?

C 교수님 면담시간에 한번 방문해 보지 그래요?

S 그건 아닌 것 같아요. 도움이 필요한 다른 학생들의 시간을 뺏는 거잖아요.

C 그런 생각하지 말아요. 그러라고 면담시간이 있는 거예요. 잠깐 들러서 인사 못할 이유는 없어요. 그러면서 겸사겸사 얼굴도 알리는 거죠. 강의에서 많은 걸 배우고 있다면 교수님께 말씀드리세요. 학생이 교수라도 그런 긍정적인 평을 들으면 흐뭇하지 않겠어요?

S 맞아요. 좋은 생각이에요.

C 그럼 교우 관계를 얘기해 보죠. 기숙사에선 어떻게 지내요?

S I don't have much in common with my roommate or anyone else I've met so far. Everyone's into sports, and I'm more artsy, you know, into music. I play the cello.

C Ahhh. Have you been playing long?

S Since age 10. It's a big part of my life. At home, I was the youngest member of our community orchestra.

C You're not going to *believe* this! There's a string quartet on campus—all students. And it so happens the cellist graduated last year. They've been searching high and low for a replacement, someone with experience. Would you be interested in auditioning?

S Absolutely! I wanted to get my academic work settled before pursuing my music here, but I think this would be a good thing for me. I guess if I really want to fit in here, I should find people who love music as much as I do. Thank you!

C My pleasure.

S 룸메이트나 지금까지 만난 누구와도 공통점이 별로 없어요. 모두들 스포츠에 열광하는데 전 예술 취향, 그러니까 음악을 좋아해요. 첼로를 연주하거든요.

C 오, 그래요. 연주한 지 오래되었나요?

S 10살부터요. 제 인생에서 중요한 부분이죠. 고향에선 지역 오케스트라 최연소 단원이었죠.

C 무슨 일이 있는지 알아요? 캠퍼스에 학생으로만 구성된 현악4중주단이 있어요. 그런데 마침 첼로 주자가 지난해에 졸업해서 경험 있는 새 단원을 백방으로 찾고 있었어요. 오디션 볼래요?

S 물론이죠! 학교 공부가 좀 자리 잡히면 음악 활동을 하려고 했지만, 이번 기회가 저한테 좋을 것 같네요. 이곳에 잘 적응하려면 저처럼 음악을 사랑하는 사람을 찾아야겠어요. 감사합니다!

C 천만에요.

어휘

on such a short notice 너무 급작스럽게   overwhelmed 위축된   culture shock 문화 충격   understatement 과소평가   academics 학업
impersonal 인간미 없는, 딱딱한   in either case 어떤 경우에라도   take it personally 상처 받다   distinguish oneself 두각을 나타내다, 이름을 떨치다
stop by ~에 들르다   office hour (대학의) 교수 면담시간   pop in ~에 잠깐 방문하다   have in common with ~와 공통점이 있다   be into ~에 빠지다, 열광하다   artsy 예술을 좋아하는   string quartet 현악4중주(단)   search high and low 샅샅이 뒤지다   replacement 교체, 대신할 사람
academic work 학업   settle 자리 잡다   fit in ~에 어울리다, 들어맞다

1. 화자들이 주로 이야기하는 내용은?

    Ⓐ 여자가 룸메이트들과 공통점이 없는 이유

    Ⓑ 여자가 학업을 따라갈 수 있는 방법

    Ⓒ 여자의 대학 생활 적응

    Ⓓ 타 대학으로 옮기려는 여자의 결정

    어휘 keep up (수준, 진도 등을) 따라가다
            adjustment to ~에 적응, 조정

2. 여자가 고향을 언급한 이유는?

    Ⓐ 현재 상황과 대조하기 위해

    Ⓑ 대도시 생활에 적응했음을 인정하려고

    Ⓒ 캠퍼스에 오래전부터 알고 지내는 사람이 몇 명 있음을
        알리려고

    Ⓓ 전에 공부를 잘했음을 강조하려고

    어휘 draw a contrast to 대조점을 도출하다

3. 사회학 시간의 일화를 통해 여자가 암시하는 바는?

    Ⓐ 틀린 대답을 해서 창피했다.

    Ⓑ 교수가 자신을 무시한 것 같아 속상했다.

    Ⓒ 교수의 강의 진행 방식이 혼란스러웠다.

    Ⓓ 다른 학생들의 발언 때문에 놀랐다.

    어휘 upset 속상한, 마음이 상한   ignore 무시하다

4. 상담 교수에 따르면, 여자가 교수 연구실을 방문해야 하는 이유는?
   두 개의 답을 고르시오

    Ⓐ 강의를 칭찬하기 위해

    Ⓑ 다른 학생들을 돕고 싶다고 제안하기 위해

    Ⓒ 자신을 소개하기 위해

    Ⓓ 좀 더 친밀한 수업 방식을 제안하기 위해

    어휘 compliment 찬사, 경의   personal 친밀감이 있는, 인간적인

5. 현악4중주단 입단에 대해 여자가 암시하는 바는?

    Ⓐ 10살 때 그만둔 취미를 계속할 수 있을 것이다.

    Ⓑ 전공 공부에 더 많은 시간을 할애할 수 있을 것이다.

    Ⓒ 학업에 대한 고민을 그치는 데 도움이 될 것이다.

    Ⓓ 관심사가 비슷한 학생들을 만나는 길이 될 것이다.

    어휘 major area 전공 분야

Questions 6~11

p.70

N Narrator **P** Professor

Script   T-19

N Listen to part of a lecture in a sociology class.

P Have you ever heard the one about alligators living in New York sewers? The story goes like this: a family went on vacation in Florida, and bought a couple of baby alligators as presents for their children, then returned from vacation to New York, bringing the alligators home with them as pets. But the alligators would escape and find their way into the New York sewer system where they started reproducing, grew to huge sizes and now strike fear into sewer workers. Have you heard this story? Well, it isn't true and it never happened, but despite that, the story's been around since the 1930s.

Or how about the song "Twinkle, twinkle, little star"? You know "Twinkle, twinkle, little star, how I wonder what you are ..." Well, we've all heard this song. Where am I going with this? Well, both the song and the story are examples of memes, and that's what we'll talk about, the theory of memes.

A mcme is defined as a piece of information copied from person to person. By this definition, most of what you know ... ideas, skills, stories, songs ... are memes. All the words you know, all the scientific theories you've learned, the rules your parents taught you to observe ... all are memes that have been passed on from person to person.

So what? ... you may say. Passing on ideas from one person to another is nothing new ... Well, the whole point of defining this familiar process as transmission of memes is so that we can explore its analogy with the transmission of *genes.*

As you know, all living organisms pass on biological information through the genes. What's a gene? A gene is a piece of biological information that gets copied, or replicated, and the copy, or replica, is passed on to the new generation. So genes are defined as replicators ...

Genes are replicators that pass on information about properties and characteristics of organisms. By analogy, *memes* also get replicated and in the process pass on cultural information from person to person, generation to generation. So memes are also replicators. To be a successful replicator, there are three key characteristics: longevity, fecundity, and fidelity. Let's take a closer look ...

First, longevity. A replicator must exist long enough to be able to get copied and transfer its information. Clearly, the longer a replicator survives, the better its chances of getting its

N 사회학 강의의 일부를 들으시오.

P 여러분은 뉴욕 하수도에 살고 있는 악어에 대해 들어본 적이 있나요? 이야기는 이렇습니다. 한 가족이 플로리다로 휴가를 갔고, 새끼 악어 한 쌍을 아이들 선물로 샀습니다. 그리고 휴가지에서 뉴욕으로 돌아올 때 악어를 애완동물로 집에 데려온 거죠. 하지만, 악어들은 탈출해서 뉴욕 하수도로 들어가 번식을 시작했고 거대한 크기로 자라나, 지금은 하수도 작업자에게 공포를 불러일으키고 있죠. 이런 얘기 들어본 적 있나요? 그런데, 이 이야기는 사실이 아니고 이런 일이 일어난 적도 없습니다. 하지만 이 이야기는 1930년대부터 인구에 회자되고 있죠.

아니면 〈반짝 반짝 작은 별〉 노래는 어떤가요? 알다시피, "반짝 반짝 작은 별 아름답게 비추네." 이 노래는 다들 들어 봤을 거예요. 자 제가 무슨 얘기를 하려는 걸까요? 이 노래와 이야기 모두 밈(meme)에 대한 예를 든 것으로 이제부터 밈이란 무엇인가, 즉 밈 이론에 대해 얘기하려고 합니다.

밈이란 사람에서 사람으로 복제되는 정보의 한 단위로 정의됩니다. 이 정의에 의하면 여러분이 아는 대부분의 것들, 생각, 기술, 이야기, 노래 등이 밈입니다. 여러분이 아는 모든 단어, 여러분이 배운 모든 과학 이론, 여러분의 부모님이 지키라고 가르친 규칙, 이 모두가 사람에서 사람으로 전달되는 밈이죠.

"그게 뭐 어쨌다는 거야?"라고 생각할 수 있어요. 한 사람이 다른 사람에게 생각을 전달한다는 것은 전혀 새로운 일이 아니니까요. 이런 익숙한 과정을 밈의 전달이라고 정의한 까닭은 바로 유전자 전달과의 유사성을 탐구하려는 것입니다.

아시다시피, 살아 있는 모든 유기체는 유전자를 통해 생물학적 정보를 전달합니다. 유전자가 뭐죠? 유전자는 복사 또는 복제되는 생물학적 정보의 한 단위죠. 이렇게 복사 또는 복제된 것이 다음 세대로 전달됩니다. 그래서 유전자를 복제자로 정의합니다.

유전자는 유기체의 형질과 특징에 대한 정보를 전달하는 복제자입니다. 비유하면, 밈 또한 복제되고, 그 과정에서 문화적 정보를 사람에서 사람으로, 세대에서 세대로 전달합니다. 그래서 밈 또한 복제자입니다. 성공적인 복제자가 되려면 세 가지 주요한 특징이 있습니다. 바로 지속성, 다산성, 정확성입니다. 조금 더 자세히 알아보죠.

먼저 지속성입니다. 복제자는 정보가 복제되고 전달할 수 있을 정도로 오래 존재해야 합니다. 확실히, 복제자가 더 오래 생존할수록, 그만큼 메시지가 복제되고 전승될 확률이 더 높아집니다. 따라서 지속성은 복제자의 핵심

message copied and passed on. So longevity is a key characteristic of a replicator. If you take the alligator story, it can exist for a long time in individual memory—let's say my memory. I can tell you the story now, or ten years from now. The same with the "Twinkle, twinkle" song. So these memes have longevity, because they're memorable, for one reason or another.

Next, fecundity. Fecundity is the ability to reproduce in large numbers. For example, the common housefly reproduces by laying several thousand eggs. So each fly gene gets copied thousands of times. Memes? Well, they can be reproduced in large numbers as well. How many times have you sung the "Twinkle, twinkle" song to someone? Each time you replicated the song—and maybe passed it along to someone who didn't know it yet, a small child maybe.

And finally, fidelity. Fidelity means accuracy of the copying process. We know fidelity is an essential principle of genetic transmission. If a copy of a gene is a bit different from the original, that's called a *genetic* mutation, and mutations are usually bad news. An organism often cannot survive with a mutated gene—and so a gene usually cannot be passed on unless it's an exact copy. For *memes*, however, fidelity is not always so important. For example, if you tell someone the alligator story I told you today, it probably won't be word for word exactly as I said it. Still, it will be basically the same story, and the person who hears the story will be able to pass it along. Other memes are replicated with higher fidelity, though—like the "Twinkle, twinkle" song? It had the exact same words twenty years ago as it does now. Well, that's because we see songs as something that has to be performed accurately each time. If you change a word, the others will usually bring you in line. They'll say, "That's not how you sing it," right?

So, you can see how looking at pieces of cultural information as replicators, as memes, and analyzing them in terms of longevity, fecundity, and fidelity, we can gain some insight about how they spread, persist, or change.

적인 특징입니다. 악어 이야기를 보면, 개인의 기억 속에 오랫동안 존재할 수 있습니다. 제 기억이라고 하죠. 저는 지금도, 10년 후에도 이 이야기를 여러분께 들려줄 수 있어요. 〈반짝 반짝 작은 별〉도 마찬가지죠. 그래서 이들 밈은 이런저런 이유로 기억하기 쉽기 때문에 수명이 깁니다.

다음은 다산성입니다. 다산성이란 다량으로 재생산할 수 있는 능력입니다. 가령, 흔히 볼 수 있는 집파리는 수천 개의 알을 낳아 번식합니다. 파리 한 마리의 유전자가 수천 번씩 복제된다는 얘기죠. 밈은 어떤가요? 이것 역시 다량으로 재생산될 수 있습니다. 여러분은 〈반짝 반짝 작은 별〉을 누군가에게 몇 번이나 불러 주었나요? 여러분이 그 노래를 복제할 때마다, 아마도 그 노래를 모르던, 아마 어린 아이겠지요, 누군가에게 전달했을 것입니다.

그럼 마지막으로 정확도를 봅시다. 이것은 복제 과정의 정확성을 의미합니다. 정확성은 유전자 전달의 필수 원칙입니다. 한 유전자의 복제물이 원본과 조금 다른 것을 돌연변이라고 부르는데, 변이는 대개 나쁜 소식입니다. 변이된 유전자를 가진 유기체는 종종 생존할 수 없습니다. 그래서 유전자는 정확한 복제물이 아니라면 대체로 전달될 수 없습니다. 그러나 밈의 경우 언제나 정확도가 그 정도로 중요하지는 않습니다. 예를 들면, 제가 오늘 들려준 악어 이야기를 여러분이 누군가에게 다시 얘기한다면, 제가 말한 것과 토씨 하나까지 똑같지는 않을 거예요. 하지만 기본적으로는 같은 이야기일 것이고, 그 이야기를 들은 사람은 다른 사람에게 전달할 수 있을 거예요. 하지만 다른 밈들은 이것보다는 더 정확하게 복제됩니다. 〈반짝 반짝 작은 별〉의 경우 그렇겠죠? 이 노래의 가사는 20년 전이나 지금이나 똑같습니다. 사람들이 노래란 매번 정확히 불러야 하는 것으로 여기기 때문입니다. 가사 한 마디를 다르게 부른다면 사람들은 으레 제대로 부르라고 할 겁니다. "그렇게 부르면 안 돼."라고 하면서 말이죠. 맞죠?

그래서 문화적 정보의 단위들을 복제자로, 밈으로 인식하고 지속성, 다산성, 정확성의 관점에서 이것들을 살펴보면 이것들이 어떻게 퍼지고, 지속하며, 변하는지에 대한 통찰력을 얻을 수 있다는 걸 알겁니다.

어휘

alligator 악어   sewer 하수도   find one's way into ~속으로 들어가다   reproduce 재생산하다, 번식하다   strike fear 공포를 불러 일으키다   be around 주변에 존재[활동]하다   meme 밈(비유전적 문화 요소)   analogy 유사점   replicate 복제하다   property 특성, 고유성   longevity 장수, 지속성   fecundity 생산력, 다산   fidelity 충실도, 정확도   accuracy 정확성   mutation 변이, 돌연변이   bring someone in line (규칙 따위에) 따르도록 만들다   persist 지속하다

6. 이 강의의 주요 목적은 무엇인가?

   Ⓐ 학생들이 새로운 정보를 기억하는 데 도움되는 방법 소개하기
   Ⓑ 정보가 사람에서 사람으로 전달되는 방식에 대한 연구 방법 소개하기
   Ⓒ 생물학적 정보와 문화적 정보의 차이 설명하기
   Ⓓ 이야기, 노래, 기타 정보 단위 간의 차이 설명하기

   어휘 method 방법

7. 교수가 악어 이야기를 한 이유는?

   Ⓐ 실화와 거짓 이야기의 차이를 설명하기 위해
   Ⓑ 악어 번식과 문화 전달 사이의 유사점을 밝히기 위해
   Ⓒ 밈으로 기능하는 정보 단위의 예를 제시하기 위해
   Ⓓ 하나의 이야기가 점차 노래로 변하는 과정을 보여주기 위해

   어휘 draw an analogy 유사성을 밝히다   gradually 점진적으로

8. 교수에 따르면, 다음 중 밈 전달의 예는? 두 개의 답을 고르시오.

   Ⓐ 친숙한 이야기 들려주기
   Ⓑ 감정 공유하기
   Ⓒ 독창적인 음악 작곡하기
   Ⓓ 과학 이론 배우기

   어휘 compose 작곡하다   original 독창적인, 색다른

9. 교수가 밈의 지속성에 관한 예로 제시한 것은?

   Ⓐ 한 이야기가 1930년대 등장한 이래로 바뀌고 있다.
   Ⓑ 한 사람이 여러 해 동안 이야기를 기억한다.
   Ⓒ 유전자는 변하지 않고 여러 세대에 걸쳐 전달된다.
   Ⓓ 한 노래가 급속도로 세계적인 인기를 얻게 된다.

   어휘 through generations 여러 세대에 걸쳐

10. 교수는 알을 많이 낳는 파리와 무엇을 비유하는가?

    Ⓐ 부모에게서 다양한 사고 방식을 배우는 아이
    Ⓑ 뉴욕 하수도에서 번식하는 악어
    Ⓒ 각기 다른 버전의 이야기를 기억하는 사람들
    Ⓓ 〈반짝 반짝 작은 별〉을 많이 불러 본 사람

    어휘 version 버전, 판

11. 강의의 일부를 다시 듣고 질문에 답하라. T-20

    > **N** *Why does the professor say this:*
    > **P** If you change a word, the others will usually bring you in line. They'll say, "That's not how you sing it," right?

    Ⓐ 밈 중 일부는 많이 변하지 않는 이유를 설명하기 위해
    Ⓑ 밈으로서 노래에 대한 학생들의 의견을 묻기 위해
    Ⓒ 밈 이론의 한 가지 문제점을 인정하기 위해
    Ⓓ 학생들에게 밈에 관한 개념을 시험해 보라고 요청하기 위해

    어휘 acknowledge 인정하다

Questions 12~17

p.72

N Narrator   P Professor   F Female Student   M Male Student

Script   T-21

N   Listen to part of a discussion in an earth science class.

P   OK. So much for sand. But before we go on to other elements of soil … any questions so far?

F   Yeah. One time we were walking down the beach, kinda sliding our feet … and with each step, we heard this … sort of squeaking sound coming from the sand … almost like the barking of a dog. What was that all about?

P   Well, when you slide your foot along the surface of the sand, there's some resistance—some friction. And that causes a vibration in the layer of sand just below—what you hear as a short squeak or bark. But that reminds me … Have you ever heard of "singing" sand dunes?

F   Singing? Oh, come on …

P   No, really.

M   Are you trying to pull our leg?

P   Not at all. These sand dunes really exist, over 40 of 'em. They're basically big piles of sand, ranging in height from less than 30 meters high to over 300. They're found in deserts all over the world: in California, Africa, Asia … Marco Polo even saw one on his travels to China 700 years ago.

F   But give me a break—they actually sing?

P   Well, their "song" has also been described as sounding like a long, drawn-out bass-note on a musical instrument … or even an airplane—the sound of a low-flying airplane. But yes, it's clearly audible … sometimes even from several kilometers away.

M   You mean … OK, I play the bass in the university orchestra …. So one of these sand dunes sounds like when I play a low note on my bass?

P   Yes. Especially when you use a bow. When you're drawing that bow across a string, there's friction and you're causing that string to vibrate, right? And the instrument resonates with a long, deep bass-note.

M   Uh-huh….

P   OK, imagine the wind piles up a large amount of new sand up along the top of a dune, and that sand gives way all of a sudden…. Now you've got this avalanche of sand sliding down the face of the dune, right? … Just like your bow slides across the string on your bass. But here, it's not a string that's vibrating, but the dune … actually, a layer of sand at the surface of the dune … that's vibrating and resonating to make this low droning sound … as the avalanche slides over it.

N   지구과학 강의의 토론 일부를 들으시오.

P   좋아요. 모래는 여기까지 하죠. 그런데 토양의 다른 요소들로 넘어가기 전에 지금까지 질문 있나요?

F   네. 한번은 해변을 걷고 있는데 발이 살짝 미끄러졌어요. 그런데 발걸음마다 이런 소리가 들렸어요. 모래에서 나는 삑삑 소리요. 흡사 개가 짖는 소리 같았어요. 도대체 무엇이었을까요?

P   자, 모래 표면을 따라 발이 미끄러지면 저항, 즉 마찰이 발생합니다. 그리고 이것이 바로 아래 모래층에서 진동을 일으키죠. 짧게 삑삑거리는 소리나 짖는 소리처럼 들리죠. 그러고 보니 생각나네요. '노래하는' 사구에 대해 들어본 적 있나요?

F   노래요? 설마요.

P   아니, 진짜예요.

M   농담이시죠?

P   아니요, 이 사구들은 실제로 존재합니다. 40개가 넘어요. 근본은 커다란 모래 더미라고 할 수 있는데, 높이가 30미터도 안 되는 것부터 300미터가 넘는 것까지 다양하죠. 이 사구들은 캘리포니아, 아프리카, 아시아 등등 전 세계 사막에서 발견됩니다. 700년 전 마르코 폴로도 중국을 여행하면서 이런 사구를 봤죠.

F   에이 말도 안 돼요. 정말 노래를 한다고요?

P   음, 사구가 부르는 '노래'는 길게 빼는 악기 저음처럼 들린다고도 하고, 저공 비행하는 비행기 소리 같다고도 합니다. 근데 분명히 소리가 들립니다. 때로는 몇 킬로미터 떨어진 곳에서도 들려요.

M   그러니까 교수님 말씀은… 그런데 저는 대학 오케스트라에서 베이스를 연주하고 있어요. 그래서 이 사구들 중 하나는 제가 베이스로 연주할 때 나는 그런 저음을 낸다는 건가요?

P   맞습니다. 특히 활을 쓸 때처럼요. 활로 현을 가로질러 그으면 마찰이 생기고 그 결과로 현이 진동하죠? 그러면 악기가 길고 깊은 저음을 내면서 공명하죠.

M   그렇군요.

P   자, 상상해 보세요. 바람이 사구 꼭대기를 따라 모래를 잔뜩 새로 쌓았어요. 그런데 모래가 갑자기 무너져요. 이제 모래사태가 사구 표면을 미끄러지듯 흘러내리겠죠? 마치 활이 베이스의 현을 가로질러 미끄러지듯이 말이죠. 하지만 여기서 진동하는 것은 현이 아니라 사구입니다. 실은 사구 표면에 있는 모래층이죠. 이 모래층은 진동하고 공명하면서 이런 낮고 단조로운 소리를 냅니다. 모래사태가 사구 위를 미끄러지듯 지나갈 때 말이죠.

M A dune has layers? Isn't it just one big hill of sand?

P Well, the sand got blown there by the wind, so the stuff on top is still pretty loosely packed … and dry. Underneath, it's not so loose, mostly due to moisture…. Even in deserts where it hasn't rained in years, there's some moisture trapped in the layer below. Now the outer layer has to be really dry or else you won't hear much of anything. But the wetter sand underneath has really different sound properties from those of the dry layer above. And the boundary between the layers acts like a mirror, in a way, to reflect sound … and so does the very outer surface of the dune. So the sound reflects back and forth inside that dry outer layer, and one particular pitch gets amplified—a monoton----e, just about, that grows louder and louder and then keeps on reverberating … long after the avalanche of sand has slid down to the bottom of the slope.

F Oh, like … the stairways in my dormitory are enclosed in concrete stairwells. And if you sing one particular note, it'll echo back and forth between the walls in there, … really loud, even after you stop singing.

P Exactly. That note, or pitch, is the frequency that resonates best in a space of those particular dimensions.

M And the pitch of the sound the sand dune makes? How high or low that is depends on the size of the dune, right? Like, … the bass I play is a lot bigger than a violin, so the sounds that resonate the loudest from it are a lot deeper than the higher pitches you get from a violin.

P Hmm. There's a certain logic to that comparison. Actually, though, it's not the height or size of the dune … but rather, it's the thickness of that outer layer of sand. In other words, it's the distance between those reflecting surfaces we talked about … the top and bottom surfaces of that layer of dry sand—the pitch depends on how far apart they are.

M 사구에 층이 있다고요? 사구는 그냥 커다란 모래언덕 아닌가요?

P 자, 모래가 바람에 날리면 꼭대기에 있는 것들은 여전히 느슨하게 뭉쳐 있죠. 그리고 건조합니다. 아래는 대체로 습기 때문에 그렇게 느슨하지 않습니다. 몇 년 동안 비가 오지 않은 사막이라도 아래층에는 습기가 약간 갇혀 있거든요. 이제 바깥층은 정말 건조해야 하겠죠. 그렇지 않으면 우리가 아무 소리도 못 들을 테니까요. 하지만 아래쪽에 있는 더 습한 모래는 위쪽에 있는 건조한 층과 소리 특성이 딴판입니다. 그리고 층 사이의 경계는 어떤 면에서 거울처럼 작용해서 소리를 반사합니다. 그리고 사구 맨 바깥쪽 표면도 마찬가지죠. 그래서 소리가 건조한 바깥층 내부에서 이리저리 반사되고, 특정 높이의 음이 증폭됩니다. 거의 단일음인데 점점 더 커지다가 모래가 경사면 아래로 쏟아져 내린 후에도 오랫동안 계속 울려 퍼지는 거죠.

F 아, 예를 들면 제가 사는 기숙사 계단은 콘크리트로 둘러싸인 계단실 안에 있어요. 그래서 특정한 음 하나를 부르면, 그 안에 있는 벽들 사이를 왔다 갔다 하면서 울려 퍼지죠. 노래를 그친 후에도 정말 큰 소리로 계속 울려요.

P 정확해요. 그 음, 즉 음높이는 특정한 크기의 공간에서 공명이 가장 잘되는 주파수조.

M 그럼 사구가 내는 소리의 음높이요? 음높이가 얼마나 높거나 낮은지는 사구의 크기에 따라 달라지나요? 가령 제가 연주하는 베이스는 바이올린보다 훨씬 크니까 베이스에서 가장 크게 울리는 소리는 바이올린에서 나는 더 높은 음보다 훨씬 깊어요.

P 음, 그렇게 비교해도 일리가 있어요. 사실, 사구의 크기나 높이가 아니라 바깥층의 두께가 중요해요. 다시 말해, 우리가 이야기했던 반사면 사이의 거리, 즉 건조한 모래층의 위쪽 표면과 아래쪽 표면 사이의 거리가 음높이에 영향을 미치죠. 음높이는 그 두 면 사이의 거리에 따라 달라집니다

어휘
....
element 요소 squeak 끼익하는 소리 resistance 저항 friction 마찰 vibration 진동 sand dune 모래 언덕 pull one's leg 놀리다, 농담을 던지다 drawn-out 너무 오래 끄는 audible 들리는 bow 활 resonate 공명하다 pile up 쌓다 avalanche 눈사태, 모래사태 boundary 경계 reflect 반사하다 pitch 음높이 amplified 증폭된 monotone 단조로운 음 reverberating 반향하는 frequency 주파수 dimension 치수, 차원 property 특성 enclosed 둘러싸인 slope 경사 comparison 비교 logic 논리 thickness 두께

12. 화자들의 대화 주제는?

    Ⓐ 사막 여행자들이 역사를 통해 들려주는 이야기

    Ⓑ 전 세계 사막에서 독특한 모래층을 찾기 위한 노력

    Ⓒ 모래가 사구 경사면을 따라 미끄러져 내려오면서 발생하는 영향

    Ⓓ 소리가 세계에서 가장 건조한 지역에서 가장 멀리 이동한다는 증거

    어휘 locate 위치를 찾다   formation 형성물

13. 교수가 사구에 대한 논의를 시작할 때 학생들의 반응을 통해 유추할 수 있는 것은?

    Ⓐ 학생들은 교수가 이전의 논의를 요약하는 특이한 방식을 높이 평가한다.

    Ⓑ 학생들은 교수가 별로 진지하지 않다고 생각한다.

    Ⓒ 학생들은 새로운 주제를 시작하기 전에 해변 모래에 대해 더 알고 싶어한다.

    Ⓓ 학생들은 오랫동안 궁금했던 주제를 교수에게 물어보려고 기다리고 있다.

14. 교수가 비행기를 언급한 이유는?

    Ⓐ 사막에서 가끔 들리는 소리를 묘사하려고

    Ⓑ 사구가 지리적으로 넓게 분포되어 있음을 강조하려고

    Ⓒ 사막에서 연구했던 일화를 소개하려고

    Ⓓ 사막 모래폭풍의 위력을 설명하려고

    어휘 anecdote 일화

15. 특이한 사구에 대한 교수의 설명에 따르면, 바깥층 모래는 대체로 아래쪽 모래와 어떻게 다른가? 정답을 2개 선택하시오.

    Ⓐ 바깥층 모래는 극도로 건조하다.

    Ⓑ 바깥층 모래는 더 느슨하게 뭉쳐 있다.

    Ⓒ 바깥층 모래는 알갱이가 더 작다.

    Ⓓ 바깥층 모래는 알갱이 크기가 균일하지 않다.

    어휘 uniform 균일한

16. 학생들 중 한 명이 기숙사 계단을 언급한 이유는?

    Ⓐ 사구 측면 경사지의 기울기를 추정하려고

    Ⓑ 과학적 입증이 단계적인 과정이라는 점을 강조하려고

    Ⓒ 사람의 목소리를 악기에 비유할 수 있음을 암시하려고

    Ⓓ 교수의 설명을 이해하고 있음을 보여주려고

    어휘 steepness 가파름, 기울기

17. 강의의 일부를 다시 듣고 질문에 답하라.

    N After a student compares different stringed instruments to sand dunes, what does the professor imply when he says this:
    P Hmm. There's a certain logic to that comparison.

    Ⓐ 대다수 전문가는 비교가 정확하다는 데 동의할 것이다.

    Ⓑ 비교가 타당해 보이지만 사실은 그렇지 않다.

    Ⓒ 학생이 자신의 논점을 명확하게 설명하지 않았다.

    Ⓓ 학생이 특이한 접근법을 사용해 교수가 내린 결론과 같은 결론에 도달했다.

Questions 18~22

p.74

N Narrator   S Student   P Professor

Script   T-23

N Listen to a conversation between a student and a professor.

S Hi. I was wondering if I could talk with you about the assignment in the Film Theory class?

P Of course, Jill.

S It seems that pretty much everyone else in the class gets what they're supposed to be doing, but *I'm* not so sure.

P Well, the class *is* for students who are really serious about film. You must have taken film courses before?

S Yeah, in high school, Film Appreciation.

P Hmm, I wouldn't think that'd be enough. Did you concentrate mainly on form, or content?

S Oh, definitely content. We'd watch, say, *Lord of the Flies*, and then discuss it.

P Oh, *that* approach … treating film as literature, ignoring what makes it unique …

S I liked it, though …

P Sure, but *that* kind of class … well, I'm not surprised you're feeling a little lost. Y'know, we have two introductory courses that are supposed to be taken before you get to *my* course—one in film art, techniques … technical stuff … and another in film history. So students in the class *you're* in should be pretty far along in film studies. In fact, usually the system blocks anyone trying to sign up for a class they shouldn't be taking, who hasn't taken the courses you're required to do *first*, as *prerequisites*.

S Well, I did have a problem with that, but I discussed it with one of your office staff and she gave me permission.

P Of course. No matter how many times I tell them, they just keep on … Well, for your own good, I'd really suggest dropping back and starting at the usual place …

S Yes, but … I've already been in this class for four weeks! I'd hate to just drop it now, especially since I find it so different, so interesting.

P I guess *so*—frankly, I can't believe you've lasted this long! These are pretty in-depth theories we've been discussing, and you've been doing OK so far, I guess. But, still, the program's been designed to progress through certain stages. Like any other professional training, we build on previous knowledge.

S Then maybe you could recommend some extra reading I can do, to catch up?

P Well, are you intending to study film, as your main concentration?

S No. No, I—I'm just interested; I'm actually in marketing, but there seems to be a connection …

N 교수와 학생의 대화를 들으시오.

S 안녕하세요. 영화이론 수업 과제 때문에 상의 드릴 게 있는데 어떠세요?

P 괜찮아, 질.

S 다른 수강생들은 수업을 잘 이해하는 것 같은데, 저는 잘 모르겠어요.

P 그 수업은 영화에 대해 아주 진지하게 접근하는 학생들을 위한 수업이야. 전에 영화 관련 과목은 들었겠지?

S 예, 고등학교에서 영화 감상 수업을 들었어요.

P 흠, 그 정도만으로는 불충분할 텐데. 형식과 내용, 어떤 걸 위주로 했죠?

S 물론 내용이죠. 이를테면 〈파리대왕〉을 보고 토론했어요.

P 아, 그런 접근이라, 영화를 문학처럼 다루고, 작품의 독특한 요소를 간과하는….

S 하지만 전 좋았는데요.

P 물론 그랬겠지. 하지만 그런 유형의 수업이었다면, 음, 내 수업에서 헤매는 게 이해는 되는군. 그런데 내 수업을 수강하기 전에 들어야 하는 개론 수업이 두 과목 있어. 하나는 영화 기술, 즉 기법, 기술적인 내용을 다루고 하나는 영화사야. 그래서 그 수업을 듣는 수강생들은 영화 공부를 꽤 많이 한 셈이지. 사실 보통은 선수 과목을 듣지 않은 상태에서 수강신청을 하면 전산에 등록이 안 되는데.

S 아, 그런 문제가 있었어요. 하지만 과 사무실 직원에게 상의했더니 허락해 주던데요.

P 아무렴 그랬겠지. 아무리 얘기해도 계속 그러니. 근데, 학생을 위해서 말인데 그냥 이 과목 취소하고 입문부터 듣지.

S 예, 하지만 벌써 4주나 들었는걸요! 그냥 여기서 그만두기는 싫은데요. 특히 교수님 수업이 참 독특하고 아주 재미있거든요.

P 그렇긴 할거야. 솔직히 여태까지 버틴 게 신기해! 그동안 꽤 심도 있는 영화이론을 논했는데 그럭저럭 잘해왔네. 하지만 이 과목은 일정한 단계를 밟아 올라가도록 짜인 거야. 다른 전공 과정들처럼 사전 지식을 바탕으로 진행돼.

S 그럼 혹시 제가 따라갈 수 있도록 따로 읽을 만한 책 좀 추천해 주시겠어요?

P 자네 영화를 전공하려는 건가?

S 아뇨. 그건 아니고 그냥 관심 있어서요. 전 마케팅 전공이에요. 그래도 연관성이 있어 보여서요.

P Oh, well, in *that* case … if you're taking the course just out of *interest* … I mean, I'd still highly recommend signing up for the introductory courses at *some* point. But in the *meantime*, there's no harm, I guess, in trying to keep up with *this* class. The interest is clearly there. Uh, instead of any extra reading just now, though, you *could* view some of the *old* introductory lectures—we have 'em on video—*that'd* give you a better handle on the subject. It's still a pretty tall order, and we'll be moving right along, so you'll really need to stay on top of it.

S OK, I've been warned. Now, could I tell you about my idea for the assignment …?

P 흠, 그렇다면 관심 차원에서 듣는 거라면, 언젠가는 꼭 입문 과정을 들어 봐. 하지만 한동안 이 수업을 따라오려고 노력하는 것도 나쁠 건 없겠지. 그리 관심이 있다고 하니. 지금 당장 뭘 읽어 보기 보단 예전 입문 강의를 좀 봐. 녹화 영상이 있으니. 그러면 주제에 대한 감이 좀 잡힐 거야. 그래도 어렵긴 할 거야. 하지만 수업 진도는 나가야 하니 훤히 꿰고 있어야 해.

S 예, 명심할게요. 참, 이제 과제에 대한 제 생각을 말씀 드려도 될까요?

어휘

film 영화 appreciation 감상 concentrate on ~에 집중하다 literature 문학 ignore 무시하다 feel lost 뭐가 뭔지 모르다, 헤매다 prerequisite 선결 조건, 선수 과목 last 지속하다 in-depth 심도 있는 handle on ~을 이해하다 tall order 어려운 주문, 무리한 요구 stay on top of ~을 훤히 알다, 완전히 파악하다

---

18. 이 대화의 주제는 무엇인가?

Ⓐ 학생이 조언을 얻고 싶어하는 과제
Ⓑ 학생이 교수의 수업을 계속 들어야 할지에 대한 우려
Ⓒ 영화이론 강좌 수강생들이 감상할 영화 선택
Ⓓ 영화과 강좌의 체계와 순서

어휘 sequence 순서

19. 학생이 고등학교 때 들은 영화 수업에 대한 교수의 태도는?

Ⓐ 자신이 가르치는 강의를 듣기에는 충분한 준비가 아니라고 생각한다.
Ⓑ 영화 수업에서 문학 작품에 대해 토론하면 안 된다고 생각한다.
Ⓒ 그런 유형의 강의는 익숙하지 않은 학생들에게는 혼란스럽다고 생각한다.
Ⓓ 그런 강의에서 취하는 접근법이 영화를 공부하는 최선의 방법이라고 생각한다.

어휘 literary work 문학 작품 inexperienced 경험 없는, 미숙한

20. 학생이 교수의 영화이론 수업에 수강 신청할 수 있었던 이유는?

Ⓐ 고등학교 때 들었던 수업이 선수 과목 요건을 충족해서
Ⓑ 대개는 학생들을 차단하는 전산이 제대로 작동하지 않아서
Ⓒ 과 사무실 직원이 지침을 따르지 않아서
Ⓓ 교수가 학생의 경우를 예외로 인정해서

어휘 fulfill 만족시키다, 충족하다
make an exception 예외로 하다

21. 학생이 수업을 계속 듣도록 교수가 허락한 이유는? 두 개의 답을 고르시오.

Ⓐ 학생이 졸업하려면 그 수업을 들어야 하므로
Ⓑ 교수가 계속 들으려는 학생의 열의에 감동해서
Ⓒ 학생이 그 과목을 수강하기에 준비가 충분하다고 교수를 설득해서
Ⓓ 학생이 영화를 전공하려는 게 아니라는 것을 알게 되어서

어휘 be impressed with ~에 감동하다 eagerness 열의
adequate 충분한

22. 수업을 따라갈 수 있도록 교수가 학생에게 해보라고 조언한 것은?

Ⓐ 입문 과정 수강
Ⓑ 녹화 영상 시청
Ⓒ 추가 교재 읽기
Ⓓ 마케팅 수업 중도 하차

어휘 drop out of ~에서 중도 하차하다

Questions 23~28

p.76

N Narrator   **P** Professor   **M** Male Student   **F** Female Student

Script   T-24

N Listen to part of a lecture in a literature class.

P Now, we can't really talk about fairy tales without first talking about *folk* tales ... because there's a strong connection between these two genres, these two types of stories. In fact, many fairy tales started out as folktales.

So, what's a *folk* tale? How would you characterize them? Jeff?

M Well, they're old stories, traditional stories. They were passed down orally within cultures, from generation to generation, so they changed a lot over time; I mean, every storyteller, or maybe every town, might have had a slightly different version of the same folktale.

P That's right, there's *local difference*, and that's why we say folktales are communal.

By "communal," we mean they reflect the traits and the concerns of a particular community at a particular time. So essentially the same tale could be told in different communities, with certain aspects of the tale adapted to fit the specific community. Um, *not* the plot ... the details of what *happens* in the story would remain constant; that was the thread that held the tale together. But all the other elements, like the location or characters, might be modified for each audience.

OK, so what about *fairy* tales? They also are found in most cultures, but how are they different from folktales? I guess the first question is what is a fairy tale? And don't anyone say, "a story with a fairy in it." Because we all know that very few fairy tales actually have those tiny magical creatures in them. But what else can we say about them? Mary?

F Well, they seem to be less realistic than folktales. Like they have something improbable happening—a frog turning into a prince, say. Oh, that's another common element, royalty ... a prince or princess. And fairy tales all seem to take place in a location that's nowhere and everywhere at the same time.

P What's the line, ah—how do all those stories start? "Once upon a time, in a faraway land ..." In the case of *folk* tales, each storyteller would specify a particular location and time, though the time and location would differ for different storytellers. With *fairy* tales, however, the location is generally unspecified, no matter who the storyteller is ... that "land faraway ..." We'll come back to this point in a few minutes.

M Um, I thought a fairy tale was just the written version of an oral folktale.

N 문학 강의의 일부를 들으시오.

P 민담에 대해서 먼저 논하지 않고서는 동화에 대해 논할 수 없습니다. 두 장르, 이 두 가지 형식의 이야기 사이에는 밀접한 연관성이 있기 때문이죠. 사실, 많은 동화들이 처음에는 민담에서 시작했습니다.

그럼 민담이란 무엇일까요? 민담을 어떻게 규정할 수 있을까요? 제프?

M 음, 옛날 이야기, 전래담이요. 문화권 내에서 세대에서 세대로 구두로 전승되어 내려오기 때문에 세월이 흐르면서 많이 바뀌죠. 즉 같은 이야기라도 이야기하는 사람마다 또는 마을마다 약간 다른 버전이 있을 수 있어요.

P 맞습니다, 지역적 차이가 있죠. 그래서 우리는 민담을 공동체적이라고 하는 겁니다. "공동체적"이라 함은 민담은 특정 시기, 특정 지역의 특성과 관심사를 투영하고 있다는 의미입니다. 그래서 기본적으로는 같은 이야기가 일부 측면만 특정 지역사회에 맞게 각색되어 타 지역사회에서 회자될 수 있죠. 줄거리는 안 바뀝니다. 이야기 속에서 일어나는 사건에 관한 내용은 늘 한결같습니다. 줄거리는 이야기를 하나로 엮는 실이죠. 하지만 그 밖의 요소를, 즉 장소나 등장인물 같은 것은 청자에 따라 변하기도 합니다.

자, 그렇다면 동화는 어떤가요? 동화도 대부분의 문화권에서 발견됩니다. 하지만 민담과 어떻게 다를까요? 첫 번째 질문은 과연 동화("fairy tale")가 무엇이냐는 겁니다. "요정(fairy)이 나오는 이야기(tale)"라고는 하지 마세요. 다들 알다시피 마법을 부리는 조그만 존재가 실제로 등장하는 동화는 극히 드무니까요. 그렇다면 뭐라고 할 수 있을까요? 메리?

F 민담보다는 좀 비현실적인 것 같아요. 있을 수 없는 일, 가령 개구리가 왕자로 변하는 일이 일어나잖아요. 아, 공통 요소가 또 있네요. 공주님, 왕자님 같은 왕족이 등장하구요. 동화 속 이야기의 장소는 세상에 없는 곳 같기도 하고 세상 어디에나 존재하는 것 같기도 해요.

P 그 말투가 뭐죠, 아 — 그런 이야기는 다 어떻게 시작하죠? "옛날 옛적, 멀고 먼 나라에 …" 민담의 경우, 화자가 특정 지역과 시대를 구체적으로 명시합니다. 비록 이야기하는 사람에 따라 시간과 장소가 바뀌곤 하지만. 그러나 동화의 경우 대체로 장소가 명시되지 않아요. 누가 얘기하던 간에 "멀고 먼 나라"라고만 하잖아요. 이 부분은 이따 다시 얘기하기로 하죠.

M 어, 동화는 그저 구전되는 민담을 글로 적은 것이라고 생각했는데요.

P Well, not exactly, though that is how many fairy tales developed. For example, in the late eighteenth century, the Grimm brothers traveled throughout what's now Germany recording local *folk* tales. These were eventually published—as *fairy* tales—but not before undergoing a process of evolution.

Now, a number of things happen when an oral tale gets written down. First, the language changes, it becomes more formal, more standard—some might say less colorful. It's like the difference in your language depending on whether you're talking to someone or writing them a letter.

Second, when an orally transmitted story is written down, an authoritative version, with a recognized author is created. The communal aspect gets lost; the tale no longer belongs to the community; it belongs to the world, so to speak. Because of this, elements like place and time can no longer be tailored to suit a particular audience, so they become less identifiable, more generalizable to any audience.

On the other hand, descriptions of characters and settings can be developed more completely. In *folk* tales, characters might be identified by a name, but you wouldn't know anything more about them. But in *fairy* tales, people no longer have to remember plots—they're written down, right? So more energy can be put into other elements of the story, like character and setting. So you get more details about the characters, and about where the action takes place, what people's houses were like, whether they're small cabins or grand palaces ... And it's worth investing that energy because the story, now in book form, isn't in danger of being lost, those details won't be forgotten. If a *folk* tale isn't repeated by each generation, it may be lost for all time. But with a fairy tale, it's always there in a book, waiting to be discovered again and again.

Another interesting difference involves the change in audience—who the stories are meant for. Contrary to what many people believe today, folktales were originally intended for adults, not for children. So why is it that fairy tales seem targeted toward children nowadays?

P 반드시 그렇진 않아요. 비록 많은 동화들이 그렇게 시작하긴 했지만. 예를 들어 18세기 말 그림형제가 지금의 독일 지역을 돌아다니면서 민담을 기록했습니다. 결국 동화집으로 출판됐죠. 변천 과정을 거친 후에 말이죠.

자, 구전 설화들이 기록되면 몇 가지 현상이 일어납니다. 우선, 언어가 바뀝니다. 더 격식을 차리고 표준화되는데, 이를 두고 생생한 맛이 떨어진다는 사람도 있습니다. 누군가에게 말로 하느냐 아니면 편지로 쓰느냐에 따라 어투가 달라지는 것과 마찬가지죠.

둘째, 구두로 전달되는 이야기가 기록되면 인정 받는 작가의 권위 있는 버전이 탄생합니다. 지역색은 사라지고 그 이야기는 더 이상 그 지역사회의 것이 아니게 됩니다. 말하자면 온 세상의 이야기가 되는 거죠. 그렇기 때문에 장소나 시대 같은 요소를 더 이상 특정한 독자층에 맞도록 조정할 수 없습니다. 그래서 그런 요소들은 식별 가능한 특색이 줄어들고 어떤 독자에게도 맞게끔 더 일반화됩니다.

반면, 등장인물과 배경에 대한 묘사는 더 완성도가 높아집니다. 민담에서 등장인물은 이름으로 구별되지만 그 밖에는 알 수 있는 것이 없습니다. 그러나 동화의 경우에 더 이상 줄거리를 기억할 필요가 없어집니다. 기록되어 있으니까요, 그렇죠? 그래서 이야기의 다른 요소인 등장인물과 배경 같은 것에 더 많은 에너지가 투여될 수 있는 것이죠. 그래서 등장인물, 행위가 발생한 장소, 등장인물의 집이 작은 오두막인지 거대한 궁전인지 등의 묘사에 자세하게 살이 붙죠. 그리고 그런 에너지를 투자할 만한 가치가 있습니다. 왜냐하면 이제는 책의 형식을 갖춘 그 이야기는 유실될 위험이 없고 상세한 내용들이 잊혀질 위험이 없으니까요. 민담은 각 세대에 의해 반복되지 않을 경우 영영 잊혀질 위험이 있습니다. 그러나 동화의 경우, 항상 책에 담겨 있으므로 언제든 계속 발견되기를 기다리고 있죠.

또 다른 흥미로운 차이점 하나는 대상 청자, 그러니까 이야기를 듣는 대상의 변화와 관련이 있습니다. 요즘 많은 사람들의 생각과 달리 민담은 원래 아이들이 아닌 어른들을 위한 것이었습니다. 그렇다면 오늘날 동화는 왜 아이들을 대상으로 하는 것처럼 보일까요?

어휘

fairy tale 동화 folktale 민담 connection 연관성 start out 처음 시작하다 characterize 규정하다, 특징[특색]을 나타내다 local difference 지역별 차이 communal 공동체적인, 집단적인 reflect 반영하다, 투영하다 trait 특징 concern 관심사, 사건 adapt 각색[번안]하다 plot 줄거리 constant 변함없는, 일관된 thread 실, 맥락 modify 변경하다, 수정하다 realistic 현실적인 improbable 있을 수 없는, 개연성이 낮은 common element 공통 요소 royalty 왕족 specify 구체적으로 명시하다 unspecified 명시되지 않은 Grimm brothers 그림형제 undergo (과정을) 겪다 evolution 진화, 점진적 변화 oral 구두의 transmit 전달하다, 전송하다 authoritative 권위 있는 tailor 맞추다 identifiable 식별할 수 있는, 인식할 수 있는 generalizable 일반화할 수 있는 worth -ing ~할 만한 가치가 있다

23. 이 강의의 주제는 무엇인가?

   Ⓐ 민담과 동화의 구전 전통
   Ⓑ 민담과 동화의 공통적 등장인물과 줄거리
   Ⓒ 민담과 동화의 차이점
   Ⓓ 민담과 동화 속에 숨은 의미들

어휘 hidden 숨은

24. 민담이 공동체적이라는 말에서 교수가 의미하는 것은?

   Ⓐ 지역사회마다 차이가 거의 없다.
   Ⓑ 한 지역사회에 속한 개인들간의 유대를 강화하는 데 기여한다.
   Ⓒ 한 지역사회 역사에서 중요한 사건들을 이야기한다.
   Ⓓ 한 지역 공동체의 필요에 따라 각색될 수 있다.

어휘 vary 다르다   ties 유대 관계   relate 이야기하다, 설명하다

25. 교수가 fairy의 개념을 명확히 하는 이유는?

   Ⓐ fairy tale이라는 말의 유래를 설명하려고
   Ⓑ fairy tale을 달리 정의할 수 있는 가능성을 배제하려고
   Ⓒ fairy tale의 기능에 대한 주장을 지지하려고
   Ⓓ 요정이 동화의 주요 요소임을 알려주려고

어휘 eliminate 제거하다, 배제하다

26. 교수는 동화의 배경에 대해 무엇이라고 하는가?

   Ⓐ 동화는 보통 불특정 장소를 배경으로 한다.
   Ⓑ 배경 장소는 이야기의 원전 국가에 따라 결정된다.
   Ⓒ 저자에게 익숙한 장소를 배경으로 한다.
   Ⓓ 화자는 청자가 누구냐에 따라 배경 장소를 바꾼다.

어휘 nonspecific 불특정의   vary 바꾸다

27. 강의에서 교수는 민담과 동화의 특징을 설명한다. 다음 중 각 이야기 유형의 특징에 해당하는 것에 표기하라.

	민담	동화
현재는 주로 어린이를 대상으로 한다.		✓
줄거리만이 안정적인 요소다.	✓	
이야기가 구전된다.	✓	
공인된 하나의 판본이 존재한다.		✓
등장인물이 충분히 발전한다.		✓
비교적 격식을 차리는 언어다.		✓

어휘 stable 안정적인

28. 강의의 일부를 다시 듣고 질문에 답하라.

 T-25

> **F** And fairy tales all seem to take place in a location that's nowhere and everywhere at the same time.
> **P** What's the line, ah—how do all those stories start? "Once upon a time, in a faraway land..."
>
> **N** *Why does the professor say this:*
> **P** What's the line, ah—how do all those stories start? "Once upon a time, in a faraway land..."

   Ⓐ 학생이 한 말을 지지하려고
   Ⓑ 학생에게 분명히 진술하라고 요구하려고
   Ⓒ 그 구절이 나오는 이야기를 학생이 알고 있는지 알아보려고
   Ⓓ 동화 속 시간과 장소의 관계를 명확하게 설명하려고

어휘 clarify 명확히 하다   statement 진술, 성명

SPEAKING

Question 1

p.80

Narrator T-26

Do you agree or disagree with the following statement? Why or why not? Use details and examples to explain your answer.

아래 주장에 찬성 또는 반대 의견을 말하고 그 이유를 설명하시오. 상세한 설명과 예를 들어 답하시오.

It is more important to study math or science than it is to study art or literature.

예술이나 문학을 공부하는 것보다 수학이나 과학을 공부하는 것이 더 중요하다.

준비 시간 : 15초
답변 시간 : 45초

중요 포인트

이 유형의 문제에는 제시된 문장에 대한 의견을 분명히 밝혀야 한다. 만일 수학이나 과학 공부가 더 중요하다고 생각한다면, "It is used in many important areas, such as engineering, and is necessary to make calculations when building structures." ("공학 등 중요한 분야에 활용되고 구조물을 세울 때 계산에 필요하다.")라고 답변할 수 있다. 자신의 개인적 사례를 들어, "I prefer math because it has helped me in certain situations, such as planning my personal finances." ("개인 재무 설계 같은 특정 상황에 도움이 되므로 수학을 선호한다.")라고 할 수도 있다.

아니면 반대로 예술 공부가 얼마나 쓸모 없는 것인지에 대해 말할 수도 있다. 제시된 명제에 반대하는 경우에도 마찬가지로 구체적으로 논증한다. "Math and science are not actually important because not many people need to know math very well." ("많은 사람들이 수학에 통달할 필요는 없으므로 수학이나 과학은 별로 중요하지 않다.") 또는 "Most people need to know only a little math or science to do their jobs." ("대부분의 사람들은 일에 필요한 수준의 수학 또는 과학 지식만 있으면 된다.")라고 대답할 수도 있다. 그런 다음 예술이나 문학이 왜 더 중요한지에 대한 예를 들어야 한다. 예가 될 수 있는 것들은 많으며, 의견을 잘 뒷받침할 수 있는 것이라면 어떤 예를 들었는지는 중요하지 않다.

Question 2

p.80

Narrator T-27

The university has announced a new policy regarding dining services. Read an article about it in the student newspaper. You have 50 seconds to read the article. Begin reading now.

대학은 새로운 식당 서비스 방침을 발표했다. 학생신문에 실린 관련 기사를 50초 동안 읽으시오. 지금 읽으시오.

Campus Dining Club Announced

Starting this year, the university dining hall will be transformed into The Campus Dining Club for one week at the end of each semester. During the last week of each semester, the dining hall will feature special meals prepared by the university's culinary arts students. The school feels that this will give students who are studying cooking and food preparation valuable experience that will help them later, when they pursue careers. The university has announced that it will charge a small additional fee for these dinners in order to pay for the special gourmet food ingredients that will be required.

캠퍼스 정찬 클럽 공지

올해부터 대학 식당이 각 학기말 일주일 동안 캠퍼스 정찬 클럽으로 변모한다. 학기의 마지막 일주일 동안 식당에서 본 대학의 조리학과 학생들이 준비한 특별 메뉴를 제공한다. 이는 요리 및 음식 관련 전공 학생들이 졸업 후 취업 활동에 도움이 될 수 있는 값진 경험을 제공할 것으로 학교측은 보고 있다. 학교는 특별 고급 음식의 재료비를 충당하기 위해 소액의 추가 요금을 받을 것이라고 발표했다.

어휘

transform A into B A가 B로 바뀌다   culinary arts 요리법
gourmet food 특식, 미식가 메뉴

Narrator T-28

Now listen to two students discussing the article.

기사에 대한 두 학생의 논의를 들으시오.

Script

F Did you see that article?

M Yeah—and it sounds like a great idea. It's really good for the students in that program.

F Don't they cook in class anyway?

M Well, yeah, they do … but my cousin was in the program a few years ago, and she said that it's very different to cook for a lot of people in that kind of atmosphere than to cook for classmates.

F Why is that?

M Well, in class you can take your time. But, cooking for more people, there's more pressure—I mean, you're in a rush, people are waiting …. and it might be easy to make a mistake with all that stress …

F Then they'll think you're a bad chef, right?

M Absolutely!

F So, OK, it's good practice. But what about the extra cost?

M Well, look at it this way. You've eaten at some of the fancier restaurants in town, right?

F Yeah, there are some great places to eat around here.

M Well, these students … they'll be making fantastic meals. And it's gonna be cheaper than going out to one of those restaurants.

F Much cheaper actually …

M So, you know, it'll be worth it. The meals will be as good as the ones in those expensive restaurants.

F 그 기사 봤니?

M 응. 아주 좋은 생각 같아. 프로그램 참여 학생들에게 정말 좋을 거야.

F 그런데 수업 중에도 요리하잖아?

M 하기야 하지. 그런데 사촌이 몇 년 전에 그 프로그램에 참여했는데 그런 분위기에서 많은 사람들의 요리를 하는 게 학급 친구들을 위해 요리하는 거랑 많이 다르다고 하더라고.

F 왜 그렇지?

M 수업 중엔 여유가 있잖아. 하지만 이건 많은 사람들을 위해 요리하는 거고, 부담감도 더 하지. 그러니까 사람들이 기다리니까 서두르게 되고 그런 스트레스로 실수하기도 쉽거든.

F 그럼 사람들이 형편없는 요리사라고 여길 테고?

M 그렇지!

F 그렇다면 괜찮은 실습이 되겠네. 하지만 추가 요금 내는 건?

M 그럼 이렇게 생각해 봐. 시내에 있는 고급 레스토랑에서 먹어 본 적

있지?

F 그래. 이 주변에 괜찮은 곳들이 좀 있지.

M 학생들은 환상적인 요리를 만들 텐데, 가격은 그런 곳에 가는 것보다 더 저렴하지 않겠어.

F 훨씬 싸겠네 정말….

M 그래서 그만한 가치가 있는 거야. 비싼 레스토랑 음식 못지않게 괜찮을 거야.

어휘

atmosphere 분위기   pressure 심적 부담감   in a rush 아주 급하게
extra cost 추가 요금

Narrator

The man expresses his opinion about the plan described in the article. Briefly summarize the plan. Then state his opinion about the plan and explain the reasons he gives for holding that opinion.

남자는 기사에 실린 계획에 대한 자신의 의견을 말한다. 그 계획을 간략히 설명하고, 남자의 의견이 무엇인지, 그리고 남자가 그렇게 주장하는 근거를 설명하시오.

준비 시간 : 30초
답변 시간 : 60초

중요 포인트

먼저 문제의 지시대로 독해 지문에 대학의 계획, 즉 대학 식당에서 조리학과 학생들이 만든 저녁을 판매하려는 계획에 대해 요약해야 한다. 이어서 대학이 그런 시도를 하려는 이유, 즉 요리 전공학생들에게 실습 경험을 제공하려는 것에 대해 간단히 언급할 수 있다. 단, 요약에 시간을 너무 소비하면 안 된다. 요약은 채점자가 대학의 계획을 명확히 이해할 수 있는 정도면 된다.

이어서 남학생의 의견을 말한다. 이 경우 남학생은 대학의 제안에 찬성하고 있으므로 남학생이 언급한 두 가지 이유에 대해 설명한다. 완성도 있는 답을 하기 위해 대화에서 얻은 정보와 독해 지문에서 나온 내용을 잘 연결해야 한다. 먼저 남학생은 수업 시간에 요리하는 것과 실제로 여러 사람들이 먹을 것을 준비해야 하는 부담스러운 상황에서 요리하는 것은 다르므로 조리학과 학생들에게 좋은 경험이 된다고 생각해서 찬성하고 있다. 또한 남학생이 대학의 계획에 찬성하는 두 번째 이유도 언급해야 한다. 이 학생은 학생 식당에서 판매하는 저녁 값이 좀 비싸지긴 하지만 그 정도는 지불할 가치가 있다고 생각한다. 요리 전공학생들이 조리하는 것인 만큼 시내의 고급 레스토랑 음식 못지 않을 것이라고 믿기 때문이다.

Narrator T-29

Read the passage about target marketing. You will have 45 seconds to read the passage. Begin reading now.

표적 마케팅에 관한 글을 45초 동안 읽으시오. 지금 읽으시오.

Target Marketing

Advertisers in the past have used radio and television in an attempt to provide information about their products to large, general audiences; it was once thought that the best way to sell a product was to advertise it to as many people as possible. However, more recent trends in advertising have turned toward target marketing. Target marketing is the strategy of advertising to smaller, very specific audiences— audiences that have been determined to have the greatest need or desire for the product being marketed. Target marketing has proved to be very effective in reaching potential customers.

표적 마케팅

과거 광고주들은 불특정 다수의 소비자들에게 정보를 제공하려는 시도에서 라디오나 텔레비전을 이용했다. 한때 제품을 파는 최선의 방법은 최대한 많은 사람들에게 제품을 광고하는 것이라 생각했기 때문이다. 하지만 최근의 광고 추세는 표적 마케팅으로 선회했다. 표적 마케팅은 소수의 특정 사람들, 즉 판매 대상 제품을 가장 사고 싶어하거나 가장 필요할 것으로 판단되는 사람들에게 광고하는 전략이다. 표적 마케팅은 잠재 고객들에 대한 전달효과가 매우 좋은 것으로 입증되었다.

어휘

target marketing 표적 마케팅 audience (TV, 영화 등) 시청자, 독자, 관람객 effective 효과적인 potential 잠재적인

Narrator T-30

Now listen to part of a lecture on this topic in a marketing class.

이 주제에 관한 마케팅 강의의 일부를 들으시오.

Script

P Nowadays, something you notice more and more is television commercials that are made specifically for certain television programs. So, let's say a company wants to sell a telephone … a cell phone. Now, during TV shows that young people watch— you know, shows with pop music or teen serials— they create a commercial that emphasizes how fun the phone is. You know, the phone has bright colors, and they show kids having a good time with their friends. And, well, the company wants the kids watching TV at this time to want to buy this phone—this phone that's made especially for them. But, the same company will make a different commercial to be shown during, say, a program about business or a business news show. Now, for this group of people, businesspeople, the company will have to show how efficient their phone is, how it can handle all business easily and maybe even save money. And here's the thing—it's basically the same phone; the company has just made two different commercials to appeal to different groups of people.

P 요즘 특정 TV 프로그램에 특화해 만든 TV 광고가 점점 더 많이 눈에 띌 겁니다. 예를 들어 한 회사가 전화기, 휴대폰을 팔려고 한다 합시다. 이제 젊은 청소년들이 보는 대중음악프로나 10대 연속극 같은 TV 프로그램이 방영되는 동안 이 회사는 휴대폰이 얼마나 재미있는지를 강조한 광고를 만듭니다. 화사한 색의 휴대폰이 등장하고 아이들이 친구들과 즐거운 시간을 보내는 장면을 연출합니다. 회사는 그 시간대에 TV를 보는 청소년들이 이 휴대폰, 그러니까 그들을 위해 특별히 만든 휴대폰을 사고 싶게 만들려는 거죠.
그러나 같은 회사는 경제 관련 프로그램이나 경제 뉴스 시간에 방영하기 위한 또 다른 광고를 만들 겁니다. 이제 이 부류의 사람들, 사업가들을 대상으로 자사의 휴대폰이 얼마나 효율적인지, 이 휴대폰으로 모든 일 처리가 얼마나 쉬운지, 심지어 비용도 절감할 수 있다는 걸 보여줘야 할 것입니다. 근데 말이죠 – 요컨대 같은 휴대폰인데 회사는 다른 고객군에게 호소하기 위해 두 가지 광고를 만든 겁니다.

어휘

serial 연속극 efficient 효율적인 here's the thing 있잖아요, 그런데 말이죠

Narrator

Using the professor's examples, explain the advertising technique of target marketing.

교수가 든 예를 이용하여 표적 마케팅의 광고 기법을 설명하시오.

준비 시간 : 30초
답변 시간 : 60초

중요 포인트

먼저 독해 지문에 나온 표적 마케팅의 기법에 대해 설명해야 한다. 지문에 따르면 표적 마케팅이란 특정 집단의 사람들에게 호소하는 광고를 기획하여 제작하는 것이다. 그리고 나서 교수가 강의에서 표적 마케팅을 설명하려고 들었던 예시를 활용한다. 교수는 휴대폰 제조사의 예를 들면서 두 가지 TV 프로그램 방영 시간에 내보낼 광고를 각기 다르게 제작한다고 설명했다. 음악프로 같은 젊은 층 시청 시간대에 내보낼 광고는 젊은 취향에 맞게 오락적 요소를 가미하고, 반대로 경제, 비즈니스 관련 프로그램에 나갈 광고에서는 휴대폰의 효율성 등 사업가들이 중시할 요소를 가미한다고 했다.

Question 4

p.82

Narrator T-31

Now listen to part of a lecture in a psychology class.

심리학 강의의 일부를 들으시오.

P   Why do we do the things we do? What drives us to participate in certain activities … to buy a certain car … or even to choose a certain career? In other words, what motivates us to do what we do?
Well, in studies of motivation, psychologists distinguish between two very different types. Our reasons for doing something, our motivations, can be *extrinsic*—in other words, based on some kind of *external* reward like praise or money … or they can be *intrinsic* … meaning we engage in the activity because it pleases us *internally*. Both create strong forces that lead us to behave in certain ways; however, intrinsic motivation is generally considered to be more long-lasting than the other.
As I said, extrinsic motivation is … *external*. It's the desire to behave in a certain way in order to obtain some kind of external reward. A child, for example, who regularly does small jobs around the house does them not because she enjoys taking out the garbage or doing the dishes but because she knows if she does these things, she'll be given a small amount money for doing them. But how motivated would the child be to continue doing the work if her parents suddenly stopped giving her money for it?
With intrinsic, or internal, motivation we want to do something because we enjoy it, or get a sense of accomplishment from it. Most people who are internally motivated get pleasure from the activity … so they just feel good about doing it. For example, I go to the gym several times a week. I don't go because I'm training for a marathon or anything. I just enjoy it. I have more energy after I exercise and I know it's good for my health so it makes me feel good about myself. And that's what's kept me going there for the past five years.

P   우리는 우리가 하는 일을 왜 할까요? 무엇이 우리를 특정 활동에 참여하게 만드는 걸까요? 특정 차를 사게 하고 혹은 심지어 특정 직업을 선택하게 할까요? 다시 말해, 우리가 무엇을 하도록 만드는 동기는 무엇일까요?
동기에 대한 연구에서 심리학자들은 두 가지 유형의 동기를 구별하고 있습니다. 뭔가를 하는 이유, 즉 동기에는 '외적 요인'이 있다고 합니다. 즉 칭찬이나 돈처럼 일종의 외적인 보상을 기저로 하는 것이죠. 또는 '내적' 동기가 있을 수 있는데요, 우리가 어떤 활동을 하는 이유는 그걸 함으로써 '내적으로' 즐거워지기 때문이라는 겁니다. 두 가지 모두 우리가 특정 방식으로 행동하도록 하는 강력한 추진력을 만들어냅니다. 하지만 내적 동기는 대체로 외적 동기보다 지속성이 더 길다고 간주됩니다.
앞서 말했듯, 외적 동기는 외부에서 옵니다. 이것은 어떤 종류의 외적 보상을 얻기 위해 특정 방식으로 행동하려는 욕구입니다. 예를 들어, 자주 집안일을 돕는 아이가 있습니다. 이 아이는 쓰레기를 버

61

거나 설거지하는 게 좋아서가 아니라 그렇게 하면 용돈을 좀 받을 수 있다는 걸 알기 때문이죠. 그러나 아이의 부모가 갑자기 용돈 주기를 중단한다면 이 아이에게는 하던 일을 계속할 동기가 과연 얼마나 부여될까요?

내재적 혹은 내적 동기가 있는 경우, 뭔가를 하는 동기는 정말 좋아하거나, 아니면 그 일에서 성취감을 얻기 때문입니다. 내적 동기가 있는 경우 대부분의 사람들은 그 활동에서 즐거움을 얻습니다. 그래서 그 일을 하는 것만으로도 기분이 좋아지죠. 예를 들면, 저는 일주일에 몇 번씩 헬스장에 가는데요, 마라톤 같은 걸 위해 훈련을 받는 건 아닙니다. 그냥 좋아서 가는 거죠. 운동을 하고 나면 활력도 더 생기고, 건강에 좋다는 걸 아니까 그만큼 자긍심도 생기고요. 이게 바로 제가 지난 5년간 꾸준히 운동하게 만든 원동력입니다.

어휘

drive (어떤 행동을 하도록) 만들다   motivation 동기 (부여)   distinguish between ~ 사이를 구별하다   extrinsic 외재적인, 외부의   external 외부의   reward 보상   intrinsic 내재적인   internally 내적으로   long-lasting 오래 지속하는   regularly 자주   sense of accomplishment 성취감   feel good about oneself 자긍심을 느끼다, 스스로 뿌듯해 하다

Narrator

Using points and examples from the talk, explain the two types of motivation.

강의에 나온 논점과 예시를 들어 두 가지 유형의 동기에 대해 설명하시오.

준비 시간 : 20초
답변 시간 : 60초

중요 포인트

내적 동기와 외적 동기를 비교해야 하는데, 강의에 나온 논점과 예시를 활용해야 하며 강의에 나오지 않는 개인적 지식을 바탕으로 답하면 안 된다.

먼저 강의 주제에 대한 요약으로 시작한다. 즉 동기에는 두 가지 유형이 있으며 각각의 명칭이 무엇인지 밝힌다. 그러고 나서 먼저 언급된 외적 동기에 대해 설명한다. 외적 동기에 이끌릴 경우 외적인 보상을 기대하고 어떤 행위를 한다고 설명한다. 그 다음 교수가 강의에서 얘기한 것처럼 용돈을 받기 위해 집안일을 돕는 어린 아이를 예로 든다. 이 경우 일하고 나서 받는 용돈이 동기가 된다.

이어서 두 번째 유형인 내적 동기에 대해 설명한다. 어떤 행위에 대한 내재적 동기가 있다는 것은 그 행위를 함으로써 기분이 좋아지기 때문이라는 개념을 설명한 뒤 교수가 언급한 예시를 든다. 즉 교수 자신이 일주일에도 몇 번 운동하는 이유는 그냥 좋아서라는 사실을 밝힌다. 또한 교수가 여러 해 동안 꾸준히 운동한 것을 볼 때 내적 동기가 더 오래 지속된다고 연결한다.

유의할 점은 강의에 나온 내용을 모두 그대로 반복할 필요는 없다는 점이다. 동기의 유형에 대한 설명이 충분할 만큼만 이야기하면 된다. 그리고 두 가지 유형에 대한 개념과 예를 고루 설명할 수 있도록 시간을 균등하게 안배해야 한다.

WRITING

Writing Based on Reading and Listening

· p.84

As early as the twelfth century A.D., the settlements of Chaco Canyon in New Mexico in the American Southwest were notable for their "great houses," massive stone buildings that contain hundreds of rooms and often stand three or four stories high. Archaeologists have been trying to determine how the buildings were used. While there is still no universally agreed upon explanation, there are three competing theories.

One theory holds that the Chaco structures were purely residential, with each housing hundreds of people. Supporters of this theory have interpreted Chaco great houses as earlier versions of the architecture seen in more recent Southwest societies. In particular, the Chaco houses appear strikingly similar to the large, well-known "apartment buildings" at Taos, New Mexico, in which many people have been living for centuries.

A second theory contends that the Chaco structures were used to store food supplies. One of the main crops of the Chaco people was grain maize, which could be stored for long periods of time without spoiling and could serve as a long-lasting supply of food. The supplies of maize had to be stored somewhere, and the size of the great houses would make them very suitable for the purpose.

A third theory proposes that houses were used as ceremonial centers. Close to one house, called Pueblo Alto, archaeologists identified an enormous mound formed by a pile of old material. Excavations of the mound revealed deposits containing a surprisingly large number of broken pots. This finding has been interpreted as evidence that people gathered at Pueblo Alto for special ceremonies. At the ceremonies, they ate festive meals and then discarded the pots in which the meals had been prepared or served. Such ceremonies have been documented for other Native American cultures.

이미 12세기에 미국 남서부 뉴멕시코 주의 차코캐니언 정착촌은 '거대한 건축물'로 유명했다. 이 대형 석조 건물에는 수백 개의 방이 있고 보통 3, 4층으로 이루어져 있다. 고고학자들은 이 건물의 용도를 밝히려 애써왔다. 보편적으로 의견이 일치하는 설명은 아직 없지만 세 가지 가설이 경합을 벌이고 있다.

한 가지 가설은 차코 건축물이 각기 수백 명을 수용할 수 있는 순전히 주거용 건물이었다는 것이다. 이 가설을 지지하는 학자들은 차코

의 거대 가옥들이 이후 남서부 지역사회에서 나타나는 건축물의 초기 형태라고 해석한다. 특히, 차코 건물들은 수세기 전부터 많은 사람들이 살고 있는 뉴멕시코 주 타오스에 있는 유명한 대형 '아파트 건물들'과 무척 흡사하다.

두 번째 가설은 차코 구조물이 식량 저장용으로 쓰였다고 주장한다. 차코 주민들의 주 농작물 중 하나가 옥수수였다. 옥수수는 오래 보관해도 상하지 않아 오래 지속되는 식량 공급원 역할을 했다. 옥수수 양식을 어딘가에 저장해야 했고 이 거대한 건축물들의 크기가 그 용도에 매우 적합했을 것이다.

세 번째 가설은 건축물들이 의식의 장소로 쓰였다는 것이다. '푸에블로 알토'라는 한 건축물 인근에서 고고학자들은 고대 물건들이 쌓여 형성된 거대한 무더기를 발견했다. 이 무더기를 발굴하자 놀랍게도 수많은 깨진 솥이 드러났다. 이런 사실은 사람들이 특별한 의식을 위해 푸에블로 알토에 모였다는 증거로 해석되고 있다. 의식에서 사람들은 축제 음식을 먹은 뒤 음식을 만들거나 담는 데 썼던 솥을 버렸다. 이런 의식들은 다른 아메리카 원주민 문화에도 기록되어 있다.

어휘

notable for ~으로 유명하다   archaeologist 고고학자   universally 보편적으로   competing 서로 경합하는, 모순된   residential 주거용의   architecture 건축, 건축물   contend 주장하다   store 저장하다   grain 곡물   maize 옥수수   serve as ~의 역할을 하다   supplies 양식, 보급품   identify 발견하다   deposit 매장물   festive 축제의   discard 버리다, 폐기하다   document 기록하다

Narrator 🎧 T-32

Now listen to part of a lecture on the topic you just read about.

방금 읽은 주제에 관한 강의의 일부를 들으시오.

(Script)

P   Unfortunately, none of the arguments about what the Chaco great houses were used for is convincing.

First—sure, *from the outside* the great houses look like later Native American apartment buildings, but the *inside* of the great houses casts serious doubt on the idea that many people lived there. I'll explain. If hundreds of people were living in the great houses, then there would have to be many *fireplaces* where each family did its daily cooking. But there're very *few* fireplaces. In one of the largest great houses there were fireplaces for only around ten families. Yet there are enough *rooms* in the great house for more than a *hundred* families. So the primary function of the houses couldn't have been residential.

Second, the idea that the great houses were used to store grain maize is unsupported by evidence. It may *sound* plausible that large, empty rooms were used for storage, but excavations of the great houses have *not* uncovered many traces of maize *or* maize containers. If the great houses were used for storage, why isn't there more spilled maize on the floor? Why aren't there more remains of big containers?

Third, the idea that the great houses were ceremonial centers isn't well supported either. Ya know that mound at Pueblo Alto? It contains lots of other materials besides broken pots, stuff you wouldn't expect from ceremonies. For example, there're large quantities of building materials— sand, stone, even construction tools. This suggests that the mound is just a *trash heap* of construction material, stuff that was thrown away or not used up when the house was being built. The pots in the pile could be regular trash, too, left over from the meals of the construction workers. So the Pueblo Alto mound is not good evidence that the great houses were used for special ceremonies.

P 유감스럽게도 차코 대형 건축물의 용도에 대한 주장 중 설득력 있는 것은 아무것도 없습니다.

첫째, 분명 이 건물은 밖에서 보면 이후 아메리카 원주민들의 아파트 건물과 흡사해 보이지만 내부를 보면 많은 사람들이 그곳에 살았다는 주장에 심각한 의구심이 생깁니다. 설명하죠. 만일 그 큰 건물에 수백 명이 거주했다면 가구마다 매일 음식을 해먹었을 화로가 많이 있었을 겁니다. 하지만 화로는 거의 없습니다. 가장 큰 건물에서도 열 가구 정도가 쓸 만한 화로 밖에 없었습니다. 하지만 방의 수는 백여 가구가 쓸 만큼 충분합니다. 그러므로 이 건축물의 주된 용도가 주거일 리가 없습니다.

두 번째로, 그 큰 건축물이 옥수수 알곡을 저장하는 데 쓰였다는 주장은 증거가 없습니다. 비어 있는 커다란 방들이 저장고로 쓰였다면 얼핏 타당하게 들릴지도 모르나 이 거대 건축물을 발굴해도 옥수수나 옥수수를 담은 용기의 흔적이 많이 나오지 않았습니다. 만약 이 거대 건물이 창고로 쓰였다면 왜 바닥에 흘린 옥수수가 그것밖에 없을까요? 커다란 보관 용기 유물이 왜 그것밖에 없을까요?

셋째, 이 거대 건축물이 의식의 장소였다는 주장 역시 증거가 부족합니다. 푸에블로 알토의 무지를 아시죠? 이곳에서 깨진 솥 외에도 많은 물건들이 있는데 의식에서 쓸 만한 것들이 아닙니다. 예를 들면, 모래, 돌, 건축 도구 같은 다량의 건축 자재들이 나왔는데요. 이 사실은 무지가 그저 건물을 짓고 남거나 버린 자재들로 쌓인 건축 자재 쓰레기 더미라는 의견을 뒷받침합니다. 쌓인 솥들 역시 건설 인부들이 식사하고 버린 생활 쓰레기일 겁니다. 그러므로 푸에블로 알토 무지는 이 거대 건축물이 특별한 의식에 쓰였다는 확실한 증거가 아닙니다.

어휘

convincing 설득력 있는   cast doubt on ~에 대해 의구심을 제기하다 fireplace (벽)난로, 화로   primary 주된   unsupported 입증되지 못하는 plausible 그럴싸한, 타당한   excavation 발굴, 굴착   spill 쏟다, 흘리다 remains 유적, 유물   mound 더미, 무지   trash 쓰레기   heap 더미, 무더기   use up 다 써버리다, 소진하다

Narrator T-33

Question 1

Summarize the points made in the lecture, being sure to explain how they cast doubt on the specific theories discussed in the reading passage.

강의의 논점을 요약하고, 강의가 독해 지문에 언급된 구체적 이론들을 어떻게 반박하는지 설명하시오.

해설

교수는 강의를 통해 지문에서 제시한 차코 건축물의 용도에 대한 세 가지 가설, 즉 주거용, 곡물 저장용 창고, 의식 거행 장소 가설을 모두 반박하고 있다는 점을 이해해야 한다. 답안 작성 시 교수가 차코 건축물의 용도에 대한 각각의 가설에 신빙성이 떨어진다고 지적하면서 언급했던 이유를 적어야 한다. 높은 점수를 받으려면 다음 표에 정리된 교수의 반박 논점들을 모두 담고 있어야 한다. 정확한 어법과 어휘력을 구사하여 표에 들어 있는 3가지 요점 모두를 명확하게 설명해야 5점을 받을 수 있다.

지문의 주요 내용	지문과 대조되는 강의 내용
The Chaco houses may have been used for residential purposes, because they are similar to residential buildings built by other societies in the American Southwest.	It is unlikely that the Chaco houses were residential, because they contain very few fireplaces, many fewer than the families living in the houses would need for cooking.
The Chaco houses may have been used to store food. The Chaco people needed a place to store their grain maize, and the Chaco houses, thanks to their large capacity, could serve that purpose.	The theory that the function of the Chaco houses was to store grain maize is undermined by the fact that very few traces of maize or maize containers have been found during excavations of the Chaco houses.
The Chaco houses may have served as ceremonial centers. The large quantity of broken pottery in a mound located near the "Pueblo Alto" house suggests that the houses hosted ceremonial feasts after which people discarded the pots in which the food was prepared and served.	The mound near the "Pueblo Alto" house also contains construction materials and tools, which suggests that such mounds were just construction trash heaps and had nothing to do with ceremonies. The pots found in the mounds were probably used by construction workers building the houses.

Writing for an Academic Discussion

p.87

Question 2

Your professor is teaching a class on public policy. Write a post responding to the professor's question.

In your response, you should do the following.

- Express and support your opinion.
- Make a contribution to the discussion in your own words.

An effective response will contain at least 100 words.

Dr. Diaz

Next week we are scheduled to discuss the economic impacts of tourism. Tourism is a source of income for many cities and regions around the world. On the other hand, tourism can also bring with it a number of well-known disadvantages. In general, do you think governments should continue to develop and encourage a tourism industry in their countries? Why or why not?

Kelly

Even considering the economic argument, I think it's time for governments to stop encouraging tourism. That's because the tourist economy is unstable. Tourists may visit a region for a while, but then people's preferences change, and tourists stop coming. It's economically better for a country to promote other industries that are more stable.

Paul

I see your point, Kelly, but I believe tourism is almost always helpful for a country—and not just for economic reasons. If a city is made more attractive for tourists, it will also become more livable for the residents. To lure tourists, cities are often made safer and cleaner, for example, and they add attractions such as museums.

교수가 공공정책에 관한 강의를 진행하고 있다. 교수의 질문에 답하는 게시글을 작성하시오.

답변은 다음 조건을 충족해야 한다.

- 의견을 표명하고 뒷받침하는 근거를 제시한다.
- 독자적인 표현과 관점으로 토론에 기여한다.

어느 정도 완성도를 갖추려면 최소 100단어 이상이어야 한다.

Dr. Diaz

다음 주에는 관광이 경제에 미치는 영향에 대해 논의할 예정입니다. 관광은 전 세계 많은 도시와 지역의 수입원이죠. 반면, 관광에는 익히 아는 수많은 단점도 따라옵니다. 대체로 여러분은 정부가 자국의 관광업을 계속 발전시키고 장려해야 한다고 생각하나요? 찬반 의견을 밝히고 이유를 설명해 주세요.

Kelly

경제적인 이유를 고려하더라도 이제는 정부가 관광 장려 정책을 중단해야 할 때라고 생각해요. 관광업은 경기가 불안정하기 때문이죠. 관광객들이 한동안 특정 지역을 방문할 수도 있지만, 이후 사람들의 취향이 바뀌면 관광객이 뚝 끊기죠. 좀 더 안정적인 다른 산업을 육성하는 편이 경제적인 측면에서 더 낫습니다.

Paul

켈리, 무슨 말인지 알겠어요. 하지만 저는 관광이 십중팔구 나라에 도움이 된다고 생각해요. 굳이 경제적인 이유가 아니라도 말이죠. 만약 관광객이 보기에 매력적인 도시로 만들면, 시민들에게도 더 살기 좋은 곳이 됩니다. 예를 들면 관광객을 끌어들이려고 도시를 더 안전하고 깨끗하게 만들기도 하고 박물관 같은 관광명소를 추가하기도 하죠.

해설

대체로 정부가 관광업을 계속 발전시키고 장려해야 하는지에 대한 토론이다. 고득점을 받으려면 이러한 토론에 기여하는 논지를 펼치며 답변해야 한다. 어느 정도 완성도를 갖추려면 최소 100단어 이상이어야 한다.

한 토론 참여자는 관광업은 경기가 불안정하므로 정부가 관광업 장려 정책을 중단해야 한다고 주장한다. 반면, 다른 토론 참여자는 관광이 주민들의 생활 수준을 개선하므로 정부가 관광업을 계속 육성해야 한다고 생각한다. 이미 서술된 개념을 포착해 더 자세히 논지를 전개해도 좋고 전혀 새로운 개념을 선보여도 좋다. 예를 들어 첫 번째 참여자의 의견에 동조하면서 날씨나 현재 사건 등 여러 다양한 요인 탓에 관광객의 발길이 끊길 수 있으므로 정부는 안정적인 산업을 발전시키는 데 집중해야 한다고 덧붙일 수 있다. 두 번째 토론 참여자의 의견에 동의하면서 관광업을 장려하려는 노력의 결과로 모든 주민을 위해 환경이 개선된 도시를 예로 들 수 있다. 새로운 주장을 덧붙일 수도 있다. 예를 들어 관광객들이 귀중한 자원을 너무 많이 사용하고 도시를 더 혼잡하게 만들고 오염시키는 문제, 지역 문화를 존중하지 않는 문제를 지적하면서 관광업을 억제해야 한다고 주장할 수 있다.

반드시 자신의 의견을 뒷받침하는 탄탄한 근거와 예시를 제시하고 명확하게 표현해야 한다. 답안이 온라인 게시물 형태로 나타나므로 여러 단락으로 나누어 구성할 필요는 없다. 하지만 개념 간 연관성이 밀접하며 조리 있고 명료해야 한다. 채점은 '학술 토론을 위한 글쓰기 평가 기준(Appendix 참조)'을 토대로 이루어진다.

READING

POWERING THE INDUSTRIAL REVOLUTION

산업혁명의 동력원　　　　　*p.92*

1. In Britain one of the most dramatic changes of the Industrial Revolution was the harnessing of power. Until the reign of George III (1760-1820), available sources of power for work and travel had not increased since the Middle Ages. There were three sources of power: animal or human muscles; the wind, operating on sail or windmill; and running water. Only the last of these was suited at all to the continuous operating of machines, and although waterpower abounded in Lancashire and Scotland and ran grain mills as well as textile mills, it had one great disadvantage: streams flowed where nature intended them to, and water-driven factories had to be located on their banks, whether or not the location was desirable for other reasons. Furthermore, even the most reliable waterpower varied with the seasons and disappeared in a drought. The new age of machinery, in short, could not have been born without a new source of both movable and constant power.

2. The source had long been known but not exploited. Early in the century, a pump had come into use in which expanding steam raised a piston in a cylinder, and atmospheric pressure brought it down again when the steam condensed inside the cylinder to form a vacuum. This "atmospheric engine," invented by Thomas Savery and vastly improved by his partner, Thomas Newcomen, embodied revolutionary principles, but it was so slow and wasteful of fuel that it could not be employed outside the coal mines for which it had been designed. In the 1760s, James Watt perfected a separate condenser for the steam, so that the cylinder did not have to be cooled at every stroke; then he devised a way to make the piston turn a wheel and thus convert reciprocating (back and forth) motion into rotary motion. He thereby transformed an inefficient pump of limited use into a steam engine of a thousand uses. The final step came when steam was introduced into the cylinder to drive the piston backward as well as forward, thereby increasing the speed of the engine and cutting its fuel consumption.

3. (A) Watt's steam engine soon showed what it could do. (B) It liberated industry from dependence on running water. (C) The engine eliminated water in the mines by driving efficient pumps, which made possible deeper and deeper mining. (D) The ready availability of coal inspired William Murdoch during the 1790s to develop the first new form of nighttime illumination to be discovered in a millennium and a half. Coal

1. 영국에서 산업혁명의 가장 극적인 변화 중 하나는 동력의 이용이다. 중세시대 이후 노동과 여행에 사용할 수 있는 동력원은 조지 3세(1760-1820)의 통치 시기까지 증가하지 않았다. 당시 동력원은 세 가지로 동물이나 인간의 힘, 보트나 풍차를 움직이는 바람, 흐르는 물이었다. 이 중 마지막 자원인 흐르는 물만 기계를 끊임없이 가동하는 데 적합했다. 랭커셔와 스코틀랜드에는 수력이 풍부하여 방직공장은 물론 곡물방앗간까지 있었지만 한 가지 큰 단점이 있었다. 즉 하천은 자연이 의도한 곳에서 흐르므로 수력에 의존하는 공장들은 그 위치가 다른 여러 가지 이유들 때문에 바람직하든 그렇지 않은 강둑에 위치할 수밖에 없었다. 더군다나 가장 믿을 만한 수력조차도 계절별로 고르지 않았고 가뭄이 들면 사라졌다. 간단히 말해, 기계가 지배하는 새로운 시대는 이동 가능하고 지속적인 새로운 동력원 없이 탄생할 수 없었다.

2. 이 동력원은 오래전부터 알려져 있었지만 이용되지는 않았다. 18세기 초 펌프를 사용하기 시작했는데 팽창된 증기가 실린더의 피스톤을 들어 올렸고, 실린더 내부의 증기가 응축하여 진공상태가 되면 기압의 영향으로 피스톤이 다시 밑으로 내려갔다. 토마스 세이버리가 발명하고 동료인 토마스 뉴커먼이 대폭 개량한 '대기압 기관'은 획기적인 원리들을 구체화했지만 속도가 너무 느리고 연료 낭비가 너무 심해서 원래 설계 목적이던 탄광 이외의 다른 곳에서는 사용할 수 없었다. 1760년대 제임스 와트가 증기를 냉각시키는 분리형 응축기를 완성하자 더 이상 피스톤이 움직일 때마다 실린더를 냉각시킬 필요가 없어졌다. 이후 와트는 피스톤으로 바퀴를 돌리는 방법을 고안해 (앞뒤로 움직이는) 반복운동을 회전운동으로 변환했다. 그리고 그 결과 제한적으로 이용할 수밖에 없던 비효율적인 펌프를 아주 다양한 방식으로 사용할 수 있는 증기기관으로 변형시켰다. 마지막 단계는 실린더에 증기를 투입해 피스톤을 앞뿐 아니라 뒤로도 움직이게 만드는 것이었는데 이를 통해 증기기관의 속도가 증가하고 연료 소비량이 줄어들었다.

3. 와트의 증기기관은 곧 그 저력을 보여줬다. 우선 산업이 흐르는 물에 의존하지 않게 되었다. 효율적인 펌프로 광산에서 물이 사라져 점점 땅속 깊숙이 채굴할 수 있게 되었다. 석탄을 언제라도 이용할 수 있다는 사실에 영감을 받은 윌리엄 머독은 1790년대 1500년 만에 처음으로 새로운 형태의 야간 조명을 개발했다. 석탄가스는 흐릿한 석유램프, 불빛이 깜박거리는 양초와 경쟁구도를 이루었고, 19세기 초 부유한 런던 사람들은 가스등을 켠 집이나 심지어 길거리에도 익숙해졌다. 목탄에 의존하고 있어 새로운 연료에 목말라 있던 제철업자들 역시 석탄 공급량이 점점 늘어나자 이득을 얻었

gas rivaled smoky oil lamps and flickering candles, and early in the new century, well-to-do Londoners grew accustomed to gaslit houses and even streets. Iron manufacturers, which had starved for fuel while depending on charcoal, also benefited from ever-increasing supplies of coal; blast furnaces with steam-powered bellows turned out more iron and steel for the new machinery. Steam became the motive force of the Industrial Revolution, as coal and iron ore were the raw materials.

4. By 1800 more than a thousand steam engines were in use in the British Isles, and Britain retained a virtual monopoly on steam engine production until the 1830s. Steam power did not merely spin cotton and roll iron; early in the new century, it also multiplied ten times over the amount of paper that a single worker could produce in a day. At the same time, operators of the first printing presses run by steam rather than by hand found it possible to produce a thousand pages in an hour rather than thirty. Steam also promised to eliminate a transportation problem not fully solved by either canal boats or turnpikes. Boats could carry heavy weights, but canals could not cross hilly terrain; turnpikes could cross the hills, but the roadbeds could not stand up under great weights. These problems needed still another solution, and the ingredients for it lay close at hand. In some industrial regions, heavily laden wagons, with flanged wheels, were being hauled by horses along metal rails; and the stationary steam engine was puffing in the factory and mine. Another generation passed before inventors succeeded in combining these ingredients, by putting the engine on wheels and the wheels on the rails, so as to provide a machine to take the place of the horse. Thus the railroad age sprang from what had already happened in the eighteenth century.

다. 증기로 움직이는 풀무가 달린 용광로에서 새로운 기계의 자재인 철강이 더 많이 생산됐다. 석탄과 철광석이 원자재가 되면서 증기는 산업혁명을 발전시키는 원동력이 되었다.

4. 1800년까지 영국제도에서 1000대 이상의 증기기관이 사용되었고 1830년대까지 영국이 증기기관 생산에서 사실상 독점을 유지했다. 증기력으로 단순히 목화 실을 자아내고 철을 압연한 것만은 아니었다. 19세기 초 증기력 덕분에 노동자 한 명의 하루 종이 생산량보다 10배나 많은 종이가 생산되었다. 같은 시기에 수작업이 아닌 증기로 돌아가는 최초의 인쇄기를 가동시킨 기사들은 수작업으로 1시간에 30장 인쇄하던 것을 증기로 1000장이나 인쇄할 수 있다는 걸 깨달았다. 증기는 운하용 보트나 도로도 완전히 해결할 수 없었던 교통 문제도 해소할 듯했다. 보트는 무거운 짐을 운반할 수 있지만 운하는 구릉성지형을 통과할 수 없었고, 반면 도로는 언덕에도 만들 수 있지만 노면이 엄청난 하중을 견딜 수 없었다. 이러한 문제들 때문에 여전히 또 다른 해결책이 필요했는데, 이를 위한 구성 요소들은 아주 가까운 곳에 있었다. 일부 공업단지에서는 말이 철로 위로 플랜지 바퀴가 달린 무거운 짐마차를 끌었고, 공장과 광산에서는 고정 증기기관에서 연기가 뿜어 나왔다. 하지만 발명가들이 이러한 요소들을 결합하는 데 성공한 것은 한 세대가 지나서였다. 그들은 기관에 바퀴를 달아 철로 위로 움직이게 만들어 말을 대체할 수 있는 기계를 제공했다. 따라서 철도시대는 이미 18세기에 발생했던 일에서 비롯되었다.

어휘

1. Industrial Revolution 산업혁명   harness 동력화하다, 이용하다   reign 통치, 지배   Middle Ages 중세(유럽 역사에서 서기 1000~1450년경)   continuous 계속되는, 지속적인   waterpower 수력   abound in ~이 풍부하다   textile mill 방직공장   disadvantage 불리한 점, 약점   drought 가뭄   movable 움직일 수 있는, 이동할 수 있는   2. exploit 개발하다, 이용하다   cylinder 실린더, 원통   condense 응축하다, 응결하다   atmospheric engine 대기압 기관   vastly 대단히, 엄청나게   embody 구체화하다, 구현하다   condenser (증기기관의) 응축기   stroke (반복 운동의) 한 동작, 한 움직임   convert 변환[전환]하다   reciprocating motion 왕복 운동   rotary motion 회전 운동   inefficient 비효율[비능률]적인   steam engine 증기기관   3. eliminate 없애다, 제거하다   illumination (불)빛, 조명   flickering 깜박거리는   well-to-do 부유한, 잘사는   grow accustomed to ~에 익숙해지다   gaslit 가스등으로 불을 밝힌   starve for ~을 갈구하다   charcoal 숯   blast furnace 용광로   bellows 풀무   ore 광석, 원광   4. retain 유지[보유]하다   monopoly 독점, 전매   multiply 늘다, 증식하다   turnpike 도로, 유료 고속도로   terrain 지형, 지역   roadbed 노면   ingredient 요인, 구성 요소   laden 잔뜩 실은, 가득한   wagon 짐마차, 4륜마차   flanged wheel 플랜지 바퀴(플랜지라는 테두리가 있어 철로를 벗어나지 않도록 장치된 바퀴)   haul 끌어 운반하다. 잡아당기다   puff (연기 따위가) 폭폭 나오다   take the place of ~을 대신하다   spring from ~로부터 일어나다, 비롯되다

67

1. 다음 중 첫 번째 단락에 음영으로 표시된 문장이 담고 있는 핵심 정보를 가장 잘 표현한 것은? 정답 외의 보기들은 의미가 상당히 왜곡되거나 필수적인 정보가 빠져 있다.

    Ⓐ 흐르는 물은 기계를 계속해서 가동할 수 있어서 공장에는 최고의 동력원이었다. 하지만 랭커셔와 스코틀랜드에만 물이 풍부해서 다른 지역에 있는 대부분의 방앗간과 공장들은 수력을 이용할 수 없었다.

    Ⓑ 수력을 이용할 때 생기는 단점은 공장부지로 가장 적합한 장소에 반드시 강물이 흐르는 것은 아니라는 사실이다. 이 점은 수력발전으로 가동되는 수많은 곡물방앗간과 방직공장이 왜 공장부지로 적합하지 않은 곳에 위치하는지를 설명한다.

    Ⓒ 흐르는 물이 풍부한 곳에서만 기계를 계속해서 가동할 수 있기 때문에 다른 공장은 물론 곡물방앗간과 방직공장이 유독 랭커셔와 스코틀랜드에만 있었다.

    Ⓓ 흐르는 물은 기계를 계속해서 돌릴 수 있는 유일한 동력원이었다. 하지만 그러려면 해당 위치가 다른 측면에서 합당한지 여부에 상관없이 물이 있는 곳에 공장이 위치해야 했다.

어휘 abundant 풍부한, 많은   regardless of ~에 상관없이

2. 다음 중 첫 번째 단락과 두 번째 단락의 관계를 가장 잘 설명한 것은?

    Ⓐ 두 번째 단락은 첫 번째 단락에서 언급한 문제가 어떻게 발생했는지 보여 준다.

    Ⓑ 두 번째 단락은 첫 번째 단락에서 언급한 문제가 어떻게 해결됐는지 설명한다.

    Ⓒ 두 번째 단락은 첫 번째 단락에서 언급한 문제를 좀 더 구체적으로 설명한다.

    Ⓓ 두 번째 단락은 첫 번째 단락에서 언급한 문제를 해결하는 것이 왜 특별히 중요한지 보여 준다.

어휘 arise 일어나다, 발생하다   technical 전문적인, 구체적인

3. 두 번째 단락에 따르면, '대기압 기관'이 느렸던 이유는?

    Ⓐ 탄광에서 사용하도록 설계됐기 때문에

    Ⓑ 피스톤이 움직일 때마다 실린더를 냉각시켜야 했기 때문에

    Ⓒ 증기를 팽창시켜 실린더의 피스톤을 들어 올렸기 때문에

    Ⓓ 엄청난 양의 연료가 공급될 때만 작동할 수 있었기 때문에

어휘 coal mine 탄광   expand 확대하다, 팽창시키다

4. 두 번째 단락에 따르면, 와트의 증기기관이 이전의 증기기관과 달랐다는 설명 중 사실이 아닌 것은?

    Ⓐ 증기로 실린더의 피스톤을 움직였다.

    Ⓑ 엄청난 속도로 움직였다.

    Ⓒ 연료를 더 효율적으로 사용했다.

    Ⓓ 다양한 방식으로 사용할 수 있었다.

5. 세 번째 단락에 따르면, 글쓴이가 윌리엄 머독이 새로운 형태의 야간 조명을 발명했다고 언급한 이유는?

    Ⓐ 와트의 증기기관이 도입되면서 중요한 발명품이 나올 수 있었음을 보여주기 위해

    Ⓑ 와트의 증기기관이 산업혁명에 중요한 유일한 발명이 아니었음을 강조하기 위해

    Ⓒ 석탄이 산업혁명의 원자재로 얼마나 중요했는지 설명하기 위해

    Ⓓ 증기를 동력원으로 사용한 18세기의 또 다른 발명품을 예로 들기 위해

어휘 power source 동력원

6. 세 번째 단락의 get accustomed to와 의미상 가장 가까운 것은?

    Ⓐ 선호하기 시작했다

    Ⓑ 갖고 싶어했다

    Ⓒ 익숙해졌다

    Ⓓ 고집했다

7. 네 번째 단락에 따르면, 다음 중 증기기관에 대한 설명으로 사실인 것은?

    Ⓐ 종이 생산에는 사용되었지만 인쇄에는 사용되지 않았다.

    Ⓑ 1800년까지 상당수가 영국 밖에서 생산됐다.

    Ⓒ 기차의 동력으로 사용하기 전 공장에서 이용했다.

    Ⓓ 운하나 도로를 만드는 데 사용했다.

어휘 production 생산, 제조   significant 상당한, 아주 큰

8. 네 번째 단락에 따르면, 말을 대체할 수 있는 기계를 제공하고자 이전에 별개였던 어떤 두 가지 구성요소를 결합했는가?

    Ⓐ 도로와 운하

    Ⓑ 고정된 증기기관과 플랜지 바퀴가 달린 짐마차

    Ⓒ 노면의 철로와 무거운 짐을 운반할 수 있는 짐마차

    Ⓓ 운하용 보트와 짐을 가득 실은 짐마차

9. 위에 제시된 지문의 일부를 보시오. 지문에 표시된 **(A)**, **(B)**, **(C)**, **(D)** 중 하나에 다음 문장이 삽입될 수 있다.

The factories did not have to go to the streams when power could come to the factories.
(동력이 공장 안으로 들어올 수 있게 되자 강이나 개울 근처에 공장을 세울 필요가 없어졌다.)

이 문장이 들어갈 가장 적당한 위치는?

(A) Watt's steam engine soon showed what it could do. **(B)** It liberated industry from dependence on running water. **(C)** The factories did not have to go to the streams when power could come to the factories. The engine eliminated water in the mines by driving efficient pumps, which made possible deeper and deeper mining. **(D)** The ready availability of coal inspired William Murdoch during the 1790s to develop the first new form of nighttime illumination to be discovered in a millennium and a half. Coal gas rivaled smoky oil lamps and flickering candles, and early in the new century, well-to-do Londoners grew accustomed to gaslit houses and even streets, Iron manufacturers, which had starved for fuel while depending on charcoal, also benefited from ever-increasing supplies of coal; blast furnaces with steam-powered bellows turned out more iron and steel for the new machinery. Steam became the motive force of the Industrial Revolution, as coal and iron ore were the raw materials.

Ⓐ (A)　　Ⓑ (B)　　Ⓒ (C)　　Ⓓ (D)

10. 지문을 간단히 요약하기 위한 도입 문장이 아래에 제시되어 있다. 아래 보기들 중에서 지문의 가장 중요한 개념을 표현한 문장 3개를 골라 요약을 완성하라. 보기들 중에는 지문에 나오지 않았거나 중요하지 않은 개념이기 때문에 요약문으로 적절치 않은 것들도 있다. 이 문제의 배점은 2점이다.

효율적이고, 이동 가능하며, 계속해서 사용할 수 있는 새로운 동력원이 없었다면 산업혁명은 일어날 수 없었다.

Ⓐ 18세기 초 세이버리와 뉴커먼이 팽창된 증기가 실린더의 피스톤을 들어 올리는 데 이용될 수 있다는 사실을 발견했다.

Ⓑ 1700년대 중반 제임스 와트는 비효율적인 증기 펌프를 빠르고 다루기 쉬우며 연료 효율적인 기관으로 변형시켰다.

Ⓒ 와트의 증기기관은 모든 공산품에서 생산량을 크게 늘리는 데 결정적인 역할을 했다.

Ⓓ 1790년대 윌리엄 머독은 석탄가스를 이용해 집과 거리에 불을 밝히는 새로운 방법을 발명했다.

Ⓔ 1830년대까지 영국은 세계에서 증기기관의 주요 생산국이었다.

Ⓕ 증기기관은 철로 발달의 중요한 요소로서 주요 교통 문제를 해결했다.

어휘　transform 변형시키다　flexible 다루기 쉬운, 유연성이 있는
　　　availability 이용도, 유효성

PEST CONTROL

1. Many pest species that are native to North America, such as white-footed mice and ground moles, are more nuisance pests and are usually regulated by native predators and parasites. This situation is not true for nonindigenous pests in North America, such as brown rats and cockroaches. After centuries, it is evident that these pests cannot be eradicated. The best that can be done is to introduce pest control measures that will control their numbers.

2. An ancient and popular means of pest control is chemical. For example, the Sumerians used sulfur to combat crop pests, and by the early 1800s such chemicals as arsenic were used to combat insect and fungal pests.

3. However, chemical control has its dark side. Chemical pesticides have many unintended consequences through their effects not just on the target species but on a wide array of nontarget species as well, often eliminating them and thereby upsetting the existing food webs, especially through the suppression of native predator species. The surviving pests then rebound in greater numbers than ever.

4. Perhaps more insidious is that a pesticide loses its effectiveness because the target species evolves resistance to it. As one pesticide replaces another, the pests acquire a resistance to them all. **(A)** Some species, notably certain mosquitoes, have overcome the toxic effects of every pesticide to which they have been exposed. **(B)** Insect pests need only about five years to evolve pesticide resistance; their predators do so much more slowly. **(C)** So after the pest develops resistance, pest outbreaks become even more disastrous. **(D)**

5. Farmers long ago observed that enemies of pests act as controls. As early as 300 c.e., the Chinese were introducing predatory ants into their citrus orchards to control leaf-eating caterpillars. Insect pests have their own array of enemies in their native habitats. When an animal or plant is introduced, intentionally or unintentionally, into a new habitat outside of its natural range, it may adapt to the new environment and leave its enemies behind. Freed from predation and finding an abundance of resources, the species quickly becomes a pest or a weed. This fact has led to the search for natural enemies to introduce into populations of pests to reduce their populations.

6. Because the serious pest is usually a nonnative species, biological control involves the introduction of a nonindigenous predator or parasite to control the pest. The introduction of the cactus-eating moth, a native of Argentina, into Australia effectively reduced and controlled the rapidly spreading prickly pear, which had been introduced into Australia in 1901.

1. 미국흰발붉은쥐나 땅두더지처럼 북아메리카가 원산지인 많은 유해종은 좀 성가시지만 대개는 토착 포식자와 기생충으로 조절된다. 이런 상황은 시궁쥐나 바퀴벌레처럼 북아메리카에 사는 비토착 유해종에게는 해당되지 않는다. 수세기가 지난 지금 명백한 사실은 이들 유해종을 완전히 박멸할 수 없다는 것이다. 할 수 있는 최선의 방안은 유해종의 개체 수를 억제할 방제 조치를 도입하는 것이다.

2. 고대부터 널리 쓰인 유해종 방제 수단은 화학적 방식이다. 예를 들어 수메르인들은 황을 사용해 작물 해충을 퇴치했고, 1800년대 초에는 비소 같은 화학물질이 해충과 병원성 곰팡이를 퇴치하는 데 사용됐다.

3. 그러나 화학적 방제에는 어두운 면이 있다. 화학적 방제제는 표적 종뿐만 아니라 다양한 비표적 종에도 영향을 미쳐 의도하지 않은 결과를 초래한다. 비표적 종들이 제거되거나, 특히 포식자 역할을 하는 토착종이 방제되면 기존의 먹이 사슬 시스템이 교란된다. 살아남은 유해종은 이전보다 개체 수가 더 불어나면서 다시 반등한다.

4. 아마도 더욱 은밀한 문제는 표적 종이 화학 방제제에 내성이 생겨 방제 효과가 사라진다는 점이다. 방제제를 다른 방제제로 대체하면 유해종은 두 방제제 모두에 대한 내성을 얻게 된다. 일부 종, 특히 특정 모기들은 그동안 노출된 모든 살충제가 지닌 독성 효과를 극복했다. 해충이 살충제 내성을 기르는 데는 5년 정도밖에 걸리지 않으며 녀석들의 포식자가 내성을 기르는 속도는 그보다 훨씬 느리다. 따라서 내성을 기른 해충이 대규모로 창궐하면 그 피해는 훨씬 심각하다.

5. 농부들은 오래전에 유해종의 적이 방제 역할을 한다는 사실을 관찰했다. 일찍이 서기 300년 중국인들은 잎을 먹는 애벌레를 방제하기 위해 감귤류 과수원에 포식성 개미를 도입했다. 해충이 자생하는 서식지에는 다양한 적이 있다. 의도했든 의도하지 않았든 동식물이 자생하는 지역을 벗어나 새로운 서식지에 도입되면 새로운 환경에 적응해 적에서 벗어날 수 있다. 포식에서 벗어나 풍성한 자원을 발견하면 그 종은 빠르게 유해종이나 잡초로 탈바꿈한다. 이러한 사실을 토대로 천적을 찾아 유해종 개체군에 도입해 개체 수를 줄이게 됐다.

6. 위험한 유해종은 대개 토착종이 아니므로 생물학적 방제에는 비토착 포식자나 기생충을 도입해 유해종을 방제하는 방식이 포함된다. 1901년 호주에 도입된 백년초가 빠르게 번지자 아르헨티나 토착종인 선인장 먹는 나방을 호주에 도입해 백년초를 효과적으로 줄이고 방제했다.

7. 그러나 화학적 방제와 마찬가지로 생물학적 방제에도 부작용이 있다. 선인장 먹는 나방이 호주에서 선인장 열매 방제에 성공하자 서인도 제도 몇 개 섬에도 선인장 먹는 나방이 도입됐다. 시간이 흐르면서 나방은 플로리다로 건너갔는

7. But biological control, like chemical control, can backfire. The success of the cactus-feeding moth in controlling prickly pear in Australia encouraged its introduction to several West Indies islands to control prickly pear there. In time the moth made its way to Florida, where it now threatens the existence of several native prickly pear species. The moral is that although using nonindigenous predators as biological controls can be effective, these species possess their own inherent dangers that must be assessed before they are released. They, too, can become alien invaders.

8. Because chemical, biological, and other methods used individually are obviously not the solution to pest control, entomologists have developed a holistic approach to pest control, called integrated pest management (IPM). IPM considers the biological, ecological, economic, social, and even aesthetic aspects of pest control and employs a variety of techniques. The objective of IPM is to control the pest not at the time of a major outbreak but at an earlier time, when the size of the population is easier to control. The approach is to rely first on natural mortality caused by weather and natural enemies, with as little disruption of the natural system as possible, and to use other methods only if they are needed to hold the pest below the economic injury level.

9. Successful IPM requires the knowledge of the population ecology of each pest and its associated species and the dynamics of the host species. It involves considerable fieldwork monitoring the pest species and its natural enemies by such techniques as egg counts and the trapping of adults to acquire information to determine the necessity, timing, and intensity of control measures. These control measures must be adjusted to the situation, which may vary from one location to another. The intensity of control or no control is based on the degree of pest damage that can be tolerated, the costs of control, and the benefits to be derived.

데, 현재 선인장 먹는 나방이 몇몇 토종 백년초의 생존을 위협하고 있다. 여기서 얻을 수 있는 교훈은 비토착 포식자를 생물학적 방제에 사용하면 효과가 있지만, 이런 외래종에는 고유한 위험이 내재되어 있으므로 외래종을 풀기 전에 위험부터 진단해야 한다는 점이다. 녀석들 역시 외래 침입종이 될 수 있다.

8. 화학적 방식과 생물학적 방식, 기타 방식을 따로따로 사용하는 것은 병해충 방제 해결책이 못 된다는 점이 분명해졌기 때문에 곤충학자들은 병해충종합관리(IPM)라고 부르는 총체적 접근 방식을 개발했다. IPM은 병해충 방제의 생물학적, 생태학적, 경제적, 사회적, 심지어 미적인 측면까지 고려해 다양한 기법을 활용한다. IPM의 목표는 병해충이 크게 창궐하는 시점이 아니라 개체 수를 더 쉽게 억제할 수 있는 초기 단계에서 제어하는 것이다. 이 접근 방식은 자연 체계의 교란을 최소화하면서 우선 날씨와 천적에 의한 자연적인 죽음에 의존하고, 병해충이 경제적 피해를 일으키는 수준보다 적게 유지되도록 필요한 경우에만 다른 방법을 사용한다.

9. IPM이 성공하려면 각 병해충 및 관련 종의 개체군 생태와 숙주 종의 동태에 대한 지식이 필요하다. 그러려면 상당한 현장 작업이 필요한데, 알 수 세기, 성충 포획 같은 기술로 병해충 종과 천적을 추적 관찰해 방제 조치의 필요성과 시기, 강도를 결정하기 위한 정보를 획득해야 한다. 지역마다 상황이 다를 수 있으므로 이러한 방제 조치는 지역 실정에 맞게 조정되어야 한다. 허용 가능한 병해충 피해 정도와 방세 비용, 얻을 수 있는 편익을 토대로 방제 강도 또는 방제를 하지 않는 결정이 이루어진다.

어휘

1. pest species 유해종 native 원산의, 토착의 white-footed mouse 미국흰발붉은쥐 ground mole 땅두더지 nuisance 성가신 것, 골칫거리 regulate 규제하다 predator 포식자 parasite 기생충 nonindigenous 비토착의 brown rat 시궁쥐 evident 명백한 eradicate 박멸하다 introduce 도입하다 measures 조치 **2.** sulfur 황 combat 퇴치하다 arsenic 비소 fungal 곰팡이의 **3.** unintended 의도하지 않은 wide array of 다양한 종류의 food web 먹이 사슬 시스템 suppression 억제 rebound 반등하다 **4.** insidious 서서히 퍼지는 resistance 저항 notably 특히 outbreak 발생, 창궐 disastrous 처참한, 심각한 **5.** observe 관찰하다 predatory 포식성의 orchard 과수원 caterpillar 애벌레 array 무리 adapt 적응하다 predation 포식 abundance 풍부함 weed 잡초 **6.** biological 생물학적인 cactus 선인장 moth 나방 prickly pear 선인장 열매 **7.** backfire 역효과를 낳다 threaten 위협하다 moral 교훈 inherent 내재하는 assess 진단하다 invader 침입자 **8.** entomologist 곤충학자 holistic 전체론적인 integrated 종합적인 aesthetic 미적인 aspect 측면 objective 목표 mortality 죽음 **9.** population ecology 개체군 생태 dynamics 역학, 동태 host species 숙주 종 considerable 상당한 fieldwork 현장 조사 trapping 포획 determine 결정하다 necessity 필요성 intensity 강도 adjust 조정하다 degree 정도 tolerate 허용하다 derive 유래하다

11. 첫 번째 단락에서 집쥐와 바퀴벌레 같은 비토착 유해종에 대해 유추할 수 있는 것은?

 (A) 녀석들의 개체 수를 제한하려는 시도는 성공하지 못했다.

 (B) 녀석들은 미국흰발붉은쥐나 땅두더지보다 북아메리카에서 더 오래 살았다.

 (C) 대체로 녀석들의 수는 토착 포식자와 기생충으로 억제할 수 없다.

 (D) 미국흰발붉은쥐나 땅두더지보다 인간에게 많은 문제를 일으키지는 않는다.

12. 다음 중 지문에서 음영으로 표시된 문장의 핵심 정보를 가장 잘 표현한 것은? 정답 외의 보기들은 의미가 상당히 왜곡되거나 필수적인 정보가 빠져 있다.

 (A) 화학 방제제는 종종 의도된 표적 이외의 종을 제거하고, 특히 토착 포식자 종을 방제해 먹이 그물을 어지럽힌다.

 (B) 종종 다른 유해종에게 영향을 미칠 의도로 살포한 화학 방제제 때문에 토착 포식자 종이 제거된다.

 (C) 화학 방제제는 토착종을 제거하고 외래 포식자의 수를 늘려 기존의 먹이 그물을 어지럽힌다.

 (D) 다양한 먹이 그물과 토착 포식자에 미치는 화학 방제제의 영향은 종종 의도하지 않은 결과다.

어휘 eliminate 제거하다

13. 다섯 번째 단락에 따르면, 어떤 종이 새로운 서식지에 도입됐을 때 유해종이 될 가능성이 높은 이유는?

 (A) 적으로부터 더 효과적으로 도망치게 되었으므로

 (B) 새로운 서식지에 천적이 없으므로

 (C) 자생하는 지역 밖에 있는 서식지에 적응하므로

 (D) 자원을 놓고 다른 동식물과 경쟁할 필요가 없으므로

14. 여섯 번째 단락에서 호주의 선인장 먹는 나방과 백년초에 대한 논의는 생물학적 방제에 관해 다음 중 어느 것을 예시하는가?

 (A) 외래 유해종은 일단 빠르게 퍼지기 시작하면 생물학적 수단을 통해 방제할 수 없다.

 (B) 외래 유해종은 때때로 외래 포식자의 도입으로 방제할 수 있다.

 (C) 비토착 유해종은 해당 종과 원래 서식지가 같은 포식자로만 방제할 수 있다.

 (D) 토착 유해종은 토착 또는 외래 포식자로 방제할 수 있다.

15. 지문에서 assessed와 의미상 가장 가까운 것은?

 (A) 최소화되다

 (B) 확인되다

 (C) 평가되다

 (D) 처리되다

16. 글쓴이가 '플로리다'의 선인장 먹는 나방에 대해 이야기하는 이유는?

 (A) 플로리다가 원산지인 백년초에게 토착 포식자가 없는 이유를 설명하려고

 (B) 포식자가 자생 환경보다 낯선 환경에서 더 빨리 퍼져 나가는 양상을 보여주려고

 (C) 단일한 비토착 포식자 종이 다양한 비토착 유해종에 맞서는 데 효과적이라는 사실을 지적하려고

 (D) 비토착 포식자로 유해종을 방제하면 의도하지 않은 결과를 초래할 수 있다고 주장하려고

17. 여덟 번째 단락에 따르면, 다음 중 병해충종합관리의 원칙이 아닌 것은?

 (A) 대규모로 창궐하기 전에 해충 개체 수를 억제한다.

 (B) 먼저 날씨와 천적이 병해충을 방제할 수 있는지 결정한다.

 (C) 일년 중 특정 계절에 병해충의 천적 개체 수를 늘린다.

 (D) 병해충이 경제적 피해를 입히기 시작할 때만 인위적인 병해충 방제 방식을 사용한다.

18. 아홉 번째 단락에 따르면, 다음 중 어느 정도 강도로 병해충 방제 조치를 적용할지 결정하는 데 도움이 되지 않는 것은?

 (A) 감당할 수 있는 병해충 피해 규모

 (B) 병해충 방제책에 드는 비용

 (C) 병해충 방제책을 통해 얻을 수 있는 것

 (D) 병해충 방제책을 이전에 사용했는지 여부

19. 위에 제시된 지문의 일부를 보시오. 지문에 표시된 **(A)**, **(B)**, **(C)**, **(D)** 중 하나에 다음 문장이 삽입될 수 있다.

These flare-ups continue to occur until a new pesticide is developed, at which time the cycle begins anew.

(이러한 폭증 현상은 새로운 살충제가 개발될 때까지 계속 발생하며, 이때 주기가 새로 시작된다.)

이 문장이 들어갈 가장 적절한 위치는?

Perhaps more insidious is that a pesticide loses its effectiveness because the target species evolves resistance to it. As one pesticide replaces another, the pests acquire a resistance to them all. **(A)** Some species, notably certain mosquitoes, have overcome the toxic effects of every pesticide to which they have been exposed. **(B)** Insect pests need only about five years to evolve pesticide resistance; their predators do so much more slowly. **(C)** So after the pest develops resistance, pest outbreaks become even more disastrous. **(D)** These flare-ups continue to occur until a new pesticide is developed, at which time the cycle begins anew.

Ⓐ (A)　　Ⓑ (B)　　Ⓒ (C)　　Ⓓ (D)

20. 지문을 요약하기 위한 도입 문장이 아래에 제시되어 있다. 아래 보기들 중에서 지문의 가장 중요한 개념을 표현한 문장 3개를 골라 요약을 완성하라. 보기들 중에는 지문에 나오지 않은 내용이거나 중요한 내용이 아니므로 요약문으로 적절치 않은 것들도 있다. 이 문제의 배점은 2점이다.

유해종 방제 대책은 접근 방식과 전반적인 성공 정도가 다양하다.

Ⓐ 생물학적 유해종 방제 방식은 고대 수메르인에 의해 도입되었으며 화학적 방제는 고대 중국에서 처음 사용되었다.

Ⓑ 유해종이 빠르게 내성을 갖게 되고, 의도하지 않은 종에 해를 끼칠 수 있으므로 방제제는 유용성에 한계가 있다.

Ⓒ 생물학적 방제, 예를 들어 유해종의 천적을 활용하는 방식은 외래 유해종을 억제하는 데는 효과가 있었지만 토착종의 생존도 위협할 수 있다.

Ⓓ 유해종 방제를 위한 생물학적, 화학적 접근법의 성공은 지역마다 상황이 크게 달라서 판단하기가 어렵다.

Ⓔ 병해충종합관리는 화학적, 생물학적 방제가 이미 실패한 지역에서 대규모 병해충 창궐을 억제하는 데 성공한 총체적 접근법이다.

Ⓕ 병해충 방제의 생물학적, 생태학적, 경제적, 미적 측면을 고려한 접근법인 병해충종합관리는 특정 상황에 맞게 조정된 다양한 기법을 사용한다.

LISTENING

Questions 1~5

p.108

N Narrator S Student A Administrator

Script T-34

N Listen to a conversation between a student and an employee in the university's career services office.

S Hi. Do you have a minute?

A Sure. How can I help you?

S I have a couple of questions about the career fair next week.

A OK, shoot.

S Um, well, are seniors the only ones who can go? I mean, you know, they're finishing school this year and getting their degrees and everything … and, well, it seems like businesses would want to talk to them and not first-year students like me …

A No, no. The career fair is open to all our students and we encourage anyone who's interested to go check it out.

S Well, that's good to know.

A You've seen the flyers and the posters around campus, I assume.

S Sure! Can't miss 'em. I mean, they all say where and when the fair is … just not who should attend.

A Actually, they do. But it's in the small print. We should probably make that part easier to read, shouldn't we? I'll make a note of that right now. So, do you have any other questions?

S Yes, actually I do now. Um, since I'd only be going to familiarize myself with the process—you know, "check it out"—I was wondering if there's anything you'd recommend that I do to prepare.

A That's actually a very good question. As you know, the career fair is generally an opportunity for local businesses to recruit new employees and for soon-to-be graduates to have interviews with several companies they might be interested in working for. Now, in your case, even though you wouldn't be looking for employment right now, it still wouldn't hurt for you to prepare much like you would if you were looking for a job.

S You mean like get my resume together and wear a suit?

A That's a given. I was thinking more along the lines of doing some research. The flyers and posters list all the businesses that are sending representatives to the career fair. Um, what's your major, or do you have one yet?

S Well, I haven't declared a major yet but I'm strongly considering accounting. See, that's part of the reason I want to go to the fair … to help me decide if that's what I really want to study …

N 대학교 취업지원실에서 학생과 직원이 나누는 대화를 들으시오.

S 안녕하세요. 잠시 시간 좀 내주시겠어요?

A 물론이에요. 뭘 도와 드릴까요?

S 다음 주 취업박람회에 대해 몇 가지 질문이 있어서요.

A 좋아요. 물어보세요.

S 음, 저기 4학년만 참가할 수 있는 건가요? 그러니까 올해 학교를 마치고 학위를 받는 사람을 말하는 건지. 그게, 기업이 만나려는 사람은 저 같은 신입생이 아니라 졸업예정자인 거 같아서요.

A 아니에요, 그렇지 않아요. 취업박람회는 모든 학생에게 열려 있어요. 관심 있는 학생은 누구나 가서 보도록 권한답니다.

S 아, 다행이네요.

A 캠퍼스 주변에서 광고 전단지와 포스터를 보셨을 텐데요.

S 그럼요! 안 봤을 리가 없죠. 그런데 박람회 장소와 시간만 나와 있어요. 누가 참가하는지 이야기는 없고….

A 사실 그렇긴 해요. 하지만 참가기준도 조그맣게 적혀 있어요. 그 부분을 좀 더 읽기 쉽게 바꿔야겠네요, 그렇죠? 지금 당장 메모해 두도록 하죠. 뭐 다른 질문 있나요?

S 예, 사실 또 물어보고 싶은 질문이 지금 막 생겼어요. 음, 그냥 과정에만 좀 익숙해지고 싶어서요, 그러니까 한번 '둘러보러' 가는 건데요. 무슨 준비를 하면 될지 조언해 주시겠어요?

A 정말 아주 좋은 질문이에요. 아시다시피, 일반적으로 취업박람회는 지역 기업이 신입사원을 채용하고, 졸업예정자는 일하고 싶은 여러 회사들과 면접을 볼 수 있는 기회에요. 그런데 학생처럼 지금 당장 직장을 구하는 경우가 아니더라도 실제 직장을 구하는 것처럼 준비하는 것도 나쁘지 않죠.

S 이력서도 준비하고 정장을 입으라는 말인가요?

A 그건 당연한 거고요. 조사도 좀 했으면 해요. 광고 전단지와 포스터에 이번 취업박람회에 직원을 파견하는 모든 기업의 명단이 적혀 있어요. 저, 전공이 뭐예요? 아직 정하지 않았나요?

S 그게, 전공을 확정하진 않았지만 회계학이 어떨까 숙고하고 있어요. 사실 이번 박람회에 참가하고 싶은 이유이기도 하고요. 정말 회계학을 공부하고 싶은지 결정하는 데 도움이 될 거 같아서요.

A That's very wise. Well, I suggest that you get on the computer and learn more about the accounting companies, in particular, that will be attending. You can learn a lot about companies from their Internet Web sites. Then prepare a list of questions.

S Questions … hmm. So in a way I'll be interviewing them?

A That's one way of looking at it. Think about it for a second. What do you want to know about working for an accounting firm?

S Well, there's the job itself … and salary, of course … and, um, working conditions … I mean, would I have an office or would I work in a big room with a zillion other employees? And … um … and maybe about opportunities for advancement …

A See? Those are all important things to know. After you do some research you'll be able to tailor your questions to the particular company you're talking to.

S Wow, I'm glad I came by here! So, it looks like I've got some work to do.

A And if you plan on attending future career fairs, I recommend you sign up for one of our interview workshops.

S I'll do that.

A 아주 현명하네요. 그럼, 인터넷에 접속해 특별히 이번에 참가하는 회계 법인에 대해 알아보는 게 좋을 거예요. 인터넷 홈페이지에서 회사에 관한 정보를 많이 얻을 수 있거든요. 그런 다음 질문 목록을 준비하도록 하세요.

S 음, 질문 목록이라. 그렇다면 어떤 면에선 제가 회사를 면접하는 거네요?

A 그렇다고 할 수 있죠. 잠깐 생각해 보세요. 회계 법인의 일에 대해 알고 싶은 게 뭐죠?

S 뭐, 회계업무 자체에 대해 알고 싶어요. 물론 급여나, 음, 근무 조건도 궁금해요. 그러니까 개인 사무실이 따로 있는지, 큰 사무실에서 수많은 직원들과 함께 일하는지 알고 싶어요. 그리고 혹시 승진 기회에 대해서도 알 수 있으면 좋고요.

A 무슨 말인지 알겠죠? 모두 중요한 것들이에요. 조사를 하고 나면, 면담할 특정 회사에 맞춰 질문 내용을 조정할 수 있을 거예요.

S 와, 여기 오길 잘했네요. 그러고 보니 할 일이 꽤 있네요.

A 앞으로 취업박람회에 참가할 계획이라면 면접대비 연수회에 신청해 보세요.

S 그럴게요.

어휘

career service office 취업지원실 career fair 취업박람회 shoot (명령문에서) 시작하다, 말하기 시작하다 degree 학위 flyer 광고지, 전단 familiarize oneself with ~에 정통하다 recommend 추천하다 recruit 모집하다, 뽑다 employee 종업원, 고용인 soon-to-be graduate 졸업예정자 employment 직장, 고용 resume 이력서 representative 대표자, 대리인 accounting 회계, 회계학 zillion 막대한 수의, 무수의 advancement 승진, 출세 tailor 맞추다, 조정하다 sign up for ~을 신청하다

1. 학생이 취업지원실에 간 이유는?

  Ⓐ 취업박람회 날짜와 시간을 확인하기 위해
  Ⓑ 취업박람회 장소를 알기 위해
  Ⓒ 취업박람회에 참가할 수 있는지 알기 위해
  Ⓓ 취업박람회의 면접에 대한 조언을 구하기 위해

  어휘 confirm 확인하다, 확증하다

2. 회사 직원이 자신과의 면접에 관심이 없을 거라고 학생이 생각하는 이유는?

  Ⓐ 올해 졸업하지 않아서
  Ⓑ 현재 경영학 수업을 듣지 않아서
  Ⓒ 아직 전공을 정하지 않아서
  Ⓓ 최신 이력서가 없어서

  어휘 currently 현재, 지금

3. 취업박람회 포스터와 광고 전단지의 작은 글씨에 대해 여자가 암시하는 것은?

  Ⓐ 작은 글씨로 된 정보가 불완전했다.
  Ⓑ 글씨가 생각했던 것보다 더 작았다.
  Ⓒ 작은 글씨로 된 정보를 업데이트할 것이다.
  Ⓓ 작은 글씨로 된 정보를 좀 더 눈에 띄게 표시할 것이다.

  어휘 incomplete 불완전한, 불충분한
      noticeable 눈에 띄는, 뚜렷한

4. 회사 직원과의 면접을 준비하기 위해 여자가 말한 좋은 방법은 무엇인가? 두 개의 답을 선택하라.

  Ⓐ 경영학과 수업 듣기
  Ⓑ 사전에 특정 기업 파악하기
  Ⓒ 회사직원에게 물어볼 질문 목록 작성하기
  Ⓓ 회계 법인에서 일하는 사람들과 이야기하기

  어휘 beforehand 미리, 사전에

5. 대화의 일부를 다시 듣고 질문에 답하라.

  N *Why does the student say this:*
  S So, it looks like I've got some work to do.

  Ⓐ 올해 취업박람회에 참가할 수 없다는 것을 알리기 위해
  Ⓑ 준비할 분량을 확인하게 위해
  Ⓒ 채용박람회 전에 마쳐야 할 학교 과제가 있다는 사실을 말하기 위해
  Ⓓ 지금 일하러 가야 한다는 사실을 말하기 위해

  어휘 preparation 준비, 대비   complete 끝내다, 완료하다

Questions 6~11

p.110

N Narrator **P** Professor **M** Male Student

Script T-36

N Listen to part of a lecture in a biology class.

P OK, I have an interesting plant species to discuss with you today. Uh, it's a species of a *very* rare tree that grows in Australia—*Eidothea hardeniana*—but it's better known as the Nightcap Oak.

Now, it was discovered only very recently, just a few years ago. Uh, it remained hidden for so long because it's so rare, there're only about, oh, two hundred of 'em in existence. They grow in a rain forest, in a mountain range in the north part of New South Wales, which is, uh, a state in Australia. So just two hundred individual trees in all.

Now, another interesting thing about the Nightcap Oak is that it is … it represents … a-a very old … *type*, a kind of a tree that grew … a hundred million years ago. Uh, we found fossils that old that bear a remarkable resemblance to the tree. So, it's a *primitive* tree, a living fossil, you might say. It's a relic from earlier times, and it has survived all these years without much change. And … it-it's probably a kind of tree from which other trees that grow in Australia today evolved. Just-just to give you an idea of what we're talking about, here's a picture of the leaves of the tree and its flowers.

I dunno how well you can see the flowers; they're those little clusters sitting at the base of the leaves.

OK, what have we tried to find out about the tree since we've discovered it? Hmm, well, how … why is … is it so rare is one of the first questions. Uh, how is it, uh, how does it reproduce, is another question. Uh, maybe those two questions are actually related? Jim.

M Hmm, I dunno, but I can imagine that … for instance … uh, seed dispersal might be a factor—I mean, if the, uh, y'know if the seeds cannot really disperse in a wide area then you know the tree may not, uh, *colonize* new areas, it-it can't spread from the area where it's growing.

P Right, that's-that's actually a very good answer. Uh, of course, you might think there might not be many areas where the tree could spread *into*, uh, because, uh, well it's-it's very specialized in terms of the habitat. But that's not really the case here, uh, the-the suitable habitat-habitat that is the actual rain forest is much larger than-than the few hectares where the Nightcap Oak grows. Now, this tree is a flowering tree as I showed you, uh, uh, it-it produces a fruit, much like a plum, on the inside there's a seed with a hard shell. Uh, it-it appears that the shell has to crack open or break down somewhat to allow the seed to soak up water. If the Nightcap

N 생물학 강의의 일부를 들으시오.

P 자, 오늘은 흥미진진한 식물에 관해 이야기해 보겠습니다. 음, 이 종은 호주에서 자라는 아주 희귀한 나무입니다. 학명은 '에이도테아 하르데니아나'이며 나이트캡 오크로 더 잘 알려져 있죠.

자, 이 나무는 아주 최근에 발견되었습니다. 기껏해야 몇 년밖에 안 되죠. 음, 그리고 매우 희귀해서 아주 오랫동안 눈에 띄질 않았죠. 그러니까 200그루 정도밖에 없습니다. 이 나무는 우림에서 자랍니다. 음, 호주의 뉴사우스웨일스 주 북부에 있는 산간지방에서 자라는데 모두 합쳐 200그루밖에 안 됩니다.

그런데 나이트캡 오크의 또 다른 흥미로운 점은 아주 오래된 종이라는 겁니다. 그러니까 1억 년 전 존재하던 나무인데요. 음, 이 나무와 놀라울 만큼 유사하고 그만큼 오래된 화석이 발견됐습니다. 그래서 나이트캡 오크는 '원시적인' 나무, 살아 있는 화석이라고 할 수 있죠. 이 나무는 태곳적인 유물로 오랜 세월 동안 큰 변화 없이 살아남았습니다. 아마도 이 나무에서 오늘날 호주에서 자라는 다른 나무들이 진화했을 겁니다. 자, 이해를 돕고자 다음은 나이트캡 오크의 나뭇잎과 꽃 그림입니다.

꽃이 얼마나 잘 보이는지 모르겠군요. 잎사귀 아래쪽에 조그맣게 뭉쳐 있는 것들이 꽃들입니다.

그렇다면 나이트캡 오크를 발견한 후 사람들은 무엇을 알아내려고 했을까요? 음, 아무래도 어떻게, 그리고 왜 이렇게 희귀한가 하는 것이 첫 번째 의문점이죠. 아, 또 다른 의문점은 어떻게 번식하느냐 하는 겁니다. 어쩌면 이 두 가지 의문점이 실제로 관계가 있지 않을까요? 짐.

M 음, 잘 모르겠어요. 짐작에는 이를테면 종자분산이 한 가지 요인 아닐까 싶은데요. 그러니까 실제로 종자가 광범위한 지역으로 분산될 수 없다면 나이트캡 오크는 새로운 지역에서 '대량 서식'할 수 없을 거 아니에요. 지금 자라는 곳에서 다른 곳으로 퍼져나갈 수 없는 거죠.

P 맞습니다. 아주 훌륭한 대답이에요. 음, 물론 나무가 퍼져나갈 수 있는 지역이 많지 않을 거라고 생각할 수 있어요. 사실 아주 특수한 서식지에서 자라는 나무니까요. 하지만 이 나무는 그런 경우가 아닙니다. 적절한 서식지라고 할 수 있는 실제 우림은 나이트캡 오크가 자라는 몇 헥타르의 공간보다 훨씬 넓습니다. 자, 보다시피 이 나무는 꽃나무입니다. 음, 그리고 자두와 아주 비슷한 열매를 맺는데 안에 딱딱한 껍질로 덮인 씨가 들어 있죠. 씨가 물을 흡수하려면 껍질이 어느 정도 벌어지거나 부서져야 할 것처럼 보입니다. 만약 나이트캡 오크가 그대로, 만약 씨앗이 그대로 껍질 안에 갇혀 있다면 싹이 틀

Oak remains, if their seeds remain locked inside their shell, they will not germinate. Now actually the seeds, uh, they don't retain the power to germinate for very long, maybe two years, so there's actually quite a short window of opportunity for the seed to germinate. So the shell somehow has to be broken down before this, uh, germination ability expires. And- and then there's a kind of rat that likes to feed on the seeds as well. So, given all these limitations, not many seeds that the tree produces will actually germinate. So this is a possible explanation for why the tree does not spread. It doesn't necessarily explain how it *became* so rare but it explains why it doesn't increase.

OK, so it seems to be the case that this species, uh this Nightcap Oak, is not very good at spreading. However, it seems, though we can't be sure, that it's very good at *persisting* as a population. Uh, uh, we, uh, there-there're some indications to suggest that the population of the Nightcap Oak has not declined over the last, uh, y'know, many hundreds of years. So, it's stayed quite stable; it-it's not a remnant of some huge population that has dwindled in the last few hundred years for some reason. It's not *necessarily* a species in retreat. OK, so it cannot spread very well but it's good at maintaining itself. It's rare but it's not disappearing. OK, the next thing we might wanna ask about a plant like that is what chances does it have to survive into the future. Let's look at that.

수 없을 거예요. 음, 사실 나이트캡 오크의 씨앗은 발아 능력을 가지는 기간이 길지 않습니다. 한 2년 정도죠. 그래서 발아할 수 있는 기회가 아주 잠깐밖에 없어요. 그러니까 발아능력의 기한이 끝나기 전에 껍질이 어떻게든 부서져야 합니다. 게다가 쥐의 일종으로 나이트캡 오크의 씨앗을 즐겨먹는 녀석도 있답니다. 따라서 이런 모든 제약을 고려할 때 나무에서 나온 씨앗 중 실제로 발아하는 것은 많지 않을 거예요. 이것이 나이트캡 오크가 퍼지지 않은 이유일 수 있습니다. 꼭 이런 이유로 희귀종인 것은 아니겠지만 개체가 늘어나지 않는 이유는 설명합니다.

좋습니다. 음, 따라서 이 나이트캡 오크 종은 잘 퍼져나가지 못하는 것으로 보입니다. 그러나 확신할 순 없어도 하나의 개체군으로서 생존력 하나는 끝내줍니다. 저, 그러니까 나이트캡 오크의 그루수가 지난 수백 년간 감소하지 않았다는 여러 가지 징후가 있거든요. 그래서 그루수가 꽤 안정적으로 유지되고 있어요. 과거에는 엄청나게 많았던 개체군이 지난 수백 년간 여러 가지 이유로 줄어들어 지금 상태가 된 게 아니라는 거죠. 나이트캡 오크가 쇠락하고 있다고 볼 수 만은 없어요. 자, 그러므로 퍼져나가는 데는 서툴지만 생존력 자체는 훌륭한 나무예요. 희귀하지만 멸종되지는 않는 거죠. 좋습니다, 이제 이런 나무가 앞으로 살아남을 가능성이 얼마나 되는지 궁금할 겁니다. 저걸 보세요.

어휘

species 종(생물 분류의 기초 단위) Nightcap Oak 나이트캡 오크 in existence 존재하는, 생존하는 rain forest 열대우림 mountain range 산맥, 산간 지방 resemblance 닮음, 유사함 primitive 원시의, 초기의 living fossil 살아 있는 화석 relic 유물, 유적 evolve 진화[발달]하다 I dunno= I don't know cluster (꽃이나 과실 따위의) 송이, 다발 reproduce 생식[번식]하다 dispersal 분산 disperse 흩어지다, 분산하다 colonize 대량 서식하다 habitat 서식지 plum 자두 crack open 열리다, 벌어지다 soak up 빨아들이다, 흡수하다 germinate 싹트다, 발아하다 retain 유지[보유]하다 germination (종자 따위의) 발아 expire 만료되다, 기한이 끝나다 limitation 한계, 제약 persist 존속하다, 살아남다 indication 표시, 징후 remnant 나머지, 잔존물 dwindle 줄어들다, 점차 감소하다 retreat 후퇴, 철수

6. 교수는 주로 나이트캡 오크의 어떤 점을 이야기하는가? 두 개의 답을 선택하라.

    ☐A 나무가 자라는 서식지의 크기와 관련된 요인들
    ☐B 지난 수백 년간 나이트캡 오크 개체군의 규모
    ☐C 나이트캡 오크가 생존할 수 있는 요인
    ☐D 지난 1억 년간 나이트캡 오크가 많이 변하지 않은 이유

    어휘 ensure 보증하다, 확실하게 하다   survival 생존, 존속

7. 교수에 따르면, 과학자들이 나이트캡 오크를 원시적이라고 규정한 이유는?

    Ⓐ 오늘날 호주에서 자라는 다른 나무들의 진화와 관련이 없기 때문에
    Ⓑ 비효율적인 번식 체계 때문에
    Ⓒ 꽃이 잎사귀 아래쪽에 있기 때문에
    Ⓓ 어떤 고대화석과 비슷하기 때문에

    어휘 evolutionary 진화의, 발달의

8. 교수가 나이트캡 오크의 서식지에 대해 강조하는 것은?

    Ⓐ 크기가 제한되어 있지만 안정적이다.
    Ⓑ 많은 식물의 서식지와 달리 확장하고 있다.
    Ⓒ 최근 변화로 나이트캡 오크가 적응하는 데 어려움을 겪는다.
    Ⓓ 나이트캡 오크가 자라는 지역보다 훨씬 넓다.

    어휘 struggle 크게 노력하다, 애쓰다   adapt 적응하다

9. 교수에 따르면, 나이트캡 오크 개체군의 확산을 방해하는 두 가지 요인은? 두 개의 답을 선택하라.

    ☐A 나무가 열매를 맺기 위한 조건이 복잡해서
    ☐B 껍질 안에 갇혀 있는 동안은 씨앗이 발아할 수 없어서
    ☐C 씨앗이 발아능력을 유지하는 기간이 제한적이어서
    ☐D 좀 더 최근에 진화한 다른 나무들과 경쟁해서

    어휘 complex 복합적인, 복잡한   competition 경쟁, 시합

10. 교수는 왜 지난 몇 백 년 동안 존재한 나이트캡 오크의 개체 수를 언급하는가?

    Ⓐ 나이트캡 오크의 개체 수가 앞으로 증가할 수 있는 이유를 설명하기 위해
    Ⓑ 나이트캡 오크의 제한적인 번식 성공률에도 개체 수가 줄어들지 않음을 지적하기 위해
    Ⓒ 나이트캡 오크가 주요한 환경 변화를 견딜 수 있다는 증거를 제시하기 위해
    Ⓓ 나이트캡 오크가 다른 나무들을 파괴하는 질병에 저항할 수 있다는 점을 지적하기 위해

    어휘 tolerate 견디다   resist 저항하다, 견디다

11. 강의의 일부를 다시 듣고 질문에 답하라.

     T-37

    > P OK, what have we tried to find out about the tree since we've discovered it? Hmm, well, how … why is … is it so rare is one of the first questions. Uh, how is it, uh, how does it reproduce, is another question. Uh, maybe those two questions are actually related?
    >
    > N *Why does the professor say this:*
    > P Maybe those two questions are actually related?

    Ⓐ 학생들이 가능한 연관성에 대해 생각하기를 원한다.
    Ⓑ 학생들에게 질문이 있는지 알고 싶어한다.
    Ⓒ 연구원들이 잘못된 질문을 하고 있음을 암시하고 있다.
    Ⓓ 두 의문점 사이에 아무런 연관성이 없음을 암시하고 있다.

    어휘 connection 연관성, 연결

Questions 12~16

p.112

N Narrator   S Student   P Professor

Script   T-38

N   Listen to a conversation between a student and a professor.

S   Professor Martin?

P   Hi, Lisa—what can I do for you?

S   Well, I've been thinking about, you know, what you were saying in class last week? About how we shouldn't wait until the last minute to find an idea and get started working on our term paper?

P   Good, good. And have you come up with anything?

S   Well, yeah, sort of—see, I've never had a linguistics class before, so I was sort of … I mean, I was looking over the course description, and a lot of the stuff you've described there, I just don't know what it's talking about, you know? Or what it means. But there was one thing that really did jump out at me …

P   Yes …?

S   The section on dialects? 'Cause, like, that's the kind of thing that's always sort of intrigued me, you know?

P   Well, that's certainly an *interesting* topic, but you may not realize, I mean, the *scope* …

S   Well, especially now, 'cause I've got, like, *one* roommate who's from the South, and *another* one from New York, and we all talk, like, *totally* different, you know?

P   Yes, I understand, but …

S   But then I was noticing, like, we don't really get into this till the end of the semester, you know? So I…

P   So you want some pointers where to go for information on the subject? Well, you could always *start* by reading the chapter in the book on sociolinguistics; that would give you a basic understanding of the key issues involved here.

S   Yeah, that's what I thought! So I started reading the chapter, you know—about how everyone speaks some dialect of their language? And I'm wondering, like, well, how do we even manage to understand each other at all?

P   Ah! Yes, an interesting question. You see …

S   So then I read the part about "dialect accommodation"—you know, the idea that people tend to adapt their speaking to make it closer to the speech of whoever they're talking to. And I'm thinking, yeah, *I* do that when I talk with my roommates! And without even thinking about it or anything, you know?

P   OK, all right—"dialect accommodation" is a more manageable sort of topic …

S   So I was thinking, like, I wonder just how much other people do the same thing? I mean, there's students here from all over

N   학생과 교수의 대화를 들으시오.

S   마틴 교수님이시죠?

P   리사. 무슨 일인가?

S   저, 지난주 수업시간에 하신 말씀에 대해 생각해 봤는데요. 아이디어가 생각날 때까지 기다리지 말고 학기말 과제를 시작하면 안 될까요?

P   좋아, 그렇게 하게. 무슨 생각이라도 있는 건가?

S   네, 그게 제가 언어학 수업을 한 번도 들어본 적이 없거든요. 그래서 강의 설명서에 교수님이 이것저것 설명하신 내용을 훑어봤는데 무슨 말을 하는 건지 모르겠어요. 그러니까 무슨 의미인지를 이해하지 못했어요. 그런데 정말 제 눈에 확 들어오는 단어가 하나 있더라고요.

P   그래?

S   사투리에 관한 부분이던가? 사실 제가 그 분야에 늘 관심이 있었거든요.

P   음, 분명 흥미로운 주제긴 하네. 하지만 자네가 깨닫지 못할 수도 있는 게, 내 말은, 그 범위가 말야….

S   그게, 제가 지금 특별히 남부출신, 뉴욕출신 룸메이트와 같은 방을 쓰거든요. 그래서 셋이 완전히 다른 말을 써요.

P   그렇군. 무슨 말인지 알겠네. 그런데….

S   그런데 말이에요. 생각해 보니 학기가 끝날 때가 되어서야 이 주제에 대해 본격적으로 배우게 된다는 걸 깨닫게 되었어요. 그래서….

P   그래서 사투리에 관한 정보를 얻을 만한 곳을 조언해 달라는 거군. 그렇다면 우선 사회언어학 책의 사투리 장을 읽어야 할 거야. 그래야 사투리의 중요한 문제들을 기본적으로 이해할 수 있거든.

S   예. 저도 그렇게 생각했어요! 그래서 그 장을 읽기 시작했는데, 어떻게 모든 사람들이 어느 정도는 사투리를 쓰는지에 관한 장부터 읽었어요. 그리고 음, 그럼 도대체 어떻게 사람들이 서로의 말을 이해하는지 궁금해졌어요.

P   아, 그렇군. 재미있는 질문이네. 알겠지만….

S   그래서 그 다음엔 '사투리 적응'에 대한 부분을 읽었어요. 이게 사람은 말할 때 상대방이 하는 말을 따라 하면서 상대방에게 맞추려 한다는 거잖아요. 그런데 정말 제가 룸메이트와 대화할 때 그러더라고요! 심지어 의식하거나 아무 생각도 하지 않는데 그래요.

P   좋아. '사투리 적응'은 그중에서도 좀 더 다루기 쉬운 주제니까….

S   그래서 생각해 봤는데요. 사람들이 어느 정도나 그렇게 하는지 궁금하더라고요. 그러니까 여기 학생들은 사방에서 왔잖아요. 누구에게 말을 거느냐에 따라 누구나 어느

the place; does everyone change the way they talk to some degree, depending on who they're talking to?

P You'd be surprised!

S So, anyway, my question is, do you think it'd be OK if I did a project like that for my term paper? You know, find students from different parts of the country, record them talking to each other in different combinations, report on how they accommodate their speech or not, that kind of thing?

P Tell you what, Lisa: Write me up a short proposal for this project—how you're going to carry out the experiment and everything, a-a design plan—and I think this'll work out just fine!

정도는 상대방의 말에 맞출까요?

P 아마 놀랄걸세!

S 그래서 어쨌든 제가 이 주제로 학기말 과제를 해도 될지 여쭙고 싶어서요. 그러니까 서로 다른 지역에서 온 학생들을 뽑은 다음, 사투리가 다른 학생들 사이의 대화를 기록하는 거예요. 그래서 어떻게 상대방의 말에 맞추는지를 보고하는 건데 어떨까요?

P 그렇다면 리사, 자네가 제출해야 할 것이 있네. 이번 과제에 대한 짧은 제안서를 작성해서 제출하게. 가령 실험은 어떻게 할 것이며 그 밖의 모든 계획을 정리한 일종의 설계서지. 그러면 과제를 잘할 수 있을 걸세!

어휘

term paper 학기말 과제   come up with 찾아내다, 내놓다   linguistics 언어학   course description 강의 설명서   jump out 눈에 띄다, 분명하다
dialect 방언, 사투리   intrigue 호기심을 자극하다, 흥미를 돋우다   scope 범위   semester 학기   pointer 충고, 조언   sociolinguistics 사회 언어학
accommodation 조정, 적응   adapt 맞추다, 조절하다   manageable 다루기 쉬운, 관리할 수 있는   to some degree 약간은, 어느 정도는   combination
결합, 조합   accommodate 부응하다, 맞추다   proposal 제안, 제의   carry out 수행하다   experiment 실험

12. 학생이 교수를 찾아간 이유는?
   Ⓐ 학기말 과제의 주제를 찾느라 애를 먹고 있다.
   Ⓑ 참고자료를 찾기 위해 도움이 필요하다.
   Ⓒ 학기말 과제 제출기간 연장을 부탁하고 싶어한다.
   Ⓓ 학기말 과제에 대한 계획을 허락 받고 싶어한다.

   어휘 material 자료   extension 연장, 확대
      approve 허가하다, 승인하다

13. 학생이 사투리에 관해 더 공부하고 싶어하는 이유는?
   Ⓐ 다른 학생들의 말을 종종 잘 이해하지 못하기 때문에
   Ⓑ 자신의 말투를 바꾸려고 하기 때문에
   Ⓒ 룸메이트들과 서로 다른 사투리로 말하기 때문에
   Ⓓ 사투리가 다른 여러 지역에서 어린 시절을 보냈기 때문에

14. 이 대화를 토대로 '사투리 적응'에 대해 내릴 수 있는 결론은? 두 개의 답을 선택하라.
   Ⓐ 주로 잠재의식에서 일어나는 과정이다.
   Ⓑ 일부 사투리에만 적용되는 과정이다.
   Ⓒ 아주 일반적인 현상이다.
   Ⓓ 광범위하게 탐구되지 않은 주제다.

   어휘 subconscious 잠재의식의   phenomenon 현상
      explore 조사하다, 탐구하다

15. 교수는 학생이 다음으로 무엇을 하길 원하는가?
   Ⓐ 자신이 추천한 논문들 읽기
   Ⓑ 전체 학생들 앞에서 제안서 발표하기
   Ⓒ 프로젝트에 대한 계획서 제출하기
   Ⓓ 다른 방언들의 녹음 듣기

   어휘 article 논문   submit 제출하다

16. 대화의 일부를 다시 듣고 질문에 답하라.

 T-39

S The section on dialects? 'Cause, like, that's the kind of thing that's always sort of intrigued me, you know?
P Well, that's certainly an *interesting* topic, but you may not realize, I mean, the *scope*...

N *What can be inferred about the professor when he says this:*
P Well, that's certainly an *interesting* topic, but you may not realize, I mean, the *scope*...

   Ⓐ 주제가 자신의 전문 지식을 넘어선다고 생각한다.
   Ⓑ 주제가 학생이 다루기에 너무 광범위하다고 생각한다.
   Ⓒ 주제가 언어학 수업과 관련이 없다고 생각한다.
   Ⓓ 다른 학생들이 같은 주제를 선택했을지도 모른다고 생각한다.

   어휘 relevant 관련 있는, 적절한

N Narrator **P** Professor

Script T-40

N Listen to part of a lecture in a creative writing class.

P All right everybody. The topic for today is, well … we're gonna take a look at how to start creating the characters for the stories you're writing. One way of doing that is to come up with what's called a character sketch. I don't mean a sketch like a drawing. I guess that's obvious. It's, um … a sketch is a way of getting started on defining your characters' personalities.

To begin, how do we create fictional characters? We don't just pull them from thin air, do we? I mean, we don't create them out of nothing. We base them—consciously or unconsciously—we base them on real people. Or, we, um … blend several people's traits … their attributes … into one character.

But when people think fiction, they may assume the characters come from the author's imagination. But the writer's imagination is influenced by … by real people. Could be anyone, so pay attention to the people you meet … someone in class, at the gym, that guy who's always sitting in the corner at the coffeehouse … uh, your cousin who's always getting into dangerous situations. We're pulling from reality … gathering bits and pieces of real people. You use these people … and the bits of behavior or characteristics as a starting point as you begin to sketch out your characters.

Here's what you should think about doing first. When you begin to formulate a story, make a list of interesting people you know or have observed. Consider *why* they're unique … or annoying. Then make notes about their unusual or dominant attributes. As you create fictional characters, you'll almost always combine characteristics from several different people on your list to form the identity and personality of just one character.

Keeping this kind of character sketch can help you solidify your character's personality … so that it remains consistent throughout your story. You need to define your characters … know their personalities so that you can have them acting in ways that're predictable … consistent with their personalities. Get to know them like a friend. You know your friends well enough to know how they'll act in certain situations, right?

Say you have three friends, their car runs out of gas on the highway. John gets upset, Mary remains calm, Teresa takes charge of handling the situation. And, let's say … both John and Mary defer to her leadership. They call you to explain what happened. And when John tells you he got mad, you're

N 문예창작 수업의 일부를 들으시오.

P 좋아요, 여러분. 아, 오늘은 여러분이 쓰려는 이야기 속의 인물을 창조하는 방법에 대해 살펴보려 합니다. 한 가지 방법은 인물 스케치를 짜는 겁니다. 데생 같은 스케치를 의미하는 것이 아닙니다. 그것만은 확실하죠. 음, 여기서 말하는 스케치란 인물의 성격 규정에 착수하는 한 가지 방법입니다.

우선 어떻게 허구의 인물들을 창조할까요? 인물이 하늘에서 뚝 떨어지는 건 아니잖아요, 그렇죠? 무(無)에서 인물을 창조할 순 없다는 말입니다. 우리는 의식적으로든 무의식적으로든 실존 인물을 바탕으로 만듭니다. 아니면 음, 몇 사람의 특징들, 태도들을 섞어서 하나의 인물로 만듭니다.

하지만 소설이라고 하면 사람들은 으레 작가의 상상을 통해 탄생한 인물을 떠올립니다. 하지만 작가의 상상력은 실존 인물들의 영향을 받습니다. 누구든지 대상이 될 수 있어요. 이를테면 교실이나 헬스장에서 만나는 사람, 항상 커피숍 구석에 앉아 있는 남자, 음, 걸핏하면 위험한 상황에 처하는 사촌도 있겠네요. 이렇게 현실에서 실제 사람들의 이런저런 모습을 끌어다 모으는 거죠. 인물의 윤곽을 그리는 출발점으로 이런 사람들, 그리고 행위나 특성의 단편들을 활용할 수 있죠.

여러분이 맨 먼저 고려해야 할 것들이 있습니다. 이야기를 써내려 가기 시작하면 주변 지인이나 관찰해온 사람들로 흥미로운 인물 목록을 만드세요. 그 사람들이 왜 독특한지, 혹은 왜 짜증스러운지 생각해 보세요. 그 다음 인물의 특이하거나 두드러진 태도를 기록하세요. 허구의 인물을 창조할 때 여러분은 거의 대부분 목록에서 각기 다른 여러 명의 성격을 결합하여 한 사람의 정체성과 인격을 창조하게 됩니다.

이런 식으로 인물 스케치를 하다 보면 인물의 성격을 확정하는 데 도움이 됩니다. 그래야 소설을 전개하는 동안 인물에 일관성이 있어요. 여러분은 인물의 특성을 정의하고, 성격을 파악해야 합니다. 그러면 인물이 예측 가능한 방식으로 행동하고 성격이 한결같지요. 인물에 대해 친구처럼 알아야 합니다. 친구라면 특정 상황에서 어떻게 행동할지 잘 알잖아요, 그렇죠?

자, 친구 세 사람이 있는데 고속도로를 달리다 기름이 떨어졌다고 합시다. 존은 화를 내고 메리는 침착하며 테레사는 책임지고 상황을 해결하죠. 그리고 존과 메리가 테레사의 지시대로 따른다고 합시다. 이제 친구들이 당신에게 연락해 무슨 일이 있었는지 설명합니다. 존이 불같이 화를 냈다고 말하는데 놀랍지 않죠. 그 친구는 항

not surprised because he always gets frustrated when things go wrong. Then he tells you how Teresa took charge, calmed him down, assigned tasks for each person, and got them on their way. Again you're not surprised. It's exactly what you'd expect. Well, you need to know your characters like you know your friends … if you know a lot about a person's character, it's easy to predict how they'll behave. So if your characters' personalities are well defined, it'll be easy for you as the writer to portray them realistically … believably in any given situation.

While writing character sketches, *do* think about *details*. Ask yourself questions, even if you don't use the *details* in your story … uh, what does each character like to eat, what setting does each prefer … the mountains? The city? What about educational background? Their reactions to success … or defeat? Write it all down.

But here I need to warn you about a possible pitfall. Don't make your character into a stereotype. Remember, the reader needs to know how your character is different from other people who might fall in the same category. Maybe your character loves the mountains and has lived in a remote area for years. To make sure he's not a stereotype, ask yourself how he sees life differently from other people who live in that kind of setting. Be careful not to make him into the cliché of the rugged mountain dweller.

OK. Now I'll throw out a little terminology … it's easy stuff. *Major* characters are sometimes called *round* characters. *Minor* characters are sometimes called … well, just the opposite. *Flat*. A round character is fully developed. A flat character isn't—character development is fairly limited. The flat character tends to serve mainly as a, um, a motivating factor. For instance, you introduce a flat character who has experienced some sort of defeat … and then your round … your main character, who loves success and loves to show off, comes and boasts about succeeding … and jokes about the flat character's defeat in front of others … humiliates the other guy. The flat character is introduced solely for the purpose of allowing the round character to show off.

상 문제가 생기면 불안을 터뜨리거든요. 그러고는 테레사가 나서서 존을 진정시키며 각자가 할 일을 정해줘서 무사히 가던 길을 갔다고 말합니다. 이번에도 놀랍지 않습니다. 정확하게 예상했던 대로거든요. 자, 여러분은 친구를 알듯 인물의 성격을 파악해야 합니다. 한 인물의 특성을 많이 알면 어떻게 행동할지 예측하기가 쉬워요. 따라서 인물의 성격이 제대로 규정되면 작가는 인물을 현실적으로, 그러니까 어떤 상황에서도 그럴듯하게 묘사하기가 쉬울 겁니다.

인물 스케치를 하는 동안 세부적인 것들도 생각해야 합니다. 그런 세세한 것들을 이야기에 써먹지 않더라도 자문해 보세요. 음, 각각의 인물이 좋아하는 음식은? 선호하는 장소는? 산일까? 도시일까? 학력은? 성공할 때나 패배할 때 반응은? 이런 걸 모두 적으세요.

하지만 이때 여러분이 주의해야 할 함정이 있습니다. 상투적인 인물로 만들어서는 안 됩니다. 명심하세요. 독자들은 등장인물이 같은 범주에 속하는 다른 사람들과 어떻게 다른지 알아야 합니다. 혹시 인물이 산을 좋아해서 오랫동안 벽지에 살고 있다고 합시다. 틀에 박힌 인물이 안 되게 하려면 이런 경우 비슷한 환경에 사는 다른 사람들과 인생관이 어떻게 다를까 자문해야 합니다. 거친 산사람처럼 상투적인 인물이 되지 않도록 주의하세요.

자, 이제 전문용어 몇 가지를 설명하죠. 간단합니다. 때때로 주요 인물을 입체적 인물이라고 합니다. 음, 그래서 주변 인물은 반대로 평면적 인물이라고 부릅니다. 입체적 인물은 충분히 변화, 발전합니다. 평면적 인물은 그렇지 않죠. 변화, 발전하는 정도가 상당히 제한적입니다. 음, 평면적 인물은 주로 동기 요인으로 쓸모가 있습니다. 예를 들어 어떤 패배를 경험한 평면적 인물이 등장합니다. 그 다음 입체적 인물이, 즉 성공에 미치고 으스대기 좋아하는 주요인물이 나타나 자신의 성공을 자랑하는 거예요. 또 다른 사람들 앞에서 평면적 인물의 패배를 조롱하고 창피를 줍니다. 이때 평면적 인물은 오로지 입체적 인물이 으스댈 계기를 제공하기 위한 목적으로 등장합니다.

어휘

character 등장인물　come up with (계획 등을) 짜다, 세우다　personality 개성, 성격　fictional 소설의, 허구적인　consciously 의식적으로, 자각하여　unconsciously 무의식적으로　blend 섞다, 혼합하다　trait 특성, 특징　attribute 속성, 자질　bits and pieces 이런저런 것들, 잡동사니　formulate 만들다, 고안하다　unique 독특한　annoying 성가신, 귀찮은　dominant 두드러진, 특징적인　attribute 속성, 태도　solidify 굳히다, 확고히 하다　consistent 일관성 있는　defer to ~을 좇다, 따르다　assign 맡기다, 배정하다　portray 그리다, 묘사하다　pitfall 함정, 덫　stereotype 틀에 박힌 방식, 상투 문구　cliché 상투적인[진부한] 표현　rugged 거칠고, 억센　dweller 거주자, 사는 사람　throw out ~을 말하다, 내뱉다　terminology 전문 용어　round character 입체적 인물　flat character 평면적 인물　show off ~을 자랑하다, 으스대다　humiliate 창피를 주다, 굴욕감을 주다　solely 오로지, 단지

83

17. 교수는 창작의 어떤 측면을 주로 이야기하는가?

Ⓐ 독자의 관심을 지속적으로 끄는 방법

Ⓑ 그럴듯한 인물을 창조하는 방법

Ⓒ 주요 인물과 주변 인물의 결정적인 차이점

Ⓓ 단편소설의 줄거리를 전개하는 기법

어휘 believable 믿을 수 있는, 그럴듯한   short story 단편 소설
plot 줄거리, 구성

18. 교수가 학생들에게 매일 만나는 사람들을 눈여겨보라고 조언하는
이유는?

Ⓐ 그런 사람들의 행동과 특징을 인물 스케치에 활용할 수 있다.

Ⓑ 실생활에서 사람들을 관찰하다 보면 줄거리를 위한 아이디어
가 떠오를 수 있다.

Ⓒ 낯선 사람보다 익숙한 사람의 행동을 관찰하기가 더 쉽다.

Ⓓ 학생들이 인물의 신체를 정확하게 묘사하는 데 필요한 정보를
수집할 수 있다.

어휘 accurate 정확한

19. 교수는 기름이 떨어진 세 친구를 예로 들고 있다. 교수가 이 예화를
통해 설명하려는 것은?

Ⓐ 작가는 친구만큼이나 인물에 대해 잘 알아야 한다.

Ⓑ 작가는 복합적으로 상호작용하는 인물을 창조해야 한다.

Ⓒ 친구는 언제나 예상대로 행동하지는 않는다.

Ⓓ 친구의 행동은 종종 허구적 인물의 행동보다 더 예측 가능하다.

어휘 interact 상호작용하다   predictable 예측할 수 있는

20. 교수가 산에 사는 사람에 대해 이야기하며 경고하는 것은?

Ⓐ 외딴 곳을 인물의 배경으로 삼지 마라.

Ⓑ 주요 인물을 한 명 이상 만들지 마라.

Ⓒ 특이한 인생을 사는 사람들을 모델로 사용하지 마라.

Ⓓ 틀에 박힌 인물로 만들지 마라.

21. 교수는 평면적 인물의 중요성이 무엇이라고 암시하는가?

Ⓐ 다른 인물보다 훨씬 더 예측 가능하게 행동한다.

Ⓑ 독자들이 이해하기 어렵다.

Ⓒ 주요 인물의 성격이 드러나도록 돕는다.

Ⓓ 패배를 경험할 수 있는 유일한 인물이다.

어휘 reveal 드러내다, 나타내다

22. 강의의 일부를 다시 듣고 질문에 답하라.

 T-41

> **P** One way of doing that is to come up with what's called a character sketch. I don't mean a sketch like a drawing. I guess that's obvious. It's um … a sketch is a way of getting started on defining your characters' personalities.
>
> **N** *Why does the professor say this:*
> **P** I don't mean a sketch like a drawing.

Ⓐ 자신이 원하는 데생의 종류를 설명할 참이라고 언질하기 위해

Ⓑ 헷갈리는 용어에 대한 학생들의 이해를 돕기 위해

Ⓒ 앞서 틀린 단어를 사용했다고 말하기 위해

Ⓓ 학생들이 더 잘하도록 동기를 부여하기 위해

어휘 confusing 혼란스러운, 헷갈리는
motivate 동기를 부여하다

Questions 23~28

p.116

N Narrator   **P** Professor   **F** Female Student   **M** Male Student

N Listen to part of a lecture in an earth science class.

P We're really just now beginning to understand how *quickly drastic* climate change can take place. We can see past occurrences of climate change that took place over just a few hundred years. Take, uh, the Sahara desert ... in Northern Africa.
The Sahara was really different 6,000 years ago. I mean, you wouldn't call it a tropical paradise or anything—ah, or maybe you *would* if you think about how today in some parts of the Sahara it only rains about once a century. Um, but basically, you had greenery and you had water. And what *I* find *particularly* interesting, amazing, really what *really* indicates how *un*-desert-like the Sahara was thousands of years ago, was something painted on a rock: prehistoric art—*hippopotamuses*. As you know, hippos need a lot of water, and hence ... Hence what?

F They need to live near a large source of water year-round.

P That's right.

M But how's that proof that the Sahara used to be a lot wetter? I mean, the people who painted those hippos ... well, couldn't they have seen them on their travels?

P OK, in principle they could, Carl. But the rock paintings aren't the only evidence. Beneath the Sahara are huge *aquifers*, basically a sea of fresh water that's perhaps a million years old, filtered through rock layers. And, ah, and-and then there's fossilized pollen from low shrubs and grasses that once grew in the Sahara. In fact these *plants* still grow, ah, but hundreds of miles away in more vegetated areas. Anyway, it's this fossilized pollen, along with the aquifers, *and* the rock paintings—these three things are all evidence that the Sahara was once much greener than it is today, that there were hippos and probably elephants, and giraffes, and so on.

M So, what happened?

P How did it happen? Well now we're so used to hearing about how human activities are affecting the climate, right; but that takes the focus away from the natural variations in the Earth's climate. Like the Ice Age, right? The planet was practically covered in ice just a few thousand years ago. Now, as far as the Sahara goes, there's some recent literature that points to the migration of the monsoon in that area.

M/F Huh?

N 지구과학 강의의 일부를 들으시오.

P 이제 곧 얼마나 빨리 기후가 급격하게 변할 수 있는지 이해하게 될 겁니다. 불과 수백 년 사이에 발생한 기후 변화의 과거 사례를 볼 수 있습니다. 음, 북아프리카의 사하라 사막을 보죠.
6000년 전 사하라는 지금과 아주 딴판이었습니다. 그렇다고 열대 낙원으로 부를 정도라는 말은 아니에요. 아, 오늘날 사하라 일부 지역은 백 년에 한 번 정도 비가 온다는 점을 감안하면 뭐 그렇게 부를 수도 있겠네요. 음, 아무튼 원래 사하라 사막에는 초목과 물이 있었습니다. 특별히 흥미롭고 놀라운 사실은 수천 년 전 사하라가 얼마나 사막하고 거리가 멀었는지 보여 주는 실질적인 증거가 있다는 것입니다. 바로 암벽화인데 선사시대 미술로 하마를 그린 그림입니다. 아시다시피 하마는 물이 많이 필요하죠. 이게 무슨 말일까요?

F 하마는 일 년 내내 커다란 수원(水源) 근처에 살아야 합니다.

P 맞습니다.

M 하지만 그게 어째서 사하라 지역에 비가 많이 왔다는 증거가 되나요? 그러니까 하마를 그린 사람들이, 음, 여행하다가 하마를 봤을 수도 있잖아요?

P 그렇습니다. 원론적으로는 그랬을 수도 있죠, 칼. 하지만 암벽화가 유일한 증거는 아닙니다. 사하라 사막 밑에 거대한 대수층이 있거든요. 아마 이것은 원래 백만 년 동안 암석층으로 스며든 담수해일 겁니다. 아, 그리고 한때 사하라 지역에서 자란 키 작은 관목과 풀에서 나온 꽃가루 화석도 있습니다. 사실 이런 식물은 지금도 자랍니다만, 사막에서 수백 마일 떨어진 초목이 좀 더 무성한 곳에 있죠. 어쨌든 대수층, 암벽화, 그리고 꽃가루 화석, 이렇게 세 가지 모두는 한때 사하라 사막에 지금보다 훨씬 녹지가 많았다는 증거입니다. 하마도 살고 아마 코끼리, 기린 따위도 있었을 거예요.

M 그런데 어떻게 된 거죠?

P 어떻게 사막으로 변했을까요? 자, 우리는 인간의 행동이 기후에 미치는 영향에 대해 귀가 따갑도록 듣습니다. 맞는 말이죠. 하지만 지구의 기후가 자연적으로 변한다는 사실에는 주목하지 않습니다. 가령 빙하시대처럼 말이에요, 그렇죠? 불과 수천 년 전 실제로 지구는 얼음으로 뒤덮여 있었어요. 그리고 사하라 사막의 경우 몬순이 이동했다고 지적하는 일부 문헌이 있습니다.

M/F 네?

P What do I mean? OK. A monsoon is a seasonal wind that can bring in a large amount of rainfall. Now, if the monsoon *migrates*, well *that* means the rains move to another area, right?

So what *caused* the monsoon to migrate? Well, the answer is the dynamics of Earth's motions—the same thing that caused the Ice Age, by the way. The Earth's *not always* the same distance from the Sun. *And* it's *not always tilting* toward the Sun at the same angle. There're slight variations in these two parameters. They're gradual variations, but their *effects* can be pretty abrupt, and *can* cause the climate to change in *just* a few hundred years.

F That's abrupt?

P Well, yeah, considering that other climate shifts take *thousands* of years, this one's pretty abrupt. So these changes in the planet's motions, they caused the climate to change; but it was also *compounded*. What the Sahara experienced was a sort of *runaway drying* effect.

As I said, the monsoon migrated south—so there was less rain in the Sahara. The *land* started to get *drier*—which in turn caused a huge *decrease* in the amount of *vegetation*, because vegetation doesn't grow as well in dry soil, right? And then, less vegetation means the soil can't hold water as well—the soil *loses* its ability to *retain* water when it *does* rain. So then you have less moisture to help clouds form ... nothing to evaporate for cloud formation. And then the cycle continues—less rain, drier soil, less vegetation, fewer clouds, less rain, etcetera, etcetera.

M But what about the people who made the rock paintings?

P Good question. No one really knows. But there might be some connection to ancient Egypt. At about the same time that the Sahara was becoming a desert, mmm ... 5,000 years ago, Egypt *really* began to flourish out in the Nile River Valley. And that's not that far away. So it's only *logical* to hypothesize that a lot of these people migrated to the Nile Valley when they realized that this was more than a temporary drought. And some people take this a step further—and that's OK, that's science—and they hypothesize that this migration actually provided an important impetus in the development of ancient Egypt. Well, we'll stay tuned on that.

P 무슨 뜻일까요? 그렇습니다. 몬순은 엄청난 양의 비를 뿌릴 수 있는 계절풍입니다. 자, 몬순이 이동한다는 건 비가 다른 지역으로 움직인다는 말이에요, 그렇죠? 그렇다면 몬순의 이동을 유발한 원인은 무엇일까요? 음, 정답은 지구 움직임의 역학적 원리 때문입니다. 그런데 빙하시대를 불러온 것도 똑같은 이유예요. 지구와 태양의 거리가 언제나 똑같지는 않습니다. 그리고 태양을 향해 기울어진 지구의 각도 역시 늘 같지는 않아요. 이 두 가지 요인에 살짝 변화가 있는 거죠. 그런데 이런 변화는 점진적인데도 그 결과는 아주 급작스러울 수 있어요. 따라서 불과 몇 백 년 만에 기후가 변할 수 있죠.

F 그게 갑작스러운 건가요?

P 음, 네. 다른 기후변화의 경우 수천 년이 걸린다는 점을 감안하면 꽤 갑작스러운 거죠. 그래서 이처럼 지구 움직임의 변화가 기후변화를 일으킨 거예요. 하지만 더 심각했죠. 사하라 지대에는 일종의 걷잡을 수 없는 건조효과가 나타났습니다.

말했다시피 몬순이 남쪽으로 이동하자 사하라에 비가 줄었어요. 그 땅이 점점 건조해지기 시작하자 식물의 수가 엄청나게 감소했습니다. 식물은 마른 땅에서 잘 자라지 않잖아요, 그렇죠? 그리고 식물이 적다는 건 토양 역시 수분을 유지할 수 없다는 의미죠. 다시 말해 비가 올 때 땅이 물을 잡아두는 능력을 상실하는 겁니다. 따라서 구름을 만들 수분이 적어지는 거죠. 구름 형성을 위해 증발할 물이 없으니까요. 그리고 이런 순환 과정이 지속되면, 그러니까 비가 적게 오고, 땅이 건조해지고, 식물은 줄어들고, 구름이 없어지고, 비가 적게 오고, 그리고 또….

M 하지만 암벽화를 그린 사람들은요?

P 좋은 질문이에요. 사실 아무도 모릅니다. 하지만 고대 이집트와 관련이 있을지도 모릅니다. 사하라 지역이 사막화되던 때와 같은 시기에, 음, 5000년 전 이집트는 실제로 나일 강 계곡에서 번성하기 시작했어요. 사하라 지역에서 그리 멀지 않습니다. 따라서 일시적인 가뭄이 아니라는 것을 깨닫자 사하라 지역의 수많은 사람들이 나일 계곡으로 이동했다고 가정할 수밖에 없습니다. 그런데 일부 사람들은 여기서 한걸음 더 나아갑니다. 괜찮습니다. 그게 과학이니까요. 이들은 이 이동이 고대 이집트의 발전에 중요한 동력을 제공했다고 봅니다. 자, 이 부분은 계속 살펴보겠습니다.

어휘

drastic 급격한, 극단적인　occurrence 발생, 나타남　tropical 열대 지방의　greenery 푸른 잎(나무)　prehistoric 선사시대의　hippopotamus 하마　aquifer 대수층(지하수를 품고 있는 지층)　fresh water 담수, 민물　pollen 꽃가루, 화분　shrub 관목　variation 변화, 변동　migration 이동, 이주　monsoon 몬순, 계절풍　rainfall 강우(량)　dynamics 역학 관계　tilt 기울다, 경사지다　angle 각도　parameter 요인, 특성　abrupt 갑작스러운　climate shift 기후변화　compound 악화시키다, 더 심각하게 만들다　runaway 순식간의, 걷잡을 수 없는　decrease 감소, 하락　vegetation 식물, 초목　retain 유지[보유]하다　evaporate 증발시키다　hypothesize 가설을 세우다　temporary 일시적인, 임시의　drought 가뭄　impetus 자극제, 추동력

23. 강의는 주로 무엇에 관한 것인가?

    Ⓐ 급격한 기후변화의 예

    Ⓑ 기후변화의 두 가지 구조 비교하기

    Ⓒ 오늘날 사하라의 기후 조건

    Ⓓ 사하라 사막에서 최근 이루어진 지질학적 발견

어휘 mechanism 메커니즘, 구조   geological 지질학의

24. 얼마 전까지 사하라의 기후는 지금과 달랐다. 교수는 이 사실을 뒷받침하고자 어떤 증거를 언급하는가? 세 개의 답을 선택하라.

    Ⓐ 고대 꽃가루

    Ⓑ 큰 동물의 뼈

    Ⓒ 암벽화

    Ⓓ 고대 이집트의 농업

    Ⓔ 지하수

어휘 agriculture 농업   underground water 지하수

25. 강의에서 빙하시대와 사하라 사막의 형성은 과거의 기후변화에 대해 무엇을 설명하는가? 두 개의 답을 선택하라.

    Ⓐ 일부 기후변화는 문명의 발달에 이바지했다.

    Ⓑ 일부 기후변화는 인간의 행위 때문이 아니었다.

    Ⓒ 일부 기후변화는 대기 중의 수분 감소가 원인이었다.

    Ⓓ 일부 기후변화는 지구 움직임과 위치의 변화가 원인이었다.

어휘 benefit 이익이 되다   civilization 문명
    atmosphere 대기

26. 북아프리카 사하라 지역의 사막화를 불러온 걷잡을 수 없는 효과를 일으킨 것은?

    Ⓐ 우세풍이 더 강해졌다.

    Ⓑ 계절성 강우가 다른 지역으로 이동했다.

    Ⓒ 식물이 넓은 지역에서 죽기 시작했다.

    Ⓓ 토양이 빗물을 잡아두는 능력을 상실했다.

어휘 prevailing wind 우세풍

27. 교수는 사하라 지역에서 이주한 사람들이 이집트 문명의 발전에 중요했다는 이론을 언급한다. 이 이론에 대한 교수의 태도를 가장 잘 설명한 것은?

    Ⓐ 최근의 고고학적 발견을 완벽하게 설명하기 때문에 흥미롭다.

    Ⓑ 일반적으로 활용할 수 있는 자료에서 지나치게 벗어나기 때문에 문제가 있다.

    Ⓒ 흥미로운 가능성을 제기하므로 더 많은 증거를 보고 싶어한다.

    Ⓓ 이주자들이 이집트에 도달한 방법을 설명하기 전까지는 진지하게 고려할 수 없다.

어휘 archaeological 고고학의   problematic 문제가 많은

28. 강의의 일부를 다시 듣고 질문에 답하라.

 T-43

> **P** I mean, you wouldn't call it a tropical paradise or anything—ah, or maybe you *would* if you think about how today in some parts of the Sahara it only rains about once a century.
>
> **N** *Why does the professor say this:*
> **P** Or maybe you *would* if you think about how today in some parts of the Sahara it only rains about once a century.

    Ⓐ 사하라의 기후에 대해 잘못 말한 것을 정정하기 위해

    Ⓑ 현재 사하라 사막의 건조 상태가 과장되었음을 암시하기 위해

    Ⓒ 과거 사하라 사막의 기후에 대해 과학자들의 의견이 일치하지 않는다는 것을 말하기 위해

    Ⓓ 사하라의 현재 기후와 과거 기후의 차이를 강조하기 위해

어휘 misstatement 잘못 말하기, 그릇된 진술
    exaggerated 과장된, 부풀린

SPEAKING

Question 1

p.120

Narrator T-44

Some people have one career throughout their lives. Other people do different kinds of work at different points in their lives. Which do you like is better? Explain why.

평생 직업이 하나인 사람도 있고 시기마다 다양한 일을 하는 사람도 있다. 어느 쪽이 더 좋은가? 그 이유도 설명하시오.

준비 시간 : 15초
답변 시간 : 45초

중요 포인트

이런 유형의 질문에는 먼저 자신의 의견을 명확히 밝힌 다음 자신의 의견을 뒷받침할 여러 가지 이유를 제시해야 한다. 한 가지 일만 하는 것이 더 좋다고 생각한다면 "If you have a career that you love, there is no reason to change." ("좋아하는 일을 하는데 굳이 직업을 바꿀 이유가 없다.")라고 말할 수 있다. 또는 "Many people enjoy doing one thing that they are very good at." ("많은 사람들이 자기가 아주 잘하는 한 가지 일만 하고 싶어한다.")라고 대답할 수도 있다. 그리고 경력이 쌓이면 돈도 많이 벌고 승진의 기회가 생긴다는 식의 다른 장점들을 말하는 것도 좋다. 구체적인 예를 많이 들수록 의견을 설명하기가 수월하다. 가령 "A doctor has gone to school for a long time and it takes a long time to learn to be a good doctor, so in this case changing careers would not make sense." ("의사는 학교도 오래 다니고 좋은 의사가 되려면 긴 세월이 걸린다. 이런 경우 직업을 바꾸는 것은 말이 안 된다.")라고 말할 수 있다.

다양한 일을 하는 것이 더 좋다고 생각하는 경우도 비슷한 방법으로 의견을 밝혀야 한다. "Doing one job for your whole life would not be interesting, and that as technology progresses, many new fields to work in become available." ("평생 한 가지 일만 하면 재미도 없고, 기술이 발전하면서 일할 수 있는 새로운 분야가 많이 생겼다.")라고 말할 수 있다. 가령 새로운 컴퓨터 기술과 관련된 업종처럼 새로운 분야에 대한 구체적인 정보를 제공하는 것이 좋다.

이런 유형의 질문에는 정답이 없다는 점을 이해하자. 어떤 의견이든 타당한 예를 들어 논리 정연하게 설명해야 한다.

Question 2

p.120

Narrator T-45

Now read a letter that a student has written to the university newspaper. You have 50 seconds to read the letter. Begin reading now.

한 학생이 대학신문에 쓴 편지를 50초 동안 읽으시오. 지금 읽으시오.

History Seminars Should Be Shorter

Currently, all of the seminar classes in the history department are three hours long. I would like to propose that history seminars be shortened to two hours. I make this proposal for two reasons. First, most students just cannot concentrate for three hours straight. I myself have taken these three-hour seminars and found them tiring and sometimes boring. Also, when a seminar lasts that long, people stop concentrating and stop learning, so the third hour of a three-hour seminar is a waste of everyone's time. Two-hour seminars would be much more

---

efficient.
Sincerely,
Tim Lawson

역사 세미나 시간 단축 요청

현재 역사학과의 모든 세미나 수업은 3시간 동안 진행됩니다. 저는 역사 세미나를 2시간으로 단축해야 한다고 제안하고 싶습니다. 제가 이렇게 제안하는 이유는 두 가지입니다. 첫째, 대부분의 학생들은 3시간 연속으로 집중할 수 없습니다. 저 역시 3시간짜리 세미나를 들어봤는데 피곤하고 때때로 지루했습니다. 또한 세미나가 그렇게 길어지면 사람들이 집중하기를 그만두고 배우는 것을 그만두게 됩니다. 따라서 3시간짜리 세미나 수업의 마지막 한 시간은 모두에게 시간 낭비입니다. 2시간짜리 세미나 수업이 훨씬 효율적입니다.

팀 로슨

어휘

currently 현재, 지금   shorten 단축하다, 짧게 하다   proposal 제안, 제의   concentrate 집중하다, 전념하다   efficient 효율적인, 능률적인

Narrator T-46

Now listen to two students discussing the letter.

편지에 관해 두 학생이 나누는 대화를 들으시오.

Script

F I totally disagree with Tim's proposal.

M Why?

F Well, look. Tim's my friend, but he's not your typical student. He stays up late partying every night—weeknights too.

M If he parties every night, no wonder he can't pay attention.

F Yes, and most students aren't like that. They come to class prepared and rested, and they can concentrate.

M So you're saying the problem is really Tim.

F Yes. He was in one of my classes last year and whenever I looked at him, he was actually sleeping.

M I guess if he's sleeping, he can't really know what's happening, what other people in class are doing.

F Right. And you want to know what does happen in that last hour of seminar? In a lot of seminars that I've been in, that's when things get interesting.

M Really?

F Yes. That's usually when students get really involved in the discussion and start exchanging important ideas. And if the history department actually did what Tim suggests, well, if they did that, what would happen is you'd lose what might be the most worthwhile part of a seminar.

F 난 팀의 제안에 절대 동의할 수 없어.

M 왜?

F 음, 생각해 봐. 팀은 내 친구지만 평범한 학생은 아니야. 녀석은 매일 밤늦도록 파티를 해. 주말은 물론이고.

M 매일 밤 파티를 한다면 당연히 수업에 집중할 수 없겠네.

F 그렇지, 학생들 대부분은 그렇지 않지. 다른 사람들은 수업준비도 하고 쉬고 들어오니까 집중할 수 있다고.

M 그러니까 진짜 문제는 팀이라는 말이구나.

F 응, 지난해 팀이랑 수업 하나를 같이 들었는데 내가 볼 때마다 자더라니까.

M 잠을 잔다면 정말 무슨 일이 일어나는지, 수업시간에 다른 사람들이 뭘 하는지도 모르겠네.

F 맞아, 세미나 마지막 시간이 어떤지 알아? 내가 들었던 많은 세미나들은 바로 그 마지막 시간이 흥미로웠어.

M 정말?

F 그렇다니까, 보통 마지막 시간에 학생들이 실제로 토론에 참여해서 서로 중요한 의견을 나누기 시작하거든. 역사학과에서 정말 팀의 제안대로 한다면 어쩌면 세미나에서 가장 귀중한 부분을 잃을 거야.

어휘

disagree 동의하지 않다, 의견이 다르다   typical 전형적인, 평범한   stay up 안 자다, 깨어 있다   get involved 관여하다   discussion 토론, 토의   exchange 주고받다, 나누다   worthwhile 가치 있는, 보람 있는

Narrator

The woman expresses her opinion about the proposal described in the letter. Briefly summarize the proposal. Then state her opinion about the proposal and explain the reasons she gives for holding that opinion.

편지의 제안에 대해 여학생이 자신의 입장을 밝힌다. 편지의 제안을 간략히 요약하시오. 그 다음 여학생의 입장이 무엇인지 말하고, 그런 입장을 취하는 이유를 설명하시오.

준비 시간 : 30초
답변 시간 : 60초

중요 포인트

먼저 역사 세미나를 두 시간으로 단축하자는 편지의 제안에 대한 여학생의 의견을 설명해야 한다. 이 경우 여학생은 편지를 쓴 팀의 제안에 동의하지 않는다.

여학생이 팀의 제안에 동의하지 않는다는 사실을 말한 후, 그런 입장을 취하는 두 가지 중요한 이유를 설명해야 한다. 완벽하게 답변하려면 두 학생의 대화 내용과 편지에서 알게 된 정보를 적절히 연결해야 한다. 여학생은 역사 세미나 시간을 단축하자는 첫 번째 이유, 다시 말해 사람들이 세 시간 동안 집중할 수 없다는 이유가 타당하지 않다고 말한다. 여학생에 따르면, 편지를 쓴 팀은 밤늦게까지 잠을 안 자고 종종 수업시간에 자기 때문이다.

여학생이 팀의 제안에 동의하지 않는 두 번째 이유 역시 설명해야 한다. 팀은 마지막 시간에 학생들이 아무것도 배우지 않으므로 이 시간이 낭비라고 말한다. 하지만 여학생은 마지막 시간에 이루어지는 토론이 가장 흥미롭고 세미나의 가장 중요한 부분이라고 생각한다.

Question 3

p.121

Narrator T-47

You have 45 seconds to read a passage from a psychology textbook. Begin reading now.

심리학 교재의 한 부분을 45초 동안 읽으시오. 지금 읽으시오.

Explicit Memories and Implicit Memories

In everyday life, when people speak of memory, they are almost always speaking about what psychologists would call explicit memories. An explicit memory is a conscious or intentional recollection, usually of facts, names, events, or other things that a person can state or declare. There is another kind of memory that is not conscious. Memories of this kind are called implicit memories. An individual can have an experience that he or she cannot consciously recall yet still display reactions that indicate the experience has been somehow recorded in his or her brain.

외현 기억과 암묵 기억

사람들이 일상생활에서 이야기하는 기억은 대개 심리학자들이 외현 기억이라고 부르는 것이다. 외현 기억은 의식적이거나 의도적인 기억으로 주로 진술하거나 분명히 말할 수 있는 사실이나 이름, 사건 등을 말한다. 또 다른 유형의 기억으로 무의식적 기억이 있다. 이런 유형의 기억을 암묵 기억이라고 부른다. 사람은 의식적으로 기억하지 못하면서도 반응을 보이는데 이는 그 경험이 어쨌든 뇌에 기록되었다는 것을 나타낸다.

어휘

explicit memory 외현 기억   implicit memory 암묵 기억
psychologist 심리학자   conscious 의식적인, 자각하는
intentional 의도적인, 계획적인   recollection 기억, 상기
display 드러내다, 보이다   reaction 반응

Narrator T-48

Now listen to part of a lecture on this topic in a psychology class.

이 주제에 관한 심리학 강의의 일부를 들으시오.

(Script)

P   OK, the first kind of memory, we're all very familiar with this, right? You probably remember what you had for dinner last night. You have a conscious memory of last night's dinner, so, um, if I ask you "What did you eat last night?" you could tell me.

But these other kind of memories—implicit memories. They work differently.

Let's take an example from the world of advertising. When you're driving along a highway, you see plenty of billboards—you know, roadside advertisements. You certainly don't remember them all. But they still affect you. Marketing researchers have shown ... well, to be specific, let's say there's a billboard on the highway advertising a car called "the Panther." The ad shows a big picture of the car. And above the car in huge letters is the name of the car: "Panther." A lot of people drive by the billboard. But ... ask those drivers later if they saw any advertisements for cars, and, well, they'll think about it, and a lot of them will say no. They honestly don't remember seeing any. They have no conscious memory of the "Panther" billboard. So you ask these same people a different question: You ask, um, OK, ah, you ask them to name an animal starting with the letter P. What do you think they will answer? Do they say "pig"? Pig is the most common animal that starts with the letter P. But they don't say "pig." They say "panther." The billboard had an effect, even though the drivers don't remember ever seeing it.

P   자, 첫 번째 유형의 기억은 모두에게 아주 친숙합니다, 그렇죠? 아마 여러분은 어젯밤 저녁식사로 무엇을 먹었는지 기억할 겁니다. 음, 따라서 어젯밤 저녁식사에 대한 의식적 기억을 갖고 있을 거예요. 그러니까 제가 '어젯밤 뭘 먹었죠?'라고 물으면 대답할 수 있을 겁니다. 하지만 또 다른 종류인 암묵 기억은 전혀 다르게 작용합니다.

광고계를 예로 들어 보죠. 고속도로를 운전하다 보면 수많은 광고판이 보입니다. 말하자면 대로변에 설치된 광고들이죠. 우리는 그것들을 모두 기억하지는 못해요. 하지만 영향력은 미칩니다. 시장조사 전문가들이 보여 줬어요. 구체적으로 예를 들어 고속도로에 'Panther(퓨마)'라는 자동차를 선전하는 광고판이 있다고 칩시다. 이 광고판에는 커다란 자동차 사진이 있어요. 그리고 차 위로 아주 커다란 글씨로 'Panther'라는 차 이름이 적혀 있죠. 많은 사람들이 차를 몰고 이 광고판을 지나칩니다. 하지만 나중에 자동차 광고를 봤냐고 물어보면 한참을 생각하다가 대부분 못 봤다고 말할 겁니다. 솔직히 전혀 기억하지 못하죠. 'Panther' 광고판에 대한 의식적 기억이 전혀 없습니다. 그래서 이번에는 같은 사람들에게 다른 질문을 합

니다. 음, 알파벳 P로 시작하는 동물 이름을 대보라고 하는 거예요. 사람들이 어떻게 대답할 것 같나요? 'pig(돼지)'라고 말할까요? 'pig'는 알파벳 P로 시작하는 가장 흔한 동물이죠. 하지만 사람들은 'pig' 대신 'panther'를 말합니다. 운전자들은 광고판을 본 것조차 기억하지 못하지만 광고가 영향을 미친 겁니다.

중요 포인트

우선 지문에 설명된 암묵 기억의 개념을 설명해야 한다. 암묵 기억은 무의식적이며 기억할 수 없지만 뇌에 기록된 기억이다. 또한 암묵 기억과 의식적으로 기억할 수 있는 외현 기억을 대조 설명하는 방법도 좋다. 하지만 여기에 시간을 많이 허비해서는 안 되며 교수의 예를 논의하는 데 충분한 시간을 확보해야 한다.

그 다음 교수가 암묵 기억을 설명하기 위해 제시한 예를 사용해야 한다. 교수의 예에서 운전자가 광고판을 지나치며 'Panther(퓨마)'라는 자동차 광고를 본다. 이후 같은 사람에게 P로 시작하는 동물 이름을 대라고 하자 'Panther'라는 단어를 떠올린다. 영어로 돼지를 뜻하는 'pig'가 알파벳 p로 시작하는 훨씬 흔한 동물인데도 말이다. 이를 통해 광고판이 운전자의 기억에 영향을 미친 것을 알 수 있다.

지문과 강의 내용을 일일이 상세하게 반복할 필요는 없지만 지문과 강의 내용의 요점을 통합해서 말해야 한다.

어휘

familiar 친숙한, 익숙한   advertising 광고, 광고업   billboard 광고게시판   advertisement 광고   affect 영향을 미치다, 작용하다   specific 구체적인, 명확한   honestly 솔직히   effect 영향, 효과

Narrator

Using the example of the car advertisement, explain what is meant by implicit memory.

자동차 광고의 예를 사용해서 암묵 기억의 의미를 설명하시오.

준비 시간 : 30초
답변 시간 : 60초

Question 4

p.122

Narrator T-49

Now listen to part of a talk in an education class.

교육학 강의의 일부를 들으시오.

P One of the hardest parts of teaching is keeping your students' attention. Now, the key to doing this is understanding the *concept* of attention.

Basically, there are two types of attention. The first type is active. Active attention is voluntary—it's when you intentionally make yourself focus on something. And since it requires effort, it's hard to keep up for a long time. OK, so, um, let's say you're teaching a ... a biology class. And today's topic is frogs. All right, you're standing at the front of the room and lecturing: "A frog is a type of animal known as an amphibian ..." Well, this isn't necessarily going to keep the students' interest. But most of them will force themselves to pay active attention to your lecture ... but it's only a matter of time before they get distracted.

Now, the other type of attention is *passive* attention—when it's involuntary. Passive attention requires no effort, because it happens naturally. If something's really interesting, students don't have to *force* themselves to pay attention to it—they do it without even thinking about it. So back to our biology lecture. You start talking about frogs, and then you pull a live frog out of your briefcase. You're describing it while you hold it up ... show the students how long its legs are and how they're used for jumping, for example. Then maybe you even let the frog jump around a bit on the desk or the floor. In this case, by doing something unexpected ... something more engaging, you can tap into their passive attention. And it can last much longer than active attention; as long as the frog's still there, your students will be interested.

P 가르칠 때 가장 어려운 부분 중 하나가 학생들이 계속 주목하도록 만드는 것입니다. 자, 그러려면 주목의 '개념'을 이해하는 것이 가장 중요해요.

기본적으로 주목에는 두 가지 종류가 있습니다. 첫 번째 유형은 능동적입니다. 능동적 주목은 자발적이라서 말하자면 무언가에 의도적으로 집중하는 거예요. 이 경우 노력이 필요하기 때문에 오래 지속하기가 어렵죠. 자, 그렇다면 음, 예를 들어 생물학 수업을 한다고 합시다. 오늘의 주제는 개구리입니다. 자, 여러분이 교실 앞에서 "개구리는 양서류라고 하는 동물이에요…"하며 가르친다고 칩시다. 음, 이런 강의로는 학생들의 눈길을 계속 붙잡아 두기가 어려울 거예요. 하지만 대부분은 억지로라도 수업에 집중하려고 하겠죠. 그래도 주의가 산만해지는 건 시간 문제죠.

자, 또 다른 종류는 수동적 주목인데요. 무의식적인 경우입니다. 수동적인 주목은 자연스럽게 일어나므로 노력할 필요가 없어요. 정말 흥미로우면 학생들은 억지로 주목할 필요가 없거든요. 굳이 의식하지 않아도 저절로 되는 거죠. 그렇다면 다시 생물 수업을 예로 들어 볼까요. 개구리 이야기를 시작하더니 가방에서 살아 있는 개구리 한 마리를 꺼냅니다. 그리고 개구리를 들어 보이며 학생들에게 설명하는 거죠. 가령 개구리 다리는 얼마나 길며 다리를 써서 어떻게 도약하는지 설명합니다. 그 다음 책상이나 바닥 위에서 개구리가 폴짝폴짝 뛰어다니도록 놔둘 수도 있겠네요. 이 경우 예기치 않은, 좀 더 흥미진진한 일을 통해 학생들의 수동적인 주목을 끌 수 있습니다. 그리고 수동적인 주목은 능동적인 주목보다 훨씬 오래 지속됩니다. 그래서 개구리가 교실에 있는 동안은 학생들이 관심을 가질 거예요.

어휘

concept 개념, 관념   active attention 능동적인 주목   voluntary 자발적인, 임의의   intentionally 의도적으로, 고의로   biology 생물학   amphibian 양서류   distracted 주의가 산만해진   passive attention 수동적인 주목   involuntary 무의식의, 무심결의   briefcase 서류 가방   tap into ~을 활용(이용)하다

Narrator

Using points and examples from the talk, explain the difference between active and passive attention.

이 강의 내용에 나온 논지와 예를 사용해서 능동적인 주목과 수동적인 주목의 차이를 설명하시오.

준비 시간 : 20초
답변 시간 : 60초

중요 포인트

답변에는 교수가 설명한 두 가지 종류의 주목에 대한 요약이 포함되어야 한다. 어느 유형을 먼저 설명하든 두 가지 모두 충분히 설명하고 서로의 차이점을 명확히 제시해야 한다.

교수의 설명에 따르면 능동적 주목은 의도적으로 억지로 집중하는 것이다. 개구리에 대한 지루한 강의를 듣기 위해 학생들은 능동적으로 주목해야 한다. 하지만 이 경우 오랫동안 집중할 수 없다.

그 다음 수동적인 주목에 대해 설명해야 한다. 수동적 주목은 무의식적이며 능동적인 주목과 달리 노력할 필요가 없다. 수동적인 주목은 내용에 자연스럽게 흥미를 느낄 때 발생한다. 선생님이 살아 있는 개구리를 꺼내서 보여준다면 학생들은 더 흥미를 보이며 계속 수동적으로 주목한다.

시간을 적절히 분배해 두 가지 유형의 주목에 대해 잘 요약하고, 두 경우 모두에서 개구리 강의의 예를 설명할 수 있어야 한다.

WRITING

Writing Based on Reading and Listening

p.124

Communal online encyclopedias represent one of the latest resources to be found on the Internet. They are in many respects like traditional printed encyclopedias: collections of articles on various subjects. What is specific to these online encyclopedias, however, is that any Internet user can contribute a new article or make an editorial change in an existing one. As a result, the encyclopedia is authored by the whole community of Internet users. The idea might sound attractive, but the communal online encyclopedias have several important problems that make them much less valuable than traditional, printed encyclopedias.

First, contributors to a communal online encyclopedia often lack academic credentials, thereby making their contributions partially informed at best and downright inaccurate in many cases. Traditional encyclopedias are written by trained experts who adhere to standards of academic rigor that nonspecialists cannot really achieve.

Second, even if the original entry in the online encyclopedia is correct, the communal nature of these online encyclopedias gives unscrupulous users and vandals or hackers the opportunity to fabricate, delete, and corrupt information in the encyclopedia. Once changes have been made to the original text, an unsuspecting user cannot tell the entry has been tampered with. None of this is possible with a traditional encyclopedia.

Third, the communal encyclopedias focus too frequently, and in too great a depth, on trivial and popular topics, which creates a false impression of what is important and what is not. A child doing research for a school project may discover that a major historical event receives as much attention in an online encyclopedia as, say, a single long-running television program. The traditional encyclopedia provides a considered view of what topics to include or exclude and contains a sense of proportion that online "democratic" communal encyclopedias do not.

온라인 공용 백과사전은 인터넷에서 찾을 수 있는 최신 자료 중 하나다. 여러 가지 면에서 온라인 백과사전은 전통적인 종이 백과사전과 비슷하다. 다시 말해 다양한 대상에 관한 글을 모아놓은 것이다. 하지만 온라인 백과사전의 특징은 인터넷 사용자라면 누구나 새로운 글을 올리거나 기존의 내용을 편집하고 수정할 수 있다는 것이다. 그 결과 온라인 백과사전의 저자는 인터넷 사용자들 전체 집단이다. 이 개념은 듣기에 멋질 수도 있다. 하지만 온라인 공용 백과사전은 여러 가지 중요한 문제 때문에 전통적인 종이 백과사전보다 훨씬 가치가 떨어진다.

첫째, 온라인 공용 백과사전의 제작에 참여한 사람들은 종종 학력이 낮아서 기껏해야 일부분만 제대로 알고 있고 많은 경우 완전히 틀린 사실을 알려준다. 전통적인 백과사전의 경우 아마추어는 감히 흉내 낼 수 없는 엄격한 학문적 표준을 고수하는 숙련된 전문가들이 저술한다.

둘째, 온라인 백과사전의 원래 정보가 정확하다 할지라도 공용이라는 특성상 파렴치한 인터넷 사용자, 문화 파괴자나 해커들이 온라인 백과사전의 정보를 조작하고 삭제하며 변질시킬 수 있다. 일단 백과사전의 원문이 변경되면 아무것도 모르는 사용자들은 원래 내용이 조작되었다는 것을 알 수 없다. 전통적인 백과사전에서는 결코 있을 수 없는 일이다.

셋째, 공용 백과사전은 너무나 자주, 그리고 너무나 심도 있게 사소하고 통속적인 주제에 치중하므로 무엇이 중요하고 무엇이 중요하지 않은지에 대한 잘못된 인상을 심어 준다. 학교 과제를 하기 위해 자료를 검색하던 어린이는 중요한 역사적 사건이 온라인 백과사전에서는 장수한 텔레비전 프로그램 하나와 동일한 비중의 관심을 받는다는 것을 발견하게 된다. 전통적인 백과사전은 어떤 주제를 포함하고 제외할지에 대한 신중한 관점을 제공하며 '민주적인' 온라인 공용 백과사전에서는 볼 수 없는 균형 감각이 있다.

어휘

communal 공용의, 공동의   encyclopedia 백과사전   respect 측면, 점   traditional 전통적인   collection 수집, 모음집   article 글, 기사   contribute (글·기사 따위) 기고하다   editorial 편집의, 편집상의   contributor 기고가, 기여자   academic credential 학위, 학력   downright 완전한, 절대의   inaccurate 틀린, 잘못된   adhere to ~을 고수하다   rigor 엄함, 엄격한 적용   unscrupulous 부도덕한, 파렴치한   vandal 예술[문화] 파괴자, 공공기물을 함부로 파괴하는 사람   fabricate 날조하다, 조작하다   corrupt 부패, 변질시키다   unsuspecting 의심치 않는   tamper with ~을 건드리다, 조작하다   trivial 사소한, 하찮은   impression 인상   a sense of proportion 균형 감각

Narrator T-50

Now listen to part of a lecture on the topic you just read about.

방금 읽은 주제에 관한 강의의 일부를 들으시오.

P The communal online encyclopedia will probably never be perfect, but that's a small price to pay for what it *does* offer. The criticisms in the reading are largely the result of prejudice against and ignorance about how far online encyclopedias have come.

First, errors: It's hardly a fair criticism that encyclopedias online have errors. Traditional encyclopedias have never been *close* to perfectly accurate. If you're looking for a *really* comprehensive reference work without *any* mistakes, you're not going to find it—on- *or* off-line. The real point is that it's easy for errors in factual material to be corrected in an online encyclopedia—but with the printed and bound encyclopedia, the errors remain for decades.

Second, hacking: online encyclopedias have recognized the importance of protecting their articles from malicious hackers. One strategy they started using is to put the crucial facts in the articles that nobody disputes in a *"read-only"* format, which is a format that no one can make changes to. That way you're making sure that the crucial facts in the articles are reliable. Another strategy that's being used is to have special editors whose job is to monitor all changes made to the articles and eliminate those changes that are clearly malicious.

Third, what's worth knowing about: The problem for traditional encyclopedias is that they have limited space, so they have to decide what's important and what's not. And in practice, the judgments of the group of academics that make these decisions don't reflect the great range of interests that people really have. But space is definitely *not* an issue for online encyclopedias. The academic articles are still represented in online encyclopedias, but there can be a great variety of articles and topics that accurately reflect the great diversity of users' interests. The diversity of views and topics that online encyclopedias offer is one of their strongest advantages.

P 아마 온라인 공용 백과사전은 결코 완벽할 수 없을 거예요. 하지만 온라인 백과사전이 제공하는 것에 비하면 아주 작은 대가에 불과하죠. 앞서 지문에서 제기한 비판들은 대부분 온라인 백과사전이 이룩한 것에 대한 편견과 무지의 산물이에요.

첫째, 오류인데요. 온라인 백과사전에 오류가 있다는 건 정당한 비판이 아닙니다. 전통적인 백과사전 역시 완벽한 정확성에 근접한 적이 결코 없거든요. 오류가 전혀 없는 진정한 종합 참고서를 찾는다면 온라인이든 오프라인이든 어디서도 발견할 수 없을 겁니다. 정말 중요한 건 온라인 백과사전에서는 사실적 자료에서 발견된 오류를 수정하기 쉽다는 거예요. 하지만 인쇄되고 제본된 백과사전의 경우 수십년간 오류가 남아 있죠.

두 번째는 해킹인데요. 온라인 백과사전은 악의적인 해커로부터 정보를 보호하는 것이 중요하다는 점을 인식하고 있습니다. 그래서 쓰기 시작한 한 가지 전략이 백과사전에서 아무도 반박할 수 없는 중요한 사실을 '읽기 전용' 난에 넣는 것입니다. 아무도 변경할 수 없는 형태죠. 그런 식으로 온라인 백과사전의 중요한 사실을 신뢰하도록 만드는 겁니다. 활용되고 있는 또 다른 전략은 특별 편집자를 두어 백과사전에 변경된 모든 내용을 검열하고 명확하게 악의적인 내용을 제거하는 겁니다.

세 번째로 무엇이 가치 있는 정보인가라는 것인데요. 전통적인 백과사전의 문제는 공간의 제약이 있어서 중요한 정보인지 아닌지를 결정해야 합니다. 실제로 이런 결정을 내리는 교수 집단의 판단은 실제 사람들의 폭넓은 관심사를 반영하지 않습니다. 하지만 확실히 온라인 백과사전에서는 공간이 문제가 되지 않아요. 온라인 백과사전에도 학술적인 내용은 있습니다. 하지만 엄청나게 다양한 사용자의 관심사를 정확하게 반영한 폭넓은 항목들과 주제들이 있을 수 있죠. 온라인 백과사전이 제공하는 다양한 관점과 주제야말로 가장 강력한 장점 중 하나예요.

어휘

criticism 비판, 비난   prejudice 편견   ignorance 무지, 무식
comprehensive reference 종합 참고서   factual 사실에 기반한
malicious 악의적인, 적의 있는   strategy 전략, 계획   crucial 중대한, 결정적인   reliable 신뢰할 수 있는   editor 편집자   eliminate 없애다, 제거하다   definitely 확실히, 틀림없이   diversity 다양성

Narrator T-51

Question 1

Summarize the points made in the lecture, being sure to explain how they oppose the specific points made in the reading passage.

방금 들은 강의 내용의 논지를 요약하고 독해 지문의 논지와 어떤 점에서 상충되는지 설명하시오.

해설

강의를 통해 교수가 지문에 제기된 온라인 공용 백과사전에 대한 여러 가지 비판에 동의하지 않는다는 사실을 이해해야 한다. 온라인 공용 백과사전에 대한 비판은 다음과 같다. 즉 정보가 정확하지 않으며, 인터넷 사용자가 백과사전의 정보를 조작할 수 있다. 그리고 온라인 공용 백과사전은 중요한 주제와 그렇지 않은 내용을 구분하지 않는다. 답안을 작성할 때, 교수가 설명한 대로 온라인 공용 백과사전에 대한 여러 가지 비판을 납득할 수 없는 이유를 적어야 한다. 고득점을 받으려면 교수가 지문 내용에 의구심을 가졌던 다음 사항들을 포함해야 한다.

Since entries in communal online encyclopedias are not always written by experts, they can be inaccurate and unreliable.

Because anyone can make revisions to the content of online encyclopedias, unscrupulous users, vandals, and hackers can intentionally corrupt the content of articles in the encyclopedias.

No encyclopedia is perfectly accurate. What really matters is how easily and quickly the mistakes can be corrected. In this regard, online encyclopedias are better than the traditional ones, because inaccurate content in online encyclopedias can be revised much faster.

Online encyclopedias have taken steps to protect their content from unscrupulous users, vandals, and hackers. Some important content is presented in a "read-only" format that cannot be revised. Also, special editors now monitor changes made to articles and eliminate revisions that are malicious.

Communal online encyclopedias often give equal space to articles on trivial topics and articles on serious topics. This creates a false impression about which information is important and which is not.

The fact that online encyclopedias contain information on all kinds of subjects is not a weakness but a strength. Diversity of topics covered by online encyclopedias is a true reflection of the diversity of people's interests. In contrast, traditional encyclopedias have limited space, and editors who choose which entries to include do not always take diverse interests into account.

Writing for an Academic Discussion

Question 2

Your professor is teaching a class on advertising. Write a post responding to the professor's question.

In your response, you should do the following.

- Express and support your opinion.
- Make a contribution to the discussion in your own words.

An effective response will contain at least 100 words.

Dr. Achebe

Let's discuss advertising for organizations that do charitable work. Many of these organizations use images, particularly photographs, in their advertisements to motivate people to donate money or goods to support their charity. Some use sad images, for example, photographs of people who are in difficult situations and need help. Others use happy or inspirational images, for example, of people already receiving help. In your view, which strategy is more effective to bring in donations—using sad or happy images? Why?

Claire

I think you've got to show the problem if you want people to understand that it's serious and help is truly needed. Consider a charity that builds schools and provides school supplies. If their advertisements only show happy children attending nice schools, why is my donation necessary?

Paul

Let's not forget that people often see lots of advertisements from many different charities—too many to even keep track of. Honestly, many potential donors may not want to look at advertisements containing unpleasant or sad images. In my opinion, inspirational images of all the good a charity does will get more attention and ultimately bring in more donations.

교수가 광고에 관한 강의를 진행하고 있다. 교수의 질문에 답하는 게시글을 작성하시오.

답변은 다음 조건을 충족해야 한다.
- 의견을 표명하고 뒷받침하는 근거를 제시한다.
- 독자적인 표현과 관점으로 토론에 기여한다.

어느 정도 완성도를 갖추려면 최소 100단어 이상이어야 한다.

Dr. Achebe

자선사업을 하는 단체를 위한 광고에 대해 이야기해 봅시다. 이런 단체들 중 많은 곳들이 광고에서 자선활동을 지원하는 돈이나 물품을 기부하도록 유도하기 위해 이미지, 특히 사진을 쓰곤 하죠. 일부는 슬픈 이미지, 예를 들어 어려운 상황에 처해 도움이 필요한 사람들의 사진을 사용합니다. 다른 단체들은 행복하거나 희망을 주는 이미지, 예를 들어 이미 도움을 받고 있는 사람들의 이미지를 사용하죠. 여러분이 보기에 슬픈 이미지와 행복한 이미지 중 어떤 전략이 기부를 이끌어내는 데 더 효과적인가요? 그렇게 생각하는 이유는 무엇인가요?

Claire

문제가 심각하고 정말로 도움이 필요하다는 것을 사람들에게 이해시키려면 문제를 보여줘야 한다고 생각해요. 학교를 짓고 학용품을 제공하는 자선단체를 생각해 보세요. 만약 광고에서 행복한 아이들이 근사한 학교에 다니는 모습만 보여준다면, 제 기부가 왜 필요하죠?

Paul

사람들은 종종 다양한 자선단체가 내는 광고를 많이 보는데, 너무 많아서 기억하기도 힘들 정도죠. 솔직히 기부를 고려하는 많은 사람이 불쾌하거나 슬픈 이미지가 담긴 광고는 보고 싶지 않을 겁니다. 제 생각에는 자선단체가 하는 온갖 좋은 일을 보여주며 희망을 주는 이미지가 관심을 더 많이 받고 결국 기부금을 많이 유치할 것 같아요.

해설

행복한 이미지와 슬픈 이미지(기분 좋은 이미지와 불편한 이미지) 중 어느 쪽이 자선단체에 더 좋은 광고인지에 관한 토론이다. 고득점을 받으려면 이러한 토론에 기여하는 논지를 펼치며 답변해야 한다. 어느 정도 완성도를 갖추려면 최소 100단어 이상이어야 한다.

한 토론 참여자는 문제의 심각성을 보여주려면 슬픈 이미지가 필요하다고 주장하고 이것을 행복한 이미지의 제한된 효과와 대비한다. 다른 토론 참여자는 사람들은 대체로 행복한 이미지에 더 끌리므로 이런 이미지를 보면 자선단체를 지원하고 싶은 마음이 든다고 주장한다. 토론 참여자들이 이미 서술한 개념을 확장해도 좋고 전혀 새로운 개념을 선보여도 좋다. 행복한 이미지와 슬픈 이미지 중에서 선택하거나 특정 조건에서 어떤 이미지가 더 효과적인지 설명할 수도 있다. 두 가지 유형의 이미지가 주는 감정적 또는 심리적 효과와 이러한 효과가 자선단체 지원과 어떻게 연관되는지 설명할 수도 있다. 또한 특정한 실제 사건이나 문제, 또는 자선단체와 관련된 특정 이미지가 어떻게 사용되는지 설명할 수 있다. 사람들이 자선단체와 관련해 겪은 경험과 광고 이미지가 이들에게 개인적으로 어떤 영향을 미쳤는지 설명할 수 있다.

반드시 자신의 의견을 뒷받침하는 탄탄한 근거와 예시를 제시하고 명확하게 표현해야 한다. 답안이 온라인 게시물 형태로 나타나므로 여러 단락으로 나누어 구성할 필요는 없다. 하지만 개념 간 연관성이 밀접하며 조리 있고 명료해야 한다. 채점은 '학술 토론을 위한 글쓰기 평가 기준(Appendix 참조)'을 토대로 이루어진다.

READING

UNDERSTANDING ANCIENT MESOAMERICAN ART

1. Starting at the end of the eighteenth century and continuing up to the present, explorers have searched for the ruins of ancient Mesoamerica, a region that includes Central America and central and southern Mexico. With the progress of time, archaeologists have unearthed civilizations increasingly remote in age. It is as if with each new century in the modern era an earlier stratum of antiquity has been revealed. Nineteenth-century explorers, particularly John Lloyd Stephens and Frederick Catherwood, came upon Maya cities in the jungle, as well as evidence of other Classic cultures. Twentieth-century research revealed a much earlier high civilization, the Olmec. It now scarcely seems possible that the frontiers of early Mesoamerican civilization can be pushed back any further, although new work—such as in Oaxaca, southern Mexico—will continue to fill in details of the picture.

2. The process of discovery often shapes what we know about the history of Mesoamerican art. New finds are just as often made accidentally as intentionally. (A) In 1971 workers installing sound and light equipment under the Pyramid of the Sun at Teotihuacán stumbled upon a remarkable cave that has since been interpreted by some scholars as a royal burial chamber. (B) Archaeology has its own fashions too: the isolation of new sites may be the prime goal in one decade and the excavation of pyramids the focus in the next. In a third decade, outlying structures rather than principal buildings may absorb archaeologists' energies. (C) Nor should one forget that excavators are vulnerable to local interests. (D) At one point, reconstruction of pyramids to attract tourism may be desired; at another, archaeologists may be precluded from working at what has already become a tourist attraction. Also, modern construction often determines which ancient sites can be excavated. In Mexico City, for example, the building of the subway initiated the excavations there and renewed interest in the old Aztec capital.

3. But the study of Mesoamerican art is not based exclusively on archaeology. Much useful information about the native populations was written down in the sixteenth century, particularly in central Mexico, and it can help us unravel the pre-Columbian past (the time prior to the arrival of Columbus in the Americas in 1492). Although many sources exist, the single most important one to the art historian is Bernardino de Sahagún's *General History of the Things of New Spain*. A Franciscan friar (member of the Roman Catholic religious order), Sahagún recorded for posterity many aspects of pre-Hispanic life in his encyclopedia of twelve books, including history, ideology, and cosmogony (theories of the origin of the universe), as well as detailed information on the materials and

1. 18세기 말부터 지금까지 탐험가들은 중앙아메리카와 멕시코 중남부를 포함하는 지역인 고대 메소아메리카의 유적을 찾아 탐사를 계속하고 있다. 세월이 흐르면서 고고학자들은 더 까마득히 먼 시대의 문명을 발굴해 내고 있다. 마치 현대에서 새로운 세기가 시작될 때마다 더 오래된 고대의 층이 드러나는 듯하다. 19세기 탐험가들, 특히 존 로이드 스티븐스와 프레데릭 캐터우드는 정글에서 마야 도시들과 전성기를 누린 다른 문화의 증거도 발견했다. 20세기에 이루어진 연구로 훨씬 오래된 고등 문명인 올멕 문명이 드러났다. 현재로서는 초기 메소아메리카 문명의 기원을 더 먼 과거까지 거슬러 올라갈 수는 없을 듯하지만, 오악사카에서 새로 진행되는 연구가 그림의 세부 사항을 계속 채워 나갈 것이다.

2. 종종 발견 과정을 통해 메소아메리카 예술사에 대한 우리의 지식이 모양새를 갖춰 간다. 새로운 발견은 의도적으로 이루어지기도 하지만, 그만큼 우연히 이루어지기도 한다. 1971년 테오티우아칸 태양의 피라미드 아래에 음향장비와 조명장비를 설치하던 인부들은 우연히 진기한 동굴을 발견했는데, 이후 일부 학자들은 이곳을 왕가 묘실로 해석한다. 고고학에도 나름 유행이 있다. 10년 정도 새로운 유적지 발견이 중요한 목표가 되다가, 다음 10년 동안에는 피라미드 발굴이 주안점이 된다. 또 다음 10년 동안은 주된 건물보다 변방에 있는 구조물이 고고학자들의 진을 빼놓기도 한다. 발굴자들이 지역 이해관계에 취약하다는 점도 잊지 말아야 한다. 어떤 시점에는 피라미드 재건이 관광객 유치를 위한 숙원사업일 수도 있고, 또 어떤 시점에는 이미 관광명소가 되어서 고고학자들이 작업을 못하도록 막을 수도 있다. 또한 많은 경우 오늘날 벌어지는 건설 공사로 어떤 고대 유적지가 발굴될지 결정되기도 한다. 예를 들어 멕시코시티에서는 지하철 건설로 발굴이 시작됐고 오래된 아즈텍 수도에 대한 관심이 다시 일어났다.

3. 하지만 메소아메리카 예술 연구는 고고학에만 의존하지 않는다. 원주민에 관한 대량의 유용한 정보가 16세기에 기록되었는데, 특히 멕시코 중부에서 기록된 정보는 선콜럼버스 시대(콜럼버스가 아메리카에 도착한 1492년보다 이전 시기)를 이해하는 데 유용하다. 수많은 자료가 존재하지만 예술사 학자에게 가장 중요한 자료는 베르나르디노 데 사아군의 『신 스페인 문물일반사』이다. 프란치스코회 수사(로마 가톨릭 수도회 소속)인 사아군은 12권으로 구성된 백과사전에서 역사, 이데올로기, 우주론(우주의 기원에 대한 이론) 등 스페인 정복 이전 시대의 많은 측면을 후세에 남겼으며, 숙련된 원주민 장인들이 쓰는 재료와 방식에 관한 상세한 정보도 기록했다. 더욱이 메소아메리카 원주민들 사이에 전통적인 생활방식이 여전히 남아 있어 학자들은 연구를 거듭할수록 오늘날

methods of the skilled native craft workers. Furthermore, traditional ways of life survive among the native peoples of Mesoamerica, and scholars have increasingly found that modern practice and belief can decode the past. Remarkably, some scholars have even turned this process around, teaching ancient writing to modern peoples who may use it to articulate their identity in the twenty-first century.

4. During the past 40 years, scholars also have made great progress in deciphering and interpreting ancient Mesoamerican writing systems, a breakthrough that has transformed our understanding of the pre-Columbian mind. Classic Maya inscriptions, for example—long thought to record only calendrical information and astrological incantations—can now be read, and we find that most of them glorify family and ancestry by displaying the right of individual sovereigns to rule. The carvings can thus be seen as portraits or public records of dynastic power. Although scholars long believed that Mesoamerican artists did not sign their works, Mayanist scholar David Stuart's 1986 deciphering of the Maya glyphs (written symbols) for "scribe" and "to write" opened a window on Maya practice; now we know at least one painter of ceramic vessels was the son of a king. Knowledge of the minor arts has also come in large part through an active art market. Thousands more small-scale objects are known now than in the twentieth century, although at a terrible cost to the ancient ruins from which they have been plundered.

의 관습과 신념으로 과거를 해독할 수 있다는 사실을 깨닫고 있다. 놀랍게도 일부 학자들은 이 과정을 거꾸로 돌려 현대인에게 고대 문자를 가르치고 있으며 이들은 21세기에 고대 문자를 이용해 자신의 정체성을 표현하고 있다.

4. 지난 40년 동안 학자들은 고대 메소아메리카 문자 체계를 해독하고 해석하는 데 큰 진전을 이루었으며, 이는 선콜럼버스 시대의 정신에 대한 이해를 완전히 바꾸어 놓는 돌파구가 되었다. 예를 들어 전성기 마야 문서는 오래도록 달력 정보와 점성술 주문만을 기록한 것으로 간주되었는데 이제는 해독이 가능해서 대다수 문서가 개별 군주의 통치권을 과시해 가족과 조상을 찬양하는 내용임을 알게 되었다. 따라서 조각품들은 왕조의 권력을 나타내는 인물상이나 공적 기록으로 간주할 수 있다. 오랫동안 학자들은 메소아메리카 예술가들이 이 작품에 서명하지 않았다고 믿었으나, 마야 연구자인 데이비드 스튜어트가 1986년 '필경사'와 '쓰다'를 의미하는 마야 상형문자(문자 기호)를 해독하면서 마야 관습을 이해하는 창이 열렸다. 이제 우리는 적어도 도자기 화가 한 사람이 왕의 아들이었다는 사실을 알게 되었다. 소규모 예술품에 대한 지식 또한 전해져 들어왔는데, 이는 대체로 활발한 미술시장을 통해서였다. 비록 고대 유적지에서 유물이 약탈당하는 엄청난 대가를 치렀지만 지금은 20세기에 비해 수천 점 많은 소형 유물이 세상에 알려지게 됐다.

어휘

1. explorer 탐험가 ruins 유적 Mesoamerica 메소아메리카 (중앙아메리카와 멕시코 일부 지역을 포함하는 고대 문명 지역) archaeologists 고고학자 unearth 발굴하다 civilization 문명 remote 먼 stratum 층 antiquity 고대 Maya 마야 (고대 메소아메리카 문명) Olmec 올멕 (고대 메소아메리카 문명) scarcely 거의 ~하지 않다 frontier 경계 Oaxaca 오악사카 (멕시코의 지역) 2. accidently 우연적으로 intentionally 의도적으로 stumble upon 우연히 발견하다 remarkable 진기한 burial chamber 묘실 prime goal 중요한 목적 decade 10년 excavation 발굴 outlying 외곽의 principal 주요한 vulnerable to ~에 취약한 interests 이해관계 reconstruction 재건 preclude ~하지 못하게 하다 3. exclusively ~에만, 독점적으로 unravel 이해하다 pre-columbian 콜럼버스 이전의 Bernardino de Sahagún 베르나르디노 데 사가군 (16세기 스페인 선교사 및 역사학자) Franciscan 프란체스코 수도회 (가톨릭 수도회) friar 수도사 posterity 후세 encyclopedia 백과사전 ideology 이데올로기, 집단적 관념 cosmogony 우주론 craft worker 공예사 practice 관습 decode 해독하다 articulate 표현하다 4. decipher 해독하다 breakthrough 돌파구 inscription 문서 calendrical 달력의 astrological 점성술의 incantations 주문 glorify 찬미하다 sovereign 군주 portrait 인물상 dynastic 왕조의 glyphs 그림문자, 상형문자 scribe 서기관 ceramic vessel 도자기 그릇 plunder 약탈하다

1. 다음 중 초기 메소아메리카 문명의 규명과 관련하여 첫 번째 단락과 부합하는 내용은?

   Ⓐ 마야 문명과 올멕 문명은 거의 같은 시기에 탐험가들에게 발견되었다.

   Ⓑ 메소아메리카 문명에 대해 우리가 알고 있는 내용 대부분은 20세기에 이루어진 발견에서 비롯된다.

   Ⓒ 멕시코 남부 오악사카에서 발견된 것들은 올멕 문명이 그곳에서 기원했다는 것을 보여준다.

   Ⓓ 멕시코 오악사카에서 아직 발견되지 않은 증거는 초기 메소아메리카의 고등 문명에 관해 추가 정보를 제공할 가능성이 높다.

   어휘 approximately 거의

2. 지문의 outlying과 의미상 가장 가까운 것은?

   Ⓐ 의례의
   Ⓑ 임시의
   Ⓒ 중심지에서 멀리 떨어진
   Ⓓ 단순한

3. 두 번째 단락에서 글쓴이가 테오티우아칸 태양의 피라미드를 논하는 이유는?

   Ⓐ 특정 유형의 메소아메리카 예술에 대한 논의를 시작하려고
   Ⓑ 우연한 발견의 중요성을 설명하려고
   Ⓒ 체계적인 연구의 필요성을 강조하려고
   Ⓓ 고고학 분야에서 현대 장비 사용에 반대하려고

   어휘 systematic 체계적인

4. 두 번째 단락에서 고고학 발견 과정에 영향을 미치는 요인으로 언급되지 않은 것은?

   Ⓐ 세월이 흐르면서 변하는 유행
   Ⓑ 학문 분야로서 고고학의 인기
   Ⓒ 지역 주민의 이해관계
   Ⓓ 현대 구조물의 건축

5. 지문의 exclusively와 의미상 가장 가까운 것은?

   Ⓐ 정확히
   Ⓑ 오로지
   Ⓒ 전통적으로
   Ⓓ 주로

6. 세 번째 단락에 따르면, 베르나르디노 데 사아군이 메소아메리카 예술 연구에 중요한 이유는?

   Ⓐ 16세기에 원주민에 대한 상세한 정보를 기록했다.
   Ⓑ 멕시코 중부에서 중요한 고고학적 발견을 했다.
   Ⓒ 자신의 예술 기반으로 숙련된 메소아메리카 공예가들의 방식과 재료를 연구했다.
   Ⓓ 원주민에게 전통적인 생활방식을 보존하라고 권유했다.

7. 세 번째 단락에 따르면, 다음 중 고대 메소아메리카 문자에 대해 사실인 것은?

   Ⓐ 메소아메리카 사람들의 현대 문자와 흡사하다.
   Ⓑ 애초 생각했던 것만큼 오래되지 않았다.
   Ⓒ 현대인들이 자신의 정체성을 표현하는 데 사용될 수 있다.
   Ⓓ 숙련된 원주민 공예가들이 가장 완벽하게 이해하고 있다.

8. 네 번째 단락에 따르면, 다음 중 마야 학자 데이비드 스튜어트의 1986년 발견에 대해 사실이 아닌 것은?

   Ⓐ 과거 학자들이 가지고 있던 신념을 뒤집었다.
   Ⓑ 왕조에 대한 방대한 기록을 드러냈다.
   Ⓒ 학자들이 처음으로 두 가지 상형문자를 이해할 수 있게 되었다.
   Ⓓ 적어도 마야 화가 한 명이 왕의 아들이라는 것을 밝혀냈다.

9. 위에 제시된 지문의 일부를 보시오. 지문에 표시된 **(A)**, **(B)**, **(C)**, **(D)** 중 하나에 다음 문장이 삽입될 수 있다.

This chance discovery has done as much for our understanding of the pyramid as any systematic study would have.
(이 우연한 발견은 어떤 체계적인 연구만큼이나 피라미드를 이해하는 데 많은 역할을 했다.)

이 문장이 들어갈 가장 적당한 위치는?

　　The process of discovery often shapes what we know about the history of Mesoamerican art. New finds are just as often made accidentally as intentionally. **(A)** In 1971 workers installing sound and light equipment under the Pyramid of the Sun at Teotihuacán stumbled upon a remarkable cave that has since been interpreted by some scholars as a royal burial chamber. **(B)** This chance discovery has done as much for our understanding of the pyramid as any systematic study would have. Archaeology has its own fashions too: the isolation of new sites may be the prime goal in one decade and the excavation of pyramids the focus in the next. In a third decade, outlying structures rather than principal buildings may absorb archaeologists' energies. **(C)** Nor should one forget that excavators are vulnerable to local interests. **(D)** At one point, reconstruction of pyramids to attract tourism may be desired; at another, archaeologists may be precluded from working at what has already become a tourist attraction. Also, modern construction often determines which ancient sites can be excavated. In Mexico City, for example, the building of the subway initiated the excavations there and renewed interest in the old Aztec capital.

　Ⓐ (A)　　　Ⓑ (B)　　　Ⓒ (C)　　　Ⓓ (D)

10. 지문을 요약하기 위한 도입 문장이 아래에 제시되어 있다. 아래 보기들 중에서 지문의 가장 중요한 개념을 표현한 문장 3개를 골라 요약을 완성하라. 보기들 중에는 지문에 나오지 않은 내용이거나 중요한 내용이 아니므로 요약문으로 적절치 않은 것들도 있다. 이 문제의 배점은 2점이다.

Our knowledge of Mesoamerican art has grown since explorers first began searching for ruins of ancient Mesoamerica.
탐험가들이 고대 메소아메리카의 유적을 처음 찾아 나선 이래로 메소아메리카 예술에 대한 우리의 지식은 늘어났다.

Ⓐ 존 로이드 스티븐스와 프레데릭 캐터우드는 정글에 있는 마야 도시 유적을 마야 문명이 올멕 문명보다 더 오래되었다는 증거로 사용했다.

Ⓑ 종종 우연히 발견되는 메소아메리카 피라미드에는 수많은 원주민 예술의 표본이 있을 뿐 아니라 관광객을 끌어들이기도 한다.

Ⓒ 전성기 마야의 글귀는 주로 달력 정보, 점성술 주문, 예술가의 서명을 기록했다.

Ⓓ 우연한 발견, 고고학의 유행, 그리고 지역 이해관계를 통해 메소아메리카 예술에 대한 우리의 지식이 모양새를 갖춘다.

Ⓔ 메소아메리카 예술에 대한 정보 대부분은 16세기 저술과 메소아메리카에 남아 있는 전통과 관습 속에 존재한다.

Ⓕ 고대 문자 체계 해독의 진전과 활발한 미술시장은 메소아메리카 예술에 대한 지식에 기여했다.

WHAT IS A COMMUNITY?

1. The Black Hills forest, the prairie riparian forest, and other forests of the western United States can be separated by the distinctly different combinations of species they comprise. It is easy to distinguish between prairie riparian forest and Black Hills forest—one is a broad-leaved forest of ash and cotton-wood trees, the other is a coniferous forest of ponderosa pine and white spruce trees. One has kingbirds; the other, juncos (birds with white outer tail feathers). The fact that ecological communities are, indeed, recognizable clusters of species led some early ecologists, particularly those living in the beginning of the twentieth century, to claim that communities are highly integrated, precisely balanced assemblages. This claim harkens back to even earlier arguments about the existence of a balance of nature, where every species is there for a specific purpose, like a vital part in a complex machine. Such a belief would suggest that to remove any species, whether it be plant, bird, or insect, would somehow disrupt the balance, and the habitat would begin to deteriorate. Likewise, to add a species may be equally disruptive.

2. One of these pioneer ecologists was Frederick Clements, who studied ecology extensively throughout the Midwest and other areas in North America. He held that within any given region of climate, ecological communities tended to slowly converge toward a single endpoint, which he called the "climatic climax." This "climax" community was, in Clements's mind, the most well-balanced, integrated grouping of species that could occur within that particular region. Clements even thought that the process of ecological succession—the replacement of some species by others over time—was somewhat akin to the development of an organism, from embryo to adult. Clements thought that succession represented discrete stages in the development of the community (rather like infancy, childhood, and adolescence), terminating in the climatic "adult" stage, when the community became self-reproducing and succession ceased. Clements's view of the ecological community reflected the notion of a precise balance of nature.

3. Clements was challenged by another pioneer ecologist, Henry Gleason, who took the opposite view. Gleason viewed the community as largely a group of species with similar tolerances to the stresses imposed by climate and other factors typical of the region. Gleason saw the element of chance as important in influencing where species occurred. His concept of the community suggests that nature is not highly integrated. Gleason thought succession could take numerous directions, depending upon local circumstances.

1. 블랙힐스 숲, 대초원 강기슭의 숲, 그 밖에 미국 서부의 숲은 각각 서식하는 종들의 조합이 달라 확연히 구분된다. 대초원 강기슭의 숲과 블랙힐스 숲은 구별하기 쉽다. 블랙힐스 숲은 물푸레나무와 미루나무로 이루어진 활엽수림이며, 대초원 강기슭의 숲은 폰데로사 소나무와 흰가문비나무로 이루어진 침엽수림이다. 블랙힐스 숲에는 왕산적딱새가 살고 대초원 강기슭의 숲에는 (바깥 꼬리털이 하얀) 검은방울새가 산다. 실제로 생태군집이 분간할 수 있는 종들의 무리라는 사실에서 일부 초기 생태학자들, 특히 20세기 초에 살았던 생태학자들은 군집들이 아주 통합적이며 정확하게 균형 잡힌 집합체라고 주장했다. 이러한 주장은 훨씬 오래전 자연이 균형을 이룬다는 주장, 즉 모든 종은 복잡한 기계의 핵심 부품처럼 특별한 목적을 위해 존재한다는 주장을 상기시킨다. 이러한 믿음에 따르면, 식물이든 새든 곤충이든 어느 하나라도 없어지면 어떤 식으로든 균형이 깨지고 서식지의 환경이 악화되기 시작할 것이다. 마찬가지로 종이 추가되어도 똑같이 균형이 무너질 수 있다.

2. 이들 선구적인 생태학자들 중 한 사람이 프레더릭 클레멘츠로, 그는 북미 중서부와 그 밖의 지역에서 생태계를 광범위하게 연구했다. 그는 어느 기후 지역에서나 생태군집이 서서히 하나의 종점을 향해 나아가는 경향이 있다고 생각했고 그 종점을 '기후 극상'이라고 불렀다. 클레멘츠는 '극상(極相)' 군집이 특정 지역 내에서 생길 수 있는 최고로 균형 잡히고 통합된 종들의 배합이라고 보았다. 클레멘츠는 심지어 시간이 흐르면서 일부 종이 다른 종으로 대체되는 생태 천이 과정이 배아에서 성체로 성장하는 생물의 발달과 어느 정도 비슷하다고 생각했다. 클레멘츠는 천이가 군집의 발달 단계(마치 유아기, 아동기, 청소년기처럼)를 뚜렷하게 드러내며 기후가 극상인 '성인' 단계에 이르면 그 군집은 자가생식이 가능해지고 천이가 종료된다고 생각했다. 생태군집에 대한 클레멘츠의 견해는 자연이 정확하게 균형을 이룬다는 생각을 반영했다.

3. 역시 선구적인 생태학자인 헨리 글리슨은 정반대의 관점에서 클레멘츠에게 이의를 제기했다. 글리슨은 대체로 생태군집을 지역의 전형적인 기후 및 다른 요소들이 가하는 스트레스에 비슷한 내성을 보이는 종들의 집합체로 보았다. 글리슨은 종들이 어디에서 발생하는지에 영향을 미치는 요소로 우연을 중요하게 여겼다. 생태군집에 대한 글리슨의 개념에 따르면, 자연은 고도로 통합된 형태가 아니다. 글리슨은 지역 환경에 따라 다양한 방향으로 천이가 발생한다고 생각했다.

4. **(A)** Who was right? **(B)** Many ecologists have made precise measurements, designed to test the assumptions of both the Clements and Gleason models. **(C)** For instance, along mountain slopes, does one life zone, or habitat type, grade sharply or gradually into another? **(D)** If the divisions are sharp, perhaps the reason is that the community is so well integrated, so holistic, so like Clements viewed it, that whole clusters of species must remain together. If the divisions are gradual, perhaps, as Gleason suggested, each species is responding individually to its environment, and clusters of species are not so integrated that they must always occur together.

5. It now appears that Gleason was far closer to the truth than Clements. The ecological community is largely an accidental assemblage of species with similar responses to a particular climate. Green ash trees are found in association with plains cottonwood trees because both can survive well on floodplains and the competition between them is not so strong that only one can persevere. One ecological community often flows into another so gradually that it is next to impossible to say where one leaves off and the other begins. Communities are individualistic.

6. This is not to say that precise harmonies are not present within communities. Most flowering plants could not exist were it not for their pollinators—and vice versa. Predators, disease organisms, and competitors all influence the abundance and distribution of everything from oak trees to field mice. But if we see a precise balance of nature, it is largely an artifact of our perception, due to the illusion that nature, especially a complex system like a forest, seems so unchanging from one day to the next.

4. 누구의 주장이 옳았을까? 많은 생태학자들이 클레멘츠와 글리슨 모형의 가설을 시험하기 위해 정밀하게 진단했다. 예를 들어 산비탈을 따라 생물분포대나 서식지 유형의 경계가 뚜렷한가 아니면 서서히 넘어가는가? 경계가 뚜렷하다면 아마도 생태군집이 아주 통합이 잘 되어 총체적이기 때문일 것이다. 따라서 클레멘츠의 관점처럼 종들의 집합체 전체가 고스란히 유지되어야 한다. 반대로 경계가 점진적이라면 아마도 글리슨의 제안대로 각각의 종이 환경에 개별적으로 반응하고 있으며 따라서 종들의 집합체는 늘 함께 발생할 정도로 통합적이지는 않다.

5. 오늘날 글리슨이 클레멘츠보다 사실이 더 가까웠던 것으로 밝혀지고 있다. 생태군집은 대체로 특정 기후에 비슷하게 반응하는 종들이 우연히 모인 집합체다. 푸른 물푸레나무와 평원의 미루나무가 공존하는 것은 둘 다 범람원에서 잘 생존하고 어느 한쪽만 버틸 수 있을 정도로 둘 사이의 경쟁이 심하지 않기 때문이다. 종종 하나의 생태군집이 다른 생태군집으로 아주 점진적으로 흘러 들어가므로 하나의 생태군집이 끝나고 갑자기 다른 생태군집이 시작된다는 건 거의 불가능하다. 군집은 개체주의적이다.

6. 그렇다고 군집 내에 정밀한 조화가 없다는 말은 아니다. 대부분의 속씨식물은 꽃가루매개자 없이 존재할 수 없으며 그 반대도 마찬가지다. 포식자, 병균, 경쟁자가 다 함께 떡갈나무에서 들쥐까지 모든 생물들의 풍도(豊度)와 분포에 영향을 미친다. 하지만 자연에서 정밀한 조화를 본다면 그것은 대부분 사람의 관념이 만들어낸 것으로 자연, 특히 숲처럼 복잡한 조직은 하루하루 전혀 변하지 않는 것처럼 보이는 착각 때문이다.

어휘

1. community (동식물) 군집, 군락 prairie (북미·캐나다의) 대초원 riparian 강기슭에 사는, 강가의 distinctly 뚜렷이, 명백히 species 종(생물 분류의 기초 단위) broad-leaved 잎이 넓적한, 활엽수의 ash tree 물푸레나무 cottonwood 미루나무 coniferous 침엽수의 ponderosa pine 폰데로사 소나무 white spruce tree 흰가문비나무 kingbird 왕산적딱새 junco 검은방울새 cluster 무리, 집단 ecologist 생태학자 integrated 통합된, 조직적인 assemblage 집합체, 모임 harken 귀를 기울이다 deteriorate 악화되다, 더 나빠지다 disruptive 붕괴시키는, 파괴적인 2. pioneer 개척자, 선구자 extensively 광범위하게, 널리 converge 모이다, 집중하다 endpoint 종점 climate climax 기후 극상(지역의 기후 조건에 가장 알맞은 안정적인 군락) climax 극상(생물학적 천이의 최종 단계) ecological succession 생태 천이(시간의 흐름에 따라 군집이 점차 안정된 구조를 향해 가거나 변하는 과정) replacement 대체, 교체 akin to ~과 같은, 흡사한 embryo 배아, 태아 discrete 별개의, 분리된 infancy 유아기 adolescence 청소년기 terminate 끝내다, 마치다 self-reproducing 자가생식, 자가번식 cease 그치다, 끝나다 3. tolerance 내성, 저항력 chance 우연 integrated 통합된 4. assumption 가설, 가정 life zone 생물분포대(온도, 강수량 등 기후조건에 따른 생물 분포 단위) division 구분, 경계 holistic 전체론의, 전체론적인 5. accidental 우연한, 우발적인 floodplain 범람원 persevere 인내하다, 견디다 individualistic 개인주의적인, 개체주의적인 6. pollinator 꽃가루매개자, 수분자 vice versa 반대의 경우도 마찬가지 predator 포식자, 포식 동물 disease organism 병균 abundance 풍부, 풍도(특정 장소와 시간에 존재하는 생물이나 종의 수) distribution 분포 artifact 인위적인 결과, 인공 산물 perception 자각 illusion 오해, 착각

11. 첫 번째 단락에서 글쓴이는 왜 대초원 강기슭의 숲과 블랙힐스 숲을 구별하는가?

   Ⓐ 생태학자들마다 생태군집의 속성에 대한 견해 차이가 있음을 강조하기 위해

   Ⓑ 일부 생태학자들이 생태군집을 고도로 통합된 형태로 보는 이유를 설명하기 위해

   Ⓒ 어떤 숲은 다른 숲보다 종 다양성이 훨씬 더 크다는 사실을 보여 주기 위해

   Ⓓ 두 숲이 미국의 다른 숲들과 어떻게 다른지 보여 주기 위해

   어휘 variety 다양성, 변화

12. 첫 번째 단락에 따르면, 20세기 초 이전의 생태군집에 대한 공통된 주장은?

   Ⓐ 한 군집의 모든 종은 그 군집 안에서 특정한 역할이 있다.

   Ⓑ 특정 종을 제거해 군집을 보호하는 것이 중요하다.

   Ⓒ 생태군집 내에서 정밀한 조화가 유지되기는 어렵다.

   Ⓓ 생태군집이 발달하면서 반드시 새로운 종이 신속하게 추가되어야 한다.

   어휘 specific 구체적인, 특정한

13. 첫 번째 단락에 따르면, 자연의 균형을 믿는다면 다음 중 생태군집에서 특정 종을 없앴을 때 나타나는 효과는?

   Ⓐ 그 군집에 남아 있는 종들 간에 경쟁이 줄어든다.

   Ⓑ 이전과 다르지만 동일하게 균형 잡힌 군집이 탄생한다.

   Ⓒ 그 군집이 쇠퇴한다.

   Ⓓ 그 군집에 종이 추가되는 것보다 더 피해가 크다.

   어휘 competition 경쟁, 시합

14. 다음 중 두 번째 단락에서 프레더릭 클레멘츠가 생각하는 생태군집을 가장 잘 설명한 것은?

   Ⓐ 한 군집의 모든 종이 발달상 번식 단계에 있을 때만이 정확하게 균형을 이룬다.

   Ⓑ '기후 극상'에 도달하면 쇠퇴하기 시작한다.

   Ⓒ 모든 기후에는 비슷한 극상 군집이 존재한다.

   Ⓓ 생태군집이 결국 그 지역에서 가능한 최고 수준의 균형에 도달한다.

   어휘 reproductive 번식하는, 생식하는
       maximum 최대의, 최고의

15. 세 번째 단락에서 글리슨에 따르면, 특정 군집에서 종의 발생은 무엇의 영향인가?

   Ⓐ 예측 불가능한 사건들

   Ⓑ 종의 개체주의적인 성향 정도

   Ⓒ 존재하는 다른 종들의 수

   Ⓓ 다른 종들의 스트레스 내성

   어휘 unpredictable 예측 불가능한, 종잡을 수 없는

16. 네 번째 단락에서 생태학자들이 진단해서 판단하고 싶었던 것은?

   Ⓐ 서로 다른 종들이 같은 환경에서 경쟁하는지 여부

   Ⓑ 서식지가 뚜렷하게 분리되는지 혹은 서서히 변하는지 여부

   Ⓒ 서식지 유형에 따라 천이가 다른지 여부

   Ⓓ 통합된 군집이 독립적인 군집보다 생존율이 높은지 여부

17. 다섯 번째 단락의 persevere와 의미상 가장 가까운 것은?

   Ⓐ 번식하다

   Ⓑ 실패하다

   Ⓒ 확장하다

   Ⓓ 지속하다

18. 다음 중 여섯 번째 단락에 음영으로 표시된 문장이 담고 있는 핵심 정보를 가장 잘 표현한 것은? 정답 외의 보기들은 의미가 상당히 왜곡되거나 필수적인 정보가 빠져 있다.

   Ⓐ 우리가 자연이 정밀하게 균형을 이룬다고 보는 이유는 자연이 변하지 않기 때문이다.

   Ⓑ 자연 체계의 복잡성 때문에 자연의 정밀한 조화는 불가능하다.

   Ⓒ 자연이 정밀하게 균형을 이룬다는 생각은 자연이 변하지 않는다는 착각에서 비롯된 것이다.

   Ⓓ 자연은 정밀하게 균형을 이루기 때문에 복잡한 구조가 변하지 않는 것처럼 보인다.

   어휘 complexity 복잡성, 복잡함

19. 위에 제시된 지문의 일부를 보시오. 지문에 표시된 **(A)**, **(B)**, **(C)**, **(D)** 중 하나에 다음 문장이 삽입될 수 있다.

Their research has helped to decide between the two views because it has focused on questions to which Clements and Gleason would give opposing answers.

(그들의 연구는 두 견해들 사이에서 결정하는 데 도움이 되었다. 왜냐하면 클레멘츠와 글리슨이라면 상반된 대답을 내놓았을 질문들에 초점을 맞추었기 때문이다.)

이 문장이 들어갈 가장 적당한 위치는?

(A) Who was right? **(B)** Many ecologists have made precise measurements, designed to test the assumptions of both the Clements and Gleason models. **(C)** Their research has helped to decide between the two views because it has focused on questions to which Clements and Gleason would give opposing answers. For instance, along mountain slopes, does one life zone, or habitat type, grade sharply or gradually into another? **(D)** If the divisions are sharp, perhaps the reason is that the community is so well integrated, so holistic, so like Clements viewed it, that whole clusters of species must remain together. If the divisions are gradual, perhaps, as Gleason suggested, each species is responding individually to its environment, and clusters of species are not so integrated that they must always occur together.

Ⓐ (A)   Ⓑ (B)   Ⓒ (C)   Ⓓ (D)

어휘 opposing 정반대의, 대립하는

20. 지문을 간단히 요약하기 위한 도입 문장이 아래에 제시되어 있다. 아래 보기들 중에서 지문의 가장 중요한 개념을 표현한 문장 3개를 골라 요약을 완성하라. 보기들 중에는 지문에 나오지 않았거나 중요하지 않은 개념이기 때문에 요약문으로 적절치 않은 것들도 있다. 이 문제의 배점은 2점이다.

시간이 흐르면서 생태군집의 구조에 대한 다양한 의견들이 나왔다.

Ⓐ 클레멘츠는 생태군집이 특정 기후 지역에서 지배권을 두고 경쟁하는 유기체와 같다고 생각했다.

Ⓑ 클레멘츠는 생태군집이 철저하게 상호의존적인 종들의 집합체로 단 하나의 기후 군집으로 진보한다고 보았다.

Ⓒ 글리슨은 하나의 기후 지역 내에서 다양한 지역적 요소들 때문에 생태군집이 다양한 방향으로 발전한다고 생각했다.

Ⓓ 글리슨은 서식지가 다른 종들 사이에 뚜렷한 경계가 있다고 믿었다.

Ⓔ 오늘날 생태학자들은 생태군집이 영구적으로 정밀하게 균형을 이루어야 한다고 인정한다.

Ⓕ 오늘날의 견해는 생태군집이란 개체주의적이며 비슷한 필요와 내성을 가진 종들이 우연히 모인 집합체라는 것이다.

어휘 dominance 지배, 우세
interdependent 상호의존적인, 서로 의존하는
permanently 영구히, 불변으로

LISTENING

Questions 1~5

p.146

N Narrator **C** Coordinator **S** Student

Script T-52

N Listen to a conversation between a student and the volunteer coordinator at the university art museum.

C Michael, do you remember the advertisement for your position here, the ad we ran in the student newspaper?

S Uh, yeah, vaguely.

C It said that, in addition to leading public tours of the museum, volunteer docents might be asked to perform other duties.

S Oh, I do remember that. Is that what you wanted to chat with me about?

C Yes. The museum has partnered with the local school district to run a poetry contest for high school students.

S A poetry contest. Cool. But, um... what does poetry have to do with museum tours?

C A lot, since it's going to be an ekphrastic poetry contest.

S Ek-ekphrastic?

C Yes, an ekphrastic poem is one that's inspired by a piece of artwork. Like, um, William Carlos Williams' poem *The Hunter in the Snow*. It was written in the 1960s and was inspired by a painting made by Pieter Bruegel in the 1500s.

S I know Bruegel's work! Beautiful panoramic scenes. I can see how they'd inspire a poet.

C Good. So the students'll be submitting poems based on paintings in our museum. We're calling the contest *The Art of Poetry*; we hope to make it an annual thing.

S Interesting! So can the students write about any painting they want?

C Oh, that might get too unwieldy for the judges, y'know, and for the docents. There's also time limitations, because anyone who registers for the contest must attend a special educational tour focusing on the Art of India exhibit. And that's why we need you.

S OK. Eh, when will the tour take place?

C Tours. We're setting them up for the third week in March ... about one month from now, uh, Monday through Friday from 4 to 5 p.m. May I sign you up for one or more of those days?

S Sure. I guess Tuesday and Thursday would work, since I have all morning classes those days. Did you want me ... should I just give my regular talk about the Indian art?

C Uh, that's the thing, Michael. You'll have a whole hour. So, instead of spending ten minutes in that exhibit, as you normally do, you'll spend the entire time talking about as many Indian paintings as possible and answering questions.

S Wait. Eh, but I've only been trained to discuss three of those paintings! And there's gotta be at least thirty in that exhibit!

N 대학 미술관에서 학생과 자원봉사 담당자가 나누는 대화를 들으시오.

C 마이클, 지금 맡은 자리 구인 광고 기억나요? 우리가 학생신문에 실었던 광고 말이에요.

S 어, 네. 어렴풋이 기억나요.

C 자원봉사 안내원은 미술관의 일반 투어를 인솔하는 일 외에도 다른 업무를 맡을 수도 있다고 밝혔죠.

S 아, 기억나요. 하실 말씀이 이건가요?

C 그래요. 미술관에서 지역 학구와 협력해서 고등학생을 위한 시작 대회를 열어요.

S 시작 대회라. 멋지네요. 하지만 음, 시가 미술관 투어와 무슨 상관이죠?

C 밀접한 관련이 있어요. 엑프래스틱 시를 짓는 대회니까요.

S 엑프래스틱?

C 맞아요. 엑프래스틱 시는 예술작품에서 영감받은 시예요. 가령 윌리엄 카를로스 윌리엄스의 시 〈눈 속의 사냥꾼〉처럼 말이죠. 이 시는 1960년대 작품인데 1500년대 피터르 브뤼헐이 그린 그림에서 영감을 받았어요.

S 브뤼헐 작품 알아요! 파노라마 같은 아름다운 풍경이죠. 제가 봐도 시인에게 영감을 줄 만해요.

C 좋아요. 그러니까 학생들이 우리 미술관에 있는 그림을 바탕으로 시를 써서 제출할 거예요. 이 대회를 '시의 예술'이라고 부르는데 해마다 열리는 행사로 만들고 싶어요.

S 재미있겠네요! 그러면 어떤 그림이든 학생들이 원하는 그림에 대해 쓸 수 있나요?

C 아, 그러면 심사위원과 안내원이 너무 부담스러울 거예요. 시간제한도 있어요. 대회에 등록한 사람은 누구나 인도 미술 전시회에 초점을 맞춘 특별 교육 투어에 참석해야 하거든요. 그래서 마이클이 필요해요.

S 그렇군요. 어, 투어는 언제 진행되나요?

C 여러 번 진행해요. 3월 셋째 주로 준비하고 있는데, 지금부터 한 달쯤 뒤죠. 어, 월요일부터 금요일 오후 4시부터 5시까지예요. 이 날짜들 중 하루나 여러 날에 마이클을 배정해도 될까요?

S 그럼요. 화요일과 목요일이 괜찮을 것 같아요. 그때는 오전 수업뿐이거든요. 그냥 평소처럼 인도 미술에 대해 이야기하면 될까요?

C 그게 문제예요, 마이클. 한 시간 내내 해야 하거든요. 그러니까 평소처럼 전시회에서 10분을 보내는 대신, 그 시간 내내 가능한 한 많은 인도 그림에 대해 이야기하고 질문에 답해야 해요.

S 잠깐만요. 어, 그런데 설명하도록 교육받은 그림이 겨우 3점뿐이에요! 전시회에는 적어도 30점은 있을 텐데요!

C It's okay. I'll e-mail all the background you'll need for the rest of them, and you won't have to go into too much depth. I'll also be giving you a list of questions and scenarios for students to think about and discuss, questions like, "Who are the people in the painting?" and "Imagine yourself as one of those people." You can facilitate these discussions.

C 괜찮아요. 나머지 그림에 필요한 배경지식을 모두 이메일로 보낼게요. 그리고 너무 깊이 파고들 필요도 없어요. 또한 학생들이 생각하고 토론할 거리인 질문 목록과 시나리오도 줄 게요. "그림 속 인물들은 누구인가요?", "자신을 이 인물들 중 한 사람이라고 상상해 보세요." 이런 질문 말이죠. 토론을 원활하게 이끌 수 있어요.

어휘

docent (박물관 등의) 자원봉사 해설자   ekphrastic 예술 작품에서 영감을 받은   panoramic 전경의, 광범위한   unwieldy 다루기 힘든   facilitate 진행하다, 돕다

1. 여자가 남자에게 이야기하려는 이유는?

   Ⓐ 남자가 안내원이 되는 데 필요한 정보를 주려고
   Ⓑ 곧 있을 글쓰기 대회에서 남자의 역할에 대해 논의하려고
   Ⓒ 여자가 계획하고 있는 대회에 대한 남자의 의견을 들으려고
   Ⓓ 인도 전시회에 대한 남자의 지식을 알아보려고

2. 여자가 언급하는 신문 광고의 주안점은 무엇이었는가?

   Ⓐ 여자가 개설에 도움을 준 엑프라스틱 시 강좌
   Ⓑ 미술관의 새로운 인도 미술 소장품
   Ⓒ 지역 고등학교의 교생 일자리
   Ⓓ 미술관의 시간제 자원봉사 일자리

3. 윌리엄 카를로스 윌리엄스의 시 〈눈 속의 사냥꾼〉에 대해 여자가 한 말은?

   Ⓐ 화가가 눈 내리는 광경을 그리도록 영감을 주었다.
   Ⓑ 오래된 풍경화에서 영감을 얻었다.
   Ⓒ 윌리엄스의 가장 긴 시이다.
   Ⓓ 윌리엄스의 가장 유명한 시이다.

4. 학생들이 시 대회에서 시를 쓸 그림에 대해 명시된 것은?

   Ⓐ 학생 1명이 그림을 3점까지 선택할 수 있다.
   Ⓑ 학생들은 그림 1점에 대해 1편 이상의 시를 쓸 수 있다.
   Ⓒ 모든 그림이 하나의 특정 전시회와 연결되어 있다.
   Ⓓ 모든 그림이 피터르 브뤼헐의 작품이다.

5. 인도 미술 전시회에서 한 시간 동안 투어를 인솔하게 됐다는 사실을 알게 된 남자의 태도는?

   Ⓐ 그곳 그림 대다수에 익숙하지 않아서 긴장된다.
   Ⓑ 좋아하는 전시회가 아니라서 실망한다.
   Ⓒ 이야기할 그림을 선택할 수 있어서 의욕이 넘친다.
   Ⓓ 인도 미술 전시회가 상대적으로 규모가 작아서 놀란다.

   어휘 Enthusiastic 열정 넘치는

N Narrator   P Professor

Script T-53

N   Listen to part of a lecture in an economics class.

P   When attempting to understand international trade, some things seem so obvious that they can hardly be controverted, and other points that are important are invisible unless you've thought about the subject carefully.

Consider the following: if there's an increase in imports, let's say, um, let's say imports of furniture, and the domestic producers of furniture find this new competition very difficult and are cutting production and employment, then it seems obvious and easy to understand and many people conclude from this that increasing imports will cause generally greater unemployment at home.

What is not so obvious is that how much we import and how much we export … those are interdependent and you can't understand the one without the other. But the exports that are generated are not easily discernable, so most people don't see them. They see only the imports of furniture rising and employment in domestic furniture production falling.

So as a result, many people argue that we ought to protect jobs by limiting imports—either by tariffs, quotas, regulations, or whatever—without realizing that this also has the effect of reducing potential future exports to the rest of the world, things that we can produce very, very … cost effectively and therefore profitably.

The fundamental proposition in international economics is that it makes sense to import those things that we … that can be produced more economically abroad than at home and export things to the rest of the world that we can produce more cost effectively than produced elsewhere in the world. Therefore, if we limit imports, we put ourselves in danger of not being able to export.

The details of this relationship will take much longer to explain than I can fully go into now but the point of the matter is that gains—the benefits of gains—from international trade result from being able to get things cheaper by buying them abroad than you can make them at home. Now there're some things that we can make at home that are … that we can do more economically than they can do abroad.

In the case of the United States, typically high-technology products, uh … are things that Americans have innovated in and started firms doing that sort of thing at which they do very well. Whereas goods that produce … that use a lot of relatively low skill labor, like furniture production, cotton production, sugar production … those are things that are

N   경제학 강의의 일부를 들으시오.

P   국제무역에 대해 이해하려고 할 때 어떤 부분은 너무 명확해서 논박할 여지가 없어 보입니다. 그런가 하면 중요한데도 주의 깊게 생각하지 않으면 눈에 보이지 않는 부분도 있죠.

이런 경우를 생각해 봅시다. 수입이 늘어나면, 그러니까, 가구 수입이 증가한다고 칩시다. 그러면 국내 가구 생산업자들은 새로운 경쟁 상대가 어렵다고 보고 생산량과 고용을 줄일 겁니다. 이 상황은 명확하고 이해하기 쉬워 보이죠. 그래서 많은 사람들은 수입이 증가하면 대체로 국내 실업률이 높아진다고 결론을 내립니다.

분명하지 않는 것은 수입량과 수출량입니다. 이 둘은 상호의존적이라 하나를 빼고 다른 하나를 이해할 수 없죠. 하지만 수출은 발생해도 쉽게 인식할 수 없기 때문에 대부분의 사람들이 알아차리지 못하죠. 따라서 가구 수입량이 늘어나면서 국내 가구 생산업계의 고용이 줄어드는 것만 보는 겁니다.

그 결과 많은 사람들이 수입을 제한해 일자리를 보호해야 한다고 주장합니다. 말하자면 관세부과, 쿼터제, 규제 등 무슨 조치라도 취하라는 거죠. 이런 조치로 향후 가구의 해외 수출 역시 감소할 수 있다는 사실은 모르죠. 국내에서 아주, 아주 비용효율적으로 생산해서 수익이 나는 그런 물건들 말이죠.

국제경제학의 기본적인 명제는 국내보다 해외에서 훨씬 경제적으로 생산할 수 있는 물건은 수입하고, 해외보다 국내에서 더 효율적인 가격으로 생산할 수 있는 제품은 전 세계로 수출하는 것이 타당하다는 겁니다. 따라서 수입을 제한하면 수출이 불가능해지는 위험을 자처하는 거예요.

이 관계를 자세히 설명하자면 지금 이야기하려는 것보다 훨씬 더 길어질 거예요. 하지만 문제의 핵심은 이윤입니다. 국내에서 만드는 것보다 해외에서 사는 게 더 싸면 이윤이 남죠. 이래서 국제무역이 생깁니다. 그리고 국내에서 만들면 해외에서 만드는 것보다 훨씬 경제적으로 생산할 수 있는 제품들도 있죠.

미국의 경우 일반적으로 첨단기술 제품들, 어, 미국이 처음으로 만들고 기업을 시작한 이런 첨단기술 제품들은 미국이 잘 만드는 제품이죠. 반면 가구, 면화, 설탕 생산처럼 상대적으로 저숙련 노동력을 대량 투입해 생산하는 제품도 있습니다. 이런 제품은 흔히 임금이 낮고 자본 사용 비용이 아주 높은 곳에서 더 저렴하게 생산됩니다.

frequently made more inexpensively in places where wage rates are low and the cost of using capital is very high.

However, in Florida they produce a lot of sugar, but the costs are so high, if we didn't have extensive restrictions on imports of sugar, the output of sugar would decline dramatically. But the sugar industry in the U.S. doesn't produce high-paying jobs, it uses resources in ineffective ways and it blocks the import of more cost-effectively produced sugar. It, it's a very bad bargain for the people in the United States to want to protect low-paying jobs thereby halting the growth of world trading and international … uh, more international specialization. It would be better to remove restrictions on imports and allow other countries in the world … countries that can produce them more cheaply … let them specialize in producing those products.

Now, I agree that people who are directly affected by imports, what they focus on … is, is that their prospects … their job prospects are being reduced, and their economic circumstances are getting worse. And that's a relevant problem and an important problem; what isn't so obvious is … that by retraining and relocating people to places and industries where jobs are expanding rather than contracting, we can make the whole economy function more effectively and productively than by trying to block imports.

Um, what is interesting to note is that, even if there were no international trade issues, like imports, any changes that occur in a country's economy—any new technology, change in preferences, change in regulations or whatever—will lead to "adjustments" that lead some sectors of the economy to decline and others to expand.

And that's what we have to figure out, and that's a hard problem to deal with in detail, is how to facilitate people adjusting from sectors where their job prospects are not so good, and in particular where real wages aren't so high, to acquire skills that will permit them to move into higher-paying jobs in other parts of the economy either by retraining or relocating. Helping pay for the relocation of these people would be very helpful, but trying to block the changes is really counterproductive. It makes people in our country poorer, and it makes people elsewhere in the world poorer as well.

하지만 플로리다 주에서는 엄청난 양의 설탕을 생산하면서도 비용이 아주 높아서 만약 설탕 수입을 대대적으로 규제하지 않는다면 설탕 생산량이 급격하게 줄어들 겁니다. 하지만 미국의 설탕 산업은 고임금 일자리를 창출하지 못해요. 비효율적인 방식으로 자원을 쓰면서 훨씬 비용효율적으로 생산된 설탕의 수입을 막고 있죠. 저임금 일자리를 보호하려고 세계 무역의 성장과, 어, 국제 분업화의 진전을 막는 것은 미국 국민들에게는 아주 불리한 흥정입니다. 수입규제를 풀고 세계의 다른 나라들이, 이 제품을 값싸게 생산할 수 있는 나라가 특화 생산하도록 하는 편이 훨씬 나을 겁니다.

자, 수입에 직접적인 영향을 받는 사람들이 걱정하는 문제에는 동의합니다. 전망, 그러니까 취업 전망이 줄어들고 경제 환경이 더 악화되니까요. 이건 의미가 있는 문제고 중요한 문제입니다. 다만 명확하게 드러나지 않는 것이 있다면… 인력을 재교육하고, 일자리가 줄어드는 곳 대신 늘어나는 곳과 그러한 산업에 인력을 재배치하면, 수입을 막으려고 하는 것보다는 전체 경제가 더 효율적이고 생산적으로 작동한다는 겁니다.

음, 흥미로운 점은 수입 같은 국제무역 문제가 없더라도 한 나라의 경제에 변화가 생기면, 가령 새로운 기술, 선호도 변화, 규제 변화 등으로 변화가 생기면 '조정'으로 이어지는데 조정을 통해 경제의 어떤 부문은 쇠퇴하고 다른 부문은 팽창합니다.

바로 이 점이 우리가 생각해야 할 부분인데 상세하게 다루기 어려운 문제예요. 말하자면 취업 전망이 좋지 않고 특히 실질 임금이 그다지 높지 않은 부문의 사람들이 조정 과정을 거쳐갈 때, 재교육이나 재배치를 통해 다른 경제 부문의 고임금 일자리로 이동할 수 있는 기술을 쉽게 습득할 수 있게 해 주는 방법을 찾아야 합니다. 이들을 재배치하도록 재정적으로 지원하면 크게 도움이 될 겁니다. 하지만 변화를 막으려고 하면 실제로 역효과만 나타납니다. 우리나라 국민은 물론 다른 나라 국민들도 훨씬 가난해질 거예요.

어휘

international trade 국제무역 obvious 분명한, 명백한 controvert 논쟁하다, 논박하다 invisible 보이지 않는, 볼 수 없는 import 수입 domestic 국내의, 자국의 employment 고용, 취업 unemployment 실업, 실직 export 수출 interdependent 상호 의존적인 discernable 인식[식별]할 수 있는 tariff 관세 quota (수출입 등에 공식적으로 허용되는) 한도, 쿼터 regulation 규제, 통제 potential 잠재적인, 가능성이 있는 effectively 효과적으로, 유효하게 profitably 이익이 되게, 유익하게 fundamental 근본[본질]적인 proposition 제안, 제의 economically 경제적으로, 효율적으로 high-technology 첨단 기술의 innovate 처음으로 받아들이다, 도입하다 capital 자본금, 자금 extensive 대규모의, 엄청난 restriction 규제, 제한 dramatically 극적으로 bargain 흥정, 협상 halt 중단시키다 international specialization 국제 분업, 국제 특화 prospect 가능성, 가망 relevant 관련 있는, 적절한 retrain 재교육하다 relocate 재배치하다 contract 줄어들다, 수축하다 preference 선호 adjustment 조정, 조절 sector 부문 facilitate 가능하게[용이하게]하다, 촉진하다 adjust 조정[조절]하다 counterproductive 역효과를 낳는

6. 이 강의는 주로 무엇에 관한 것인가?

Ⓐ 국제무역의 확장을 제한하는 방법들
Ⓑ 국제무역 규제가 경제에 끼칠 수 있는 폐해
Ⓒ 수출 분배에 영향을 미치는 요소들
Ⓓ 최근 몇 년 동안 국제무역이 확대된 이유

어휘 expansion 확장, 확대   distribution 분배, 배급

7. 교수에 따르면, 많은 사람들이 수입규제를 원하는 이유는?

Ⓐ 국내 제품의 가격 상승을 위해
Ⓑ 수출 가격의 경쟁력을 높이기 위해
Ⓒ 국내 실업률 상승을 막기 위해
Ⓓ 특정 산업의 경제 성장을 장려하기 위해

어휘 increase 증가, 상승   competitive 경쟁력 있는

8. 교수에 따르면, 수입 제한에 따른 부정적인 결과는?

Ⓐ 기술 혁신의 속도가 느려진다.
Ⓑ 국내의 저임금 일자리 수가 감소한다.
Ⓒ 사람들이 임금이 더 낮은 영역으로 이동한다.
Ⓓ 잠재적인 수출 소득이 줄어든다.

어휘 innovation 혁신, 쇄신

9. 교수가 플로리다 주의 설탕 산업에 대해 암시하는 것은?

Ⓐ 고임금 일자리를 창출하는 좋은 원천이다.
Ⓑ 수입에 따른 경쟁을 피하려고 보호해서는 안 된다.
Ⓒ 국제 분업의 효과를 보여 주는 좋은 예다.
Ⓓ 비용효율적으로 관리된다.

어휘 high-paying 임금이 높은, 고임금의
     cost-effectively 비용효율적으로

10. 교수가 수입 증가의 효과에 대해 암시하는 것은?

Ⓐ 결국 수출이 감소할 것이다.
Ⓑ 반드시 경제에 나쁜 것만은 아니다.
Ⓒ 쉽게 해결되는 국내 경제 문제들이 생긴다.
Ⓓ 경제에 미치는 영향이 즉각적이며 분명하다.

어휘 impact 영향, 효과   apparent 분명한, 명백한

11. 실업자 재교육과 재배치에 대한 교수의 견해는?

Ⓐ 시간이 흐르면 수입을 막는 것보다 훨씬 비싸다.
Ⓑ 때때로 의도하지 않은 결과가 발생할 수 있다.
Ⓒ 수입 증가에 적응하는 한 가지 방법이다.
Ⓓ 비효율적인 산업의 조업도를 유지한다.

어휘 consequence 결과, 영향   adapt to ~에 적응하다
     production level 조업도(일정 기간의 조업률)

Questions 12~16

p.150

N Narrator   S Student   P Professor

Script T-54

N Listen to a conversation between a student and a professor.

S Hi, uh … Professor Anderson … wondering if you had a couple of minutes …

P Of course, Paula …

S Thanks … uh, you sent me a letter recently about doing, uh, an honors project—inviting me to come in and talk about …

P Right, right, well, as your academic advisor, it's my job to look out for your academic interests, and based on your grades, and some very positive feedback I've heard from your professors, I wanted to formally invite you to consider doing an honors project …

S Yeah … well, thanks … uh, actually I kinda wanted to ask you … quite frankly—like how much work it would probably be? I mean, I'm gonna be spending a lot of time applying to law schools next semester and …

P Well, let me tell you how it works … and then you can decide from there.

S OK.

P Basically, the honors project is an opportunity to do … some in-depth work on a topic you're interested in before graduating college. You register for the class, but it doesn't work the same way a regular class does—you find a professor who you want to work with—you ask the professor—a sort of mentor who's knowledgeable on the topic you're interested in—the topic you're gonna write your honors thesis on …

S Writing a *thesis*? That's part of the *project*? Ah, like how many pages are we talking?

P Usually about 50 … but it's a valuable experience, writing a thesis paper.

S So, basically, after I register for the class, I need to ask a professor who'll sorta help me …

P Actually, you need to do that—a professor needs to agree to oversee your honors project—before you register.

S Oh, OK …

P I mean, I know it sounds kinda daunting, but that's what the professor's there for—to help guide you through the different steps of the process and … uh … most students are very pleased with the experience … they're able to demonstrate advanced research skills, which is important; especially in your case, writing an honors thesis would be a big plus …

S You think so?

P Absolutely. Especially considering your plans, since you're applying to law schools. It shows initiative, that you've done well as an undergraduate—to be allowed to do the honors

N 학생과 교수의 대화를 들으시오.

S 안녕하세요. 저, 앤더슨 교수님. 시간 좀 있으세요?

P 물론이지, 폴라.

S 감사합니다. 저, 교수님께서 최근에 그러니까 우등과정 프로젝트에 참여해 보라고 편지를 보내셨어요. 와서 얘기해 보자고.

P 맞아, 그랬지. 지도교수로서 자네의 학문적인 관심을 찾는 게 내 일이거든. 그래서 자네의 학점과 자네를 가르친 여러 교수들의 긍정적인 반응을 보니 우등과정 프로젝트에 참여하면 어떨까 정식으로 제안하고 싶었네.

S 예, 감사해요. 저, 실은 교수님께 여쭙고 싶은 게 있는데 솔직히 말해서 그러려면 어느 정도 공부해야 하나요? 실은 다음 학기에 로스쿨에 지원하려면 거기 시간이 많이 들 것 같아요.

P 음, 우등과정 프로젝트가 어떻게 진행되는지 얘기해 줄 테니 들어 보고 결정하게.

S 좋아요.

P 기본적으로 우등과정 프로젝트는 좋은 기회라네. 그러니까 대학을 졸업하기 전 관심 주제를 심도 있게 연구할 수 있는 기회이지. 수강신청을 해야 하는데 진행 방식은 정규 수업과 달라. 함께 연구하고 싶은 교수를 찾고 교수에게 부탁해야 해. 자네가 관심 있는, 그러니까 앞으로 우등과정 논문을 쓰게 될 주제에 정통한 일종의 멘토이지.

S 논문을 쓴다고요? 그것도 프로젝트의 일부인가요? 아, 분량은 어느 정도죠?

P 보통 50페이지 정도라네. 하지만 논문을 써 보는 건 귀중한 경험이 될 거야.

S 그렇다면 기본적으로 수강신청을 한 후 도와주실 교수님께 부탁해야겠네요….

P 사실 수강신청 전에 교수의 동의가 필요하네. 자네의 우등과정 프로젝트를 교수가 감독하겠다고 동의해야 하거든.

S 아, 알겠어요.

P 음, 벅차 보인다는 건 아네. 하지만 그래서 교수가 있는 거고. 교수는 자네가 이 과정의 여러 단계들을 통과할 수 있도록 도와줄 거야. 그리고 대부분의 학생이 이 경험에 매우 흡족해 한다네. 진일보한 연구능력을 발휘할 수 있는데, 이 점이 중요하거든. 특히 자네의 경우 우등과정 논문을 썼다는 게 큰 이점으로 작용할거야.

S 그렇게 생각하세요?

P 물론이지. 특히 로스쿨에 지원하겠다는 자네의 계획을

project … that you're able to work independently and, of course, you would graduate with honors …

S Yeah, it *does* sound good—it's just, you know, I've never written something like that before, so …

P Well, you choose something you're interested in—maybe you can even expand a shorter research paper from another class or …

S So, like, maybe … You know, I took this course from Professor Connelly—his course on Comparative Governments last semester and, uh … did pretty well—I wrote a paper actually, on political parties in Venezuela and—and he seemed to like my research. Anyway, he, uh, I got an A in the course.

P Good, so it sounds like you do have a general idea for a topic, and you might know what professor you want to work with … and look, it's still a couple weeks before registration, maybe you should talk to Professor Connelly and then get back to me.

S Yeah, I will—thanks. I'll come by again sometime next week.

P That's fine. Good luck.

고려하면 더욱 그래. 우등과정 프로젝트에 참여할 수 있었다는 건 진취적이고, 학부생으로서 우수했다는 점을 보여주거든. 독립적으로 연구할 수 있는 능력도 보여 주고, 게다가 당연히 우등으로 졸업하게 될 거고….

S 네, 정말 좋네요. 그런데 아시겠지만 제가 한 번도 논문 같은 걸 써 보질 않아서요, 그래서….

P 음, 자네가 관심 있는 분야에서 선택하면 돼. 어쩌면 다른 수업시간에 제출한 짤막한 연구 보고서를 늘리는 방법도 있으니까 아니면….

S 그렇다면, 실은 제가 코넬리 교수님의 수업을 들었거든요. 지난 학기에 코넬리 교수님의 비교정치학 수업을 들었는데 꽤 괜찮았어요. 실은 베네수엘라의 정당들에 관한 리포트를 썼는데 교수님이 제 연구를 마음에 들어 하시는 듯했어요. 어쨌든 A학점을 받았어요.

P 좋아, 그렇다면 연구 주제도 대강 있는 듯하고 함께 연구하고 싶은 교수도 알고 있으니. 자, 아직 수강신청까지 몇 주 남았으니까 코넬리 교수와 이야기해 보고 다시 내게 오면 되겠어.

S 예, 그렇게 할게요. 고맙습니다. 다음 주에 다시 한 번 들를게요.

P 좋아, 행운을 비네.

어휘

honors project 우등과정 프로젝트   academic advisor 지도교수   positive feedback 긍정적인 반응[의견]   formally 정식으로, 공식적으로   kinda=kind of 약간, 무언가   apply to 지원하다, 신청하다   in-depth 상세한, 심도 있는   register for 등록하다, 신청하다   knowledgeable 정통한, 많이 아는   thesis 학위 논문   valuable 귀중한, 쓸모 있는   sorta=sort of 일종의   oversee 감독[감시]하다   daunting 벅찬, 쉽지 않은   absolutely 그럼, 물론이지(강한 동의·허락을 나타냄)   initiative 진취성, 자주성   undergraduate 학부생, 대학생   independently 독립적으로, 자주적으로   expand 확장[확대]하다   Comparative Governments 비교정치학   political party 정당   registration 등록, 신고

12. 학생이 지도교수인 앤더슨 교수를 만나러 간 이유는?

    Ⓐ 앤더슨 교수가 연구를 도와주기 원해서

    Ⓑ 앤더슨 교수의 초청에 응하기 위해

    Ⓒ 다른 교수에게 불만이 있어서

    Ⓓ 로스쿨 추천서를 받고 싶어서

어휘 complaint 불평, 불만 recommendation 추천, 권고

13. 학생이 코넬리 교수의 수업을 언급한 이유는?

    Ⓐ 그 수업에서 받은 학점이 불만이어서

    Ⓑ 그 수업에서 수행한 연구를 확장할 수 있을 듯해서

    Ⓒ 지금까지 들어본 수업들 중 가장 어려운 수업이라서

    Ⓓ 코넬리 교수가 학생들을 데리고 베네수엘라로 여행을 가서

14. 학생은 다시 만나기 전까지 앤더슨 교수에게 무엇을 하겠다고 말하는가?

    Ⓐ 코넬리 교수의 수업을 수강신청할 것이다.

    Ⓑ 우등과정 논문을 쓰기 시작할 것이다.

    Ⓒ 코넬리 교수에게 우등과정 프로젝트를 제출할 것이다.

    Ⓓ 코넬리 교수와 우등과정 프로젝트에 대해 이야기할 것이다.

어휘 turn in ~을 제출하다

15. 대화의 일부를 다시 듣고 질문에 답하라.

 T-55

> **N** *What does Professor Anderson imply when he says this:*
> **P** ... they're able to demonstrate advanced research skills, which is important; especially in your case, writing an honors thesis would be a big plus ...

    Ⓐ 우등과정 논문을 써 보라는 제안을 받는 학생이 거의 없다.

    Ⓑ 여자는 과거에 연구능력이 형편없었다.

    Ⓒ 여자가 로스쿨에 입학하는 데 우등과정 논문이 도움이 될 수 있다.

    Ⓓ 여자는 연구능력을 개괄적으로 설명하는 제안서를 작성해야 한다.

어휘 proposal 제안, 제의 outline 개요를 말하다

16. 대화의 일부를 다시 듣고 질문에 답하라.

 T-56

> **N** *What does the woman imply when she says this:*
> **P** Yeah, it does sound good—it's just, you know, I've never written something like that before ... so ...

    Ⓐ 여자는 우등과정 논문을 쓸 수 있을지 자신이 없다.

    Ⓑ 여자는 우등과정 논문이 자신에게 유용하다고 생각하지 않는다.

    Ⓒ 여자는 스스로 글을 잘 쓴다고 생각한다.

    Ⓓ 여자는 과거에 연구 보고서를 한 번 썼다.

어휘 uncertain 불확실한, 확신이 없는

N Narrator   **P** Professor   **F** Female student   **M** Male student

Script T-57

N Listen to part of a lecture in a journalism class. The professor has been discussing newspapers.

P About 40 years ago, half of all Americans felt they'd be lost without a daily newspaper. But today, only one in *ten* Americans say they'd be lost without a paper. In fact, today, half of all Americans say they don't need a newspaper at all. And so people in the newspaper industry are trying to figure out how they can get more people reading the newspaper more often. They're trying to crack journalism's riddle for the ages: what makes people read newspapers? OK, well, let me ask you—as a journalism student, what do *you* think is the answer to this question? Elizabeth?

F Um, I would probably try to improve the content of the newspaper.

P Better content. Hmm. You mean like *well-written* editorials and articles?

F Well, I mean provide more *interesting* content, like, I would first try to find out what readers really want to read ... and then put *that* into the paper.

P Yes, in fact, not too long ago, there was an extensive study conducted to investigate what draws people to newspapers. Uh, they found out that there's a clear, strong link between satisfaction with *content* and overall readership. Those newspapers that contained what the readers wanted most brought in the most readers. No big surprise there, right? So, what kind of content brings in readers? The study found that *people-centered local news* ranks at the top of the list ... stories about *ordinary* people. For example, you could write about the experiences of those who were involved in a news story, and their friends and relatives ... The vantage points would be those of *ordinary* people, not of police or other officials ... OK? Now the study also showed that people want more stories about movies, TV, and weather, and *fewer* stories and photos about natural disasters and accidents ... So, to get reader satisfaction, you need to select the right topics, and within those topics, the right news events or stories to cover. Yes, James?

M It seems to me that a lot of what you just mentioned doesn't line up with the principles of good journalism. Catering to readers' tastes may improve overall readership, but what about the social responsibilities that newspapers have? I mean, there are some topics that newspapers *need* to write about in order to serve the public interest. Those topics may not always be fun and interesting for the average reader, but it's still the newspaper's responsibility to make that information available to the public.

N 신문방송학 강의의 일부를 들으시오. 교수는 신문에 대해 이야기하고 있다.

P 약 40년 전 전체 미국인의 절반이 일간신문이 없으면 무력감을 느낄 거라고 생각했습니다. 하지만 오늘날에는 미국인 10명중 1명만이 신문이 없으면 무력감을 느낄 거라고 하네요. 사실 현재 전체 미국인의 절반은 신문이 전혀 필요 없다고 말합니다. 그래서 신문업계 종사자들은 더 많은 사람들이 신문을 더 자주 보게 만들 방법을 알아내려고 하죠. 오랜 세월 풀리지 않은 언론의 수수께끼를 풀고 있는 거죠. 바로 이겁니다. 어떻게 해야 사람들이 신문을 읽을까? 그렇다면 음, 신문방송학과 학생들인 여러분에게 질문해 보죠. 이 질문의 해답이 뭐라고 생각하나요? 엘리자베스?

F 저, 신문의 내용을 개선해 보려 할 거 같아요.

P 더 좋은 내용이라. 음. 훌륭한 사설이나 기사를 말하는 건가요?

F 그게, 좀 더 흥미로운 내용을 싣는 거죠. 저라면 먼저 독자들이 정말 읽고 싶어하는 내용을 찾을 거예요. 그런 다음 신문에 그 내용을 싣는 거죠.

P 맞아요, 사실 얼마 전 사람들이 신문을 보는 이유를 조사하는 폭넓은 연구가 있었어요. 음, 연구를 통해 내용에 대한 만족도와 전체 구독자수 사이에 강력하고 명확한 연관성이 있음이 밝혀졌는데요. 독자들이 가장 원하는 내용이 실린 신문에 사람들이 많이 몰렸어요. 크게 놀랄 일은 아니에요. 그렇죠? 그렇다면 어떤 내용이 독자들을 모을까요? 연구에 따르면, 사람을 중점적으로 다룬 지역 뉴스, 그러니까 보통 사람들의 이야기가 리스트 상위에 올랐다고 하네요. 예를 들어 보도기사와 관련된 사람이나 친구, 가족들의 경험을 기사화한다고 합시다. 그러면 기사의 관점이 경찰이나 공무원의 관점이 아닌 이런 평범한 사람들의 관점이 되겠죠, 그렇죠? 자, 또한 연구결과에 따르면, 사람들이 영화, TV, 날씨에 관한 기사를 선호하며 자연재해, 사고와 관련된 기사나 사진은 덜 좋아한다고 하네요. 따라서 독자들을 만족시키려면 적절한 주제를 선택한 후 그 안에서 보도할 수 있는 뉴스 사건이나 이야기를 다루어야 해요. 네, 제임스?

M 교수님이 방금 말씀하신 내용의 상당 부분이 훌륭한 저널리즘의 원칙과 맞지 않는 것 같아요. 독자의 취향에 영합하면 전체 구독자수는 늘겠죠. 하지만 신문의 사회적인 책임은 어떡하죠? 제 말은 신문이 공익을 위해 반드시 보도해야 할 주제들이 있잖아요. 이러한 주제가 항상 평균적인 독자에게 재미있거나 흥미롭지 않을 수도 있고요. 그래도 여전히 그런 정보를 대중이 접할 수 있

P That's a good point. You need a good mix of content. You can't just rush towards an attractive topic and forget about the reporting role of newspapers. There's a danger of going soft—newspapers *do* have to perform their obligations to citizens. So what newspapers sometimes do is to combine serious journalism with a reader-friendly *presentation*. Um, let me give you an example: When the justice department opened an investigation on the local police—some pretty serious stuff that could be boring to some readers—well, one local newspaper ran a lead story on their front page, but they also simplified the format by including small breakout boxes that presented—in a nutshell—the highlights of the story. That way, they could report the serious stories they needed to report, and, and still hold their readers' attention. OK? Uh, going back to the research on readership growth we were talking about ... Uh, the most vital step of all, the study shows, may be making the paper easier to *use*. How can we make the paper "easier to *use*"? Well, it means stories need to include information, such as phone numbers, times, dates, addresses, Web sites and the like, so that readers can "go and do" things based on what they've read.

F Professor Ellington? Um, when you said we need to make the paper "easier to use," I thought you were gonna say something about use of graphics, colors, and stuff like that.

P Well, I guess those things do help in a way, but it turned out that those contemporary touches, uh, such as more attractive designs, extensive use of color, and informational graphics matter much less than you'd expect. Surprising, isn't it?

F Yeah, it is ... Um, how about service? Does the study say anything about improving service? I don't think people are gonna subscribe if the paper doesn't arrive, or shows up late ...

P Or shows up wet, which by the way, happened to me this morning. Oh, absolutely. Service affects readership. In fact, improving your service is much more likely to increase your readership than making changes in your editorial content ... Not only on-time delivery in good condition, but also things like efficient billing, affordability, um... Yes?

F They could also, like, increase the number of sites where they sell single copies.

P Certainly that's one way to improve service.

도록 하는 게 신문의 책임이죠.

P 좋은 지적이에요. 내용을 적절히 조합해야 합니다. 무작정 흥미로운 주제에만 매달려 신문이 가진 보도의 임무를 망각할 순 없어요. 내용이 가벼워질 위험이 있거든요. 신문은 시민에 대한 의무를 다해야 해요. 따라서 때때로 신문들은 진지한 저널리즘과 독자의 기호에 맞춘 보도 방법을 결합하기도 하죠. 음, 예를 들어 볼까요. 법무부가 지역 경찰에 대한 수사에 착수했어요. 어떤 독자들에게는 지루할 수 있는 아주 심각한 사건이죠. 자, 한 지역 신문이 이 사건을 일면 머리기사로 실었습니다. 하지만 작은 상자 안에 사건의 주요 내용을 요약해 보여 주는 방식으로 서식을 간소화했어요. 이런 식으로 하면 반드시 전해야 할 심각한 기사를 보도하면서도 여전히 독자들의 관심을 끌 수 있어요. 알겠죠? 자, 구독자수를 늘리기 위한 연구 이야기로 다시 돌아가겠습니다. 음, 연구에 따르면, 무엇보다 가장 필수적인 조치는 신문을 이용하기 쉽게 만드는 것이라고 합니다. 어떻게 신문을 '이용하기 쉽게' 만들 수 있을까요? 자, 신문기사에 전화번호, 시간, 날짜, 주소, 웹사이트 등의 정보를 실어야 한다는 거예요. 그래야 독자들이 읽은 내용을 바탕으로 '바로바로 실행에 옮길 수' 있거든요.

F 엘링턴 교수님? 저, 신문을 '이용하기 쉽게' 만들어야 한다고 하실 때 그래픽이나 색깔 등을 활용하는 방법을 말씀하시겠구나 생각했어요.

P 뭐, 그런 것들도 어느 정도 도움이 될 겁니다. 하지만 그러한 현대 기법들이 음, 가령 더 멋진 디자인이나 다채로운 색깔, 정보가 담긴 그래픽이 생각보다 그다지 중요하지 않은 것으로 나타났어요. 놀랍죠?

F 네, 그렇군요. 그렇다면 서비스는요? 연구가 서비스 향상에 대해서는 언급하지 않았나요? 신문이 배달되지 않거나 늦게 오면 사람들이 구독하지 않을 거 같은데요.

P 신문이 젖어서 오는 경우도 있죠. 오늘 아침 제게 일어난 일이에요. 물론이죠. 서비스는 구독에 영향을 미칩니다. 실제로 서비스가 향상되면 사설 내용을 바꾸는 것보다 구독자수가 늘어날 가능성이 훨씬 크죠. 제시간에 좋은 상태로 배달되는 건 물론 효율적인 청구서 발부, 적당한 가격…. 얘기해 보세요.

F 신문을 한 부씩 파는 장소를 늘리는 방법도 있겠어요.

P 물론 그것도 서비스를 향상시키는 하나의 방법이죠.

어휘

figure out ~을 알아내다, 생각해 내다 riddle 수수께끼, 불가사의 content 내용 editorial 사설, 논설 article 글, 기사 overall 전체의, 종합적인 readership 구독자수 ordinary 보통의, 평범한 vantage point 관점 natural disaster 자연재해 cover 취재[보도]하다 line up with ~와 일치하다 principle 원칙, 원리 cater to ~에 영합하다, 입맛에 맞추다 responsibility 책임, 맡은 일 go soft 말랑말랑하게 만들다 obligation 의무, 책무 reader-friendly 독자의 기호에 맞춘 presentation 제시 방식, 설명 justice department 법무부 investigation 수사, 조사 lead story (신문, 방송 등의) 머리기사, 톱뉴스 simplify 간소화하다 in a nutshell 간단히 vital 필수적인 contemporary 현대의, 당대의 extensive 광범위한, 폭넓은 subscribe 구독하다 delivery 배달, 인도 efficient 효율적인, 효과가 있는 affordability 감당할 수 있는 비용, 구매할 수 있는 가격

17. 이 강의는 주로 무엇에 관한 것인가?

　Ⓐ 일부 신문들이 서비스를 향상하지 않는 이유
　Ⓑ 신문이 구독자수를 늘리는 방법
　Ⓒ 지역 신문이 주요 신문과 경쟁할 수 없는 이유
　Ⓓ 몇 년 사이 독자들의 관심 주제가 바뀐 경위

18. 교수에 따르면, 신문 독자들이 가장 관심을 갖는 주제는? 두 개의 답을 선택하라.

　Ⓐ 정치 문제
　Ⓑ 연예와 날씨
　Ⓒ 자연재해와 사고
　Ⓓ 보통 사람들

19. 교수에 따르면, 심각한 기사를 보도록 독자의 관심을 끌 수 있는 방법은?

　Ⓐ 배경 지식을 제공하는 사진 넣기
　Ⓑ 기사 내용 살짝 수정하기
　Ⓒ 구독자들의 관심을 더 끌 수 있는 서식 만들기
　Ⓓ 심각한 기사의 수를 점차적으로 늘리기

　어휘 revision 수정, 개정　appeal to ~의 관심을 끌다

20. 신문의 색깔 사용에 대해 교수가 암시하는 것은?

　Ⓐ 독자의 선호도에 따라 크게 영향을 받는다.
　Ⓑ 초창기 연구가 시사하는 것보다 더 효과적이다.
　Ⓒ 구독자수를 크게 늘리지는 못했다.
　Ⓓ 저널리즘 연구에서 간과되었다.

　어휘 effective 효과적인, 효력이 있는　significant 상당한, 아주 큰
　　　 neglect 무시하다, 간과하다

21. 강의의 일부를 다시 듣고 질문에 답하라.

 T-58

　N *What does the student imply when he says this:*
　P It seems to me that a lot of what you just mentioned doesn't line up with the principles of good journalism. Catering to readers' tastes may improve overall readership, but what about the social responsibilities that newspapers have?

　Ⓐ 교수의 말에 전적으로 동의한다.
　Ⓑ 교수의 견해에 놀랐다.
　Ⓒ 교수가 이야기하는 주제가 낯설다.
　Ⓓ 논의 중인 문제의 해결책을 제안할 수 있다.

　어휘 completely 완전히, 전적으로　point of view 관점, 견해
　　　 solution 해결책

22. 강의의 일부를 다시 듣고 질문에 답하라.

 T-59

　F I don't think people are gonna subscribe if the paper doesn't arrive, or shows up late ...
　P Or shows up wet, which by the way, happened to me this morning. Oh, absolutely. Service affects readership.

　N *What does the professor imply when he says this:*
　P Or shows up wet, which by the way, happened to me this morning. Oh, absolutely.

　Ⓐ 학생의 말을 전적으로 지지한다.
　Ⓑ 오늘 아침 겪은 일은 뜻밖이었다.
　Ⓒ 오늘 아침 일어난 일에 충격 받지 않았다.
　Ⓓ 학생이 불평해서는 안 된다.

　어휘 statement 진술　unexpected 뜻밖의, 예기치 못한
　　　 be affected 충격 받다, 감동 받다

Questions 23~28

p.154

N Narrator   **P** Professor

Script   T-60

N Listen to part of a lecture in a geology class.

P Um, beginning in the late 1960s, geologists began to uncover some evidence of a rather surprising kind when they looked … um … at various places around the world. What they found out when they examined rocks from about a … the period from about 750 million years ago to about 580 million years ago, they found that … it seemed that glaciers covered the entire surface of the Earth—from pole to pole, including the tropics.

Um … how did they come to this astonishing conclusion? What was the evidence for this? Especially when glaciers today are found only at the poles … or in the mountains.

Well, uh … basically when glaciers grow and move they leave behind a distinctive deposit consisting of primarily … of, at least on the top level, of ground up little bits of rock … almost … they almost look like rocks that have been deposited by streams, if you've ever seen those. And that's caused because, although the glacier is ice, it is actually flowing very slowly and as it moves it grinds the top layer of rock, it breaks off pieces and carries them away. So when you have glaciation you have a distinctive pattern of these pieces of rock which are called "erratics."

Erratics are rocks … they're the stones that are often carried long distances by glaciers.

So, in the 1960s and onward up through the 1990s, we keep finding evidence for glaciation, no matter what the latitude … even in tropical latitudes. Now, today there are glaciers in the tropics but only at very high elevations. But 750 million years ago, apparently there were glaciers even at sea level in the tropics.

How could this have happened?

Well, first … the growth of glaciers, uh, benefits, if you will, from a kind of a positive feedback loop called the "ice-albedo effect."

With the ice-albedo effect, glaciers—'cause they're white—reflect light and heat more … much more than does liquid water … or soil and rock, which are dark and absorb heat. So, the more glaciers there are, the more heat is reflected, so the climate gets cooler, and glaciers grow even more.

However … normally, on a global scale, there is a major process that functions to curb the growth of glaciers. And, that process involves carbon dioxide.

Now, we're all familiar with the notion that carbon dioxide is what we call a "greenhouse gas." The more carbon dioxide there is in the atmosphere, the more heat the atmosphere

N 지질학 강의의 일부를 들으시오.

P 음, 1960년대 후반에 들어서자 지질학자들은 세계 곳곳을 살펴보고 꽤 놀라운 증거들을 밝혀내기 시작했어요. 지질학자들은 대략 7억 5천만 년 전부터 5억 8천만 년 전까지의 시기에 형성된 암석을 조사하여 발견했죠. 빙하가 지구 표면 전체를 덮고 있었던 것 같다고. 열대지방을 비롯해 북극부터 남극까지 전체가 말이죠.

음, 지질학자들은 어떻게 이런 놀라운 결론을 내리게 되었을까요? 그 증거는 무엇이었을까요? 특히 오늘날 빙하는 극지방이나 산지에서나 볼 수 있는데 말이에요.

자, 어, 기본적으로 빙하가 커져 움직이면 뚜렷한 퇴적물을 남기게 됩니다. 퇴적물의 성분은 주로, 최소한 꼭대기에는 잘게 부서진 암석조각을 남기는데 대체로…. 혹시 전에 본 적이 있다면, 시내가 흐르면서 퇴적되는 암석들과 아주 흡사하죠. 빙하 퇴적물이 생기는 이유는 빙하가 얼음인데도 실제로 아주 서서히 이동하기 때문이에요. 빙하가 이동하면서 암석의 표층을 으깨는데 이때 떨어져 나온 암석 조각들을 빙하가 운반합니다. 그래서 빙하 작용이 있는 곳에서 '표석(漂石)'이라는 독특한 유형의 암석조각들을 볼 수 있어요.

표석은 암석이에요. 흔히 빙하가 먼 곳까지 운반해온 돌이죠.

그래서 1960년대 이후 1990년대까지 빙하작용을 입증하는 증거를 꾸준히 발견했습니다. 지역에 상관없이 심지어 열대지방에서도 발견했죠. 자, 오늘날에도 열대지방에 빙하가 있지만 해발이 아주 높은 지역에만 있죠. 하지만 7억 5천만 년 전에는 분명히 열대지방의 해수면에도 빙하가 있었답니다.

어떻게 이런 일이 가능했을까요?

자, 우선 빙하의 확장은 음, 말하자면 '빙하-알베도 효과'라는 일종의 양성 피드백 고리의 도움을 받습니다.

빙하는 흰색이라서 빙하-알베도 효과 때문에 빛과 열을 물보다 훨씬 더 많이 반사하죠. 또는 어두운 색이라 열을 흡수하는 토양이나 암석보다도 더 많이 반사합니다. 따라서 빙하가 많은 곳일수록 더 많은 열이 반사되어 기후가 점점 서늘해지고 빙하도 훨씬 더 커지게 됩니다.

하지만 보통 세계적으로 빙하의 확장을 억제하도록 작용하는 중요한 과정이 있어요. 그리고 이 과정은 이산화탄소와 관련이 있죠.

자, 이산화탄소가 소위 '온실가스'라는 건 다들 익히 알고 있을 겁니다. 대기 중에 이산화탄소가 많을수록 대기 중에 더 많은 열이 보존되는데요. 이것이 바로 온실가스가 하는 일이죠. 따라서 온실가스 효과는 알베도 효과의

retains. That's what a greenhouse gas does. So, the greenhouse-gas effect is kinda the opposite of the albedo effect.

Now as it happens … when silicate rocks, which is a very common class of rock, when they're exposed to the air and to normal weathering, they erode. Carbon dioxide is attracted to these eroding rocks and binds to them, forming calcium carbonate.

Calcium carbonate is eventually washed into the ocean where it settles to the bottom. This process, this forming of calcium carbonate, has the effect of sucking the carbon dioxide out of the air and storing it at the bottom of the ocean.

Now, follow me here. The process that's sucking carbon dioxide out of the air, keeping the greenhouse gas levels low, cannot happen if the rock is covered with ice.

So, while glaciers reflect light and heat … cooling the Earth, they at the same time cover rocks so there's less calcium carbonate formed … which leaves more carbon dioxide in the atmosphere. Higher levels of carbon dioxide keep the atmosphere warm … which slows the growth of glaciers. So, it's a balance, and the glacier growth remains pretty much under control.

Now, what happened 750 million years ago to upset that balance? It seems a relatively simple explanation actually …

750 million years ago … all the major continents are rocky, bare, and pretty much lined up along the equator; they hadn't yet moved to where they are today. So, what happened was, perhaps a slight cooling of … the very slight and temporary cooling of the Sun—which still happens from time to time—and the Earth starts to cool, the ice starts to spread on the oceans … starting at the poles.

Now, by the time the ice reaches about two-thirds of the way to the equator, it's too late.

See … because the continents are the last things to be covered by glaciers, they continue weathering … the rocks keep eroding and the carbon dioxide levels keep falling …

So, the ice-albedo effect from the glaciers is increasing in strength while the atmosphere continues to lose its ability to retain heat making glacier growth unstoppable. Now you have what's called a "runaway freeze." And for perhaps as long as 50 million years, possibly with some interludes, the Earth was frozen from pole to pole, like a giant snowball.

반대라고 할 수 있죠.

가장 흔한 암석인 규산염 암이 대기에 노출되어 정상적인 풍화과정을 통해 침식되는데요. 이산화탄소는 이처럼 침식된 암석에 달라붙어 결합해 탄산칼슘을 형성하죠.

결국 탄산칼슘은 바다까지 씻겨 내려와 해저로 가라앉는데요. 탄산칼슘이 형성되는 이 과정은 대기 중의 이산화탄소를 빨아들여 해저에 저장하는 효과가 있어요.

자, 잘 들어요. 대기 중의 이산화탄소를 빨아들여 온실가스 수치를 낮게 유지하는 과정은 암석이 얼음으로 덮여 있으면 절대 일어날 수 없는 과정이죠.

따라서 빙하가 빛과 열을 반사하면 지구가 서늘해지는데 동시에 빙하가 암석을 덮고 있어서 탄산칼슘이 덜 형성되고 그러면 대기 중에 더 많은 이산화탄소가 남게 되어요. 이산화탄소 수치가 높아지면 대기가 따뜻해지고 그 결과 빙하의 확장 속도가 느려집니다. 따라서 균형 작용으로 빙하의 확장을 상당 부분 통제하게 돼요.

그렇다면 7억 5천만 년 전 무슨 일로 균형이 무너졌을까요? 사실 비교적 간단한 설명 같은데요.

7억 5천만 년 전, 큰 대륙들은 하나같이 암석이 많고 맨땅인데다 대부분 적도를 따라 늘어서 있었어요. 게다가 아직 오늘날의 위치로 이동하지 않은 상태였죠. 따라서 당시 발생한 상황이란 태양이 아마도 살짝 서늘해졌을 거예요. 아주 살짝 일시적으로 식은 건데 이런 일은 오늘날에도 가끔 발생해요. 그러면 지구가 식기 시작해서 극지방부터 얼음이 바다를 뒤덮기 시작합니다.

그런데 빙하가 적도까지 3분의 2 정도 도달할 무렵이면 너무 늦어요.

그게 빙하가 마지막으로 덮는 것이 대륙이거든요. 대륙은 지속적인 풍화작용으로 암석이 침식되고 이산화탄소 수치가 계속해서 떨어져요. 따라서 대기가 열을 보존하는 능력을 계속 상실하면서 빙하의 확장이 걷잡을 수 없어지고 빙하의 빙하-알베도 효과가 점점 강력해집니다. 오늘날 이것을 '통제 불가능한 한파' 라고 해요. 그래서 어쩌면 5천만 년이나 되는 긴 시간 동안 몇 번의 간빙기와 함께 남극에서 북극까지 지구 전체가 하나의 커다란 눈덩이처럼 얼어붙어 있었을 거예요.

어휘
....

geologist 지질학자   uncover 드러내다, 폭로하다   glacier 빙하   surface 표면, 표층   tropics 열대지방   astonishing 놀라운   distinctive 독특한, 구별되는   deposit 침전물, 퇴적물   grind 잘게 부수다, 마멸시키다   glaciation 빙하 작용, 빙결   erratic (빙하에 의한) 표석   latitude 위도, 지역   elevation 고도, 해발 높이   positive feedback loop 양성 피드백 고리, 양의 강화 효과   ice-albedo effect 빙하-알베도 효과   reflect 반사하다   curb 억제[제한]하다   carbon dioxide 이산화탄소   greenhouse gas 온실가스   retain 유지[보유]하다   silicate rock 규산염 암   weathering 풍화작용   erode 침식되다, 마멸되다   calcium carbonate 탄화칼슘   suck 빨아들이다   under control 제어되는, 통제되는   upset 뒤흔들다, 망치다   bare 헐벗은, 노출된   equator 적도   temporary 일시적인   runaway 통제할 수 없는, 고삐 풀린   interlude 사이, 중간

23. 이 강의는 주로 7억 5천만 년 전 지구의 어떤 양상에 관한 것인가?

    Ⓐ 대륙의 위치 변화

    Ⓑ 대기 중의 온실가스 효과

    Ⓒ 해류에 영향을 미친 요소

    Ⓓ 전 지구적 한파의 요인

어휘 continent 대륙, 육지　freeze 혹한, 한파

24. 교수에 따르면, 지질학자들은 열대지방에 존재하는 표석을 어떻게 해석하는가?

    Ⓐ 한때 열대지방의 이산화탄소 수치가 높았음을 보여 준다.

    Ⓑ 지구 전체가 얼어붙었다는 증거다.

    Ⓒ 앞으로 언젠가 지구가 서늘해질 수 있음을 보여 준다.

    Ⓓ 일부 빙하가 열대지방에서 형성되었다는 증거다.

어휘 originate 비롯되다, 시작되다

25. 빙하-알베도 효과란?

    Ⓐ 바닷속의 이산화탄소로 지구온난화의 균형이 유지된다.

    Ⓑ 대기 중에 보존된 태양 복사열이 빙하를 녹인다.

    Ⓒ 대기에서 엄청난 양의 이산화탄소가 제거된다.

    Ⓓ 빙하가 반사한 열이 빙하의 확장을 돕는다.

어휘 solar radiation 태양 복사열　remove 없애다, 제거하다
　　　reflection 반사, 반향

26. 이산화탄소와 규산염 암은 어떤 관계인가?

    Ⓐ 규산염 암은 대부분 이산화탄소로 이루어진다.

    Ⓑ 규산염 암 때문에 이산화탄소가 발생한다.

    Ⓒ 규산염 암의 침식으로 대기 중의 이산화탄소 수치가 감소한다.

    Ⓓ 규산염 암이 형성되면 바다에 이산화탄소가 없어진다.

어휘 be composed of ~로 구성되다　erosion 침식, 부식

27. 7억 5천만 년 전 통제 불가능한 한파가 발생하게 된 지구의 한 가지 특징은?

    Ⓐ 바다의 이산화탄소 수치가 낮았다.

    Ⓑ 대륙들이 적도 가까이에 있었다.

    Ⓒ 빙하가 이동하면서 엄청난 양의 암석을 운반했다.

    Ⓓ 대기 중의 온실가스 수치가 높았다.

어휘 quantity 양, 수량

28. 강의의 일부를 다시 듣고 질문에 답하라.

 T-61

> P　Well, uh ... basically when glaciers grow and move they leave behind a distinctive deposit consisting of primarily ... of, at least on the top level, of ground up little bits of rock ... almost ... they almost look like rocks that have been deposited by streams, if you've ever seen those.
>
> N　*Why does the professor say this:*
> P　... they almost look like rocks that have been deposited by streams, if you've ever seen those.

    Ⓐ 낯선 사물을 친근한 사물에 비유하기 위해

    Ⓑ 사신의 주장과 모순되는 증거를 밝히기 위해

    Ⓒ 빙하 퇴적물이 어떤 형태를 띠는지 불확실하다는 길 보여 주기 위해

    Ⓓ 학생들에게 개울의 암석들을 조사하도록 만들기 위해

어휘 unfamiliar 낯선, 생소한　contradict 모순되다, 부정하다
　　　uncertainty 불확실성, 확신이 없음

SPEAKING

Question 1

p.158

Narrator T-62

When some people visit a city or country for the first time, they prefer to take an organized tour. Other people prefer to explore new places on their own. Which do you prefer and why?

처음으로 낯선 도시나 나라를 방문할 때 단체여행을 선호하는 사람이 있는가 하면 스스로 새로운 곳을 탐험하려는 사람도 있다. 어느 쪽을 선호하는가, 그리고 그 이유는?

준비 시간 : 15초
답변 시간 : 45초

중요 포인트

이 질문에 정답은 없다. 어느 쪽을 선택하든지 자신의 의견을 명확히 밝히고 뒷받침할 수 있는 여러 가지 이유를 제시해야 한다. 단체여행이 더 좋다고 생각한다면, "A tour is better, especially if you do not know much about the new place. You might not know where to go or what to see. Plus, the guide will have more knowledge than you do." (새로운 장소에 대해 잘 모르므로 단체여행이 더 낫다. 관광할 장소나 대상을 모를 수 있고 더욱이 여행가이드가 더 많은 정보를 알고 있을 것이다.")라고 말할 수 있다. 혼자서 떠났던 여행 경험을 구체적인 예로 드는 것도 좋다.

스스로 새로운 곳을 탐험하는 것이 더 좋다면, "A tour would limit you, because you would be told where to go. There might be a situation where you want to stay in one place for a longer time, but the tour would not allow this." ("단체여행은 목적지를 정해 주므로 제약이 있다. 한곳에서 오래 머무르고 싶어도 단체여행에서는 불가능하다.")라고 설명할 수 있다. 이 경우 혼자 여행하면서 좋았던 이유를 구체적인 예로 설명하는 것이 좋다.

Question 2

p.158

Narrator T-63

A university professor is switching to a new position. Read the article from the university about the professor. You will have 45 seconds to read the article. Begin reading now.

한 대학 교수가 새로운 보직으로 옮기려고 한다. 그 교수에 관해 대학이 실은 기사를 45초 동안 읽으시오. 지금 읽으시오.

Professor Fox Accepts New Position

We are happy to announce that Professor Fox will be filling the vacant Dean of Students position. Strong organizational skills are important for this position. Professor Fox has demonstrated such skills in her role as Head of the Philosophy Department, where she has coordinated department affairs for five years. Additionally, the Dean of Students must be someone who is able to work well with students, since responsibilities include counseling and advising students who are dealing with personal problems. As our head women's soccer coach, Professor Fox has proven to be a supportive role model for team members, always offering assistance when they ask for personal guidance.

폭스 교수 새로운 보직 수락

폭스 교수가 공석인 학생처장 자리를 맡게 되었음을 발표하게 되어 기쁩니다. 이 직위는 체계적인 일 처리 능력이 중요한 자리입니다. 폭스 교수는 철학과 학과장으로서 5년 동안 과 업무를 조정하며 이러한 능력 보여 주었습니다. 덧붙여 학생처장은 학생들과 원만하게 일할 수 있는 사람이어야 합니다. 개인적인 문제로 찾아온 학생들을 상담하고 조언하는 것도 학생처장의 책무이기 때문입니다. 폭스 교수는 여학생 축구팀의 수석코치로서 팀원들이 개별적인 지도를 부탁하면 언제나 도와주는 등 주변에 힘이 되는 귀감임이 입증되었습니다.

어휘

vacant 비어 있는, 공석의 Dean of Students 학생처장 position 지위, 자리 organizational skill 조직력, 조직 기술 Head of Philosophy Department 철학과 주임교수 coordinate 조정하다, 조직화하다 additionally 게다가 supportive 도와주는, 힘을 주는 assistance 도움, 지원

Narrator T-64

Now listen to two students discussing the article.

기사에 관해 두 학생이 나누는 대화를 들으시오.

Script

F I don't like this at all.

M Why not? She's done a lot for the philosophy department … like, well, hiring some great new teaching assistants … and putting together seminars.

F Well, she has trouble organizing schedules.

M Whadda'ya mean?

F Well, she only realized last minute that she didn't have enough teaching assistants in the department, so some classes got cancelled.

M Oh!

F And I wanted to take a special two-week philosophy course in Europe … she was supposed to sign all the paperwork, but she didn't do it in time so I missed the whole trip!

M Oh, wow. So organization's not her strong point, I guess.

F Yeah. Besides, she's always critical. A lot of us on the team have complained to the university about her aggressive coaching style.

M Oh, really? I met her … I mean, I thought she was nice.

F Humph! Well, my friend … she had some serious problems in her family. She went to talk to Professor Fox and …

M Yeah? What happened?

F Well, she wanted emotional support from someone she looked up to, but instead Professor Fox made all kinds of critical comments. Maybe she's good at philosophy, but she's not a counselor. When students go to the dean, they go because they need someone to talk to, not so someone can criticize them.

F 정말 마음에 안 들어.

M 왜 그래? 폭스 교수님은 철학과를 위해 많은 일을 하셨어. 있잖아 음, 훌륭한 새 조교들도 채용하시고 세미나도 준비하시고.

F 그게, 일정을 엉망으로 짜시거든.

M 무슨 말이야?

F 음, 교수님이 철학과 조교가 부족하다는 걸 막판에 아셔서 강좌 몇 개가 취소됐어.

M 저런!

F 그리고 내가 2주간 유럽에서 철학 특별과정을 듣고 싶었는데 그러려면 모든 문서에 폭스 교수님의 서명이 필요하거든. 그런데 교수님이 제때 처리하지 않아서 그 과정 전체를 놓쳤어!

M 세상에. 그렇다면 체계적인 일 처리가 강점은 아니겠구나.

F 맞아. 게다가 늘 비판적이셔. 축구팀의 상당수 학생들이 폭스 교수의 공격적인 지도 스타일에 대해 대학에 항의했어.

M 어, 정말? 나도 교수님을 뵀는데 친절하시던데.

F 흥! 음, 내 친구는 집안에 심각한 문제가 있었어. 그 친구가 상담하러 폭스 교수님을 찾아갔는데….

M 그래? 어떻게 됐어?

F 음, 친구는 자신이 존경하는 사람에게 정서적으로 위로 받고 싶었어. 하지만 폭스 교수님은 위로 대신 온갖 잔소리만 늘어놓으셨지. 교수님이 훌륭한 철학자일지는 모르지만 상담자는 아니야. 학생들이 학생처장을 찾아갈 땐 대화 상대가 필요해서야. 잔소리하는 사람이 아니고.

어휘

teaching assistant 조교   Whadda'ya mean?=what do you mean? 무슨 말이야? cancel 취소하다 philosophy 철학 critical 비판적인, 비난하는 aggressive 공격적인 emotional 감정적인, 정서적인 look up to ~을 존경하다, 우러러보다   comment 언급, 논평 counselor 상담자, 카운슬러 criticize 비판[비난]하다

Narrator

The woman expresses her opinion about the change described in the article. Briefly summarize the change. Then state her opinion about the change and explain the reasons she gives for holding that opinion.

여자가 기사에 실린 변화에 대해 의견을 말하고 있다. 변화의 내용을 간략히 요약한 다음 여자의 의견이 무엇이며 그런 입장을 취하는 이유를 설명하시오.

준비 시간 : 30초
답변 시간 : 60초

중요 포인트

여학생이 폭스 교수를 공석인 학생처장 자리에 임명한다는 대학의 결정에 동의하지 않는다는 사실을 말한 후, 그런 입장을 취하는 두 가지 중요한 이유를 설명해야 한다. 완벽한 답변을 위해 두 학생의 대화 내용과 기사에서 알게 된 정보를 연결해야 한다.

여학생은 폭스 교수를 학생처장으로 임명하는 첫 번째 이유, 다시 말해 폭스 교수의 일 처리가 뛰어나다는 건 타당하지 않다고 말한다. 폭스 교수가 철학과 조교를 충분히 확보하지 못해 강좌 몇 개가 취소되었고, 서류를 제때 처리하지 않아서 여학생이 유럽에서 진행되는 철학 특별과정을 놓쳤다는 사례를 설명해야 한다.

여학생이 대학의 결정에 동의하지 않는 두 번째 이유 역시 설명해야 한다. 여학생은 폭스 교수가 학생들을 잘 다룰 수 있는 사람이라는 데 동의하지 않는다. 이를 뒷받침하고자 여학생은 폭스 교수의 공격적인 지도 스타일을 이유로 든다. 또한 여학생은 위로가 필요한 한 친구에게 폭스 교수가 비판만 했다는 예도 든다. 이러한 사례에서 폭스 교수가 훌륭한 학생처장이 될 수 없을 것이라는 여학생의 견해를 알 수 있다.

121

답변에는 여학생이 대학의 결정에 동의하지 않는 두 가지 이유가 모두 제시되어야 한다. 그렇다고 지문의 내용을 일일이 상세하게 설명하거나 한 가지 이유에만 너무 치중해서도 안 된다. 충분한 시간을 갖고 두 가지 이유를 모두 설명해야 한다.

Question 3

p.159

Narrator T-65

Read the following paragraph from a psychology textbook. You will have 45 seconds to read the passage. Begin reading now.

심리학 교재의 지문을 45초 동안 읽으시오. 지금 읽으시오.

Critical Period

It is generally believed that for many organisms, there is a specific time period, a so-called "window of opportunity," during which the organism must receive crucial input from its environment in order for normal development to occur. This period is called the *critical period*. If the needed environmental input is not received during this period, the normal development of certain physical attributes or behaviors may never occur. In other words, if the organism is not provided with the needed stimulus or influence during the critical period, it may permanently lose the capacity to ever obtain a particular physical attribute or behavior.

임계기

많은 생물에게는 이른바 '기회의 창'이라는 특정 기간이 있다는 것이 일반적인 믿음이다. 말하자면 생물이 정상적으로 발달하려면 이 기간 동안 환경에서 중요한 자극을 받아야 한다는 것이다. 이 기간을 임계기라고 한다. 이 기간 동안 환경에서 자극을 받지 못하면 특정한 신체적 특징이나 행동이 결코 정상적으로 발달하지 못할 수도 있다. 다시 말해 임계기 동안 생물이 필요한 자극이나 영향을 받지 못하면 특정한 신체적 특징이나 행동을 습득할 수 있는 능력을 영원히 상실할 수 있다.

어휘

critical period 임계기 organism 생물, 유기체 specific 특정한,

구체적인 crucial 중대한, 결정적인 input 투입, 제공 physical 신체의, 육체의 attribute 속성, 특질 behavior 행동, 습성 stimulus 자극 influence 영향 permanently 영구히, 불변으로 capacity 능력, 잠재력

Narrator T-66

Now listen to part of a lecture in a psychology class.

심리학 강의의 일부를 들으시오.

(Script)

P Let's start with a physical attribute, say, uh, in kittens. Adult cats have extremely good vision, especially at night. But in order for a kitten's eyesight to develop normally, the kitten must be exposed to light during the first four months of its life. Without that, its eyesight will not develop correctly, it will never be able to see as well as it should. Even if the kitten is exposed to plenty of light *after* those four months of darkness, it won't matter, its vision will *never* develop normally.

As far as behavior's concerned, well, have you ever seen how little baby geese line up and then, single-file, they follow their parent goose around? Well, what would happen if they didn't see a parent goose within the first two days of their lives?

Actually, for normal behavior to develop, they must see what to follow within these first two days. What happens is, whatever large moving object they first see during those two days, they'll adopt that object as their parent ... forever. It can never be changed. For example, suppose after the baby geese were hatched, the only other animal around was, I don't know, say a dog. OK? So the baby geese see a dog, but no other geese. Even though the dog is a totally different species, the geese will adopt it as their parent—they'll follow it around. And even if the parent geese reappear later, it won't matter to the babies—they'll follow the dog. After two days the behavior is fixed and they'll never exhibit the normal behavior of following their real parent—a goose.

P 자, 새끼 고양이의 신체적 특징부터 이야기할게요. 어른 고양이는 시력이 아주 좋습니다. 특히 밤에 더 그렇죠. 하지만 새끼 고양이의 시력이 정상적으로 발달하려면 생후 4개월 동안 빛에 노출되어야 합니다. 그렇지 않으면 결코 정상 시력만큼 잘 볼 수 없을 겁니다. 생후 4개월간 어둠 속에 있다가 나중에 많은 빛에 노출돼도 소용없어요. 결코 시력이 정상적으로 발달하지 못합니다.

자, 특정 행동을 예로 들자면 새끼 거위들이 일렬종대로 줄지어 어미 거위 뒤를 졸졸 따라다니는 모습을 본 적이 있나요? 음, 만약 새끼 거위들이 생후 이틀 내에 어미를 보지 못하면 어떻게 될까요?

실제로 정상적인 행동발달이 나타나려면 새끼 거위들이 생후 이틀 내에 따라갈 상대를 보아야 합니다. 새끼 거위들은 생후 이틀 사이에 처음 보는 움직이는 커다란 물체가 무엇이든 그 물체를 어미로 받아들입니다. 영원히 말이죠. 절대 변하지 않습니다. 가령 새끼 거위들이 알에서 깨어난 뒤 주변에 다른 동물이라고는 없고, 뭐라고 할까요, 개 한 마리뿐이었다고 합시다. 알겠죠? 그러면 새끼 거위들은 개만 보고 다른 거위들을 보지 못하겠죠. 비록 개가 거위와 전혀 다른 종이지만 새끼들은 개를 어미로 받아들이고 주변을 졸졸 따라다닐 거예요. 그리고 나중에 어미 거위가 다시 나타난다 해도 새끼들은 아랑곳하지 않고 개를 따라갈 겁니다. 생후 이틀 후면 이 행동이 고정되기 때문에 진짜 어미인 거위를 따라가는 정상적인 행동이 결코 나타나지 않습니다.

어휘

extremely 극히, 극심하게   eyesight 시력   be exposed to ~에 노출되다   single-file 한 줄로, 일렬종대로   adopt 받아들이다, 취하다   hatch 부화하다   reappear 다시 나타나다   exhibit 나타내다, 보이다

Narrator

Using the examples of kittens and geese, explain the idea of a critical period.

새끼 고양이와 거위의 예를 활용해 임계기의 개념을 설명하시오.

준비 시간 : 30초
답변 시간 : 60초

중요 포인트

우선 지문에 설명된 임계기의 개념을 설명해야 한다. 임계기는 많은 생물에게 필요한 특정 기간이다. 즉 생물이 정상적으로 발달하려면 이 기간 동안 외부 환경이 제공하는 중요한 자극을 공급 받아야 한다. 하지만 지문의 모든 내용을 요약하느라 시간을 많이 허비해서는 안 된다.

그 다음 교수가 임계기를 설명하기 위해 제시한 예를 사용해야 한다. 첫 번째 예에서 교수는 신체적 특징에 영향을 미치는 임계기를 설명한다. 고양이의 경우 생후 4개월 내에 빛에 노출되지 않으면 시력이 정상적으로 발달하지 않는다. 두 번째 예에서 교수는 특정 행동에 영향을 미치는 임계기를 설명한다. 새끼 거위의 경우 생후 이틀 내에 처음으로 본 움직이는 커다란 물체를 어미로 받아들인다. 그래서 심지어 전혀 다른 종인데도 새끼 거위는 처음으로 본 물체를 어미로 따른다. 그리고 나중에 진짜 어미 거위가 나타난다 해도 이 행동은 바뀌지 않는다.

Question 4

p.160

Narrator T-67

Now listen to part of a lecture in a business ethics class. The professor is discussing advertising.

기업 윤리 강의의 일부를 들으시오. 교수는 광고에 대해 이야기하고 있다.

P Advertisers often try to sell you things by exaggerating about the quality of their products. It helps them get your attention. And exaggeration in advertising is usually considered acceptable, but not always. In the United States, there are laws to help determine what advertisers can say about their products. Basically, the law says advertisers can exaggerate as long as no one's gonna actually believe the exaggeration and take it literally. So, the exaggeration has to be very extreme. If it's not extreme enough and someone would actually buy the product because they believed the exaggeration, that advertisement may be illegal.

Take this example: a vacuum cleaner manufacturer made a vacuum cleaner that didn't weigh very much, and they wanted to get the point across about how light it was. So they made a TV commercial showing the vacuum cleaner floating in the air while cleaning the house. Well, that was a visual exaggeration. It got people's attention. And because a floating vacuum cleaner is obviously impossible, the commercial was legal because no one would actually believe the visual exaggeration and buy the vacuum cleaner because they thought it floated in the air.

But what if the company wanted to show that the vacuum cleaner was very powerful? What if it made a television commercial where a person uses the vacuum cleaner to perfectly clean this really big and really dirty carpet in, uh, just a few seconds. Well that would really grab your attention. But the thing is, even though that the commercial is an exaggeration, you can imagine someone actually believing it and buying the vacuum cleaner and then being very disappointed because the vacuum cleaner couldn't do that. So advertisers can't use an exaggeration like that because it's actually not extreme enough and someone might believe it.

P 흔히 광고주들은 제품의 품질을 과장해서 소비자에게 판매하려고 합니다. 그래야 소비자들의 관심을 끌 수 있거든요. 보통은 과장광고가 용인되는 것으로 보지만 항상 그렇지만은 아니에요. 미국에는 광고주들이 제품에 대해 말할 수 있는 내용을 판단하도록 도와주는 법이 있어요. 기본적으로 이 법에 따르면, 소비자가 실제로 과장된 내용을 믿거나 있는 그대로 받아들이지 않는 한 광고주들이 과장할 수 있습니다. 따라서 과장된 내용이 아주 극단적이어야 해요. 그렇지 않으면 어떤 사람들은 과장된 내용을 믿고 실제로 제품을 살 수도 있거든요. 그러면 그 광고는 불법이 될 수 있죠.

예를 들죠. 진공청소기 제조사가 무겁지 않은 진공청소기를 만들었는데 청소기가 가볍다는 점을 중점적으로 전달하고 싶었어요. 그래서 집안을 청소하는 동안 공중에 진공청소기가 둥둥 떠다니는 TV 광고를 만들었어요. 음, 시각적인 과장이었죠. 이 광고는 사람들의 눈길을 끌었어요. 누가 봐도 진공청소기가 둥둥 떠다니는 건 불가능하기 때문에 그 광고는 합법이었죠. 시각적인 과장을 정말 믿고 진공청소기가 공중에 떠다닌다고 생각해서 청소기를 살 사람은 없으니까요.

하지만 제조사가 진공청소기의 강력한 성능을 보여 주고 싶었다면 어땠을까요? 한 사람이 진공청소기로 정말 크고 아주 더러운 카펫을 음, 그것도 단 몇 초 만에 완벽하게 청소하는 TV 광고를 만들었다면? 이 광고 역시 정말 관심을 끌었을 거예요. 하지만 광고가 과장임에도 불구하고 누군가 정말로 광고를 믿고 진공청소기를 샀는데 청

소기의 성능이 광고와 달라 크게 실망하는 그런 일이 있겠죠. 따라서 광고주들은 실제로 지나치게 극단적이지 않아서 사람들이 믿을 수 있는 이런 과장은 할 수 없어요.

Narrator

Using the example of the vacuum cleaner, explain when it is legally acceptable to use exaggeration in advertising and when it is not.

진공청소기의 예를 사용해서 과장광고가 합법으로 용인되는 경우와 그렇지 않은 경우를 설명하시오.

준비 시간 : 20초
답변 시간 : 60초

중요 포인트

먼저 강의 내용을 요약해야 한다. 즉 과장광고에 대해 말해야 하는데 합법적인 과장광고와 불법적인 과장광고를 예로 들어 설명해야 한다.

처음에는 강의의 일반적인 내용으로 시작해야 한다. 가령 광고에서 과장은 아무도 믿을 수 없을 만큼 아주 극단적이어야 한다고 말한다. 그 다음 교수가 제시한 첫 번째 예를 설명하는 것이다. 청소기가 가볍다는 점을 중점적으로 전달하고 싶은 광고주가 진공청소기가 공중에 떠다니는 TV 광고를 선보였다. 이런 식의 광고는 진짜로 진공청소기가 공중에 떠다닌다고 믿는 사람이 아무도 없기 때문에 합법적이다.

그 다음 교수가 제시한 두 번째 예를 설명해야 한다. 교수는 크고 더러운 카펫을 단 몇 초 만에 완벽하게 청소하는 진공청소기 광고가 과장광고이며 사람들이 진짜로 믿을 수 있기 때문에 용인될 수 없다고 말한다. 누군가 청소기를 사서 광고와 성능이 다르다며 실망할 수도 있기 때문이다.

WRITING

Writing Based on Reading and Listening

p.162

Many people dream of owning their own business but are afraid of the risks. Instead of starting a new business, however, one can buy a franchise. A franchise is a license issued by a large, usually well-known, company to a small business owner. Under the license, the owner acquires the right to use the company's brand name and agrees to sell its products. In return, the franchising company receives a percent of the sales.

A major problem for first-time business owners is finding reliable suppliers of the goods and services they need: equipment, raw materials, maintenance, etc. It is easy to choose the wrong supplier, and doing so can be costly. Buying a franchise eliminates much of this problem. Most franchising companies have already found reliable suppliers, and franchise contracts typically specify which suppliers are to be used. This protects franchise owners from the risk of serious losses.

Another advantage of a franchise is that it can save a new business a lot of money on advertising. Advertising one's product to potential customers is a crucial factor in a business's success. A franchise owner, however, sells an already popular and recognized brand and also gets the benefit of sophisticated and expensive advertising paid by the parent company.

Finally, a franchise offers more security than starting an independent (nonfranchise) business. The failure rate for starting independent businesses is very high during the first few years; the failure rate for starting franchises is much lower. Finding one's own way in today's competitive business environment is difficult, and buying a franchise allows an inexperienced business owner to use a proven business model.

많은 사람들이 자기 사업체 소유를 꿈꾸면서도 위험을 두려워한다. 하지만 새로운 사업을 시작하는 대신 프랜차이즈를 살 수 있다. 프랜차이즈는 보통 유명한 대기업이 소규모 자영업자에게 발행하는 인가증이다. 이 인가증으로 자영업자는 대기업의 상표명을 사용할 권리를 갖고 제품을 판매하는 데 합의한다. 그 대가로 프랜차이즈 회사는 매상에서 일정 비율을 가져간다.

처음 창업하는 사람들에게 가장 큰 문제는 필요한 제품과 서비스를 제공할 믿을 만한 납품업체를 찾는 일이다. 즉 장비, 원자재, 보수 유지 등을 믿고 맡길 곳이 필요하다. 하지만 잘못된 납품업체를 선택하기가 쉽고 그러다 보면 비용이 많이 나갈 수 있다. 프랜차이즈를 사면 이런 문제가 상당 부분 없어진다. 대부분의 프랜차이즈 회사는 이

미 믿을 만한 납품업체를 확보하고 있으며, 보통 프랜차이즈 계약서에 어떤 납품업체를 쓸 지 상세히 명시한다. 이를 통해 프랜차이즈 가맹주가 막대한 손실을 입지 않도록 보호한다.

프랜차이즈의 또 다른 이점은 새로운 사업에 들어가는 엄청난 광고비를 절약할 수 있다는 것이다. 잠재 고객에게 상품을 광고하는 것은 사업 성공의 결정적인 요인이다. 하지만 프랜차이즈 가맹주는 이미 대중적이고 알려진 브랜드를 팔고 모기업이 돈을 들여 제작한 세련되고 값비싼 광고로 덕을 본다.

마지막으로 프랜차이즈는 (프랜차이즈가 아닌) 자영업을 시작할 때보다 훨씬 더 안전하다. 자영업의 경우 처음 몇 년간 실패할 확률이 매우 높지만 프랜차이즈로 시작하면 실패 확률이 훨씬 낮다. 오늘날의 경쟁적인 사업 환경에서 독자적인 길을 찾기가 어려운데 프랜차이즈를 사면 경험이 부족한 사업주는 검증된 사업모델을 활용할 수 있다.

어휘

risk 위험 franchise 프랜차이즈, 가맹점 영업권 license 허가증, 인가증 small business owner 소규모 자영업자 acquire 취득하다, 얻다 reliable 신뢰할 수 있는, 믿을 만한 supplier 공급자, 납품업체 equipment 장비, 용품 raw material 원자재, 원료 maintenance 유지, 보수 관리 eliminate 없애다, 제거하다 contract 계약, 계약서 typically 보통, 일반적으로 specify (구체적으로) 명시하다 potential customer 잠재 고객 crucial 중대한, 결정적인 sophisticated 세련된 security 안전, 보안 competitive 경쟁의, 경쟁적인 inexperienced 경험이 부족한, 미숙한

Narrator 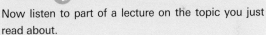 T-68

Now listen to part of a lecture on the topic you just read about.

방금 읽은 주제에 관한 강의의 일부를 들으시오.

Script

P Many people think that if you want to go into business for yourself, it's best to buy a franchise. But recently a study looked closely at franchises, and some of the findings call that idea into question.

One interesting point was that many franchise contracts force franchise owners to ... to buy very specific goods and services, and those goods and services tend to be overpriced. In other words, even though there are equivalent goods and services available on the market, uh, that are considerably cheaper, the owners aren't *allowed* to buy them.

Another point was about advertising. When you buy a franchise, you agree to pay up to six percent of your sum total in sales—that's quite a lot of money. One thing you're supposed to get in return for this money is that the company does the advertising for you. But the company doesn't advertise your business. What gets advertised is the *company's* brand, the *company's* products, which are sold by many other businesses in many other places. It turns out, individual franchise owners mostly get very little benefit—*much* less than they would get by spending even half that money to advertise their own business directly.

Finally, the biggest issue: security. Starting a franchise is not the most secure option out there. True, it's less risky than starting an independent business. But there's a *third* option that the passage didn't talk about. You can buy an *already existing independent* business from a previous owner. And the study showed that independent businesses bought from previous owners have *twice* as much chance of success during the first four years as franchises.

P   자기 사업을 하고 싶으면 프랜차이즈를 사는 것이 최선이라고 많은 이들이 생각합니다. 하지만 최근 프랜차이즈를 면밀히 조사한 연구에서 이런 생각에 의문을 던지는 몇 가지 점이 발견되었어요.

한 가지 흥미로운 점은 많은 프랜차이즈 계약서에 가맹주가 특정 제품과 서비스를 구매해야 하는 강제조항이 있는데 그런 제품과 서비스의 가격이 높게 책정되는 경향이 있습니다. 다시 말해 시장에서 동질의 제품과 서비스를 상당히 저렴하게 이용할 수 있는데도 가맹주는 그런 제품을 살 수가 없습니다.

또 한 가지 점은 광고입니다. 프랜차이즈를 사면 총 매출의 6퍼센트를 지불한다는 합의사항이 있어요. 꽤 많은 돈이죠. 이 돈을 내는 대가로 받는 것이 바로 회사가 하는 광고예요. 하지만 회사는 가맹주의 사업을 광고하는 게 아니에요. 광고되는 것은 회사의 브랜드와 회사의 제품인데 이것들은 이미 많은 곳에서 다른 사업주들이 판매하고 있죠. 프랜차이즈 가맹주 개인이 얻는 혜택은 거의 없는 것으로 나타났어요. 절반의 비용으로 자기 사업체를 직접 광고하는 것보다 훨씬 못하다는 겁니다.

마지막으로 가장 큰 문제인데요. 바로 안전성이에요. 프랜차이즈를 시작하는 것이 가장 안전한 선택이 아니거든요. 사실이에요. 프랜차이즈가 자영업을 시작하는 것보다는 덜 위험해요. 하지만 앞의 글에서 언급하지 않은 제3의 선택이 있어요. 이전 주인에게 기존 사업체를 인수하는 방법이죠. 연구에 따르면, 이전 업주에게 기존 사업체를 인수하는 경우 첫 4년 동안 사업 성공률이 프랜차이즈의 두 배라고 해요.

어휘

go into business 사업에 뛰어들다   overprice 너무 비싼 값을 매기다
equivalent 동등한, 맞먹는   considerably 많이, 상당히   in return for
~의 대가로, ~와 맞바꾸어   turn out ~으로 드러나다   directly 직접적으로   option 선택, 선택권   previous 앞의, 이전의

Narrator T-69

Question 1

Summarize the points made in the lecture, being sure to explain how they challenge specific points made in the reading passage.

방금 들은 강의의 논점들을 요약하되 이 논점들이 독해 지문의 구체적 논점들을 어떻게 반박하고 있는지 설명하시오.

해설

강의를 통해 교수가 지문에 제기된 프랜차이즈 사업의 여러 가지 장점에 동의하지 않는다는 사실을 이해해야 한다. 지문에 제기된 프랜차이즈의 장점은 가맹주가 납품업체를 찾을 필요가 없으며 모기업이 제작한 광고로 이익을 얻는데다 다른 형태의 자영업보다 훨씬 더 안전하다는 것이다.

답안을 작성할 때, 교수가 설명한 대로 프랜차이즈 사업이 자영업자가 되는 최선의 길이 못 되는 이유들을 언급해야 한다. 고득점을 받으려면 교수가 지문에서 의구심을 가졌던 다음의 내용들을 포함하여 대답해야 한다.

지문의 주요 내용	지문과 대조되는 강의 내용
Since franchising companies have already selected reliable suppliers for franchise owners to use, a new franchise owner does not run the risk of working with unreliable suppliers.	A franchise owner is forced to use the suppliers identified by the parent company. Such suppliers often charge too much for their goods and services. A franchise owner cannot use cheaper suppliers that may be available.
Franchise owners save money on advertising because they sell well-known brands and because they get the benefit of advertising paid for by the parent companies.	In fact, franchise owners have to pay a portion of their income to the parent company in return for advertising services. However, advertising by the parent company focuses on the brand and not on the owner's individual business. Owners would get greater benefit for less money if they did their own advertising.
Buying a franchise offers very good security. The failure rate of starting franchises is much lower than the failure rate of starting independent businesses.	There is in fact an option for starting business owners that is more secure than buying a franchise: buying an already-existing independent business. Independent businesses bought from previous owners have twice as much chance of success as new franchises.

Writing for an Academic Discussion

p.165

Question 2

Your professor is teaching a class on sociology. Write a post responding to the professor's question.

In your response, you should do the following.

- Express and support your opinion.
- Make a contribution to the discussion in your own words.

An effective response will contain at least 100 words.

Dr. Diaz

As we discuss rules that societies expect their members to follow, let's focus specifically on how young people perceive those rules. Sometimes young people consider those rules to be too strict or unfair, and they take action to try to loosen the rules or change them. How important is it for young people to try to change rules that they consider to be unfair?

Kelly

It is so easy for some young people to get into trouble with illegal things. Parents should create rules to prevent that, and kids should not challenge those rules. Kids do not have the life experience to understand how, for example, their parents' rules about not staying out late at night are helping them stay out of trouble.

Paul

As a young person, I think the society I live in has certain rules that are in many respects unwise and unfair; for example, the rules in my country do not allow teachers to discuss certain controversial subjects in school that are important to young people. Young people should challenge those rules.

교수가 사회학 강의를 진행하고 있다. 교수의 질문에 답하는 게시글을 작성하시오.

답변은 다음 조건을 충족해야 한다.

– 의견을 표명하고 뒷받침하는 근거를 제시한다.
– 독자적인 표현과 관점으로 토론에 기여한다.

어느 정도 완성도를 갖추려면 최소 100단어 이상이어야 한다.

Dr. Diaz

사회가 구성원들이 지키기를 기대하는 규칙에 대해 논의하고 있는데요. 특히 젊은이들이 그런 규칙을 어떻게 인식하는지에 초점을 맞춥시다. 이따금 젊은이들은 그런 규칙이 지나치게 엄격하거나 부당하다고 생각하고, 규칙을 완화하거나 바꾸려고 행동을 취하죠. 젊은이들이 부당하다고 생각하는 규칙을 바꾸려고 노력하는 것이 얼마나 중요한가요?

Kelly

어떤 젊은이는 불법적인 일에 쉽게 휘말립니다. 부모는 이를 방지하기 위해 규칙을 만들어야 하고, 아이들은 그 규칙에 도전하지 말아야 해요. 아이들은 인생 경험이 부족하니까 예를 들면 밤늦게까지 밖에 돌아다니지 말라는 부모의 규칙이 말썽에 휘말리지 않도록 도와준다는 점을 이해하지 못해요.

Paul

젊은이로서 제가 살고 있는 사회에 여러 면에서 어리석고 부당한 규칙들이 있다고 생각해요. 예를 들어 우리나라 규칙에는 젊은이에게 중요하지만 논란거리가 되는 특정 주제에 대해 토론하는 것을 교사가 허용하지 않죠. 젊은이들은 그런 규칙에 도전해야 해요.

해설

젊은이들이 사회적 규칙을 바꾸는 것이 중요한지에 관한 토론이다. 고득점을 받으려면 이러한 토론에 기여하는 논지를 펼치며 답변해야 한다. 어느 정도 완성도를 갖추려면 최소 100단어 이상이어야 한다.

한 토론 참여자는 젊은이들이 규칙을 변경해서는 안 된다고 주장한다. 그 이유는 이러한 규칙을 부모가 정했는데, 부모는 젊은이보다 경험이 많고 규칙을 정한 이유에는 젊은이가 말썽에 휘말리지 않도록 하려는 이유가 포함되어 있기 때문이다. 다른 토론 참여자는 사회가 정한 많은 규칙이 부당하므로 젊은이들이 도전해야 한다고 주장한다. 이미 서술된 개념을 포착해 더 자세히 논지를 전개해도 좋고 전혀 새로운 개념을 선보여도 좋다. 예를 들어 세상은 항상 유동적이므로 젊은이들이 규칙을 바꿔야 하며, 시대가 변하면 규칙도 바뀌어야 한다고 주장할 수 있다.

반드시 자신의 의견을 뒷받침하는 탄탄한 근거와 예시를 제시하고 명확하게 표현해야 한다. 답안이 온라인 게시물 형태로 나타나므로 여러 단락으로 나누어 구성할 필요는 없다. 하지만 개념 간 연관성이 밀접하며 조리 있고 명료해야 한다. 채점은 '학술 토론을 위한 글쓰기 평가 기준(Appendix 참조)'을 토대로 이루어진다.

READING

HABITATS AND CHIPMUNK SPECIES

서식지와 줄무늬다람쥐 종   *p.170*

1. There are eight chipmunk species in the Sierra Nevada mountain range, and most of them look pretty much alike. But eight different species of chipmunks scurrying around a picnic area will not be found. Nowhere in the Sierra do all eight species occur together. Each species tends strongly to occupy a specific habitat type, within an elevational range, and the overlap among them is minimal.

2. The eight chipmunk species of the Sierra Nevada represent but a few of the 15 species found in western North America, yet the whole of eastern North America makes do with but one species: the Eastern chipmunk. Why are there so many very similar chipmunks in the West? The presence of tall mountains interspersed with vast areas of arid desert and grassland makes the West ecologically far different from the East. The West affords much more opportunity for chipmunk populations to become geographically isolated from one another, a condition of species formation. Also, there are more extremes in western habitats. In the Sierra Nevada, high elevations are close to low elevations, at least in terms of mileage, but ecologically they are very different.

3. Most ecologists believe that ancient populations of chipmunks diverged genetically when isolated from one another by mountains and unfavorable ecological habitat. These scattered populations first evolved into races—adapted to the local ecological conditions—and then into species, reproductively isolated from one another. This period of evolution was relatively recent, as evidenced by the similar appearance of all the western chipmunk species.

4. Ecologists have studied the four chipmunk species that occur on the eastern slope of the Sierra and have learned just how these species interact while remaining separate, each occupying its own elevational zone. The sagebrush chipmunk is found at the lowest elevation, among the sagebrush. The yellow pine chipmunk is common in low to mid-elevations and open conifer forests, including pinon and ponderosa and Jeffrey pine forests. The lodgepole chipmunk is found at higher elevations, among the lodgepoles, firs, and high-elevation pines. The alpine chipmunk is higher still, venturing among the talus slopes, alpine meadows, and high-elevation pines and junipers. **(A)** Obviously, the ranges of each species overlap. **(B)** Why don't sagebrush chipmunks move into the pine zones? **(C)** Why don't alpine chipmunks move to lower elevations and share the conifer forests with lodgepole chipmunks? **(D)**

1. 시에라네바다 산맥에는 8종의 줄무늬다람쥐가 서식하는데, 녀석들의 생김새는 비슷비슷하다. 하지만 8종이 한꺼번에 한 유원지 구역을 종종걸음으로 정신없이 돌아다니는 모습은 찾아볼 수 없다. 시에라네바다 산맥 어디에도 8종이 함께 출몰하는 지역은 없다. 각각의 종은 어떤 한 표고 범위 내의 특정한 서식지를 차지하는 경향이 높으며 겹치는 서식지는 아주 미미하다.

2. 시에라네바다 산맥에 서식하는 8종의 줄무늬다람쥐는 북미 서부에서 발견되는 15종 가운데 일부지만, 북미 동부 전역을 통틀어 아쉽게도 동부 줄무늬다람쥐 1종만 서식한다. 서부에는 왜 생김새가 비슷한 다람쥐들이 그렇게 다양한 것일까? 광활하게 펼쳐진 건조한 사막과 초원 속에 분포된 높은 산맥으로 서부의 생태 환경은 동부와 크게 달라졌다. 서부에는 줄무늬다람쥐 개체군들이 지리적으로 서로 고립될 기회, 즉 종이 형성될 수 있는 조건이 훨씬 많았다. 더불어 서부 서식지에는 극단적인 환경이 더 많다. 시에라네바다 산맥의 고지대와 저지대는 거리상으로는 가깝지만, 생태 환경은 크게 다르다.

3. 생태학자들은 줄무늬다람쥐의 조상 개체군이 산맥 및 불리한 생태 서식지에 의해 서로 고립되면서 유전적으로 분화했다고 믿는다. 이렇게 흩어진 개체군들은 우선 그 지역의 환경 조건에 적응한 종족으로 진화한 다음, 서로 격리된 채 번식을 거듭해 분리된 종으로 진화했다. 서부에 서식하는 줄무늬다람쥐 종의 생김새가 전부 비슷비슷한 것으로 보아 이러한 진화는 비교적 최근에 일어났다.

4. 생태학자들은 시에라네바다 산맥 동쪽 사면에 출몰하는 4종의 줄무늬다람쥐를 연구했고, 각각의 종이 서로 떨어져 고유한 표고 범위를 차지하며 어떻게 상호작용하는지 알아냈다. 산쑥 줄무늬다람쥐는 산쑥과의 식물이 자라는 가장 낮은 지대에 서식한다. 옐로우파인 줄무늬다람쥐는 저지대에서 중간 지대까지 피뇽소나무와 폰데로사소나무, 제프리소나무가 듬성듬성 자라는 침엽수림에서 흔히 볼 수 있다. 로지폴 줄무늬다람쥐는 로지폴소나무와 전나무, 고산소나무가 자라는 고지대에 서식한다. 알파인 줄무늬다람쥐는 애추사면, 고산 초원, 고산소나무와 향나무 사이를 누비면서 훨씬 높은 지대에 서식한다. 분명 각 종의 영역들은 겹친다. 산쑥 줄무늬다람쥐는 왜 소나무 숲으로 가지 않을까? 알파인 줄무늬다람쥐는 왜 표고가 더 낮은 곳으로 가서 로지폴 줄무늬다람쥐와 침엽수림을 공유하지 않을까?

5. The answer, in one word, is aggression. Chipmunk species actively defend their ecological zones from encroachment by neighboring species. The yellow pine chipmunk is more aggressive than the sagebrush chipmunk, possibly because it is a bit larger. It successfully bullies its smaller evolutionary cousin, excluding it from the pine forests. Experiments have shown that the sagebrush chipmunk is physiologically able to live anywhere in the Sierra Nevada, from high alpine zones to the desert. The little creature is apparently restricted to the desert not because it is specialized to live only there but because that is the only habitat where none of the other chipmunk species can live. The fact that sagebrush chipmunks tolerate very warm temperatures makes them, and only them, able to live where they do. The sagebrush chipmunk essentially occupies its habitat by default. In one study, ecologists established that yellow pine chipmunks actively exclude sagebrush chipmunks from pine forests; the ecologists simply trapped all the yellow pine chipmunks in a section of forest and moved them out. Sagebrush chipmunks immediately moved in, but yellow pine chipmunks did not enter sagebrush desert when sagebrush chipmunks were removed.

6. The most aggressive of the four eastern-slope species is the lodgepole chipmunk, a feisty rodent indeed. It actively prevents alpine chipmunks from moving downslope, and yellow pine chipmunks from moving upslope. There is logic behind the lodgepole's aggressive demeanor. It lives in the cool, shaded conifer forests, and of the four species, it is the least able to tolerate heat stress. It is, in other words, the species of the strictest habitat needs: it simply must be in those shaded forests. However, if it shared its habitat with alpine and yellow pine chipmunks, either or both of these species might outcompete it, taking most of the available food. Such a competition could effectively eliminate lodgepole chipmunks from the habitat. Lodgepoles survive only by virtue of their aggression.

5. 그 이유는 한마디로 공격성 때문이다. 줄무늬다람쥐들은 이웃 종의 침입으로부터 생태 구역을 적극적으로 방어한다. 옐로우파인 줄무늬다람쥐는 산쑥 줄무늬다람쥐보다 훨씬 더 공격적인데, 아마도 몸집이 약간 더 크기 때문인 듯하다. 옐로우파인 줄무늬다람쥐는 진화상 사촌뻘인 이 작은 동물들을 괴롭혀 소나무 숲에서 내쫓는다. 실험 결과는 산쑥 줄무늬다람쥐가 생리적으로 고산 지대에서 사막까지 시에라네바다 산맥의 어느 곳에서든 서식할 수 있다는 사실을 보여준다. 이 조그만 동물이 사막에 갇혀 살게 된 이유는 원래 사막에서만 살 수 있어서가 아니라 사막이 다른 줄무늬다람쥐들은 살 수 없는 유일한 서식지이기 때문이다. 산쑥 줄무늬다람쥐는 더위를 잘 견딜 수 있기 때문에 지금의 서식지에서, 녀석들끼리만 살게 되었다. 산쑥 줄무늬다람쥐는 싸우지도 않고 남은 서식지를 차지한 셈이다. 한 연구에서 생태학자들은 옐로우파인 줄무늬다람쥐가 산쑥 줄무늬다람쥐를 적극적으로 소나무 숲에서 내쫓는다는 사실을 밝혀냈다. 생태학자들은 옐로우파인 줄무늬다람쥐를 전부 숲 한쪽으로 몬 다음 다른 곳으로 빼냈다. 산쑥 줄무늬다람쥐는 즉시 숲으로 들어갔지만, 옐로우파인 줄무늬다람쥐는 산쑥 줄무늬다람쥐가 사라진 산쑥 사막에 발을 들여놓지 않았다.

6. 동쪽 사면에 서식하는 4종 중에서 가장 공격적인 종은 로지폴 줄무늬다람쥐라는 아주 혈기 왕성한 설치류다. 이 종은 알파인 줄무늬다람쥐는 아래쪽으로 내려오지 못하게, 옐로우파인 줄무늬다람쥐는 위쪽으로 올라가지 못하게 아주 적극적으로 막는다. 로지폴 줄무늬다람쥐의 공격적인 태도에는 그럴 만한 이유가 숨어 있다. 로지폴 줄무늬다람쥐는 시원하고 그늘진 침엽수림에서 서식하며, 4종 가운데 가장 더위에 약하다. 다시 말해 서식지 조건이 가장 까다롭다. 간단히 말해 그늘진 숲이라야 살 수 있다. 하지만 알파인 줄무늬다람쥐나 옐로우파인 줄무늬다람쥐가 녀석들과 서식지를 공유한다면 어느 한쪽 혹은 둘 다가 경쟁에서 승리해 먹이 대부분을 빼앗고 말 것이다. 이렇게 경쟁이 붙는다면 로지폴 줄무늬다람쥐는 그 서식지에서 사실상 제거될 것이다. 로지폴 줄무늬다람쥐는 오로지 공격성 덕분에 살아남는다.

어휘

1. habitat 서식지   chipmunk 줄무늬다람쥐   scurry 종종걸음을 치다, 총총[허둥지둥] 가다   elevational range 표고 범위   overlap 겹치는 부분
2. represent 대표하다, 나타내다   make do with ~으로 임시변통하다, 아쉬운 대로 ~뿐이다   presence 존재, 참석   intersperse (사이에) 배치하다   arid 건조한   population (동식물) 개체군, 인구   isolate 고립시키다   formation 형성   3. diverge 분화하다, 갈라지다   genetically 유전적으로   ecological 생태계의   scattered 흩어진   reproductively 생식[번식]상   evolution (생물) 진화, (점진적) 발전   appearance 생김새   4. occupy (공간 등을) 차지하다, 점령하다   sagebrush 산쑥   open forest 나무가 듬성듬성한 숲, 소림(疏林)   conifer 침엽수   talus slope 애추사면(풍화 작용으로 생긴 암석 파편이 산지 사면을 따라 낙하하여 퇴적된 퇴적지형)   meadow 초원   juniper 향나무   5. aggression 공격성   encroachment 잠식, 침략, 침해   bully (약자를) 괴롭히다   physiologically 생리적으로   tolerate (힘든 환경 등을) 견디다   by default (경기·시합에서) 부전승으로   exclude from ~에서 몰아내다   trap in (빠져나가지 못하도록) ~에 가두다   6. aggressive 공격적인   feisty 혈기 왕성한, 거침없는   rodent 설치류   demeanor 태도   outcompete 경쟁에서 이기다   eliminate 제거하다, 없애다   by virtue of ~ 덕분으로

1. 두 번째 단락에서 글쓴이가 북미 서부에 매우 다양한 줄무늬다람쥐 종이 서식하는 이유로 언급한 것은?

Ⓐ 일찍이 북미 동부로부터 줄무늬다람쥐의 대이동이 있었기 때문에

Ⓑ 줄무늬다람쥐들이 북미 동부의 고산 지대에 적응할 수 없었기 때문에

Ⓒ 서부의 생태적 다양성과 극단적 환경들이 줄무늬다람쥐들을 지리적으로 고립시켰기 때문에

Ⓓ 동부에는 줄무늬다람쥐의 종 형성을 방해하는 거대한 인간 집단이 거주하지 않았기 때문에

어휘 migration (사람·철새·동물의 대규모) 이동
inability 무능, 불능 absence 결석, 부재
discourage 방해하다, 좌절시키다

2. 세 번째 단락의 diverged와 의미상 가장 가까운 것은?

Ⓐ 줄어들었다
Ⓑ 경쟁했다
Ⓒ 발달했다
Ⓓ 분리되었다

3. 다음 중 네 번째 단락에서 음영으로 표시된 문장이 담고 있는 핵심 정보를 가장 잘 표현한 것은? 정답 외의 보기들은 의미가 상당히 왜곡되거나 필수적인 정보가 빠져 있다.

Ⓐ 생태학자들은 시에라네바다 산맥 동쪽 사면의 지리적 특성이 줄무늬다람쥐의 사회적 발달에 어떤 영향을 미쳤는지 연구했다.

Ⓑ 생태학자들은 시에라네바다 산맥 동쪽 사면에서 각기 따로 서식하는 줄무늬다람쥐 종끼리 정확히 어떤 관계에 있는지 알아냈다.

Ⓒ 생태학자들은 시에라네바다 산맥 동쪽 사면의 줄무늬다람쥐들이 다른 종으로부터 위협을 받으면 표고가 더 높은 지대를 침입하고 점유한다는 사실을 발견했다.

Ⓓ 생태학자들은 시에라네바다 산맥 동쪽 사면의 줄무늬다람쥐가 어떻게 동종 개체들과의 상호작용을 회피하는지 연구했다.

어휘 invade 침입하다, 침략하다 threaten 위협하다

4. 네 번째 단락에 따르면, 옐로우파인 줄무늬다람쥐는 시에라네바다 산맥 동쪽 사면에 서식하는 다른 종과의 관계를 감안할 때 어디에서 발견될 수 있는가?

Ⓐ 산쑥 줄무늬다람쥐보다 낮은 곳
Ⓑ 알파인 줄무늬다람쥐보다 높은 곳
Ⓒ 산쑥 줄무늬다람쥐와 같은 고도
Ⓓ 로지폴 줄무늬다람쥐보다 낮은 곳

5. 다섯 번째 단락의 encroachment와 의미상 가장 가까운 것은?

Ⓐ 완전한 파괴
Ⓑ 점진적 침입
Ⓒ 과도한 개발
Ⓓ 대체

6. 다섯 번째 단락에 따르면, 산쑥 줄무늬다람쥐와 서식지의 관계에 대한 다음 설명 중 사실이 아닌 것은?

Ⓐ 산쑥 줄무늬다람쥐는 시에라네바다 산맥의 어느 서식지에서든 살아남을 수 있다.

Ⓑ 산쑥 줄무늬다람쥐는 다른 종과 경쟁할 필요가 없기 때문에 지금의 서식지를 차지하고 있다.

Ⓒ 산쑥 줄무늬다람쥐는 다른 줄무늬다람쥐 종들보다 더위를 더 잘 견딜 수 있다.

Ⓓ 산쑥 줄무늬다람쥐는 따뜻한 계절에는 표고가 더 높은 고산 지대에 머문다.

7. 다음 중 다섯 번째 단락 끝부분에서 언급한 실험 결과가 뒷받침하는 내용은?

Ⓐ 옐로우파인 줄무늬다람쥐의 서식지는 다른 종들도 선호하지만, 산쑥 줄무늬다람쥐의 서식지는 다른 종들이 선호하지 않는다.

Ⓑ 옐로우파인 줄무늬다람쥐를 서식지에서 몰아내는 것보다 산쑥 줄무늬다람쥐를 서식지에서 몰아내는 것이 훨씬 더 어려웠다.

Ⓒ 옐로우파인 줄무늬다람쥐와 산쑥 줄무늬다람쥐가 서식지에 필요로 하는 환경 조건은 동일하다.

Ⓓ 서식지의 온도는 옐로우파인 줄무늬다람쥐에게도, 산쑥 줄무늬다람쥐에게도 중요한 요인이 아니다.

어휘 desirable 바람직한, 호감 가는

8. 여섯 번째 단락에 따르면, 로지폴 줄무늬다람쥐가 경쟁 관계에 있는 줄무늬다람쥐들로부터 녀석들의 서식지를 매우 적극적으로 보호하는 이유는?

Ⓐ 특수한 먹이가 필요해서
Ⓑ 추위를 잘 견딜 수 없어서
Ⓒ 숲의 나무가 드리우는 그늘이 필요해서
Ⓓ 내리막과 오르막 사이를 오갈 수 있는 것을 좋아해서

어휘 specialized 특수한 requirement 필요한 것

9. 위에 제시된 지문의 일부를 보시오. 지문에 표시된 **(A)**, **(B)**, **(C)**, **(D)** 중 하나에 다음 문장이 삽입될 수 있다.

Yet each species remains within a fairly well-defined elevational zone.
(하지만 각각의 종은 상당히 경계가 분명한 표고 범위에 머무른다.)

이 문장이 들어갈 가장 적당한 위치는?

Ecologists have studied the four chipmunk species that occur on the eastern slope of the Sierra and have learned just how these species interact while remaining separate, each occupying its own elevational zone. The sagebrush chipmunk is found at the lowest elevation, among the sagebrush. The yellow pine chipmunk is common in low to mid-elevations and open conifer forests, including piñon and ponderosa and Jeffrey pine forests. The lodgepole chipmunk is found at higher elevations, among the lodgepoles, firs, and high-elevation pines. The alpine chipmunk is higher still, venturing among the talus slopes, alpine meadows, and high-elevation pines and junipers. **(A)** Obviously, the ranges of each species overlap. **(B)** Yet each species remains within a fairly well-defined elevational zone. Why don't sagebrush chipmunks move into the pine zones? **(C)** Why don't alpine chipmunks move to lower elevations and share the conifer forests with lodgepole chipmunks? **(D)**

Ⓐ (A)   Ⓑ (B)   Ⓒ (C)   Ⓓ (D)

어휘 well-defined 경계가 분명한

10. 지문을 간단히 요약하기 위한 도입 문장이 아래에 제시되어 있다. 아래 보기들 중에서 지문의 가장 중요한 개념을 표현한 문장 3개를 골라 요약을 완성하라. 보기들 중에는 지문에 나오지 않았거나 중요하지 않은 개념이기 때문에 요약문으로 적절치 않은 것들도 있다. 이 문제의 배점은 2점이다.

북미 서부에는 다양한 다람쥐 종이 서식한다.

Ⓐ 시에라네바다 산맥의 생태적 다양성은 줄무늬다람쥐 종의 분화를 낳았다.

Ⓑ 북미 동부에 서식하는 줄무늬다람쥐는 오직 한 종뿐이다.

Ⓒ 시에라네바다 산맥의 줄무늬다람쥐 종들은 다양한 고도에서 생존할 수 있을지라도 각각 특정 구역에만 서식한다.

Ⓓ 줄무늬다람쥐들은 다른 종의 침입으로부터 서식지를 적극적으로 방어한다.

Ⓔ 실험 결과에 따르면, 산쑥 줄무늬다람쥐는 생리적 요구 조건 때문에 사막에서 산다.

Ⓕ 가장 공격적인 줄무늬다람쥐 종은 로지폴 줄무늬다람쥐다.

어휘 variation 변화, 변이   differentiation 분화, 파생, 차별

A MODEL OF URBAN EXPANSION 도시 성장 모델 *p.177*

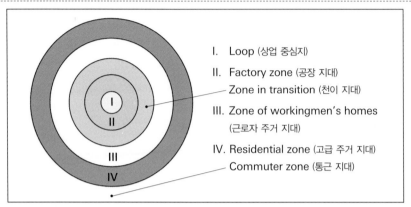

I. Loop (상업 중심지)

II. Factory zone (공장 지대)
— Zone in transition (천이 지대)

III. Zone of workingmen's homes
(근로자 주거 지대)

IV. Residential zone (고급 주거 지대)
— Commuter zone (통근 지대)

1. In the early twentieth century, the science of sociology found supporters in the United States and Canada partly because the cities there were growing so rapidly. It often appeared that North American cities would be unable to absorb all the newcomers arriving in such large numbers. Presociological thinkers like Frederick Law Olmsted, the founder of the movement to build parks and recreation areas in cities, and Jacob Riis, an advocate of slum reform, urged the nation's leaders to invest in improving the urban environment, building parks and beaches, and making better housing available to all. These reform efforts were greatly aided by sociologists who conducted empirical research on the social conditions in cities. In the early twentieth century, many sociologists lived in cities like Chicago that were characterized by rapid population growth and serious social problems. It seemed logical to use empirical research to construct theories about how cities grow and change in response to major social forces as well as more controlled urban planning.

2. The founders of the Chicago school of sociology, Robert Park and Ernest Burgess, attempted to develop a dynamic model of the city, one that would account not only for the expansion of cities in terms of population and territory but also for the patterns of settlement and land use within cities. They identified several factors that influence the physical form of cities. As Park stated, among them are "transportation and communication, tramways and telephones, newspapers and advertising, steel construction and elevators—all things, in fact, which tend to bring about at once a greater mobility and a greater concentration of the urban populations."

3. Park and Burgess based their model of urban growth on the concept of "natural areas"—that is, areas such as occupational suburbs or residential enclaves in which the population is relatively homogeneous and land is used in similar ways without deliberate planning. Park and Burgess saw urban expansion as occurring through a series of "invasions" of successive zones or areas surrounding the center of the city.

1. 20세기 초, 사회학은 미국과 캐나다에서 환영 받았는데, 부분적인 이유는 그 일대의 도시들이 매우 급속히 성장하고 있었기 때문이다. 대개 북미 도시들은 그처럼 대량으로 유입되는 인구를 전부 흡수할 수 없을 듯했다. 도시에 공원과 휴식 공간을 만들자는 운동의 창시자인 프레더릭 로 옴스테드, 빈민가 개혁 운동의 주창자인 제이콥 리스 같은 사회학 이전 시대의 사상가들은 국가 지도층에 도시 환경을 개선하고, 공원과 해변을 조성하고, 모든 시민에게 더 나은 주택을 공급하는 일에 투자할 것을 촉구했다. 이러한 개혁 운동은 도시의 사회적 조건에 관한 실증적 연구를 하던 사회학자들의 도움을 크게 받았다. 20세기 초, 많은 사회학자들은 급속한 인구 팽창과 심각한 사회 문제들이 나타났던 시카고 같은 도시에 살았다. 더 세심하게 관리되는 도시 계획뿐 아니라 주요 사회력에 대응하여 도시가 어떻게 성장하고 변하는지에 대한 이론을 정립하기 위해 실증적 연구를 이용한 것은 당연한 귀결이었다.

2. 사회학의 시카고학파를 창시한 로버트 파크와 어니스트 버제스는 인구와 영역이라는 관점에서 도시의 팽창은 물론 도시 내의 정착 패턴과 토지 이용 패턴까지 설명할 수 있는 역동적인 도시 모델을 수립하고자 했다. 그들은 도시의 물리적 형태에 영향을 미치는 몇몇 요인들을 찾아냈다. 파크의 주장에 따르면, 거기에는 "교통과 통신, 전차와 전화, 신문과 광고, 철골 구조와 엘리베이터에 이르는 모든 것, 사실상 기동성을 높이는 동시에 도시 인구 집중을 심화시킬 만한 모든 것"이 포함된다.

3. 파크와 버제스의 도시 성장 모델은 "자연 지역"이라는 개념에 뿌리를 두고 있다. 자연 지역이란 인위적인 계획 없이도 비슷한 방식으로 토지를 이용하며 비교적 동질성을 띠는 사람들이 모여 사는 직업과 관련된 교외 지역 또는 소수 민족 집단 거주지 등을 말한다. 파크와 버제스는 도심을 둘러싸고 있는 연이은 구역이나 지역을 연속적으로 "침입"하는 과정을 통해 도시 팽창이 일어난다고 보았다. 예를 들면, 농촌 지역이나 타국에서 온 사람들은 집값이 저렴한 지역으로 "침입했다". 그런 지역들은 대체로 직장에서 가까운 편이었

For example, people from rural areas and other societies "invaded" areas where housing was inexpensive. Those areas tended to be close to the places where they worked. In turn, people who could afford better housing and the cost of commuting "invaded" areas farther from the business district.

4. Park and Burgess's model has come to be known as the "concentric-zone model" (represented by the figure). Because the model was originally based on studies of Chicago, its center is labeled "Loop," the term commonly applied to that city's central commercial zone. Surrounding the central zone is a "zone in transition," an area that is being invaded by business and light manufacturing. The third zone is inhabited by workers who do not want to live in the factory or business district but at the same time need to live reasonably close to where they work. The fourth or residential zone consists of upscale apartment buildings and single-family homes. And the outermost ring, outside the city limits, is the suburban or commuters' zone; its residents live within a 30- to 60-minute ride of the central business district.

5. Studies by Park, Burgess, and other Chicago-school sociologists showed how new groups of immigrants tended to be concentrated in separate areas within inner-city zones, where they sometimes experienced tension with other ethnic groups that had arrived earlier. Over time, however, each group was able to adjust to life in the city and to find a place for itself in the urban economy. **(A)** Eventually many of the immigrants moved to unsegregated areas in outer zones; the areas they left behind were promptly occupied by new waves of immigrants.

6. The Park and Burgess model of growth in zones and natural areas of the city can still be used to describe patterns of growth in cities that were built around a central business district and that continue to attract large numbers of immigrants. **(B)** But this model is biased toward the commercial and industrial cities of North America, which have tended to form around business centers rather than around palaces or cathedrals, as is often the case in some other parts of the world. **(C)** Moreover, it fails to account for other patterns of urbanization, such as the rapid urbanization that occurs along commercial transportation corridors and the rise of nearby satellite cities. **(D)**

다. 한편 비싼 집값과 통근 비용을 부담할 수 있는 사람들은 업무 지구에서 좀 더 멀리 떨어진 지역으로 "침입했다".

4. 파크와 버제스의 모델은 (도형에 나타난 것처럼) "동심원 모델"로 명명되었다. 원래 시카고에 대한 연구를 기반으로 한 모델이었기 때문에 중심부는 시카고의 중심 상업 지구를 부르던 용어인 "루프"라고 부른다. 중심부를 에워싼 지대는 "천이 지대"로 업무와 경공업의 침입을 받고 있다. 세 번째 지대는 공장이나 업무 지구에서 살기는 싫지만 직장에서 꽤 가까운 곳에 살아야 하는 근로자들이 거주한다. 네 번째 고급 주거 지대는 고급 아파트와 단독주택이 들어선다. 가장 바깥쪽 원, 즉 도시 외곽은 교외 또는 통근 지대라고 하는데, 이곳 주민들은 중심 업무 지구까지 차로 30분에서 60분을 넘지 않는 거리에 거주한다.

5. 파크와 버제스를 비롯한 시카고학파 사회학자들의 연구 결과는 새로 유입된 이주민 집단이 도심 내 별개의 지역들에 모여 살게 되고, 때로 이들이 그곳에 먼저 자리 잡았던 다른 민족 집단들과 갈등을 겪는 경위를 보여 주었다. 하지만 시간이 지나면서 각 집단은 점차 도시 생활에 적응하며 도시 경제의 한 축을 차지해 나갔다. 결국, 이주민들 중 많은 이들이 인종 차별이 없는 외곽 지역으로 이동했으며 빈자리는 신속히 다른 이주민들로 채워졌다.

6. 도시 내 지대들과 자연 지역의 성장에 관한 파크와 버제스의 모델은 중심 업무 지구 주변에 형성되며 엄청난 수의 인구가 계속 유입되는 도시의 성장 패턴을 설명하는 데는 여전히 유용하다. 하지만 이 모델은 상업과 산업이 발달한 북미 도시들에 치우쳐 있는데, 세계 일부 지역에서는 흔히 왕궁이나 대성당 주변에 도시가 형성되지만 북미 도시들은 업무 지구 주변에 형성되는 경향이 있다. 더욱이 이 모델은 도로교통망을 따라 발생하는 급속한 도시화나 인근 위성도시의 출현 같은 다른 도시화 패턴은 설명하지 못한다.

어휘

1. absorb 흡수하다 presociological thinker 사회학 이전 시대의 사상가 founder 창시자, 창립자 advocate 옹호자 slum 빈민가 reform 개혁 urban 도시의 empirical 실증적, 경험에 의거한 construct (이론) 구축하다, 정립하다 in response to ~에 부응[대응]하여 social force 사회력(사회를 움직이는 힘) controlled 통제된, 주의 깊게 관리되는 2. account for ~을 설명하다 expansion 확장, 팽창 settlement 정착 factor 요인, 요소 tramway 전차 bring about ~을 가져오다, 일으키다 mobility 기동성 3. occupational 직업의, 특정 직업과 관련된 enclave 소수 민족 거주지 homogeneous 동족의, 동질성을 띠는 deliberate 인위적인, 의도적인 successive 연속적인 rural 시골의, 농촌의 invade 침입하다 commuting 통근 4. concentric 동심원의 commercial zone 상업지구 zone in transition 천이 지대 light manufacturing 경공업 upscale (수입·교육·사회적 지위가) 평균 이상의 outermost 가장 바깥쪽의 5. concentrate 집중하다, 모으다 tension 갈등, 긴장 ethnic group 민족 집단 unsegregated 인종 차별 없는 promptly 즉시 6. biased 편향된, 치우친 cathedral 대성당 urbanization 도시화 transportation corridor 도로교통망 satellite city 위성도시

11. 다음 중 첫 번째 단락에서 옴스테드와 리스의 공통점에 대해 추론할 수 있는 것은?

    Ⓐ 둘 다 도시에 관한 실증적 연구를 토대로 이론을 정립했다.

    Ⓑ 둘 다 북미 도시로 엄청나게 몰려든 이주민에 속했다.

    Ⓒ 둘 다 도시의 생활 조건을 개선하고 싶어했다.

    Ⓓ 둘 다 대도시의 급속한 팽창을 줄이고 싶어했다.

어휘 newcomer 새내기, 이민자

12. 다음 중 옴스테드, 리스와 사회학의 관계를 가장 잘 기술한 것은?

    Ⓐ 그들의 목표는 나중에 사회학자들이 실시한 연구로 뒷받침되었다.

    Ⓑ 그들의 접근법 때문에 실증적 사회학 연구에 반대하게 되었다.

    Ⓒ 그들의 작업이 사회학 연구만큼 중요하다는 것을 입증하는 데 어려움을 겪었다.

    Ⓓ 그들은 사회학 연구의 근거를 이용해 국가 지도층에 도시 개발에 투자하라고 촉구했다.

어휘 urge 촉구하다

13. 다음 중 두 번째 단락에서 음영으로 표시된 문장이 담고 있는 핵심 정보를 가장 잘 표현한 것은? 정답 외의 보기들은 의미가 상당히 왜곡되거나 필수적인 정보가 빠져 있다.

    Ⓐ 파크와 버제스가 창시한 사회학의 시카고학파는 팽창하는 도시의 인구가 도시 주변부의 토지를 보호하도록 돕고자 했다.

    Ⓑ 파크와 버제스가 만든 모델은 시카고 같은 도시의 인구와 지역이 왜 확대되는지는 물론 도시의 토지가 어떤 방식으로 이용되거나 정착되는지를 설명하고자 했다.

    Ⓒ 사회학의 시카고학파를 창시한 학자들은 시카고를 토지 이용과 정착 방법에서 타 도시들의 본보기가 될 역동적인 모델로 만들고 싶어했다.

    Ⓓ 파크와 버제스는 인구가 늘어나고 새로운 지역에 정착함에 따라 시카고 같은 도시들이 바람직한 토지 이용 모델을 따라야 한다고 생각했다.

어휘 found 창시하다, 창립하다   settle 정착하다

14. 두 번째 단락에서 글쓴이가 로버트 파크의 진술을 인용한 이유는?

    Ⓐ 파크와 버제스는 동의하지 않았을지도 모르는 특정 주제를 규명하기 위해

    Ⓑ 신중한 계획이 필요했던 시카고 개발의 면면을 부각하기 위해

    Ⓒ 도시 개발의 패턴에 영향을 미치는 몇몇 요인을 명시하기 위해

    Ⓓ 도시의 물리적 형태에 대한 파크와 버제스의 정의와 비교하기 위해

어휘 physical 물리적인

15. 다음 중 세 번째 단락에서 파크와 버제스가 생각한 "자연 지역"에 대한 설명으로 사실이 아닌 것은?

    Ⓐ 자연 지역에서 토지 이용은 일관된 패턴을 따르지만 대체로 계획되진 않는다.

    Ⓑ 자연 지역에 사는 사람들은 높은 동질성을 보이는 경향이 있다.

    Ⓒ 자연 지역은 보통 다른 지역에 사는 사람들의 "침입"을 받지 않는다.

    Ⓓ 자연 지역은 파크와 버제스가 개발한 모델의 중요한 기본 개념이다.

어휘 consistent 일관된   component 구성 요소

16. 네 번째 단락에 따르면, 동심원 모델에서 "루프"라는 용어를 사용하는 이유는?

    Ⓐ 모델에서 각 지대 사이에 연결 지대가 많음을 시사한다.

    Ⓑ 지대가 자주 천이 과정에 놓이고 빈번하게 바뀐다는 사실을 시사한다.

    Ⓒ 모델이 시카고라는 도시를 염두에 두고 정립되었다는 사실을 반영한다.

    Ⓓ 사람들이 종종 원래 살던 지대로 돌아간다는 사실을 강조한다.

어휘 with ~ in mind ~을 염두에 두고

17. 다섯 번째 단락의 promptly와 의미상 가장 가까운 것은?

    Ⓐ 빨리

    Ⓑ 보통

    Ⓒ 결국

    Ⓓ 쉽게

18. 여섯 번째 단락에서 파크와 버제스의 모델을 현대 북미 도시들에 적용할 때 암시하는 것은?

    Ⓐ 국제 개발 모델로 활용된 도시들에 특히 유용하다.

    Ⓑ 일부 도시 지역의 개발을 설명하는 데는 아직도 유용하지만, 모든 도시에는 그렇지 않다.

    Ⓒ 상업 중심지가 있는 도시들과 왕궁과 대성당이 중심에 있는 도시들에 똑같이 적용될 수 있다.

    Ⓓ 이주 패턴에 변화가 생겼기 때문에 현대 도시들에는 잘 맞지 않는다.

어휘 applicable 해당되는, 적용되는

19. 위에 제시된 지문의 일부를 보시오. 지문에 표시된 **(A)**, **(B)**, **(C)**, **(D)** 중 하나에 다음 문장이 삽입될 수 있다.

Typical of this kind of urban growth is the steel-producing center of Gary, Indiana, outside of Chicago, which developed because massive heavy industry could not be located within the major urban center itself.

(이러한 도시 성장의 전형은 인디애나 주의 게리라는 제철 공업 중심지로, 규모가 큰 중공업 지구는 주요 도심에 자리잡을 수 없었기 때문에 시카고 외곽에 발달했다.)

이 문장이 들어갈 가장 적당한 위치는?

   Studies by Park, Burgess, and other Chicago-school sociologists showed how new groups of immigrants tended to be concentrated in separate areas within inner-city zones, where they sometimes experienced tension with other ethnic groups that had arrived earlier. Over time, however, each group was able to adjust to life in the city and to find a place for itself in the urban economy. **(A)** Eventually many of the immigrants moved to unsegregated areas in outer zones; the areas they left behind were promptly occupied by new waves of immigrants.

   The Park and Burgess model of growth in zones and natural area of the city can still be used to describe patterns of growth in cities that were built around a central business district and that continue to attract large numbers of immigrants. **(B)** But this model is biased toward the commercial and industrial cities of North America, which have tended to form around business centers rather than around palaces or cathedrals, as is often the case in some other parts of the world. **(C)** Moreover, it fails to account for other patterns of urbanization, such as the rapid urbanization that occurs along commercial transportation corridors and the rise of nearby satellite cities. **(D)** Typical of this kind of urban growth is the steel-producing center of Gary, Indiana, outside of Chicago, which developed because massive heavy industry could not be located within the major urban center itself.

Ⓐ (A)   Ⓑ (B)   Ⓒ (C)   Ⓓ (D)

어휘 heavy industry 중공업

20. 지문을 간단히 요약하기 위한 도입 문장이 아래에 제시되어 있다. 아래 보기들 중에서 지문의 가장 중요한 개념을 표현한 문장 3개를 골라 요약을 완성하라. 보기들 중에는 지문에 나오지 않았거나 중요하지 않은 개념이기 때문에 요약문으로 적절치 않은 것들도 있다. 이 문제의 배점은 2점이다.

로버트 파크와 어니스트 버제스라는 두 사회학자는 도시가 어떻게 토지를 이용하고 성장하는지를 설명하는 "동심원 모델"을 개발했다.

Ⓐ 이 모델은 시카고라는 도시가 중심부에 위치한 교통 및 통신 시스템 주변에 발달한 경위를 설명하기 위해 개발되었다.

Ⓑ 이 모델은 20세기 초 미국에서 급속히 팽창하는 도시의 삶의 질에 대한 고민에서 비롯되었다.

Ⓒ 이 모델의 창시자들은 일정한 양식에 맞춘 도시 계획을 신뢰하지 않았으며, 그 대신 이른바 "자연 지역"의 팽창을 통한 성장을 옹호했다.

Ⓓ 이 모델에 따르면, 도시에 새로 유입된 집단은 중심부 인근에 함께 모여 사는 경향이 있으며 시간이 지나면 민족적, 직업적으로 훨씬 다양한 외곽 지역으로 이주한다.

Ⓔ 이 모델은 중심에 위치한 업무 지구로 엄청난 수의 근로자를 끌어들이며 성장한 도시들에 적용될 수 있다.

Ⓕ 이 모델은 결국 도심이 너무 혼잡해지면 주민들이 도시 밖의 새로운 위성도시들로 이주할 것으로 예측한다.

어휘 concern 우려, 염려   quality of life 삶의 질
      advocate 옹호하다, 변호하다

LISTENING

Questions 1~5

N Narrator   S Student   A Admissions officer

Script 🎧 T-70

N Listen to a conversation between a student and an admissions officer at City College.

S Hi. Can I ask you a few questions about starting classes during your summer session?

A Sure. Ask away! It starts next week, you know.

S Yeah, and I want to get some required courses out of the way so I can … maybe I can graduate one term earlier and get out into the job market sooner.

A That sounds like a good idea. Let me pull up the summer school database on my computer here …

S OK.

A OK, there it is. What's your student ID number?

S Oh, well, the thing is … I'm not actually admitted *here*. I'll be starting school upstate at Hooper University in the fall. But I'm down here for the summer, staying with my grandparents, 'cause I have a summer job near here.

A Oh, I see, well…

S So I'm outta luck?

A Well, you would be if you were starting anywhere but Hooper. But City College has a sort of special relationship with Hooper … a full exchange agreement … so our students can take classes at Hooper and vice versa. So if you can show me proof … um, your admissions letter from Hooper, then I can get you into our system here and give you an ID number.

S Oh, cool. So … um … I wanna take a math course and a science course—preferably biology. And I was also hoping to get my English composition course out of the way, too.

A Well all three of those courses are offered in the summer, but you've gotta understand that summer courses are condensed—you meet longer hours and all the assignments are doubled up because … it's the same amount of information presented and tested as in a regular term, but it's only six weeks long. Two courses are considered full time in summer term. Even if you weren't working, I couldn't let you register for more than that.

S Yeah, I was half expecting that. What about the schedule? Are classes only offered during the day?

A Well, during the week, we have some classes in the daytime and some at night, and on the weekends, we have some classes all day Saturday or all day Sunday for the six weeks.

S My job is pretty flexible, so one on a weekday and one on a weekend shouldn't be any problem. OK, so after I bring you my admissions letter, how do I sign up for the classes?

A Well, as soon as your student ID number is assigned and your

N 학생과 시티대학 입학 사정관의 대화를 들으시오.

S 안녕하세요. 여름 학기에 개설하는 과목에 대해 좀 여쭤봐도 될까요?

A 그럼요. 얼마든지 물어보세요! 다음 주에 개강입니다.

S 네, 필수 과목 몇 개를 미리 이수하고 싶은데, 그러면 한 학기 조기 졸업하고 취업 시장에 더 일찍 뛰어들 수 있을 것 같아서요.

A 좋은 생각이에요. 컴퓨터에 여름 학기 데이터베이스 좀 띄울게요. 잠시만요.

S 예.

A 됐습니다. 학번이요?

S 아, 저 그게 실은 이 학교에 입학 허가를 받은 건 아니고요. 주 북부에 있는 후퍼대학에 이번 가을 학기에 입학하는데요. 여름 동안은 여기 내려와서 조부모님 댁에서 지내요. 근처에 여름 일자리를 구했거든요.

A 아, 그러시군요.

S 제가 운이 없나요?

A 후퍼대학이 아닌 다른 대학에 입학하셨다면 그럴 뻔했네요. 하지만 시티대학은 후퍼대학과 특별한 협약을 맺고 있어요. 학점 교류제도라고. 그래서 본교 학생들이 후퍼대학 수업을 들을 수도 있고, 그 반대도 가능해요. 그럼 증명서, 음, 후퍼대학 입학 허가서를 보여 주시면 시스템에 등록하고 학번을 만들어 드릴게요.

S 아, 다행이네요. 그런데 저는 수학과 과학 중에서도 되도록이면 생물학을 듣고 싶은데요. 또 영작문도 미리 이수하고 싶거든요.

A 세 과목 다 여름 학기에 개설되긴 하지만, 여름 학기 수업은 압축적이라는 사실을 아셔야 해요. 수업 시간도 길고 과제도 두 배예요. 가르치고 평가하는 내용은 정규 학기랑 똑같은데 6주 만에 끝나니까요. 여름 학기에는 두 과목 이상은 수강하실 수 없어요. 설령 일을 안 하더라도 그 이상은 등록하실 수 없어요.

S 네, 저도 어느 정도 짐작은 했어요. 수업 일정은요? 수업이 주중에만 있나요?

A 주중에는 수업이 낮에도 있고 밤에도 있어요. 주말에는 6주 토요 종일반과 일요 종일반이 있어요.

S 일이 시간을 조정할 수 있는 편이라 주중에 한 과목, 주말에 한 과목 이렇게 들으면 문제없겠네요. 좋습니다. 입학 허가서를 가져온 뒤에 수강신청은 어떻게 하죠?

A 학번이 발급되고 개인 정보를 학사 정보 시스템에 입력하자마자 전화만 하면 즉시 등록할 수 있어요.

S 학자금 지원은 어떻게 되나요? 여름 학기에도 받을 수 있나요?

information is in our admissions system, you can register by phone almost immediately.

S What about financial aid? Is it possible to get it for the summer?

A Sorry, but that's something you would've had to work out long before now. But the good news is that the tuition for our courses is about half of what you're going to be paying at Hooper.

S Oh, well that helps! Thank you so much for answering all my questions. I'll be back tomorrow with my letter.

A I won't be here then, but do you see that lady sitting at that desk over there? That's Ms. Brinker. I'll leave her a note about what we discussed, and she'll get you started.

S Cool.

A 죄송합니다만, 그건 진작 알아보셨어야 해요. 그래도 수강료가 후퍼대학에서 내실 수강료의 절반밖에 안 된다는 점은 좋은 소식이죠.

S 오, 다행이네요! 답변 정말 감사합니다. 내일 입학 허가서 들고 다시 올게요.

A 내일은 제가 여기 없고요. 저기 책상 앞에 앉은 여자분 보이죠? 브링커 씨예요. 오늘 한 얘기 전달해 놓을게요. 저분이 도와주실 거예요.

S 좋아요.

어휘

admissions officer 입학 사정관   summer session 여름 계절학기   get out of the way 미리 해치우다   pull up (컴퓨터에) ~을 띄우다   upstate 주(州) 북부   exchange agreement 학점 교류제도   composition 작문   condensed 압축된, 농축된   full time 최대 이수 가능 학점   flexible 융통성 있는   financial aid 학자금 지원   tuition 수강료, 등록금

---

1. 두 사람이 주로 의논하고 있는 내용은?

Ⓐ 학자금 지원 받기
Ⓑ 학생의 4년치 수강 시간표 짜기
Ⓒ 여름 학기 수강 신청
Ⓓ 후퍼대학과 다른 두 대학의 입학 요강 차이점

어휘 admissions requirements 입학 요강

2. 학생이 시티대학에서 강의를 듣고 싶어하는 이유는?

Ⓐ 후퍼대학에는 원하는 강의가 개설되지 않아서
Ⓑ 시티대학 강의가 후퍼대학 강의보다 수강료가 저렴해서
Ⓒ 주말에도 강의를 들을 수 있어서
Ⓓ 후퍼대학에서 조기 졸업을 할 수 있어서

3. 남자가 두 과목만 수강할 수 있는 이유는?

Ⓐ 학생들은 여름 학기에 두 과목만 들을 수 있도록 제한되어 있다.
Ⓑ 남자는 토요일과 일요일에만 수업에 참석할 수 있다.
Ⓒ 학자금이 두 과목까지만 지원된다.
Ⓓ 여름 동안 일 때문에 두 과목 이상은 들을 수가 없다.

어휘 attend 참석하다   keep from -ing ~하지 못하게 막다

4. 브링커 씨가 남자를 위해 할 일은? 두 개의 답을 선택하라.

Ⓐ 남자에게 학번 발급하기
Ⓑ 남자에게 학자금 신청서 주기
Ⓒ 남자가 어떤 과목을 수강할지 상담하기
Ⓓ 남자가 후퍼대학에 지원할 수 있도록 돕기
Ⓔ 남자의 정보를 시티대학 학사 정보 시스템에 입력하기

5. 대화의 일부를 다시 듣고 질문에 답하라.

 T-71

S So I'm outta luck?

A Well, you would be if you were starting anywhere but Hooper.

N *What does the woman mean when she says this:*

A Well, you would be if you were starting anywhere but Hooper.

Ⓐ 남자는 시티대학에 지원하기 위해 너무 오래 기다렸다.
Ⓑ 남자는 후퍼대학에 다니지 말아야 한다.
Ⓒ 남자는 원하는 대로 할 수 있을 것이다.
Ⓓ 남자는 매우 운이 나쁘다.

N Narrator **P** Professor **M** Male Student

Script T-72

N Listen to part of a lecture in a world history class.

P In any introductory course, I think it's always a good idea to step back and ask ourselves "What are we studying in this class, and why are we studying it?"
So, for example, when you looked at the title of this course in the catalog—"Introduction to World History"—what did you think you were getting into ... what made you sign up for it—besides filling the social-science requirement?
Anyone ...?

M Well ... just the—the history—of everything ... you know, like starting at the beginning ... with ... I guess, the Greeks and Romans ... the Middle Ages, the Renaissance ... you know, that kinda stuff ... like what we did in high school.

P OK ... Now, what you're describing is *one* approach to world history.
In fact, there are several approaches—basic "models" or "conceptual frameworks" of what we study when we "do" history. And what you studied in high school—what I call the "Western-Heritage Model," this used to be the most common approach in U.S. high schools and colleges ... in fact, it's the model I learned with, when I was growing up back—oh, about a hundred years ago ...
Uh ... at Middletown High School, up in Maine ... I guess it made sense to *my* teachers back then—since, well, the history of western Europe was the cultural heritage of everyone in my class ... and this remained the dominant approach in most U.S. schools till ... oh, maybe ... 30, 40 years ago ... But it doesn't take more than a quick look around campus—even just this classroom today—to see that the student body in the U.S. is much more diverse than my little class in Middletown High ... and this Western-Heritage Model was eventually replaced by—or sometimes combined with—one or more of the newer approaches ... and I wanna take a minute to describe these to you today, so you can see where *this* course fits in.
OK .... so ... up until the mid-twentieth century, the basic purpose of most world-history courses was to learn about a set of values ... institutions ... ideas ... which were considered the "heritage" of the people of Europe—things like ... democracy ... legal systems ... types of social organization ... artistic achievements ...
Now, as I said, this model gives us a rather *limited* view of history. So, in the 1960s and '70s it was combined with—or replaced by—what I call the "Different-Cultures Model." The

N 세계사 수업의 강의 일부를 들으시오.

P 입문 과목을 들을 때는 "이 수업에서 무엇을 공부하는지, 왜 공부하는지?"를 항상 자문하는 것이 좋습니다.
예를 들어 수강 편람에서 '세계사 입문'이라는 과목명을 보았을 때 무엇을 기대했고, 무엇 때문에 신청하게 되었나요? 사회과학 필수 학점을 채우기 위한 것 말고요.
말해 볼 사람?

M 저, 그냥 모든 것에 대한 역사요. 그러니까 그리스 로마 시대부터 시작해서, 중세, 르네상스기처럼 고등학교 때 배운 그런 내용일 듯한데요.

P 좋습니다. 방금 세계사 접근법의 한 가지가 나왔군요. 사실 역사를 "공부"할 때는 몇 가지 접근법들이 있습니다. 그러니까 기본적인 "모델" 혹은 "개념적 틀" 말이죠. 여러분이 고등학교 때 배운 것은 이른바 "서양문화유산 모델"로 과거 미국의 고등학교와 대학교에서 가장 보편적인 접근법이었어요. 사실 제가 어릴 적에 배웠던 모델이기도 합니다. 오, 약 백 년 전이네요.
메인 주 북부 미들타운고등학교 선생님들한테는 아마 설득력 있는 모델이었겠지요. 서유럽의 역사는 우리 반 모든 학생들의 문화유산이었으니까요. 당시 미국 내 대부분의 학교에서 지배적인 접근법이었고 한 30, 40년 전까지만 해도 그랬죠. 하지만 캠퍼스를 잠깐만 둘러보면, 지금 이 교실만 해도 그렇고요, 미들타운고등학교의 작은 학급에 비해 인종 구성이 훨씬 다양해졌다는 걸 알 수 있습니다. 서양문화유산 모델은 결국 하나 또는 그 이상의 새로운 접근법들로 대체되거나 흡수되었습니다. 오늘은 이 새로운 접근법들을 소개하려고 합니다. 그러면 본 과목이 어디에 해당하는지 알 수 있겠지요.
그런데, 그러니까 20세기 중반까지도 세계사 과목 대부분의 기본적인 학습 목표는 민주주의, 사법 제도, 사회 조직 유형, 예술 작품 등 유럽인의 "문화유산"으로 간주되던 다양한 가치, 제도, 이념에 대해 배우는 것이었습니다.
아까도 말했듯이 이 모델은 역사를 다소 제한된 관점으로 봅니다. 그래서 1960~70년대에 들어서 이른바 "다문화 모델"이라는 접근법으로 흡수되거나 대체되었습니다. 60년대는 교과 과정을 오늘날에 맞게 만들라는 요구가 높아지고, 모든 학문에 팽배한 유럽 중심주의에 대한 비판이 일었던 시기입니다. 대체로 다문화 모델은 서양문화유산 모델의 기본 가정을 문제 삼지는 않았습니다. 그보다는 서유럽 외에 다른 문명들과 문화적 범주들도 기술해야 한다고 강력히 주장했죠.
즉 모든 사람들의 문화유산 말입니다. 그리스 로마 시대

'60s were a period in which people were demanding more relevance in the curriculum, and there was criticism of the *European* focus that you were likely to find in all the academic disciplines. For the most part, the Different-Cultures Model didn't challenge the basic assumptions of the Western-Heritage Model. What it did was insist on representing *other* civilizations and cultural categories, *in addition* to those of western Europe …

In other words, the heritage of *all* people: not just what goes back to the Greeks and Romans, but also the origins of African … Asian … Native American civilizations. Though more inclusive, it's still, basically, a "heritage model" … which brings us to a *third* approach, what I call the "Patterns-of-Change Model."

Like the Different-Cultures Model, this model presents a wide cultural perspective. But, with this model, we're no longer *limited* by notions of fixed cultural or geographical boundaries. So, then, studying world history is not so much a question of how a particular nation or ethnic group developed, but rather it's a look at common themes— conflicts … trends—that cut across modern-day borders of nations or ethnic groups. In my opinion, this is the best way of studying history, to better understand current-day trends and conflicts.

For example, let's take the study of the Islamic world. Well, when I first learned about Islamic civilization, it was from the perspective of Europeans. Now, with the Patterns-of-Change Model, we're looking at the past through a wider lens. So *we* would be more interested, say, in how interactions with Islamic civilization—the religion … art … literature—affected cultures in Africa … India … Spain … and so on.

Or … let's take another example. Instead of looking at each cultural group as having a separate, *linear* development from some ancient origin, in *this* course we'll be looking for the common themes that go beyond cultural or regional distinctions. So … instead of studying … a particular succession of British kings … or a dynasty of Chinese emperors … in *this* course, we'll be looking at the broader concepts of monarchy, imperialism … and political transformation.

뿐 아니라 아프리카, 아시아, 아메리카 원주민 문명의 기원까지 거슬러 올라가는 거죠. 이 모델은 더 포괄적이긴 하지만 여전히 기본적으로는 "문화유산 모델"입니다. 이제 세 번째 접근법인 "변화 패턴 모델"을 볼 차례군요.

이 모델도 다문화 모델처럼 폭넓은 문화적 관점을 제시합니다. 하지만 이 모델을 활용하면 고정불변의 문화적 개념들이나 지리적 경계에 갇히지 않아요. 그래서 세계사를 연구할 때 어떤 국가나 민족 집단이 어떻게 발전했느냐 보다는 대립이나 추세 등 오늘날의 국경이나 민족 거주지 형성에 영향을 미친 공통 주제들을 살펴봅니다. 저는 이 모델이 오늘날의 추세와 대립을 잘 이해할 수 있는 가장 훌륭한 역사 연구법이라고 생각합니다.

이슬람 세계에 대한 연구를 예로 들어보죠. 제가 이슬람 문명에 대해 처음 배웠을 때는 유럽인의 관점에서 보았습니다. 이제 우리는 변화 패턴 모델과 함께 더 큰 렌즈를 통해 과거를 들여다봅니다. 그래서 우리는 종교, 예술, 문학 등 이슬람 문명과의 교류가 아프리카, 인도, 스페인 등지의 문화에 어떤 영향을 미쳤는지에 더 관심을 둘 것입니다.

또 다른 예를 들어 보죠. 이 과목에서는 고대 문명으로부터 독립적, 단선적으로 발전해온 각 문화 집단을 살펴보는 대신 문화적, 지역적 구분을 초월한 공통 주제를 찾아낼 것입니다. 그래서 영국 왕들의 특정 계보나 중국의 황조 대신 군주제와 제국주의, 그리고 정치적 변동이라는 더 넓은 개념을 다룰 것입니다.

어휘

introductory course 입문자를 위한 강의   social-science 사회과학   approach 접근법   conceptual 개념상의   framework 틀, 체계   artistic achievement 예술 작품   heritage (국가, 사회의) 유산   dominant 우세한, 지배적인   diverse 다양한   institutions 제도   democracy 민주주의 legal systems 사법 체계   relevance 적절성, 중요성 현재의 사회 문제와의 연관성   curriculum 교과 과정   discipline (대학의) 학문, 학과목, 규율 assumption 가정, 추정   civilization 문명   origin 기원, 근원   inclusive 포괄적인   perspective 관점, 시각   ethnic 민족의   conflict 갈등, 마찰 cut across ~에도 영향을 미치다, 해당되다   literature 문학   linear 직선 모양의, 단선적인   distinction 구분   succession 계승   dynasty 통치기 monarchy 군주제   imperialism 제국주의   transformation 변동

6. 이 강의의 주요 목적은 무엇인가?

  Ⓐ 세계사 연구와 미국사 연구 비교하기
  Ⓑ 학생들에게 다음 과제 설명하기
  Ⓒ 세계사를 연구하는 다양한 접근법 설명하기
  Ⓓ 학문으로서 역사학의 기원 설명하기

  어휘 approach 접근법 academic discipline 학문

7. 교수가 고등학교 때 배웠던 서양문화유산 모델을 언급하는 이유는?

  Ⓐ 교수가 그 모델을 선호하는 이유를 설명하기 위해
  Ⓑ 그 모델이 과거에는 널리 쓰였다는 사실을 강조하기 위해
  Ⓒ 그 모델에 대한 학생의 설명에서 오류를 바로잡기 위해
  Ⓓ 고등학교 역사 수업과 대학 역사 수업을 비교하기 위해

8. 교수에 따르면, 다문화 모델의 장점은 무엇인가?

  Ⓐ 미국사에 치중한다.
  Ⓑ 가장 널리 연구된 이론에 바탕을 두고 있다.
  Ⓒ 다양한 문화 집단의 역사를 아우른다.
  Ⓓ 여러 문화 집단에 걸치는 주제별 연관성을 찾는다.

  어휘 thematic 주제와 관련된 connection 연관성

9. 교수는 이 과목에서 앞으로 이슬람 문명의 어떤 측면을 주로 토론
   하려고 하는가?

  Ⓐ 이슬람 통치자들의 계보
  Ⓑ 이슬람 건축의 고대 기원
  Ⓒ 이슬람의 영향으로부터 유럽 문화권의 고립
  Ⓓ 아프리카 문화의 이슬람 요소들

  어휘 succession 계승, 계보 ruler 통치자
       architecture 건축 isolation 고립

10. 아래의 각 주제와 이것을 토론할 가능성이 가장 높은 세계사 강의
    유형을 짝지어라. 보기를 해당되는 곳에 적으시오.

서양문화유산 모델	다문화 모델	변화 패턴 모델
C	A	B

  Ⓐ 아메리카 원주민 예술의 미국 문화에 대한 공헌
  Ⓑ 아시아와 유럽에서 독자적으로 발달한 인쇄술
  Ⓒ 미국 사법 제도의 토대가 된 고대 로마 제도

  어휘 contribution 공헌, 기여 foundation 토대, 기반

11. 대화의 일부를 다시 듣고 질문에 답하라.

T-73

> P So, for example, when you looked at the title
> of this course in the catalog — "Introduction
> to World History" — what did you think you
> were getting into … what made you sign up
> for it — besides filling the social-science
> requirement?
>
> N *What is the professor's attitude?*

  Ⓐ 교수는 이 강의가 학생들의 기대를 충족할 수 있을지 미심쩍다.
  Ⓑ 교수는 학생들이 흥미가 있어서 이 강의를 선택했기를 바란다.
  Ⓒ 교수는 이 강의가 필수 학점을 채워줄 수 있어서 기쁘다.
  Ⓓ 교수는 학생들이 이 과목의 필수 활동에 대해 잘 모를까 봐 걱
     정한다.

  어휘 expectation 기대 fulfill 충족하다

Questions 12~16

p.190

N Narrator   S Student   A Academic advisor

Script T-74

N Listen to a conversation between a student and his academic advisor.

S Excuse me, Ms. Chambers? Um, I don't have an appointment, but I was kinda wondering if you had a minute to help me with something.

A Oh, sure. Have a seat.
What's on your mind?

S Well, uh … I guess I really don't know where to start … It's not just one class. It's … I'm not doing all that great. Like on my homework assignments. And in class. And I don't know why. I mean, I just don't get it! I-I read the assignments and I do the homework and I'm still not doing too well …

A Um, which classes? You mean, like Spanish … you're taking Spanish, right?

S Oh, no, not Spanish … if it weren't for Spanish I'd really be in trouble … no, but it's really all the others, psychology and sociology especially.

A Is it the material, what you read in the textbooks? You don't understand it?

S No, that's just it—I think I understand stuff when I read it …

A You don't re …

S Remember? Well, I remember names and definitions, but … like, in class, when the professor asks us about the theories, what they're all about, I never have the answer.

A Sounds like you're trying to learn by memorizing details, instead of picking out the main points of the reading. So, tell me, how do you study?

S Well, I—I … I mean, I read the assigned chapters, and I try to underline everything … like all of the words I don't know, and I always memorize the definitions. But, I dunno, when I get back in class, it always seems like the other students've gotten a better handle on what was in the reading. So, maybe it's just me …

A Oh, it's not. Believe me. Lots of students … You know, my first year as a college student … I really had a hard time. I spent hours reading in the library … but I was just wasting time, 'cause I wasn't really studying the right things. I did the same sort of thing it sounds like you're doing, not focusing on what's really important in the reading, but on the smaller details.

S Yeah, maybe. But I spend so much time studying, it seems like I should be doing better.

A The first year of college can be a little overwhelming, I know. Point is, lots of students have trouble adjusting at first, you

N 학생과 학사 지도사의 대화를 들으시오.

S 실례합니다, 체임버스 씨? 미리 약속은 잡지 않았지만, 잠시 도와주실 수 있을지요.

A 물론이지. 앉거라. 무슨 고민인데?

S 그게, 어디서부터 시작해야 할지 정말 막막한 것 같아요. 한 과목만 문제가 아니고요. 전부 그다지 잘하고 있는 것 같지 않아요. 과제도 그렇고, 수업 시간에도 그렇고. 이유는 모르겠어요. 그냥 이해가 안 돼요! 과제물도 읽고 숙제도 하는데 여전히 헤매고 있어요.

A 음, 어떤 과목을 말하는 거니? 스페인어? 스페인어 듣는구나?

S 아, 아니요, 스페인어는 아니에요. 스페인어 과목이 없었더라면 정말 문제가 심각했을 거예요. 스페인어 말고 다른 과목이 전부 다 문제예요. 특히 심리학하고 사회학이요.

A 교재에서 읽은 내용을 이해 못하는 거니?

S 예, 맞아요. 제 생각엔 읽을 때는 이해하는 것 같거든요.

A 그럼, 외우는 게….

S 못 외우냐고요? 명칭이나 정의는 잘 외워요. 하지만 강의 시간에 교수님이 어떤 이론에 대한 핵심 내용을 물어보시면 답을 도저히 모르겠어요.

A 읽을 때 핵심 내용을 파악하기보다는 사소한 것들을 암기하는 방식으로 공부하는 것 같구나. 어떻게 공부하는지 말해 줄래?

S 전, 그러니까, 과제 부분을 읽고 모르는 단어에 전부 밑줄을 그어요. 그리고 항상 정의를 외워요. 하지만 모르겠어요. 수업에 들어가면 다른 학생들은 과제 내용을 훨씬 잘 이해한 것 같다는 느낌이 들어요. 그래서 저만 이런가….

A 그렇지 않단다. 정말이야. 많은 학생들이 그래. 있잖아, 나도 대학 신입생일 때 굉장히 고생했어. 도서관에 앉아 몇 시간 동안 책을 읽었지만, 시간 낭비였어. 공부 방법이 잘못되었던 거지. 나도 지금 너처럼 책에서 정말 중요한 부분보다는 사소하고 세세한 내용에 치중했단다.

S 네, 그럴 수도 있겠네요. 하지만 오랜 시간 공부하는 만큼 더 잘해야 하는데.

A 1학년 때는 좀 버거울 수 있어. 내 말은, 많은 학생들이 어떻게 공부할지, 어떻게 시간을 가장 효율적으로 활용할 수 있을지 알아내느라고 적응하는 데 고생한다는 거야. 읽기 과제를 하는 건 아주 잘하고 있어. 하지만 밑줄 긋고 외우는 건 불필요하다는 생각이 들어. 시간도 많이 잡아먹고, 아무튼 시간을 잘 활용하는 방법은 아닌 것 같구나. 이렇게 한번 해 보렴. 책을 읽을 때 읽어야 할

know, figuring out how to study, how to use their time, you know, to your best advantage. It's good that you do the assigned readings … but, you've … well, I think you're unnecessarily underlining and memorizing. That takes a lot of time, and, well, it's not the best use of your time. Here's something you can do: when you read, just read the assigned sections, and then … and without looking back at the text—write a summary of the key points, the main ideas in the chapter. And after you do that, it-it's good to go back and reread the text. And you look for any examples you can find to support those key points. Let me show you an example of what I mean.

부분을 일단 그냥 읽어. 그러고 나서 책을 다시 보지 말고 읽은 부분에서 가장 중심적인 생각, 핵심 요지들을 요약해서 적어 봐. 다 쓰고 나서 교재를 다시 한번 읽으면 좋아. 그리고 핵심 요지들을 뒷받침하는 구체적인 예들을 찾는 거야. 어떻게 하는 건지 보여 주마.

어휘

academic advisor 학사 지도사   appointment (특히 업무 관련) 약속   in trouble 곤경에 빠진   psychology 심리학   sociology 사회학
definition 정의, 개념   theory 이론, 학설   memorize 암기하다   underline 밑줄을 긋다   overwhelming 압도적인   adjust 적응하다
to one's best advantage 가장 유리하게

---

12. 남자가 여자를 찾아간 이유는?

   Ⓐ 교수에게 시험에 관해 이야기해달라고 부탁하려고
   Ⓑ 과제를 완성하는 데 도움을 받으려고
   Ⓒ 수업을 따라가기 힘든 이유를 이해하는 데 도움을 받으려고
   Ⓓ 어떤 과목을 수강하면 좋을지 여자의 의견을 물으려고

   어휘 complete 완료하다   take a class 수강하다

13. 남자가 스페인어 과목에 대해 암시하는 것은?

   Ⓐ 그 수업에서 다른 학생들을 도와준다.
   Ⓑ 그 수업은 잘 따라가고 있다.
   Ⓒ 과제를 다 끝낼 수 없다.
   Ⓓ 그 과목을 더 많이 공부해야 한다.

14. 남자가 읽기 과제에서 부딪히는 문제는?

   Ⓐ 읽는 내용이 재미없다.
   Ⓑ 용어의 정의를 외울 수 없다.
   Ⓒ 읽어야 할 분량이 너무 많다.
   Ⓓ 중요한 정보를 파악하기 어렵다.

   어휘 term (전문) 용어   have difficulty -ing ～하는 데 애를 먹다

15. 여자는 왜 남자에게 자신의 학창시절 경험담을 말하는가?

   Ⓐ 다른 학생들도 비슷한 문제를 겪는다는 점을 깨우쳐 주려고
   Ⓑ 도서관에서 더 많이 공부하라고 격려하려고
   Ⓒ 세부 내용 암기의 중요성을 설명하려고
   Ⓓ 공부 방법 강의를 들어보라고 설득하려고

   어휘 convince 설득하다   study-skill 공부 방법

16. 여자가 남자에게 추천한 행동은? 두 개의 답을 선택하라.

   Ⓐ 교재를 읽을 때 정의 부분에 밑줄 치기
   Ⓑ 읽은 내용에 대한 요약문 적기
   Ⓒ 내용 두 번 읽기
   Ⓓ 스스로 추가 자료 찾아 보기

Questions 17~22

p.192

N Narrator **P** Professor **F** Female student **M** Male student

Script T-75

N Listen to part of a lecture in an astronomy class.

P I'll tell you a story about how one astronomy problem was solved. It happened many years ago, but you'll see that it's interesting and still relevant. Two, three hundred years ago, astronomers already had telescopes, but they were not as powerful as those we have now. Let's say … they were at the level of telescopes amateur astronomers use today. Tell me, what do you see in the night sky when you use a telescope like that? Quick, tell me.

F Planets …

P Right …

M Even … like … the moons of Jupiter?

P Right …

F Stars.

P OK … what else? … You think that's all? … Ever heard of nebulae? … I bet you have … Well, let's just, um, put it up anyway …

Nebulae are small fuzzy patches you see in the sky, they look like little clouds. Many of them have a spiral shape, and that's why we called them *spiral* nebulae … So astronomers in the eighteenth century … *eighteenth* century … when they looked through the telescope, they could see planets—and they knew those were planets … the moons of Jupiter—and they knew they were the moons of Jupiter … and then they saw spiral nebulae and they didn't have a clue.

What could those be? So, some of them thought—"these things are cloudy and fuzzy, so they're probably small clouds of cosmic dust, and they don't have to be very far away from us." But there were others who thought, "OK, the things *look* small and fuzzy, but *maybe* they're actually distant galaxies of stars, but we can't see the stars, because they're so far away and they seem *so* tiny that they *look* like dust, and even the whole galaxy looks like a tiny little cloud."

Which of the two theories do you think was more … uh, surprising?

M The galaxy one.

P And why?

M Well, I mean it assumed that the nebulae are not what they look like at first sight. The first theory assumed that, right?

P OK. And now tell me this … which one would have seemed more likely at the time?

M Uh … They couldn't tell.

P Right. Two morals here: first, there can be different explanations for the same observation. And second,

N 천문학 수업의 강의 일부를 들으시오.

P 어떤 천문학 문제를 어떻게 풀었는지 얘기해 봅시다. 오래전 이야기지만, 흥미롭고 여전히 의미가 있다는 걸 알게 될 겁니다. 200~300년 전, 천문학자들은 이미 망원경을 갖고 있었지만 오늘날 사용하는 망원경처럼 성능이 좋지는 않았어요. 말하자면 오늘날 아마추어 천문가들이 사용하는 망원경 수준이죠. 그런 망원경을 사용하면 밤하늘에서 무엇을 볼 수 있는지 말해 볼까요? 어서 말해 보세요.

F 행성이요.

P 맞아요.

M 목성의 위성 같은 것도요?

P 맞아요.

F 별이요.

P 좋습니다. 또 있나요? 그게 다인가요? 성운(星雲)은 들어본 적 있나요? 들어 봤을 겁니다. 아무튼 이쯤에서 마무리합시다.

성운은 하늘에서 볼 수 있는 작고 흐릿한 점으로 작은 구름처럼 생겼습니다. 대부분 나선형이라서 나선 성운이라고 부릅니다. 그래서 18세기 천문학자들은, 18세기예요, 망원경으로 하늘을 관찰할 때 행성을 보고 행성인지 알았으며, 목성의 위성들을 보고 목성의 위성인지 알았지만, 나선 성운을 보았을 때는 전혀 짐작도 못했습니다.

저건 대체 뭘까 고민하던 학자들 중 일부는 "구름이 낀 듯 흐릿한 형체로 보아 우주 먼지가 모여서 생긴 작은 구름으로 추정되며 지구에서 그렇게 멀리 떨어져 있지 않다"고 생각했습니다. 하지만 달리 생각한 학자들도 있었지요. "작고 흐릿하지만, 실제로는 멀리 떨어진 은하일 수도 있는데, 별이 안 보이는 이유는 너무 멀리 떨어져 있는 데다 너무 작아서 먼지처럼 보이며, 심지어 전체 은하조차 작은 구름으로 보인다."

둘 중 어느 이론이 더 놀라운가요?

M 은하 이론이요.

P 이유는?

M 성운이 겉으로 보이는 것과 다르다고 가정하잖아요. 첫 번째 이론은 같다고 가정하고요, 그렇죠?

P 맞아요. 그럼 이렇게 말해 보죠. 당시에 어느 이론이 더 그럴듯해 보였을까요?

M 음, 당시 사람들은 알 수 없었습니다.

P 맞아요. 여기에는 두 가지 교훈이 있어요. 첫 번째는 같은 관찰을 놓고 다른 설명이 있을 수 있다는 것이고. 두 번째는 '명백한' 것이 반드시 '옳은' 것을 뜻하지는 않는다는 겁니다. 아주 오랫동안 진전이 없었습니다. 150

"obvious" doesn't necessarily mean "right" ... What happened next was ... for a long time nothing. More than 150 years. No one could decide ... Both hypotheses seemed plausible ... And a lot was at stake—because if the *galaxy* theory was right, it would be proof that the universe is enormous ... and if the *dust* theory was right ... maybe *not* so enormous. So the size of the universe was at stake ... Finally in the 1920s we came up with a telescope that was strong enough to tell us something new here. When we used it to look at the spiral nebulae, we saw ... well, we were not absolutely sure ... but it really looked like there were stars in those nebulae. So not dust after all, but stars ...

But how far away were they, really? How would you measure that? Any ideas? Laura?

F   Well, how about measuring how strong those stars shine? Because, if the star is far away, then its light would be weak, right?

P   Yes ... but there's a problem here. You need to know how bright the star is in the first place, because some stars are naturally much brighter than others. So, if you see a star that's weak ... it can mean one of two things ...

F   Oh ... it's either far away or it's just a weak star.

P   And you can't really always tell which. But you're on the right track. There is a kind of star where you can *calculate* its natural brightness ... and—you guessed it—we found some in the nebulae. It's called a *variable* star—or a "variable" for short—because its brightness *varies* in regular intervals. I won't go into detail here, but ... basically ... the longer the interval, the brighter the star, so from the *length* of those intervals we were able to calculate their natural brightness. This told us how distant they were—and many turned out to be very, very far away. So we can be sure that the spiral nebulae really *are* very distant galaxies—which is what some eighteenth-century astronomers *guessed* but didn't have the instruments to prove ...

Now, one reason I told you this story is that *today* there are still plenty of situations when we see something out there, but we really aren't sure *what* it is. An example of one such mysterious observation would be gamma-ray bursters.

We've known about these gamma-ray bursters for a long time now, but we can't all agree on what they are.

여 년이 지난 후까지. 아무도 결정할 수 없었습니다. 두 가설 모두 그럴듯해 보였죠. 많은 문제가 여기에 달려 있었죠. 은하 이론이 옳다면 우주가 거대하다는 증거가 될 것이고, 먼지 이론이 옳다면 우주가 그리 크지 않다는 증거가 될 테니까요. 그래서 우주의 크기 문제가 달려 있었죠. 마침내 1920년대에 새로운 정보를 알려줄 만큼 성능이 좋은 망원경이 나왔습니다. 이 망원경으로 나선 성운을 관찰해 보니 절대적으로 확신할 수는 없었지만, 성운 안에 정말 별이 있는 것처럼 보였습니다. 먼지가 아니라 별이었죠.

하지만 성운이 얼마나 멀리 떨어져 있었을까요? 어떻게 측정할 수 있었을까요? 말해 볼 사람? 로라?

F   별의 밝기가 얼마나 강한지 측정하는 건 어때요? 별이 멀리 떨어져 있으면 어둡잖아요, 그렇죠?

P   맞아요. 하지만 문제가 있어요. 우선 별의 원래 밝기를 알아야 합니다. 왜냐하면 어떤 별은 원래 다른 별보다 더 밝으니까요. 따라서 어두운 별이 있다면 둘 중 하나겠지요.

F   음, 거리가 멀거나 원래 어두운 별인 거네요.

P   어느 쪽인지 항상 알 수는 없습니다. 하지만 제대로 짚었어요. 고유한 밝기를 계산할 수 있는 별이 있어요. 짐작했겠지만, 성운에도 그런 별들이 있어요. 이런 별들을 '변광성', 줄여서 '변광'이라고 합니다. 밝기가 일정한 주기에 따라 변하기 때문이죠. 여기서 더 깊이 들어가지는 않겠지만, 기본적으로 주기가 길수록 별이 더 밝기 때문에 주기의 길이를 이용해 고유한 밝기를 계산할 수 있어요. 이런 식으로 별이 얼마나 멀리 떨어져 있는지 측정할 수 있었는데 많은 별들이 엄청나게 멀리 떨어진 것으로 확인되었어요. 그래서 나선 성운이 아주 멀리 떨어진 외부은하라고 확신할 수 있게 되었습니다. 18세기 천문학자들이 짐작은 했지만 증명할 도구가 없었던 가설이지요.

여러분에게 이 이야기를 들려준 한 가지 이유는 오늘날에도 존재는 확인했지만 정체를 확신할 수 없는 상황들은 여전히 아주 많기 때문입니다. 아직 신비에 싸인 관찰 대상 중 하나가 감마선 폭발원입니다.

우리는 오래전부터 감마선 폭발원을 인지했지만, 그 정체를 둘러싸고 의견이 분분합니다.

어휘

astronomy 천문학   telescope 천체 망원경   Jupiter 목성   nebulae 성운(가스와 먼지 따위로 이루어져 구름처럼 뿌옇게 보이는 천체)   fuzzy 흐릿한 patch 조각, 점   spiral shape 나선형   clue 단서   cosmic 우주의   galaxy 은하   moral 교훈   explanation 설명   observation 관찰   obvious 명백한   hypothesis 가설   plausible 타당한, 그럴듯한   at stake 성패가 달린, 위기에 처한   enormous 거대한   absolutely 절대적으로   measure 측정하다   calculate 계산하다   variable star 변광성   vary 변하다   interval 주기, 간격   instrument 도구   gamma-ray burster 감마선 폭발원 (감마선 폭발의 원인이 되는 천체)

17. 이 강의의 주제는 무엇인가?

Ⓐ 천문학자들이 관찰한 어떤 현상에 관한 정확한 해석을 찾아낸
    방법
Ⓑ 천문학자들이 두 종류의 성운을 구별하는 방법
Ⓒ 지난 300년 간의 다양한 망원경 성능 향상
Ⓓ 천문학에서 여전히 풀리지 않은 문제

어휘 interpretation 해석   distinguish 구별하다

18. 강의에 따르면, 멀리 떨어진 은하들은 18세기 천문학자들에게 어떻게 보였는가?

Ⓐ 행성의 위성처럼
Ⓑ 작은 구름처럼
Ⓒ 변광성처럼
Ⓓ 밝은 불꽃처럼

19. 천문학자들이 성운의 정체를 파악한 후 제대로 추정할 수 있게 된 것은?

Ⓐ 변광성의 지름
Ⓑ 우주 먼지의 밀도
Ⓒ 우주의 크기
Ⓓ 은하에 속한 행성의 평균 개수

어휘 diameter (원의) 지름   density 밀도, 농도

20. 교수에 따르면, 천문학자들이 1920년대 망원경 덕분에 처음으로 하게 된 일은?

Ⓐ 목성의 위성 연구
Ⓑ 감마선 폭발원 관찰
Ⓒ 성운 먼지 이론 기각
Ⓓ 은하가 놀랄 만큼 작다는 사실 증명

어휘 reject 기각하다, 거부하다   prove 증명하다

21. 18세기 천문학자와 오늘날 천문학자의 공통점은?

Ⓐ 도구를 이용해 발견한 모든 것을 설명할 수는 없었다.
Ⓑ 확인하지 못한 물체들의 정확한 거리를 알았다.
Ⓒ 나선 성운을 관찰할 만큼 성능이 좋은 도구가 없었다.
Ⓓ 변광성의 고유한 밝기를 놓고 논쟁했다.

어휘 detect 발견하다, 탐지하다   argue over ~를 놓고 논쟁하다

22. 강의의 일부를 다시 듣고 질문에 답하라.

 T-76

P But how far away were they, really? How would you measure that? Any ideas? Laura?
F Well, how about measuring how strong those stars shine? Because, if the star is far away, then its light would be weak, right?
P Yes ... but there's a problem here. You need to know how bright the star is in the first place, because some stars are naturally much brighter than others. So, if you see a star that's weak ... it can mean one of two things...
F Oh ... it's either far away or it's just a weak star.

N *What can be inferred about the student when she says this:*
F Oh ... it's either far away or it's just a weak star.

Ⓐ 정답이라고 확신한다.
Ⓑ 원래 의견에 약점이 있었음을 깨달았다.
Ⓒ 교수가 옳다고 수긍하지 않는다.
Ⓓ 교수가 자신이 말한 내용을 오해했다고 생각한다.

어휘 weakness 약점

N Narrator   P Professor

Script T-77

N Listen to part of a lecture in an art history class.

P Today we're going to talk about how to look at a piece of art, how to *"read"* it—what you should look for … what aspects of it you should evaluate. A lot of people think that if you stand in front of a work of art and gaze at it for a couple of minutes, you're evaluating it. But truly *reading* a piece of art, evaluating it *properly*, is a complex process, a process that takes *time*.

When we're confronted with a piece of art, there're several things we have to keep in mind, for example, its beauty … that's where aesthetics comes in.

Aesthetics is the philosophy that deals with the definition of beauty, which goes all the way back to ancient Greece. They, um, the early Greek philosophers said that beauty and art are based on imitation. Their feeling about art was that it's beautiful when it imitates life; they thought that the *truthfulness* of an image, how truthful it is to life, determines its value as art. Today we have a broader definition of aesthetics.

Now *don't* identify aesthetics as personal taste. Taste is bound by time; taste is tied to a society, a given set of moral values, usually. You may not like a piece of art from a different culture—it may not be your taste—but you appreciate its beauty 'cause you recognize certain aesthetic principles. Art generally adheres to certain aesthetic principles like balance, uh, balanced proportions, contrast, movement, or rhythm.

We'll discuss aesthetics more in detail when we look at some pieces of art together. Another thing to keep in mind in evaluating art is that art has a *purpose*, generally determined by the artist. You may not know what it is, and you don't need to know what it is to appreciate a piece of art, but it helps. For example, if you know what the artist's purpose is … if you know that a piece of art expresses the artist's feeling about a political or social situation, you'll probably look at it differently.

Now, besides beauty and purpose, what are the other aspects of a piece of art that need to be evaluated? Very simple—you examine a piece of art following these four formal steps. The first step is *description* … describe physical characteristics of the piece—like this painting is large, it's oil on canvas. Describe the subject—it's a person, it's a landscape—or predominant colors like, um, earth colors … that's a description.

OK? So, you've described the piece. The next step is *analysis*.

N 미술사 수업의 강의 일부를 들으시오.

P 오늘은 미술 작품을 보는 법, 작품을 "읽는" 법, 즉 무엇을 봐야 하며, 어떤 면을 평가해야 하는지에 대해 이야기할게요. 많은 사람들이 미술 작품 앞에 서서 몇 분간 유심히 바라보는 것을 평가라고 생각합니다. 하지만 진정으로 작품을 읽고 적절히 평가하는 과정은 복잡하고 시간이 걸립니다.

미술 작품을 마주할 때 염두에 두어야 하는 사항이 몇 가지 있습니다. 이를테면 아름다움 등등. 그래서 미학이 생겨났지요.

미학은 아름다움에 대한 정의를 다루는 철학으로 고대 그리스까지 거슬러 올라갑니다. 초기 그리스 철학자들은 아름다움과 미술이 모방에 뿌리를 두고 있다고 말했죠. 그들은 실물을 그대로 모방한 미술을 아름답다고 느꼈습니다. 이미지의 진실성, 즉 얼마나 실물에 가깝게 재현했느냐가 미술의 가치를 결정한다고 생각했습니다. 오늘날에는 좀 더 넓은 의미로 미학을 정의합니다.

이제 미학을 개인의 취향 문제로 보지 마세요. 취향은 시대에 얽매이고, 사회나 일단의 도덕적 가치에 얽매이는 경우가 많습니다. 혹 다른 문화권의 미술 작품이 마음에 들지 않더라도, 그러니까 여러분 취향이 아니라도 미학적 원리들을 파악할 수 있기 때문에 작품의 아름다움을 감상할 수 있습니다. 미술은 일반적으로 균형, 균형 잡힌 비율, 대조, 동세, 리듬 같은 미학적 원리를 충실히 따릅니다.

몇몇 작품을 함께 보면서 미학에 대해 더 자세히 논의해 봅시다. 미술을 평가할 때 염두에 두어야 할 또 다른 사항은 미술에는 보통 화가가 의도한 목적이 담겨 있다는 점입니다. 목적이 무엇인지 알아채지 못할 수도 있고, 작품을 감상하는 데 반드시 목적이 무엇인지 알 필요는 없지만, 알면 도움이 됩니다. 예를 들어 화가의 목적이 무엇인지 안다면, 그 미술품이 정치적, 사회적 상황에 대한 화가의 감정을 표현했다는 사실을 안다면, 분명 작품이 달리 보일 겁니다.

아름다움과 목적 외에 미술 작품의 또 어떤 면을 평가해야 할까요? 매우 간단합니다. 다음과 같은 일정한 4단계를 거치며 관찰하면 됩니다. 첫 단계는 설명으로 작품의 물리적인 특징, 이 그림은 크다든지, 캔버스에 그린 유화라든지 하는 내용을 설명합니다. 인물화인지, 풍경화인지 대상을 설명하고, 흙색 등 주조색을 설명합니다. 이것이 설명 단계입니다.

아셨죠? 이제 작품을 설명했습니다. 다음은 분석입니다. 작품에 담긴 모든 보편적인 상징, 등장인물, 주제를 관찰

You're looking at the piece for any universal symbols, characters, or themes it might contain. Certain symbols are universal, and the artist counts on your understanding of symbols. Even colors have symbolic significance, as you may know. And also *objects* depicted in a piece of art are often used to represent an abstract idea. Like wheels or spheres—they look like circles, right?—so wheels and spheres represent wholeness and continuity. I have a handout, a list of these symbols and images and their interpretations, that I'll give you later. But for now, the point is that after you describe the piece of art, you *analyze* its content ... you determine whether it contains elements that the artist is using to try to convey a certain meaning.

If it does, the next step is *interpretation*. Interpretation follows analysis very closely. You try to interpret the meaning of the symbols you identified in the piece. Almost all art has an obvious and an implied meaning. The implied meaning is hidden in the symbolic system expressed in the piece of art. What we see depicted is *one* scene, but there can be several levels of meaning. Your interpretation of these symbols makes clear what the artist is trying to tell us.

The last step is *judgment or opinion*—what do you think of the piece, is it powerful or boring?—but I give that hardly any weight. If the four steps were to be divided up into a chart, then description, analysis, and interpretation would take up 99 percent. Your opinion is not important in understanding a piece of art. It's nice to say: I like it ... I wouldn't mind hanging it over my couch, but to evaluate a piece of art, it's not critical.

OK. Now you know what I mean by "reading" a piece of art, and what it entails. Try to keep all that in mind next time you go to an art museum. I can tell you right now that you probably won't be able to look at more than 12 pieces of art during that visit.

OK, now let's look at a slide of a piece of art and try to "read" it together.

합니다. 특정한 상징들은 보편적이며, 화가는 여러분이 상징을 이해하리라 기대합니다. 다들 알겠지만, 색깔에도 상징적 의미가 있습니다. 또 미술 작품에 묘사된 사물이 추상적 관념을 표현하는 경우도 많습니다. 바퀴나 구 같은 경우, 원처럼 생겼지요? 그래서 바퀴나 구는 완전성과 연속성을 상징합니다. 이러한 상징과 이미지들에 대한 해석을 정리한 유인물을 있다가 나눠 줄게요. 우선 지금은 미술 작품을 설명한 후에 내용을 분석해야 한다는 것, 화가가 특정한 의미를 전달하려고 사용한 요소들이 담겨 있는지를 판단해야 한다는 것을 기억해 둡시다.

만약 그렇다면 그 다음 단계는 해석입니다. 해석은 분석과 아주 밀접하게 연관되어 있습니다. 작품에서 발견한 상징들의 의미를 해석하려고 합니다. 거의 모든 작품에는 명시적, 암시적 의미가 있습니다. 암시적 의미는 작품에 표현된 상징체계 속에 숨어 있죠. 묘사된 것은 한 장면이지만 여러 수준의 의미를 담고 있을 수도 있습니다. 이러한 상징들을 해석하면 화가가 말하고자 하는 의도가 무엇인지 명확히 드러납니다.

마지막 단계는 판단 혹은 의견입니다. 작품에 대한 여러분의 느낌이 어떤지, 강렬한지, 지루한지를 말합니다. 하지만 이 단계는 그리 중요하지 않습니다. 4단계를 차트에 그린다면 아마 설명, 분석, 해석이 99%를 차지할 겁니다. 여러분의 의견은 미술품을 이해하는 데 별로 중요하지 않아요. 마음에 든다, 소파 위에 걸어 두고 싶다고 말하면 듣기 좋죠. 하지만 미술 작품 평가에는 중요하지 않습니다.

자, 이제 미술 작품을 "읽는" 행위가 무엇을 뜻하는지, 어떤 일들이 수반되는지 알았을 겁니다. 다음번에 미술관에 갈 때 전부 기억해 보세요. 장담컨대, 한 번 가서 12점 이상의 작품을 보기는 아마 힘들 겁니다.

이제 미술 작품들을 슬라이드로 보면서 함께 "읽어" 보도록 합시다.

어휘

aspect 면, 양상   evaluate (가치, 품질 등을) 평가하다   gaze 응시하다   properly 적절히   confront 마주치다, 직면하다   aesthetics 미학
philosophy 철학   imitation 모방   truthfulness 진실성   taste 취향   appreciate 감상하다   principle 원리, 원칙   adhere to 고수하다
proportion 비율   contrast 대조   movement 동세   description 설명, 묘사   predominant color 주조색   earth color 흙색   universal 보편적인
significance 의미, 중요성   depict 묘사하다   abstract 추상적인   sphere 구(球), 공 모양   wholeness 완전성   continuity 연속성   implied 암시적인
take up (시간이나 공간을) 차지하다   couch 긴 의자, 소파   entail 수반하다

23. 이 강의의 주제는 무엇인가?

Ⓐ 다양한 회화 기법
Ⓑ 미술 작품의 목적을 알아내는 방법
Ⓒ 도덕적 가치들이 미술에 반영되는 방식
Ⓓ 미술 작품을 평가하는 방식

어휘 reflect 반영하다, 비추다

24. 교수에 따르면, 고대 그리스 철학자들이 미술 작품에서 소중하게 여긴 것은?

Ⓐ 실물에 대한 정확한 모방
Ⓑ 실물에 대한 독특한 관점
Ⓒ 복잡한 감정들의 표현
Ⓓ 상징주의의 활용

어휘 accurate 정확한   unusual 독특한, 흔치 않은
symbolism 상징주의

25. 교수가 개인의 취향에 대해 이야기하는 이유는?

Ⓐ 미술 평가에서 개인적 취향의 중요성을 지적하려고
Ⓑ 학생들에게 미학의 의미를 이해시키려고
Ⓒ 개인의 취향과 미학이 같음을 증명하려고
Ⓓ 다른 문화권의 미술에 대해 설명하려고

26. 교수가 바퀴와 구를 언급하는 이유는?

Ⓐ 미술 작품에서 동세가 어떻게 표현될 수 있는지 예증하려고
Ⓑ 미술 작품에서 사물이 색채보다 훨씬 중요함을 입증하려고
Ⓒ 상징적 의미가 담긴 사물을 예로 들려고
Ⓓ 어떤 사물이 미술 작품에 잘 등장하지 않는 이유를 설명하려고

어휘 demonstrate 입증하다   rarely 드물게

27. 교수는 미술 작품을 관찰할 때 필요한 4단계를 언급한다. 단계를 순서대로 배치하라.

보기를 적절한 곳에 써 넣으시오. 보기에 해당하는 알파벳을 쓰거나 문장을 옮겨 쓰시오.

1	C
2	B
3	D
4	A

Ⓐ 미술품에 대한 의견 제시하기
Ⓑ 상징이 있는지 찾기
Ⓒ 미술품에 대해 기술하기
Ⓓ 화가의 의도를 알아내기

28. 강의의 일부를 다시 듣고 질문에 답하라.

 T-78

N *What does the professor imply when he says this:*
P Try to keep all that in mind next time you go to an art museum. I can tell you right now that you probably won't be able to look at more than 12 pieces of art during that visit.

Ⓐ 교수는 12점의 미술품을 평가하라는 과제를 낼 것이다.
Ⓑ 교수는 미술관으로 단체 견학을 준비하고 있다.
Ⓒ 미술품을 평가하는 데는 시간이 많이 걸린다.
Ⓓ 학생들은 이제 미술품을 빨리 평가할 수 있을 것이다.

어휘 assign (일, 과제 등을) 부여하다
organize (행사, 회의 등을) 조직하다, 준비하다

SPEAKING

Question 1
p.198

Narrator T-79

Some people enjoy watching movies or television in their spare time. Others prefer reading books or magazines. State which you prefer and explain why.

어떤 사람들은 여가 시간에 영화나 TV를 보는 것을 좋아한다. 다른 사람들은 책이나 잡지를 읽는 쪽을 더 좋아한다. 어느 쪽을 선호하는지 밝히고 이유를 설명하시오.

준비 시간 : 15초
답변 시간 : 45초

중요 포인트

수험자는 영화나 TV 시청을 선호하는지, 책이나 잡지 읽는 쪽을 선호하는지에 대한 자신의 의견을 명확히 진술해야 한다. 그런 다음 의견을 뒷받침하는 근거를 제시해야 한다.

영화나 TV 시청을 선호한다면 "I enjoy the visual nature of films." ("나는 영화의 시각적인 속성을 좋아한다."), "I particularly enjoy seeing other places shown in films." ("나는 특히 영화에 나오는 다른 장소들을 구경하는 것을 좋아한다.")라는 식으로 근거를 제시해야 한다. 그런 다음 재미있게 보았던 여행 영화 등 특정 영화를 묘사한다거나, 영화를 보고 여행을 떠나고 싶은 충동이 일었다고 말할 수 있다.

책이나 잡지를 읽는 것을 선호한다면 "I prefer to imagine something that I read myself, rather than seeing a movie of it." ("나는 영상으로 보기보다 스스로 읽으면서 상상하기를 더 좋아한다."), "I am often disappointed when I see a movie that was based on a book because I had imagined the scenes and characters differently and this is why I prefer to read." ("나는 책을 원작으로 만든 영화를 볼 때면 자주 실망하는데, 장면과 인물이 내가 상상한 모습과 다르기 때문이다. 그래서 독서를 더 좋아한다.")라고 말할 수 있다. 특정 영화나 책을 묘사하면서 내용을 전개할 수도 있다.

이 질문에 정답은 따로 없다는 점을 염두에 두기 바란다. 어느 쪽을 선호하든 구체적인 예를 들어 답변을 뒷받침해야 한다.

Question 2
p.198

Narrator T-80

Read the announcement about City University's plans for the campus gym. You will have 45 seconds to read. Begin reading now.

시티대학 교내 체육관에 대한 공지 사항을 45초 동안 읽으시오. 지금 읽으시오.

Plans for Campus Gym

The recreational services department will receive special funding from this year's budget to increase the number of exercise machines in the campus gym. The increase is in response to numerous student complaints regarding the insufficient number of machines available. Recreational services agrees that, due to an increase in university enrollment, more students are using the gym. They, therefore, welcomed the proposal, adding that it would encourage even more students to exercise and would help to promote a healthier lifestyle among students.

교내 체육관 운영 계획

레크리에이션부는 올해 예산에서 교내 체육관에 운동 기구를 늘리기 위한 특별 지원금을 받을 예정입니다. 이렇게 결정한 배경은 운동 기구가 충분하지 않다고 불만을 제기하는 학생들이 많았기 때문입니다. 레크리에이션부는 본교 재학생이 늘어나면서 체육관 이용자 수가 늘어났다는 점에 동의합니다. 따라서 레크리에이션부는 이번 제안을 반기면서 더 많은 학생들이 운동을 하게끔 유도할 수 있고 더 건강한 생활 습관을 전파하는 데 도움이 될 것이라고 덧붙였습니다.

어휘

gym 체육관   funding 지원금, 자금   budget 예산
numerous 많은   insufficient 불충분한
enrollment 등록, 등록[재적]자 수   proposal 제안
promote 촉진하다

149

Listen to two students discussing the plan.

이 계획에 대해 두 학생이 나누는 대화를 들으시오.

Script

M Hey, have you read about this … the plans for the gym?

F Yeah, but I could sure think of better things to do with the money.

M You're kidding. I thought you'd be all for it. You go to the gym all the time.

F Yeah, but I never have any problem. Sure there's a lot of people there but I never have to wait to use the exercise bikes, or even the weight machines. Do you?

M Not really. It's not that busy.

F The other thing is … well, we have all sorts of exercise programs, a terrific swimming pool that's always open, great running paths, all kinds of sports teams. I'm just saying that a bunch of new machines in the gym aren't gonna make any difference. People like to get their exercise in different ways … and on this campus there're already plenty of choices.

M You may be right…

M 안녕, 체육관에 대한 공지 사항 읽었어?

F 응, 하지만 그 돈으로 훨씬 나은 것들을 할 수 있을 텐데.

M 무슨 소리야. 쌍수 들고 환영할 줄 알았더니. 너 체육관 자주 가잖아.

F 그래, 하지만 한 번도 문제없었어. 사람들이 좀 많기는 하지만 자전거나 운동 기구 앞에서 기다린 적은 없어. 너는?

M 나도 없었던 것 같아. 그렇게 붐비진 않잖아.

F 이유는 또 있어. 우리 학교에는 이미 다양한 운동 프로그램, 연중무휴인 시설 좋은 수영장, 훌륭한 조깅 트랙, 다양한 운동부가 있잖아. 내 말은 체육관에 새 운동 기구를 왕창 들여온다고 해서 큰 변화가 일어나지는 않을 거란 거야. 사람들은 각자 원하는 방식으로 운동하고 싶어하고, 우리 학교에는 이미 너무나 많은 선택권이 있어.

M 하긴 그러네.

어휘

exercise bike 운동용 자전거   weight machine 근력운동 기구
terrific 훌륭한   running path 조깅 트랙

Narrator

The woman expresses her opinion about the plan described in the announcement. Briefly summarize the plan. Then state her opinion about the plan and explain the reasons she gives for holding that opinion.

여자가 공지 사항의 계획에 대한 의견을 말하고 있다. 계획을 간략히 요약한 다음, 여학생의 의견이 무엇이며 그런 입장을 취하는 이유를 설명하시오.

준비 시간 : 30초
답변 시간 : 60초

중요 포인트

먼저 대학 측의 계획을 간략히 요약해야 한다. 계획은 체육관에 운동 기구를 보충하는 것이다. 그렇게 결정한 이유를 1) "Fewer machines are available because of increased student enrollment." ("재학생이 늘어나서 이용할 수 있는 운동 기구의 수가 적어졌다."), 2) "It will encourage more students to exercise." ("더 많은 학생들이 운동하게끔 유도할 수 있다.")라고 간략히 요약해도 된다. 요약에 시간을 너무 끌다가 여학생이 계획에 반대하는 두 가지 이유에 대해 얘기할 시간이 모자랄 수도 있다. 이런 문제 유형의 경우 간단한 요약이면 충분하다.

요약이 끝나면 여학생의 입장을 밝혀야 한다. 이 문제의 경우 여학생은 대학 측의 계획에 대해 반대한다. 그런 다음 여학생이 그런 입장을 취하는 두 가지 이유를 전달해야 한다. 답변을 완성하기 위해서는 대화와 지문에 있는 정보를 연결해야 한다. 여학생은 이용할 수 있는 운동 기구의 수가 적다는 논점에 반대한다. 여학생은 체육관에 사람이 많은 것은 사실이지만 기구를 이용하려고 기다릴 필요는 없다고 말한다.

그리고 여학생이 대학 측의 계획에 반대하는 두 번째 이유도 전달해야 한다. 여학생은 새 운동 기구를 보충한다고 더 많은 사람이 운동을 하진 않을 거라고 생각한다. 여학생은 시티 대학이 지금도 충분히 학생들이 운동을 하고 더 건강한 생활 습관을 유지할 기회를 제공하고 있다고 말하며 수영장, 조깅 트랙, 운동부를 예로 든다.

Question 3

p.199

Narrator T-82

Now read the passage about keystone species. You will have 50 seconds to read the passage. Begin reading now.

핵심종에 대한 지문을 50초 동안 읽으시오. 지금 읽으시오.

Keystone Species

Within a habitat, each species depends on other species, and contributes to the overall stability of that ecosystem. However, some species do more than others by providing essential services. Without the influence of these key species, the habitat changes significantly. Scientists refer to these important players in an ecosystem as *keystone species*. When a keystone species disappears from its habitat, the habitat changes dramatically. Their disappearance can then trigger the loss of other species. As some species vanish, others move in or become more abundant. The new mix of species changes the habitat's appearance and character.

핵심종

서식지 내에서 모든 종은 다른 종에 의존하며 서식지 생태계의 전반적인 안정성에 기여한다. 하지만 어떤 종들은 결정적인 역할을 함으로써 다른 종보다 훨씬 많이 기여한다. 이러한 핵심종의 역할이 없으면 서식지에는 커다란 변화가 일어난다. 과학자들은 이처럼 생태계에서 중요한 역할을 하는 종들을 핵심종이라고 부른다. 핵심종이 서식지에서 사라지면 서식지에는 극적인 변화가 일어난다. 핵심종이 사라지면 다른 종도 사라질 수 있다. 일부 종이 사라지면서 다른 종이 새로 유입되거나 개체 수가 늘어난다. 종의 구성이 바뀌면 서식지의 모습과 특징도 변한다.

어휘

keystone species 핵심종   habitat 서식지   overall 전반적인
stability 안정성   essential 결정적인   ecosystem 생태계
disappearance 소멸, 실종   trigger 촉발하다   vanish 사라지다
abundant 풍부한

Narrator T-83

Now listen to part of a lecture on this topic in a biology class.

이 주제에 관한 생물학 강의의 일부를 들으시오

Script

P   Let's take the elephant, for example. Elephants are an important species in the African grasslands. Without them, the grasslands actually stop being grasslands at all if you can believe it—they change to forests. What happens is that in the grasslands some types of seeds other than grasses can sprout and begin to grow, which ... if they're left alone ... they could eventually grow into shrubs or trees. But what happens is that elephants come along and eat the sprouting plants ... or the plants get crushed under the elephants' feet. And even if a plant or two manage to survive, it won't last long because sooner or later the elephant will knock it over or pull it out of the ground.

So what if the elephants weren't there and these plants were allowed to grow to maturity? Well, pretty soon there'd be whole clusters of trees. Their branches and leaves would shade the grasses ... and without the sunlight, the grasses won't survive. So pretty soon the grass disappears, trees grow in its place and eventually the whole grassland changes to forest.

And as you can imagine the elephant has an impact on other animal species in the habitat as well. A lot of animals in this habitat rely on the grasses for food, for example. When the grasses disappear— when their food source disappears—these animals are eventually forced to leave. Gradually, some new species come into the habitat—species that are better suited to life in the forest. These new species replace the ones that left. So you can see the influence of the elephant on the environment is significant.

151

P 코끼리를 예로 들어봅시다. 코끼리는 아프리카 초원에서 중요한 종입니다. 코끼리가 없다면 초원은 더 이상 초원으로 있지 않습니다. 믿기지 않겠지만, 숲으로 바뀝니다. 초원에는 풀이 아닌 다른 씨앗들이 움트고 자랍니다. 그대로 둔다면 결국에는 관목이나 나무가 됩니다. 하지만 코끼리가 와서 자라나는 식물을 먹어 치웁니다. 아니면 식물이 코끼리 발에 짓밟히기도 하죠. 한두 그루가 어떻게든 살아남더라도 그리 오래가지 못합니다. 머지않아 코끼리가 쓰러뜨리거나 뿌리를 뽑아버릴 테니까요.

그렇다면 코끼리가 없으면 이런 식물이 무럭무럭 자랄 수 있을까요? 금세 나무가 군락을 이룰 겁니다. 나뭇가지와 잎사귀가 그늘을 드리워 햇빛을 가리면 풀은 살아남지 못합니다. 그래서 금세 풀은 사라지고 그 자리에 나무가 자라서 결국에는 초원 전체가 숲으로 바뀝니다. 짐작하겠지만 코끼리는 서식지에 있는 다른 동물종에도 영향을 미칩니다. 이를테면 서식지에 사는 많은 동물이 풀을 먹고삽니다. 초원, 즉 녀석들의 먹이 공급원이 사라지면 이 동물들은 결국에는 어쩔 수 없이 떠나야 합니다. 점차 새로운 종들이 서식지에 들어옵니다. 숲에서 살기에 훨씬 적합한 종들이겠지요. 새로운 종들은 떠난 종들의 빈자리를 대신합니다. 코끼리가 환경에 미치는 영향이 얼마나 지대한지 알 수 있죠.

어휘

seed 싹, 씨앗   sprout 싹트다, 움트다   shrub 관목   crush 밟아 뭉개다
maturity 성숙, 다 자란 상태   cluster 무리, 다발   have an impact on
~에 영향을 미치다   be suited to ~에 적합하다

Narrator

The professor gives examples of the effects of elephants on the African grasslands habitat. Using the examples from the talk, explain why elephants are considered a keystone species.

교수는 코끼리가 아프리카 초원 서식지에 미치는 영향을 예를 들어 설명한다. 강의에 나온 예들을 이용하여 코끼리가 핵심종인 이유를 설명하시오.

준비 시간 : 30초
답변 시간 : 60초

중요 포인트

먼저 지문에 나온 핵심종의 개념을 설명해야 한다. 코끼리와 연관 지어 얘기할 수 있다. 핵심종이 중요한 이유는 핵심종이 없으면 서식지에 극적인 변화가 일어나기 때문이다. 아프리카 초원 서식지에 사는 코끼리는 핵심종의 예다.

그런 다음 교수가 든 예를 언급해야 한다. 지문과 강의에 나온 모든 세부 내용을 반복할 필요는 없지만, 완벽한 답변이 되려면 지문과 강의의 요점을 통합해야 한다.

교수는 코끼리가 사라지면 초원 서식지가 어떻게 변할지 예를 들며, "Elephants eat or destroy tree and shrub seeds and small plants, preventing many trees from growing in the grasslands. If they did not remove these trees, many trees would block sunshine, so grasses would die. The trees would eventually replace grasses, and the forest would replace the grasslands." ("코끼리는 나무와 관목의 씨앗, 작은 풀을 먹어 치우거나 짓밟아서 초원에서 나무가 마구 자라는 것을 예방한다. 코끼리가 나무를 없애지 않으면 나무들이 무성하게 자라 햇빛을 가려 풀이 죽는다. 결국 나무가 풀을 대체하고, 숲이 초원을 대체한다.")라고 말한다.

교수는 코끼리가 사라지면 서식지에 어떤 영향을 미칠지 또 다른 관점을 제시한다. 교수는 "Other animals in this habitat depend on grasses for food and survival. When grasses die, these animals leave the habitat and new species move into the habitat." ("서식지에 있는 다른 동물들은 먹이와 생존을 위해 초원에 의지한다. 초원이 사라지면 동물들이 서식지를 떠나고 새로운 종이 들어온다.")라고 말한다. 두 가지 예는 코끼리가 왜 핵심종인지를 설명한다.

이것은 한 가지 예시 답안에 불과하다. 답변을 구성하는 다른 방법들도 있다. 가장 중요한 포인트는 질문에서 요구한 구체적인 정보에 대해 언급하는 것이다. "Elephants are considered a keystone species because they have an important effect on their environment and it would change greatly without them." ("코끼리가 핵심종인 이유는 환경에 지대한 영향을 미치며, 사라질 경우 환경이 크게 변하기 때문이다.")라는 내용을 채점자가 이해하도록 해야 한다.

Question 4

p.200

Narrator T-84

Now listen to part of a lecture in a creative writing class.

문예창작 수업의 강의 일부를 들으시오.

P   As writers, you want the dialogue in your story to have impact. Well, there are many ways to do that, and I'm gonna talk about two of them— exaggeration and understatement. Now, understatement is the opposite of exaggeration, but you can actually use them both to do the same thing— to create emphasis or impact. Let's compare them and see how they do that.

OK, exaggeration. When you want your characters to emphasize a point, you can have them describe things or their feelings as bigger or more extreme than they really are. For example, your main character comes back from a very long walk and she's very tired. Well, you can have her say "Boy, I'm tired." *Or* you can have her say, "I can't take another step." Well, *of course* she can take another step, but you see, if she exaggerates, she'll make her point in a more forceful and interesting way.

But you can also create emphasis with *understatement*, and like I said it's the opposite of exaggeration, but it does the same thing. With understatement you emphasize by saying, by saying *less*, by saying less than you mean. That sounds paradoxical, so I'll give you an example. From real life.

My friend Ed is a very talented cook. So last week he cooked me a delicious meal. Now, I could've said to him, "This food is really great, Ed," but that's kinda boring. Plus, Ed *knew* I thought the food was delicious. I'd eaten three servings. So instead I said, "This food's not bad, Ed." Now clearly the food was a lot *better* than *not bad*. But by understating, by describing the food as—as *less* good than it really was, I actually made a stronger statement. The characters in your stories can do this too.

P   작가로서 여러분은 이야기 속에 인상에 남는 대사를 쓰고 싶을 겁니다. 그렇게 하는 방법은 다양한데, 오늘은 과장법과 곡언법에 대해 이야기해보려고 합니다. 곡언법은 과장법과 정반대 개념이지만, 실제로는 둘 다 강조나 임팩트를 더하는 같은 역할을 합니다. 두 수사법을 비교해 보고 어떻게 그런 역할을 하는지 알아봅시다.

자, 먼저 과장법입니다. 작중인물이 어떤 점을 강조하도록 만들려면

사물이나 감정을 실제보다 훨씬 크게 혹은 극단적으로 묘사할 수 있습니다. 예를 들면 여주인공이 오랫동안 걷다가 돌아와 매우 피곤합니다. "아, 너무 피곤해."라고 쓸 수도 있지요. 아니면 "한 발짝도 못 움직이겠어."라고 쓸 수도 있습니다. 물론 여자는 한 발짝 걸을 수 있지만, 보다시피 과장법을 이용하면 훨씬 강렬하고 흥미로운 표현이 됩니다.

한편 곡언법을 이용해 강조할 수도 있는데, 앞서 말했다시피 과장법과 정반대 개념이지만, 같은 효과를 냅니다. 곡언법을 이용하면 뜻하는 바보다 더 작게 표현함으로써 강조의 효과를 냅니다. 모순처럼 들리지만, 실생활에서 예를 들어 보겠습니다.

제 친구 에드는 아주 요리 솜씨가 좋습니다. 지난주에 저한테 맛있는 요리를 해주었지요. 이럴 때 "정말 맛있다"고 말할 수 있습니다. 하지만 너무 단조롭지요. 게다가 에드는 제가 맛있다고 생각한다는 사실을 이미 알았습니다. 세 접시나 먹었거든요. 그래서 그 대신 "이번 요리는 나쁘진 않네, 에드."라고 말합니다. 분명 그 요리는 나쁘지 않은 정도보다 훨씬 더 훌륭합니다. 하지만 절제된 표현으로 그 요리가 실제보다 덜 훌륭하다고 표현함으로써 훨씬 더 강한 표현으로 만든 것이지요. 여러분의 작중인물들도 이렇게 할 수 있습니다.

어휘

exaggeration 과장법   understatement 곡언법
paradoxical 모순적인   talented 재능이 있는   serving (음식) 1인분

Narrator

Using the examples mentioned by the professor, describe two ways that writers create emphasis when writing dialogue.

교수가 언급한 예들을 사용해서 작가들이 대사를 쓸 때 활용할 수 있는 두 가지 강조법을 설명하시오.

준비 시간 : 20초
답변 시간 : 60초

중요 포인트

이 문제는 강의 내용을 듣고 요약하는 능력을 요구한다. 작가들이 대사를 쓸 때 사용하는 두 가지 강조법인 과장법과 곡언법에 대해 언급해야 한다.

소개가 끝나면 작가가 강조할 때 쓸 수 있는 첫 번째 수사법에 대해 이야기해야 한다. 교수는 과장법이 실제보다 더 크게 혹은 더 많게 묘사함으로써 강조나 임팩트를 더할 수 있다고 말한다. 예를 들면 오랫동안 걸어서 피곤한 등장인물은 "피곤해."라고 말하지 않고 "한 발짝도 못 움직이겠어."라고 말한다. 과장법은 훨씬 강렬하고 흥미를 유발한다.

그런 다음 강조할 때 쓸 수 있는 두 번째 수사법에 대해 이야기해야 한다. 교수는 곡언법을 이용하면 뜻하는 바보다 더 작게 말함으로써 강조할 수 있다고 말한다. 예를 들면 교수는 친구의 훌륭한 요리를 두고 "나쁘지 않다."는 말로 칭찬했다. 곡언법을 이용하면 더 강한 표현이 된다.

수험자는 두 번째 예를 말할 시간을 충분히 안배해야 한다. 이 문제는 두 가지 예를 모두 언급해야 하기 때문이다.

WRITING

Writing Based on Reading and Listening

p.204

Soon technology will provide smart cars: cars that virtually drive themselves. A computer in the car determines the speed and route to the desired destination. The computer is in continuous contact with a global positioning system and other technologies that will provide extremely accurate information about the location of the car, other cars on the road, congestion, accidents, and so forth. The human driver will be little more than a passenger. Smart cars promise to make driving safer, quicker, and less expensive.

First of all, smart cars will prevent many accidents, thereby saving lives. The cars will be equipped with a variety of sensors that very accurately detect cars and other obstacles in their path, and they will have automatic programs that control braking and turning to avoid collisions. Given the hundreds of accidents that occur on highways daily, it is clear that humans do a poor job of avoiding accidents and that computer control would be a great improvement.

Second, with the wide use of smart cars, traffic problems will practically disappear. These computer-controlled cars can follow each other closely, even at high speeds. This ability will result in increased highway speeds. Today commuting by car can take hours a day. So the increased speed of smart cars will be a great benefit, welcomed by the many people who commute by car.

Finally, smart cars will bring a reduction in the costs of driving. Because smart cars are programmed to drive the most direct routes, car owners will have to spend less money on repairs and replacement parts. Expensive items such as brakes, tires, and transmissions will last much longer in smart cars than in other cars.

이제 곧 스마트 자동차 기술이 현실화될 것이다. 스마트 자동차란 컴퓨터를 이용해 스스로 주행하는 자동차를 말한다. 차량에 내장된 컴퓨터가 원하는 목적지까지 주행 속도와 경로를 결정한다. 컴퓨터는 GPS를 비롯해, 차량 위치, 도로의 교통량, 교통 혼잡, 교통사고 등에 대한 매우 정확한 정보를 제공하는 다른 장비들과 끊임없이 교신한다. 운전자는 탑승자에 불과하다. 스마트 자동차는 더 안전하고, 더 빠르고, 더 저렴한 주행을 약속한다.

우선, 스마트 자동차는 교통사고를 예방해 생명을 구할 수 있다.

자동차에는 진로에 있는 다른 차량과 장애물을 매우 정확히 감지할 수 있는 다양한 센서가 장착되고, 충돌을 피하기 위해 브레이크와 방향 전환을 자동 조종하는 프로그램이 탑재된다. 고속도로에서 매일 발생하는 수백 건의 교통사고를 볼 때, 인간은 교통사고를 피하는 데 서툴며 컴퓨터 조종이 훨씬 나은 해결책이라는 점은 자명하다.

둘째, 스마트 자동차의 보급과 함께 교통 문제는 거의 사라질 것이다. 컴퓨터로 조종되는 자동차는 빠른 속도로 주행할 때도 앞차와의 간격을 좁게 유지할 수 있다. 이렇게 되면 고속도로 소통이 원활해질 것이다. 오늘날 차로 통근하려면 하루에 몇 시간을 허비해야 한다. 따라서 스마트 자동차의 주행 속도 향상은 차로 통근하는 많은 사람들에게 환영 받는 훌륭한 혜택이 될 것이다.

끝으로, 스마트 자동차는 주행 비용 절감을 불러온다. 스마트 자동차는 최단 거리를 주행하도록 설정되기 때문에 수리 및 부품 교체 비용이 줄어들 것이다. 브레이크, 타이어, 변속기 등 고가의 부품은 일반 자동차보다 스마트 자동차에서 훨씬 수명이 오래갈 것이다.

어휘

virtually 실제로 destination 목적지 continuous 지속적인, 끊임 없는 global positioning system 위성항법장치(GPS) congestion 혼잡, 막힘 obstacle 장애물 collision 충돌 practically 사실상, 거의 reduction 절감 replacement part 교체 부품 transmission (자동차) 변속기

Narrator T-85

Now listen to part of a lecture on the topic you just read about.

방금 읽은 주제에 관한 강의의 일부를 들으시오.

Script

P   Even if computerized smart cars meet all the technological expectations set for them, it's not clear that they'd produce the benefits some have predicted.

Smart cars will still get into some accidents. After all, even the most technologically advanced devices fail occasionally. And since the smart car technology will allow cars to be more tightly packed together on the roads, these accidents will be pileups that involve many more cars and so be much worse than accidents that occur today. Overall, there is little reason to believe that smart cars will save lives or reduce the number of injuries in automobile accidents.

Second, let's talk about the potential to increase highway speeds and therefore decrease commuting time. Well, history has consistently shown that when some driving convenience is introduced, more and more people decide to drive because they expect an easier driving experience. But then the increased number of drivers in the case of smart cars of the future would not decrease commuting time. This is because the traffic congestion caused by the additional cars on the road would not allow the drivers to take advantage of the smart cars' potential for higher speeds.

And finally, it's not reasonable to expect that smart cars will save drivers money. The global positioning technology required to direct smart cars to their desired destinations is very expensive, and smart cars will need other costly technologies too, such as sensors that control how far a smart car stays behind the car in front of it. Moreover, the advanced technology of smart cars will make repairs to them more expensive than repairs on conventional automobiles. These new expenses will more than offset the expected savings on the repair and replacement of traditional mechanical car parts.

P 컴퓨터로 조종되는 스마트 자동차에서 기술적으로 기대하고 있는 모든 것이 실현되더라도 일부 사람들이 예측한 혜택들을 정말로 가져올지는 불투명합니다.

스마트 자동차는 여전히 교통사고를 일으킬 겁니다. 어쨌거나 가장 앞선 최첨단 장치들조차 가끔은 고장을 일으키니까요. 그리고 스마트 자동차 기술로 도로에서 다른 차량에 바짝 붙어 주행할 수 있게 되므로 사고가 났다 하면 연쇄추돌이 되면서 오늘날의 교통사고보다 훨씬 심각할 겁니다. 전체적으로, 스마트 자동차 덕분에 교통사고 사망자나 부상자가 감소하리라 믿을 만한 근거는 거의 없습니다.

둘째, 고속도로 소통이 원활해지고 통근 시간이 줄어들 가능성에 대해 이야기해 봅시다. 역사는 계속해서 보여 줍니다. 운전이 조금이라도 편리해질수록 운전이 쉬워졌다는 이유로 점점 더 많은 사람들이 차를 운전한다는 사실을요. 하지만 미래에 스마트 자동차를 모는 운전자 수가 늘어난다면 통근 시간은 줄어들 수 없습니다. 도로에 자동차 수가 늘어나서 교통 혼잡이 발생하면서 스마트 자동차의 주행 속도 향상이라는 가능성이 실현되지 못하기 때문입니다.

마지막으로, 스마트 자동차가 비용을 절감해 준다고 기대할 만한 근거가 없습니다. 스마트 자동차를 원하는 목적지까지 안내하는 데 필요한 GPS 기술은 매우 비싸며, 그 밖에 앞차와의 간격을 유지하는 센서 등 다른 고가의 기술도 필요합니다. 더욱이 스마트 자동차에 들어가는 첨단 기술 장비들 때문에 수리 비용이 기존의 자동차보다 훨씬 비싸집니다. 이 추가 비용은 기존의 기계 부품을 수리하고 교체하는 데서 절감할 수 있으리라 기대하는 비용을 상쇄하고도 남을 겁니다.

어휘

expectation 기대, 예측 benefit 혜택, 이득 predict 예측하다 fail 고장 나다, 실패하다 occasionally 가끔 pileup 연쇄추돌 reduce 줄이다 injury 부상 potential 가능성 decrease 줄이다, 감소시키다 convenience 편리함 traffic congestion 교통 혼잡 costly 비싼, 비용이 많이 드는 repair 수리 conventional 기존의 expense 비용 offset 상쇄하다 replacement 교체 mechanical 기계적인, 기계로 작동되는

Narrator T-86

Question 1
Summarize the points made in the lecture, being sure to explain how they challenge specific points made in the reading passage.

방금 들은 강의의 논점들을 요약하되 이 논점들이 독해 지문의 구체적 논점들을 어떻게 반박하고 있는지 설명하시오.

해설

강의에서는 독해 지문에서 설명한 스마트 자동차의 장점, 즉 "스마트 자동차가 교통사고 횟수를 줄일 것이다", "통근 시간을 줄일 것이다", "경비를 절감하게 해줄 것이다"라는 내용에 동의하지 않는다는 점을 반드시 파악해야 한다. 답안에는 스마트 자동차가 독해 지문에서 예측한 혜택들을 제공할 수 없는 이유에 대해 교수가 제시한 근거들을 반드시 포함해야 한다.

지문의 주요 내용	지문과 대조되는 강의 내용
Since smart cars will be equipped with sophisticated technology to detect obstacles and control braking and turning, many accidents that human drivers cause today will be prevented.	Technologies used in smart cars will fail occasionally, as all technologies do. Since smart cars will travel at greater speeds and closer together, such technology failures will result in accidents that will be more serious than accidents caused nowadays by human drivers.
Commuting time for many people will be reduced because smart cars will be able to travel at greater speeds and closer together.	Every improvement in driving convenience usually results in more people taking to the road. The introduction of smart cars will likely result in more cars on the roads, which will cause additional traffic congestion. Commuting time is therefore not likely to decrease.
Smart cars will be able to choose the most direct routes. With less distance traveled, smart car owners will save money on repair and part replacement costs.	Sophisticated technologies used by smart cars will make the cars more expensive to buy and also more expensive to repair. These added costs will offset the savings identified in the reading.

155

Question 2

Your professor is teaching a class on child development. Write a post responding to the professor's question.

In your response, you should do the following.

- Express and support your opinion.
- Make a contribution to the discussion in your own words.

An effective response will contain at least 100 words.

Dr. Achebe

Next week, we'll begin discussing the effect of parental monitoring on child development. We'll start by looking specifically at parental monitoring of children's access to the Internet. Some parents believe that they need to closely watch and restrict their children's online activity. Do you agree with this approach? Do you think it is important for parents to monitor and limit their children's access to the Internet? Why or why not?

Claire

In my opinion, this kind of parental monitoring is essential. If parents are aware of what their children are doing online, they can help them avoid making mistakes. For example, they can intervene if they see their child has accidentally made a big purchase from an online retailer.

Paul

I respectfully disagree with Claire. Parental monitoring hinders a child's growth and learning. Yes, children can make mistakes online, but making mistakes is how they learn. If parents always step in to correct these mistakes, it prevents children from learning from the consequences of their actions.

교수가 아동 발달에 관한 강의를 진행하고 있다. 교수의 질문에 답하는 게시글을 작성하시오.

답변은 다음 조건을 충족해야 한다.
- 의견을 표명하고 뒷받침하는 근거를 제시한다.
- 독자적인 표현과 관점으로 토론에 기여한다.
어느 정도 완성도를 갖추려면 최소 100단어 이상이어야 한다.

Dr. Achebe

다음 주부터 부모의 감시가 아동 발달에 미치는 영향에 대해 논의하겠습니다. 구체적으로 자녀의 인터넷 접속에 대한 부모의 감시를 살펴보면서 시작할게요. 어떤 부모는 자녀의 온라인 활동을 면밀히 관찰하고 제한해야 한다고 생각하죠. 여러분은 이런 접근 방식에 동의하나요? 부모가 자녀의 인터넷 접속을 감시하고 제한하는 것이 중요하다고 생각하나요? 찬반 의견을 밝히고 이유를 설명해 주세요.

Claire

제 생각에 이런 부모의 감시는 반드시 필요합니다. 자녀가 온라인에서 무엇을 하는지 부모가 알면 자녀가 실수하지 않도록 도와줄 수 있습니다. 예를 들어 자녀가 온라인 소매업체에서 실수로 비싼 물건을 구매한 사실을 안다면 개입할 수 있어요.

Paul

클레어의 의견을 존중하지만 동의하지는 않습니다. 부모의 감시는 자녀의 성장과 학습을 방해합니다. 맞습니다. 자녀가 온라인에서 실수할 수도 있죠. 하지만 실수를 통해 배웁니다. 만약 부모가 이런 실수를 바로잡느라 일일이 개입한다면, 자녀는 자신들의 행동이 빚은 결과에서 배울 수 없게 됩니다.

해설

부모가 자녀의 인터넷 접속을 감시하고 제한해야 하는지에 관한 토론이다. 고득점을 받으려면 이러한 토론에 기여하는 논지를 펼치며 답변해야 한다. 어느 정도 완성도를 갖추려면 최소 100단어 이상이어야 한다.

한 토론 참여자는 부모의 감시가 반드시 필요하며 자녀가 실수하지 않도록 돕는다고 주장하고, 다른 토론 참여자는 부모의 감시가 자녀의 성장과 실수에서 배우는 능력을 방해한다고 주장한다. 토론 참여자들이 이미 서술한 개념을 확장해도 좋고 전혀 새로운 개념을 소개해도 좋다. 부모의 감시가 온라인에서 자녀의 안전을 보장하고, 지침과 교육을 제공하며, 자녀의 온라인 활동과 오프라인 활동 사이에 건강한 균형을 촉진한다고 서술할 수 있다. 반대로 부모의 감시가 자녀의 독립성, 자율성, 사생활을 제한하고 부모와 자녀 사이의 신뢰를 좀먹는다고 말할 수 있다. 또한 부모의 감시 정도, 즉 부모의 감시가 어느 수준이면 지나치고 어느 수준이면 적절한지에 대해 논의할 수 있다. 다른 해결책을 제안할 수도 있다. 예를 들어 부모가 자녀와 건강하고 신뢰할 수 있는 관계를 구축하도록 노력해야 한다고 주장할 수 있다.

반드시 자신의 의견을 뒷받침하는 탄탄한 근거와 예시를 제시하고 명확하게 표현해야 한다. 답안이 온라인 게시물 형태로 나타나므로 여러 단락으로 나누어 구성할 필요는 없다. 하지만 개념 간 연관성이 밀접하며 조리 있고 명료해야 한다. 채점은 '학술 토론을 위한 글쓰기 평가 기준(Appendix 참조)'을 토대로 이루어진다.